Qualitative Data Analysis
Fourth Edition

Sara Miller McCune founded SAGE Publishing in 1965 to support the dissemination of usable knowledge and educate a global community. SAGE publishes more than 1000 journals and over 800 new books each year, spanning a wide range of subject areas. Our growing selection of library products includes archives, data, case studies and video. SAGE remains majority owned by our founder and after her lifetime will become owned by a charitable trust that secures the company's continued independence.

Los Angeles | London | New Delhi | Singapore | Washington DC | Melbourne

Qualitative Data Analysis
A Methods Sourcebook
Fourth Edition

Matthew B. Miles

A. Michael Huberman

Johnny Saldaña

Arizona State University

Los Angeles | London | New Delhi
Singapore | Washington DC | Melbourne

FOR INFORMATION:

SAGE Publications, Inc.
2455 Teller Road
Thousand Oaks, California 91320
E-mail: order@sagepub.com

SAGE Publications Ltd.
1 Oliver's Yard
55 City Road
London EC1Y 1SP
United Kingdom

SAGE Publications India Pvt. Ltd.
B 1/I 1 Mohan Cooperative Industrial Area
Mathura Road, New Delhi 110 044
India

SAGE Publications Asia-Pacific Pte. Ltd.
18 Cross Street #10-10/11/12
China Square Central
Singapore 048423

Printed in the United States of America

ISBN: 978-1-5443-7185-6

Acquisitions Editor: Helen Salmon
Content Development Editor: Chelsea Neve
Editorial Assistant: Megan O'Heffernan
Production Editor: Andrew Olson
Copy Editor: Liann Lech
Typesetter: C&M Digitals (P) Ltd.
Proofreader: Caryne Brown
Indexer: Jeanne Busemeyer
Cover Designer: Scott Van Atta
Marketing Manager: Susannah Goldes

This book is printed on acid-free paper.

19 20 21 22 23 10 9 8 7 6 5 4 3 2 1

BRIEF CONTENTS

DETAILED CONTENTS

PART II • DISPLAYING THE DATA

LIST OF DISPLAYS

PREFACE TO THE FOURTH EDITION

Johnny Saldaña

This fourth edition of Matthew B. Miles and A. Michael Huberman's classic SAGE Publishing text, *Qualitative Data Analysis*, continues to update the late authors' unique work for new generations of qualitative researchers as well as for the dedicated followers of their methods for almost 40 years. I am honored to join them, in spirit, as the third author of this revised text.

This book offers its readers practical guidance in recommended methods for assembling and analyzing primarily text-based data in visual arrays. *Qualitative Data Analysis: A Methods Sourcebook* is designed for researchers in virtually all fields and disciplines that honor what their human participants have to say, treasure the products and artifacts they create, and respect the complexity of social action as it happens all around us. It is intended primarily for students in graduate degree programs who are learning how to investigate the human condition through qualitative research coursework, and for established scholars and practitioners continuing their professional development by reading the literature on current methods.

> A website at **study.sagepub.com/miles4e** includes a selected bibliography compiled by author Johnny Saldaña, plus downloadable versions of the book's Appendix and display templates.

A NOTE ON THIS REVISION

My charge as third coauthor was to *adapt* Miles and Huberman's work, not to write my own book on qualitative data analysis. For this fourth edition, I have continued to maintain the general spirit and integrity of the core contents of the original 1994 authoritative work, while making the text more accessible and relevant to contemporary researchers. I have added graphics as a display modality in addition to matrices and networks, and have included several new displays to the collection in Chapters 2, 4–9, and 11–12, based on the work of fellow scholars. The chapters on "Research Design and Data Management;" "Fundamentals of Qualitative Data Analysis;" "Designing Matrix, Network, and Graphic Displays;" "Methods of Describing;" "Methods of Ordering;" and "Writing About Qualitative Research" have been substantially revised.

Peer reviewers of the third edition publication and this edition's manuscript offered constructive recommendations for revision, and I have attempted to incorporate several of those ideas into this work. I must counter, however, that just one book alone cannot address absolutely all matters related to qualitative data analysis, lest it become a massive tome or multivolume series. There are excellent works devoted exclusively to related specialized topics such as mixed methods research and digital technology, and I refer my readers to those titles for supplemental information (see the extensive annotated bibliography in the Appendix for recommended resources).

Finally, despite the open-ended leeway I was granted to revise and update Miles and Huberman's classic work for two editions, I still do not feel that this is "my" book. Thus, they remain listed as first and second coauthors. I am a privileged guest in the academic house they've built. I'm responsible for the home's traditions and upkeep, but with generous allowances for my own decorative flair in selected rooms.

ACKNOWLEDGMENTS

I am honored that Helen Salmon, acquisitions editor of SAGE Publications' College Division, commissioned me to adapt Miles and Huberman's text for its third and fourth editions. My initial contact with SAGE began with their former London office editor, Patrick Brindle, who encouraged me to develop *The Coding Manual for Qualitative Researchers*, and for his welcoming invitation to this distinguished publishing house, I am truly grateful. I also thank Chelsea Neve, Susannah Goldes, Andrew Olson, Bennie Clark Allen, Scott Van Atta, Jeanne Busemeyer, Caryne Brown, and Megan O'Heffernan at SAGE Publishing for prepublication guidance, and Liann Lech for meticulous copyediting of this manuscript.

My own qualitative research methods professors at Arizona State University significantly influenced my growth as a scholar and writer. I am indebted to Tom Barone, Mary Lee Smith, Amira De la Garza, and Sarah J. Tracy for their life-changing impact on my academic career. For their collegial friendship, mentorship, and support of my work, I also thank Ann Whitehouse, Coleman A. Jennings, Lin Wright, Harry F. Wolcott, Norman K. Denzin, Yvonna S. Lincoln, Mitchell Allen, Jai Seaman, Ray Maietta, Ronald J. Chenail, Leo A. Mallette, Linda Essig, Kakali Bhattacharya, Patricia Leavy, Liora Bresler, Joe Norris, Laura A. McCammon, Angela Hines, Matt Omasta, and Jim Simpson.

For this particular edition, I also thank Daniel Turner of Quirkos Software and David K. Woods of Transana for screenshot permissions, Taylor & Francis Ltd for figure reproduction permission, Paul J. Mack for a photograph permission, and all the scholars whose work is included in this book for their exemplary qualitative research.

My final thanks go to Matthew B. Miles and A. Michael Huberman themselves. To my knowledge, I never met them or heard them speak at professional conferences, but their data-analytic methods, which I learned intimately in my qualitative research courses, have been part of my work ever since. I always strive to meet their rigorous standards, and I frequently quote their now-classic advice to "think display." I owe much of my career trajectory to the legacy of scholars before me whose methods books and articles helped shape my own ways of working as a qualitative researcher and data analyst. Miles and Huberman are two of those esteemed scholars, and I am honored to be connected with them in this way. I hope that the fourth edition of their book pays proper tribute and homage to their significant level of scholarship.

SAGE Publishing and Johnny Saldaña are grateful for feedback on the third edition and draft manuscript of the fourth edition from the following reviewers:

Sheila J. Foley, Bay Path University

Bronwynne Evans, Arizona State University

Caroline S. Hackerott, Arkansas Tech University

Casey B. Nixon, Piedmont College

Guofang Li, University of British Columbia

Jennifer Morrison, Johns Hopkins University

Karthigeyan Subramaniam, University of North Texas

ABOUT THE AUTHORS

Matthew B. Miles, a social psychologist, had a career-long interest in strategies for educational reform. His work focused on planned change in education, group and organizational studies, and the dissemination and implementation of research findings. His first major research project was a 4-year study of six new, innovative public schools.

A. Michael Huberman's long-term interests were in scientific epistemology, and adult cognition and knowledge use. His work focused on education policy, school reform, and the practical translation of research knowledge into effective school practice. His first extensive project was a 4-year study of an experimental elementary school's implementation of Piagetian theories in classroom practice.

Johnny Saldaña, a theatre educator, has explored qualitative research methodologies ranging from coding to ethnodrama. His work focuses on young people's and adults' participation in and transformation through the arts. His first qualitative research project was a 2½-year ethnography of a beginning teacher's experiences at an inner-city fine arts magnet school.

Miles and Huberman collaborated for many years on studies of the dissemination of educational innovations and school improvement. In the course of a multisite study sponsored by the National Institute of Education, they began a study of the procedures they were using to analyze data, which provided the intellectual stimulus and the content of much of this book. Miles and Huberman led seminars based on the book in the United States, Canada, western Europe, and Australia. Their work together and with other colleagues included the study of school change agents; innovation in urban high schools; the social architecture of schools; teachers' life cycles; the use of scientific knowledge in vocational education; and educational reform in Bangladesh, Ethiopia, New Zealand, and Colombia.

Saldaña's studies have included child audience responses to theatre; teachers' perceptions of achievement standards; a survey of adults reflecting on their high school experiences; longitudinal qualitative research methodology; coding and qualitative data analysis methods; and arts-based research methodologies, including ethnodrama and ethnotheatrical play production. His methods works have been cited and referenced in more than 10,000 research studies conducted in over 130 countries. Johnny Saldaña is Professor Emeritus from Arizona State University's School of Film, Dance, and Theatre, and is the author of SAGE Publications' *The Coding Manual for Qualitative Researchers* (3rd ed.); *Thinking Qualitatively: Methods of Mind*; and, with co-author Matt Omasta, *Qualitative Research: Analyzing Life*.

THE SUBSTANTIVE START

PART I

INTRODUCTION

CHAPTER SUMMARY

This chapter introduces the reader to the coauthors' perspectives about the nature of qualitative data and the interrelated components of qualitative data analysis. We offer recommended guidance for the various audiences of this book and establish the parameters of what we cover in the text.

CONTENTS

THE PURPOSE OF THIS BOOK

We wrote this book to address a need faced by researchers in all disciplines and fields of human inquiry: The need to construct credible and trustworthy meaning from qualitative data through analytic methods that are practical and will generate knowledge that we and others can rely on.

Qualitative data are a source of well-grounded, rich descriptions of social processes. With qualitative data, one can preserve chronological flow to derive plausible explanations for outcomes. Good qualitative data also lead to serendipitous findings and interrelationships. They help researchers get beyond initial conceptions and generate new understandings. Finally, the findings from well-analyzed qualitative studies have a quality of "undeniability." Words and images, especially organized into vignettes, stories, and evocative visual representations, have a concrete, vivid, and meaningful flavor that often proves far more persuasive to a reader than pages of summary statistics.

The expansion of qualitative inquiry from the 1970s onward has been phenomenal. There are now numerous handbooks (e.g., Denzin & Lincoln's *The SAGE Handbook of Qualitative Research* [2018] and Gubrium, Holstein, Marvasti, & McKinney's *The SAGE Handbook of Interview Research* [2012]); introductory textbooks (e.g., Charmaz's *Constructing Grounded Theory* [2014] and Saldaña & Omasta's *Qualitative Research: Analyzing Life* [2018]); prestigious peer-reviewed journals (*Qualitative Inquiry, Qualitative Health Research*); online newsletters and forums (SAGE Publications' Methodspace, *The Qualitative Report*); annual conferences (International Congress of Qualitative Inquiry, International Institute for Qualitative Methodology); and qualitative special-interest groups in several major professional associations (American Educational Research Association, National Communication Association).

Although many researchers, from graduate students writing their theses and dissertations to experienced researchers, work alone on their projects and often focus on single cases, qualitative work is becoming more complex. Increasingly, we see mixed methods studies that combine qualitative and quantitative inquiry, carried out by research teams working collaboratively through specialized analytic software. And exciting new approaches to qualitative inquiry draw their inspiration from poetry, dramatic literature, visual art, dance, film, and other creative genres to present and represent social life in fresh, evocative ways.

Yet, in the flurry of this activity, we should be mindful of some pervasive issues that have not gone away. These issues include the labor intensiveness (and extensiveness over months or years) of data collection; frequent data overload; the time demands of processing and analyzing data; the adequacy of sampling when only a few cases can be managed; the generalizability and transferability of findings; the credibility, trustworthiness, and quality of conclusions; and their utility in the world of policy and action.

This book is written in the belief that, as qualitative researchers, we need to keep sharing our *craft and art*—that is, the explicit, systematic, and sometimes creative methods we use to analyze data. This is the need our book addresses. We hope that our experiences will be helpful to our colleagues, as theirs have been to us.

THE NATURE OF THIS BOOK

This is a practical methods sourcebook for all researchers who make use of qualitative data. But it is not intended as a comprehensive text; we do not address matters such as how to gain entry into a field site or how to facilitate participant interviews. Others have dealt with these issues elsewhere and well; we cite their work along the way and refer you to the appendix's annotated bibliography for more information.

For each of the methods outlined, we give specific examples with enough detail so that the reader can see how things work; try the method; and, most important, revise the method in future work. These analytic approaches are manageable and straightforward, though some displays may, at first, appear daunting. Don't let them intimidate you; they are *examples*, not exemplars or standards of practice. Each method of data analysis and display offers practical suggestions for the researcher's use and adaptation with accessible software and basic programs.

Audiences

This book is for practicing researchers in all fields whose work involves actual qualitative data analysis issues. An important subset of that audience is the *beginning researcher*—a graduate student or early-career faculty member—working with qualitative data. We have encountered many students who launch into qualitative theses, dissertations, or research projects who sometimes feel overwhelmed and undertrained. With them in mind, we keep the language accessible and supportive, and we offer suggestions for using the book in qualitative research methods courses.

Many examples used in the book are drawn from educational research, both ours and others'. But we also include relevant discussion for other disciplines—nursing, anthropology, sociology, psychology, business, the arts, organization studies, sports, social media, political science, criminology, tourism, ethnic studies, communication, family studies, program evaluation, and policy research—to underline that the methods are generic, not field limited.

Some of the methods reported here grew out of multiple case studies of organizations carried out by a research team. But do not despair if you are working alone, if your study has just one case, or if you are focusing at the small-group level. There are many relevant examples for you, along with targeted advice.

OUR ORIENTATION

It is worthwhile, we think, for researchers to make their positionality and standpoint clear. To know how a researcher construes the shape of the social world and aims to give us a credible account of it is to know our conversational partner.

We label ourselves *pragmatic realists*. We believe that social phenomena exist not only in the mind but also in the world—and that some reasonably stable relationships can be found among the idiosyncratic messiness of life. There are regularities and sequences that link together phenomena. From these patterns, we can derive the concepts that underlie individual and social life. The fact that most of those concepts—such as *negotiating, possible selves, emotional labor*, and so on—are invisible to the human eye does not make them invalid.

Human relationships and societies have unique peculiarities and inconsistencies that make a realist approach to understanding them more complex—but not impossible. We must contend with the institutions, structures, practices, and conventions that people produce, reproduce, and transform. Human meanings and intentions are worked out within the frameworks of these social structures—structures that are invisible but nonetheless real. In other words, social phenomena such as language, culture, and power exist in the world and exert strong influences over human activities because most people construe them in common ways. Things that are believed become real and can be inquired into.

We agree with interpretivists who point out that knowledge is socially constructed. We affirm the existence and importance of the subjective, the phenomenological, and the meaning making at the center of social life. Our goal is to register and transcend these processes by making assertions and building theories to account for a real world that is both bounded and perceptually laden—and to test these assertions and theories in our various disciplines.

Our tests do not use the deductive logic of classical positivism. Rather, our explanations flow from an account of how human actions produced the events we observed. We want to account for events rather than simply document their sequence. We look for an individual or a social process at the core of events that can be captured to provide a causal description of the most likely forces at work.

The paradigms for conducting social research are always shifting beneath our feet. Our view is that it is possible to develop practical methods for judging the goodness of our findings, discoveries, and conclusions. To us, research is actually more a creative craft than a slavish adherence to methodological rules. No study conforms exactly to a standard methodology; each one calls for the researcher to adapt the methodology and methods to the uniqueness of the setting or case.

Readers looking at the methods in this sourcebook will find them to be orderly ones with some degree of formalization. Many colleagues prefer more relaxed and open-ended voyages through their data, and we wish them well. We have opted for thoroughness and explicitness in this book, not just because it suits us but because vague descriptions are of little practical use to others. The overall structure of this text allows for some techniques to be used and others to be left aside. We advise you to look behind any apparent formalism and seek out what will be *useful* in your own work.

AN APPROACH TO QUALITATIVE DATA ANALYSIS

When you've been doing qualitative research as long as we have, the methodologies or genres start to blur. As pragmatic realists, we no longer adhere slavishly to one school of thought, or practice solely within the boundaries of one particular methodological approach. The data-analytic methods and techniques we've employed over the past few decades have been "a little bit of this and a little bit of that," used on an "as needed" basis. This is not to suggest that we were being improvisationally foolhardy as we figured out what to do next. On the contrary, we have been quite deliberate and diligent in our analytic methodologies and work. We resonate with ethnographer Amanda Coffey's (2018) insight that analysis "involves an ongoing dialogue with and between data and ideas" (p. 25).

Over time, the methods included in this book have become almost signature works—the "Miles and Huberman" way of analyzing qualitative data. But if you ask established qualitative researchers to describe Miles and Huberman's methods, you'll hear diverse opinions ranging from positive descriptors such as "systematic," "rigorous," and "authoritative," to negative descriptors such as "old fashioned," "confusing," and (a personal favorite) "positivists in sheep's clothing." Add Saldaña as a coauthor to the third and fourth editions of this text, and the evolution of these methods continues.

The three of us do not subscribe to any one particular genre of qualitative research—we are "shamelessly eclectic," as the popular saying goes. But our analytic sequence depicted throughout the book is probably a hybrid blend of ethnographic methods and grounded theory. It moves from one inductive inference to another by selectively collecting data, comparing and contrasting this material in the quest for patterns or regularities, seeking out more data to support or qualify these emerging clusters, and then gradually drawing inferences from the links between other new data segments and the cumulative set of conceptualizations. In the past few decades, we've found that refining and developing analysis methods on new projects had a clear payoff. Our confidence in our findings was greater, and credibility for our research, practice, and policy audiences was enhanced.

Analytic Methods: Some Common Features

We've observed features that recur in many established approaches to qualitative analysis. Here is a fairly classic set of analytic moves arranged in sequence:

1. Assigning codes or themes to a set of field notes, interview transcripts, documents, and/or visual data

2. Sorting and sifting through these coded materials to identify similar phrases, relationships between variables, patterns, categories, themes, distinct differences between subgroups, and common sequences

3. Isolating these patterns and processes, and commonalities and differences, and taking them out to the field in the next wave of data collection

4. Noting reflections or other remarks in jottings, analytic memos, and/or journals

5. Gradually elaborating a refined set of assertions, propositions, categories, themes, concepts, and generalizations that cover the consistencies discerned in the database

6. Comparing those generalizations with a formalized body of knowledge in the form of concepts or theories

The analytic challenge for all qualitative researchers is finding coherent descriptions and explanations that still include all of the gaps, inconsistencies, and contradictions inherent in personal and social life. The risk is in forcing the logic, the order, and the plausibility that constitute theory-making on the uneven, sometimes random, nature of social life.

We'll return to recurring features such as these, while acknowledging the diversity of analytic approaches now in use. Next, however, we need to take a step back to ask, what kind of data are we actually faced with in qualitative studies?

THE NATURE OF QUALITATIVE DATA

General Nature

In this book, we focus primarily on data in the form of words—that is, language in the form of extended text. Qualitative data also can appear as still or moving images, and we address these when necessary to the analytic task at hand (see the appendix for recommended titles and guidance for visual data).

The words we collect and analyze are based on *observations*, *interviews*, *documents*, *media*, and *artifacts*. These data collection activities typically are carried out in close proximity to a local setting for a sustained period of time. Such data are not usually immediately accessible for analysis but require some type of processing: Raw field notes need to be expanded and typed up, audio recordings need to be transcribed and corrected, and photographs need to be documented and analyzed.

The words we choose to document what we see and hear in the field can never truly be "objective"; they can only be our *interpretations* of what we experience. Similarly, transcription of audio recordings can be done in many ways that will produce rather different texts. And the influence of the researcher's personal *values*, *attitudes*, and *beliefs* from and toward fieldwork cannot be avoided.

To put it another way, qualitative data are not so much about behavior as they are about *actions* (which carry with them intentions and meanings and lead to outcomes or consequences). Some actions are relatively straightforward; others involve "impression management"—how people want others, including the researcher, to see them. Furthermore, those actions always occur in specific situations within a social and historical context, which deeply influence how they are interpreted by both insiders and the researcher as outsider. Thus, the apparent simplicity of qualitative data masks a good deal of complexity, requiring plenty of care, self-awareness, and reflection on the part of the researcher.

Strengths of Qualitative Data

One major feature of well-collected qualitative data is that they focus on *naturally occurring, ordinary events in natural settings*, so that we have a strong handle on what "real life" is like. Qualitative data, with their emphasis on people's *lived experiences*, are fundamentally well suited to locating the *meanings* people place on the events, processes, and structures of their lives and for connecting these meanings to the *social world* around them. There is *local groundedness*—that is, data that were collected in close proximity to a specific situation. The emphasis is on a specific *case*, a focused and bounded phenomenon embedded in its context. The influences of the *local context* are not stripped away but are taken into account. The possibility for understanding latent, underlying, or nonobvious issues is strong.

Another feature of qualitative data is their *richness and holism*, with strong potential for revealing complexity. Such data provide "thick descriptions" (Geertz, 1973) that are vivid, are nested in a real context, and have a ring of truth that has a strong impact on the reader. Furthermore, the fact that such data are typically collected over a *sustained period* makes them powerful for studying any process (including history). We can go far beyond snapshots of "what?" or "how many?" to just *how* and *why* things happen as they do—and even *assess causation* as it actually plays out in a particular setting.

We make three other claims for the power of qualitative data, to which we will return in later chapters: as *a strategy for discovery*, for *exploring new ideas*, and for *developing hypotheses*. In addition, we underline their potential for *testing hypotheses*, seeing whether specific predictions hold up. Finally, qualitative data are useful when one needs to supplement, validate, or illuminate *quantitative* data gathered from the same setting for mixed methods studies.

OUR VIEW OF QUALITATIVE DATA ANALYSIS

We see analysis as three concurrent flows of activity: data condensation, data display, and conclusion drawing/verification. We will explore each of these components in more depth as we proceed through the book. For now, we make only some overall comments.

Data Condensation

Data condensation refers to the process of selecting, focusing, simplifying, abstracting, and/or transforming the data that appear in the full corpus (body) of written-up field notes, interview transcripts, documents, and other empirical materials. By condensing, we're making data *stronger*. (We stay away from data "reduction" as a term because that implies we're weakening or losing something in the process.)

As we see it, data condensation occurs continuously throughout the life of any qualitatively oriented project. Even before the data are actually collected, anticipatory data condensation is occurring as the researcher decides which conceptual framework, which research questions, which cases, and which data collection methods to choose. As data collection proceeds, further episodes of data condensation occur: writing summaries, coding, generating categories, developing themes, and writing analytic memos. The data condensing/transforming process continues after the fieldwork is over, until a final report is completed.

Data condensation is not something separate from analysis. It is a *part* of analysis. The researcher's decisions—which data units to code and which to pull out, which category labels best summarize a number of codes, which evolving story to tell—*are all analytic choices*. Data condensation is a form of analysis that sharpens, sorts, focuses, discards, and organizes data in such a way that "final" conclusions can be drawn and verified.

By data condensation, we do not necessarily mean quantification. Yet occasionally, it may be helpful to convert the data into *magnitudes* (e.g., the analyst decides that the program being looked at has a "high" or "low" degree of effectiveness), but this is not always necessary.

Data Display

The second major flow of analysis activity is data display. Generically, a *display* is an organized, condensed assembly of information that allows analytic reflection and action. In daily life, displays vary from smartphone apps to newspaper advertisements to Facebook status updates. Looking at displays helps us understand what is happening and to do something—either analyze further or take action—based on that understanding.

The most frequent form of display for qualitative data in the past has been *extended text*. As we will note later, text (in the form of, say, 1,000 pages of field notes) is terribly cumbersome. It is dispersed, sequential rather than simultaneous, poorly structured, and extremely bulky. Using only extended text, a researcher may find it easy to jump to hasty, partial, and unfounded conclusions. Human beings are not very powerful as processors of large amounts of information or big data, as it's currently termed. Extended text overloads our information-processing capabilities and preys on our tendencies to find simplifying patterns. Or we drastically overweight vivid information, such as the exciting event that jumps out of page 124 of the field notes after a long, "boring" passage.

In the course of our work, we have become convinced that good displays are a major avenue to robust qualitative analysis. The displays discussed and illustrated in this book include many types of matrices, networks, and graphics. All are designed to assemble organized information into an immediately accessible, compact form so that the analyst can see what is happening and either draw justified conclusions or move on to the next step of analysis that the display suggests may be useful.

As with data condensation, the creation and use of displays is not separate from analysis—it is a *part* of analysis. Designing a display—deciding on the rows and columns of a matrix for qualitative data and deciding which data, in which form, should be entered in the cells—are analytic activities. In this book, we advocate more systematic, powerful displays and urge a more inventive, self-conscious, and iterative stance toward their generation and use. As we've said in our previous writings, "You know what you display."

Drawing and Verifying Conclusions

The third stream of analysis activity is conclusion drawing and verification. From the start of data collection, the qualitative analyst interprets what things mean by noting patterns, assertions, propositions, explanations, and causal flows. The competent researcher holds these conclusions lightly, maintaining openness and skepticism, but the conclusions are still there, vague at first, then increasingly explicit and grounded. "Final" conclusions may not appear until data collection is over, depending on the size of the corpus of field notes; the coding, storage, and retrieval methods used; the analytic prowess of the researcher; and any necessary deadlines to be met.

Conclusion drawing, in our view, is only half of the picture. Conclusions are also *verified* as the analyst proceeds. Verification may be as brief as a fleeting second thought crossing the analyst's mind during writing, with a short excursion back to the field notes, or it may be thorough and elaborate, with lengthy argumentation and review among colleagues to develop "intersubjective consensus," or with extensive efforts to replicate a finding in another data set. The meanings emerging from the data have to be tested for their plausibility, sturdiness, and confirmability—that is, their validity. Otherwise, we are left with interesting stories about what happened but of unknown truth and utility.

Some researchers take issue with the term "conclusions" because the nature of contemporary social life, they believe, is too uncertain, tenuous, and fluid for any notion of finality. Other preferred terms such as "findings," "discoveries," and "closure" smooth the presumptive edge of authoritative certainty. Admittedly, we too subscribe to this open-ended perspective, yet we use "conclusions" simply because it is a well-established term (and expectation) of research methodology. Also, a report that does not provide readers with *some* form of take-aways at the end serves little value to its audiences and suggests that the researcher has not fulfilled his or her analytic responsibilities.

We have presented these three streams—data condensation, data display, and conclusion drawing/verification—as interwoven before, during, and after data collection in parallel form, to make up the general activity called "analysis." The three streams can also be represented as shown in Display 1.1—our first network display. In this view, the three types of analysis activity and the activity of data collection itself form an interactive, cyclical process. The researcher steadily moves among these nodes during data collection and then shuttles among condensing, displaying, and conclusion drawing/verifying for the remainder of the study.

The coding of data, for example (*data condensation*), leads to new ideas on what should go into a matrix (*data display*). Entering the data requires further data condensation. As the matrix fills up, preliminary *conclusions* are drawn, but they lead to the decision, for example, to add another column to the matrix to test and *verify* the conclusion.

In this view, qualitative data analysis is a continuous, iterative enterprise. Issues of data condensation, display, and conclusion drawing/verification come into play successively as analysis episodes follow each other. Such a process is actually no more complex, conceptually speaking, than the analysis modes quantitative researchers use. Like their qualitative colleagues, they must be preoccupied with data condensation (calculating means, standard deviations); display (correlation tables, regression printouts); and conclusion drawing/verification (significance levels, experimental/control group differences). But their activities are carried out through well-defined, familiar methods; are guided by canons; and are usually more sequential than iterative or cyclical. Qualitative researchers are in a more fluid and more humanistic position of meaning making.

DISPLAY 1.1   ●   Components of Qualitative Data Analysis: Interactive Model

Source: Miles, M. B., & Huberman, A. M. (1994). *Qualitative data analysis: An expanded sourcebook* (2nd ed.). Thousand Oaks, CA: Sage Publications.

SUGGESTIONS FOR READERS

Recommendations for what a reader should do with any particular book are often presumptuous, mistaken, or both. Authors have no control over who reads their books or what readers may find useful. Nevertheless, we offer a few suggestions for different types of users.

Students and Other Novice Researchers

We give some direct advice here, keeping in mind that you will often be working alone, usually on a single case, and may be feeling worried about the quality of your study—thesis/dissertation or not. We emphasize that this book is not written for newcomers to qualitative inquiry; readers should have some introductory background knowledge of fundamentals such as basic fieldwork research terminology, conducting a literature review, participant observation, and interviewing participants.

1. This book focuses on *data analysis*. Use other, introductory books to help with the basics of fieldwork (see the appendix for recommended titles and resources).

2. Learn by doing. Use your own study (whether it is in the planning stage or under way) as a vehicle and apply it to relevant methods in each chapter.

3. Compensate for the problem of having to work alone by finding someone to be a critical friend or mentor to respond to your work as you proceed.

4. Keep an informal journal or analytic memo set of what you are running up against. This tactic will help your learning and will be useful when you write up your study.

5. Don't worry about the jargon-like names of particular displays; the issue is what a display can do for you.

6. The biggest enemy of your learning is the gnawing worry that you're not "doing it right." Thesis and dissertation work tends to encourage that. But any given analytic problem can be approached in many useful ways. Creative heuristics—that is, inventing your way out of a problem—is definitely the better stance.

Experienced Researchers

This is a sourcebook. Colleagues have told us that they have used it in several ways:

1. *Browsing:* The book contains a wide range of material, so simply exploring it in an unstructured way can be fruitful.

2. *Problem solving:* Anyone opening the book comes to it with more or less specifically defined problems in doing qualitative data analysis. The index has been designed to be "problem sensitive" to permit easy access to appropriate sections of the book. The table of contents can also be used in this way.

3. *"A to Z":* Some readers prefer to go through a book sequentially, from start to finish. We have organized the book so that it makes sense that way.

4. *Operational use:* For readers conducting an ongoing qualitative research project, either alone or with colleagues, it's useful to read particular sections focusing on upcoming analysis tasks (e.g., coding, time-ordered displays); then discuss them with available colleagues; and finally plan the next steps in the project, revising the methods outlined here or developing new ones.

5. *Research consulting:* The book can be used by people with an advisory or consulting role in the start-up and ongoing life of research projects. Assuming good problem identification, a research consultant can work with the client in either a problem-solving or a direct-training capacity to aid in thoughtful project design and coping with early problems.

Teachers of Qualitative Research Methods Courses

Some colleagues have used this book as a primary text, others as a supplementary one. In either case, our advice is to engage students in active data collection and analysis. For each topic, we have used a learning approach like this, carried out by individuals or working pairs, who stay together throughout an extended workshop:

1. Introductory lecture and/or reading to clarify the main conceptual points of the section

2. A brief learning task (e.g., coding a data excerpt, designing a matrix template, drawing a network or graphic, interpreting a filled-out matrix, or writing an initial analysis)

3. Comparing the products of individuals or pairs, drawing generalizations, and discussing future applications of the method

The same general principles apply when the book is used in a semester-long course, although the coverage will be deeper. Interim exercises focusing on actual research tasks, critiqued in class, are particularly productive. Active, reflective self-documentation through personal journals or analytic memos is also beneficial.

CLOSURE AND TRANSITION

This introduction provided some brief groundwork and foundations for the rest of the book. Analysis is doing, so let's proceed to the next chapter of Part One to review research design decisions that will later play important roles in qualitative data analysis. Following that chapter is a brief discussion on ethics, then an expanded chapter on analysis fundamentals.

Part Two's chapters are the heart of this book—methods of displaying data for exploring, describing, ordering, explaining, and predicting about the social worlds we study. Part Three's chapters examine how we verify and document the conclusions we draw through systematic thinking and good writing.

RESEARCH DESIGN AND DATA MANAGEMENT

CHAPTER SUMMARY

This chapter discusses how qualitative research design decisions influence and affect later data analysis. Such core topics include conceptual frameworks, methodologies, research questions, instrumentation, sampling, consideration of mixed methods, and data management with computers and software.

CONTENTS

INTRODUCTION

This book is about qualitative data analysis, but first we need to discuss how initial research design decisions may influence and affect the forthcoming analytic components of the study. Research design choices such as the conceptual framework, research methodology, research questions, data collection methods, participant sampling, and so on are analytic acts themselves. They are a sort of *anticipatory data condensation* because they rule out certain factors and relationships and attend to others. Even technical management tasks such as how data will be stored, organized, and processed, and what computer software may be used, both support and affect analysis.

We cannot deal thoroughly here with qualitative research design; see the appendix for recommended titles on the topic. In this chapter, we discuss the *analytic issues* that arise as a study is conceived and implemented. We provide specific examples but want to emphasize that these issues must be dealt with uniquely and flexibly in any particular study. Initial design decisions nearly always lead to a redesign.

LOOSE VERSUS TIGHT RESEARCH DESIGNS

Prior to fieldwork, how much shape and structure should a qualitative research design have? Some researchers keep prestructured designs to a minimum. They consider social processes too complex, too contextual, too elusive, or too fluid to be approached with explicit conceptual frameworks or standardized data collection instruments. They prefer a more loosely structured, emergent, inductively grounded approach for gathering data. Their conceptual frameworks will tend to emerge from the field during the course of the study. The important research questions will become clear only gradually; meaningful settings and participants will not be selected prior to fieldwork but only after initial orientation to the site.

Highly inductive, loosely designed studies make good sense when experienced researchers have plenty of time to explore unfamiliar cultures, understudied phenomena, or very complex social processes. But if you're new to qualitative research and are looking at a better understood phenomenon within a familiar culture or subculture, a loose, inductive design may be a waste of time. Months of fieldwork and voluminous data may yield only a few analytic banalities. Also, fieldwork may well involve multiple-case research rather than single-case studies. If different fieldworkers on a research team are operating inductively with no common framework or instrumentation, they are bound to end up with the double dilemma of data overload and lack of comparability across cases.

Tighter designs provide clarity and focus for beginning researchers worried about protocols and data overload. Tighter designs are also a wiser course for researchers working with well-delineated research questions or who wish to test or further explicate hypotheses. A standardized protocol for data collection across multiple sites gathered by multiple fieldworkers permits better cross-case comparison and analysis.

Yet in multiple-case research, the looser the initial framework, the more each researcher can be receptive to local idiosyncrasies—but cross-case comparability will be hard to get, and the costs and the information load for analysis will be colossal. Tightly coordinated designs face the opposite dilemma: They yield more economical, comparable, and potentially generalizable findings, but they are less case sensitive and may entail bending data out of contextual shape to answer a cross-case analytic question.

Then, too, we should not forget why we are out in the field in the first place: to describe and analyze a pattern of interrelationships. Starting with them (deductively) or getting gradually to them (inductively) are both possible. In the life of a study, we need both approaches to pull a mass of facts and findings into a wide-ranging, coherent set of conclusions and generalizations.

A case can be made for tight, prestructured qualitative designs and for loose, emergent ones. Whether you choose one end of the continuum or the other for your particular study must be your decision. But a midway point between the extremes is yet another position, and perhaps the one most qualitative researchers take.

DISPLAYING THE CONCEPTUAL FRAMEWORK

Description and Rationale

A conceptual framework explains, graphically and/or in narrative form, the main things to be studied—for example, the key factors, variables, phenomena, concepts, participants—and the presumed interrelationships among them—as a *network*. Conceptual frameworks are simply the current and evolving version of the researcher's "map" of the qualitative territory being investigated. As the explorer's knowledge of the terrain improves, the map becomes correspondingly more differentiated and integrated. Thus, conceptual frameworks are developed at the beginning of a study and evolve as the study progresses. This framework also becomes a template, of sorts, for how data collection and analysis begin and proceed during and after fieldwork.

A conceptual framework forces you to be selective—to decide which things are most important; which relationships are likely to be most meaningful; and, as a consequence, what information should be collected and analyzed—at least at the outset. If multiple researchers are involved, the framework helps them study the same phenomena in ways that will permit an eventual cross-case analysis.

Conceptual frameworks can be simple or elaborate, descriptive or causal, commonsensical or theory driven. Theory relies on a few general concepts that subsume a mountain of particulars. *Culture, social intelligence, coping,* and *identity* are the labels we put on intellectual "bins" containing constituent actions, experiences, variables, categories, processes, and events. Bins come from theory, from personal experience, and often from the general objectives of the study envisioned. Setting out bins, naming them, and getting clearer about their interrelationships help lead you toward a conceptual framework. It is both the process and product of analytic reflection.

A note on terminology: Some use the terms *conceptual framework* and *theoretical framework* interchangeably, but some methodologists note that there are distinct differences between the two, depending on whose definitions you read. To us, a theoretical framework utilizes theory/theories and their constituent elements as the presumed "working model" that drives the investigation and analysis of a social phenomenon. But a conceptual framework is a more inductively derived and evolutionary model that can certainly include aspects of the theoretical, but primarily incorporates case- or site-specific variables, concepts, contexts, participants, and so on. In other words, a conceptual framework grounds itself in the local elements of a particular, unique study; a theoretical framework abstracts a study's ideas based on the literature.

Example

A conceptual framework can specify who and what will (and will not) be studied. Display 2.1 is a *first-cut, first-draft* attempt at listing, in graphic form, the myriad influences on a single classroom teacher. This illustration identifies the people (state school superintendent, district reading specialists, etc.); organizations (state school board, district school board, etc.); and "things" or

DISPLAY 2.1   ●   A First-Draft Conceptual Framework for a Case Study Teacher and the Influences on Her Practice

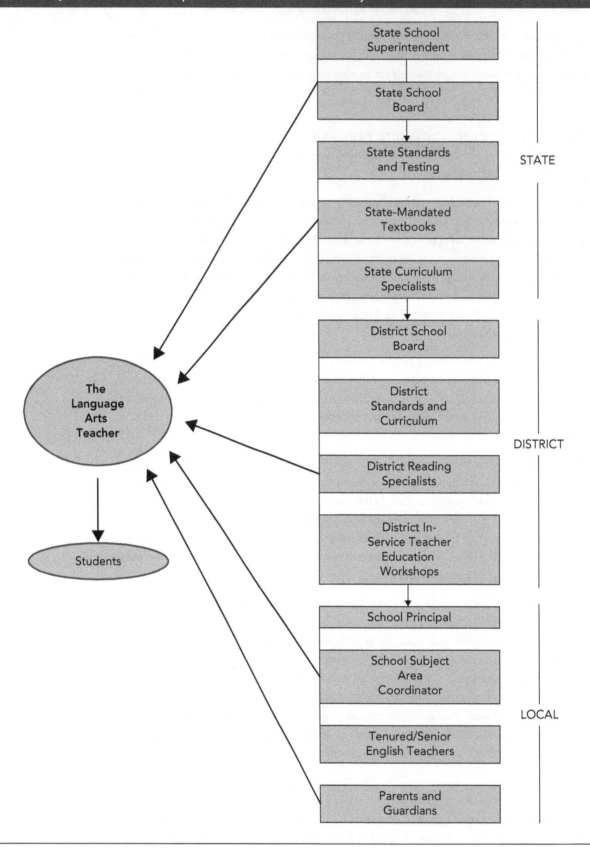

official documents/policies (state-mandated textbooks, district standards and curriculum, etc.) the researcher identified as influential on a classroom teacher's instructional practices with her students. There is a general clustering of *who*s and *what*s by level—state, district, and local—and an implied hierarchy of supervision/authority and distribution of power from top to bottom.

We see here the focusing function of a conceptual framework. Some, not all, social actors in this long list are going to be studied, along with some, not all, aspects of their activity. For example, the researcher, due to accessibility, may be unable to directly interview the state school superintendent or state school board members. But he can certainly access public documents and records of their official business from published minutes of state school board meetings. Once all permissions have been obtained, the language arts teacher herself will be interviewed several times and observed teaching in several of her classrooms. Documents such as her lesson plans, textbooks, and samples of graded student work will be reviewed. Only some relationships in this conceptual framework will be explored, certain kinds of processes documented, and certain analyses made—at least at the outset.

Now for a slightly more complex (i.e., "messy") conceptual framework using some of the same aspects of this study as they evolved. Display 2.2 includes the exact same bins and labels as Display 2.1, but their arrangement and the arrows of influence are different. There is less symmetry (support that the network reflects the "asymmetrical" social world we live in), a new hierarchy, and a different set of interrelationships.

The researcher got to this display after spending some time observing and interviewing the language arts teacher. State standards and testing were the primary factors that influenced both her practice

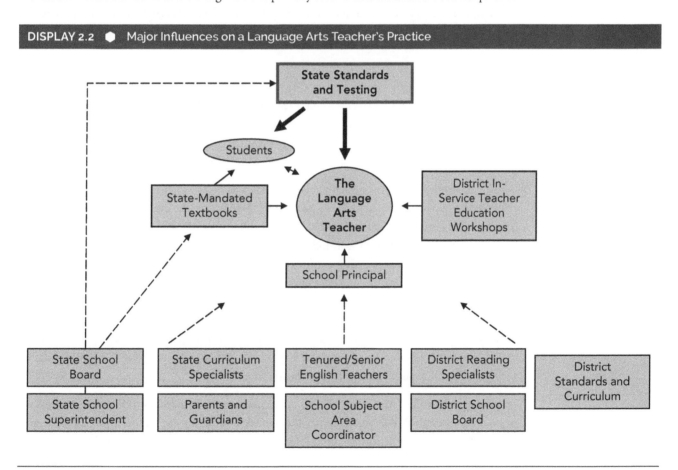

DISPLAY 2.2 ● Major Influences on a Language Arts Teacher's Practice

and the students' classroom experiences. Of all the players from Display 2.1 that were hierarchically listed, some were actually quite peripheral *according to the perspective of the language arts teacher*. These are listed at the bottom of the display, with dashed arrows toward the major bins suggesting minimal or foregrounded influence.

The other three major factors the researcher learned and interpreted as most salient were the teacher's school principal and her "obsession" with raising the school's standardized test scores, the district in-service teacher education workshops (which the teacher praised and found "extremely useful for me and my kids"), and the state-mandated textbooks (which heavily emphasized writing over literature appreciation for language arts).

A display such as this might be considered partly *confirmatory* if the researcher is able to visit other language arts teachers within the same school and within other schools outside the district to determine if their spheres of influence also include the same factors. A *working hypothesis* for field testing that the researcher developed after studying and analyzing this display is this: *The mandates of education manifest themselves primarily as prescriptive products imposed on educators and their students.* Overall, what Displays 2.1 and 2.2 illustrate is that conceptual frameworks *evolve* as a study continues and the bigger picture becomes clearer. Display 2.2 is the product of fieldwork, initial data analysis, and a processual model for testing as additional data and analysis continue.

The conceptual framework is your first analytic *display*. It is a visual representation of your main conceptual ideas about a study and how they interact and interplay with each other. Also remember that conceptual frameworks tell a *story* of some kind. They are evolving, one-page representations of your research in progress, comparable to the storyboards of filmmakers, who first draw on paper or render with software what they will eventually document on digital video.

Other Examples

We now provide two examples from published studies that illustrate the display possibilities for conceptual frameworks. Space does not permit us to discuss each one in depth, but we hope you can get the gist of the researchers' approaches by examining the bins and their proposed interaction patterns and trajectories.

Display 2.3, from Ballestra, Cardinali, Palanga, and Pacelli (2017), portrays a conceptual model of teenage students' intentions to pursue a sales career. Notice that the overall design follows a linear trajectory. But also notice that each arrow has one or more hypotheses (H1, H2, H3, etc.) attached to it. Hypothesis 1 in this study is as follows: "Understanding the changes to the salesperson's role will have a significant impact on students' feelings toward selling as a career" (p. 178). Hypothesis 8 is the following: "Studying business/economic subjects during high school has a significant impact on students' later intent to pursue a sales career" (p. 179). This conceptual framework includes nine specific hypotheses, developed from the coresearchers' literature review, to test as qualitative and quantitative data are collected and analyzed. Not only is their display a preliminary or *exploratory* model of a young adult's sales career process, it is also an analytic game plan to examine whether their participants' experiences support the theories of the field.

Display 2.4, from Chapman et al. (2017), examines the role of powerlessness among health care workers in tuberculosis infection control. This model, however, is not representative of the beginning of the study but rather the *end* of it, after the data have been collected and analyzed:

> The first cycle describes the context of powerlessness, while the second cycle represents how empowerment through evidence-based interventions can be applied in the future.

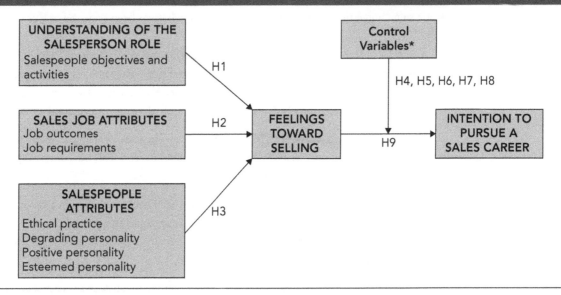

DISPLAY 2.3 ● A Conceptual Model of Students' Intention to Pursue a Sales Career

Source: Ballestra, Cardinali, Palanga, & Pacelli (2017), p. 181.

[Display 2.4] presents the HCWs' [Health Care Workers'] perceived limitations in the application of *M. tuberculosis* infection control measures in clinical practice, influencing the decision-making process and resulting in the knowledge-action gap. (Chapman et al., 2017, p. 2119)

Like Display 2.3, this too is a linear model, but notice how the bins in Display 2.4 are supported with bullet-pointed factors that detail the analytic findings. This conceptual model elegantly maps the researchers' conclusions in story form with an accompanying narrative that explains the participants' dilemmas and experiences.

DISPLAY 2.4 ● Conceptual Model That Presents HCWs' Perceived Limitations in the Application of MTB Infection Control Measures in Clinical Practice, Influencing the Decision–Making Process and Resulting in the "Knowledge–Action" Gap

Source: Chapman et al. (2017), p. 2120.

Conceptual Framework Advice

Here are some suggestions that summarize and extend what has been reviewed in this section:

1. Conceptual frameworks are best done graphically, at first, to support the accompanying narrative. Having to get the entire framework on a single page obliges you to specify the bins that hold discrete phenomena, map likely interrelationships, divide variables that are conceptually or functionally distinct, and work with all of the information at once.

2. Expect to do several versions right from the outset. There are probably as many ways of representing the main variables as there are variables to represent, but some—typically later cuts—are more elegant than others.

3. If your study has more than one researcher, have each field researcher do a cut at a framework early on and then compare the several versions. This procedure will show, literally, where everyone's head is. It usually leads to an explication of contentious or foggy areas that otherwise would have surfaced later on.

4. Avoid the no-risk framework—that is, one that defines variables at a very global level and has two-directional arrows everywhere. This avoidance amounts essentially to making no focusing decisions and is little better than the strategy of going indiscriminately into the field to see what the site has to tell. However, you can begin with a generic framework as a way of getting to a more selective and specific one.

5. Prior theorizing and empirical research are, of course, important inputs. It helps to lay out your own orienting frame and then map onto it the variables and relationships from the literature available, to see where the overlaps, contradictions, qualifications, and refinements are.

For an extended discussion of conceptual frameworks and how they influence and affect all aspects of research, see Ravitch and Riggan (2016).

METHODOLOGIES (GENRES) OF QUALITATIVE RESEARCH

Qualitative research can be conducted in dozens of ways, many approaches with long traditions behind them. Saldaña (2011b) describes more than 20 different qualitative research genres (i.e., methodologies or types) out of many more available to investigators, ranging from well-established traditions such as ethnography, grounded theory, phenomenology, case study, and content analysis, to more progressive genres of qualitative research such as poetic inquiry, narrative inquiry, ethnodrama, and autoethnography. To do them all justice is impossible here. For our purposes, the questions are as follows: What do selected genres of qualitative research have to say about *analysis*? And can we see some common themes and practices among them?

Ideally, the conceptual framework you develop for a study is the impetus for selecting the most appropriate methodological approach to investigate its major components. For example, if you conceptualize that depression is a cognitive and emotional *experience*, then a *phenomenological study* with its emphasis on *thematic analysis* may be an appropriate choice. If you conceptualize that depression is an intimate, personal, and contextual state of being, then perhaps an exemplary *case study* of an individual living with depression, holistically analyzed through *narrative vignettes*, may be in order.

Yet sometimes the methodology we select is based not on our conceptual framework but rather on our *research questions* of interest (discussed next). If we wish to get the best answers to our particular set of inquiries, then we should select the best research genre *and its accompanying methods* that will produce them. If we wish to know the details of *how* people cope with depression in their daily lives, then a series of *interviews* with participants may be more revealing than participant observation of their day-to-day routines. Interview transcripts would then be carefully *coded* to develop major *categories* of coping with mental illness (e.g., psychotropic medication, professional therapy, self-care strategies).

Some researchers, however, have a particular affinity for just one genre of research and dedicate their professional careers to studying social life through a particular framework. They may label themselves "grounded theorists," "phenomenologists," or "autoethnographers," and thus investigate the world through a specialized methodological lens and design their projects to accommodate their preferred ways of working. Over time, they also develop nuanced expertise in the genre itself and have much to offer other researchers about a particular methodology and its methods.

The point of this discussion is that the particular research methodology you select for your study will determine what types of data collection methods you employ and thus what types of analysis might be undertaken. Grounded theory, for example, uses a series of cumulative coding cycles and reflective analytic memoing to develop a core category for theory generation. Phenomenology tends to look at data thematically to extract essences and essentials of participant meanings. Mixed methods research integrates both qualitative and quantitative data and analyses for a more multidimensional approach to inquiry. Poetic inquiry, narrative inquiry, and ethnodrama adopt and adapt the conventions of fictional literature to render nonfiction participant experiences in poetic, prosaic, and dramatic forms, as opposed to the traditional and conventional formats of scholarly/academic writing.

The purpose of this section is not to describe every single methodology of qualitative research available to you but to focus on some common features that occur in most genres of qualitative inquiry. We list some of them here, aware that some exemplars are missing:

1. Qualitative research is conducted through intense and/or prolonged contact with participants in a naturalistic setting to investigate the everyday and/or exceptional lives of individuals, groups, organizations, cultures, and/or societies.

2. The researcher's role is to gain a holistic (systemic, encompassing, and integrated) overview of the context under study: its social arrangement, its ways of working, and its explicit and implicit rules.

3. The researcher attempts to capture data on the perceptions of local participants from the inside through a process of deep attentiveness, empathetic understanding, and suspension or bracketing of preconceptions about the topics under discussion.

4. Relatively little standardized instrumentation is used, though audio-recorded interviews with participants tend to be used most often. The researcher himself or herself is essentially the main instrument in the study.

5. Most of the analysis is done with words. The words can be assembled, subclustered, or broken into segments. They can be reorganized to permit the researcher to compare, contrast, analyze, and construct patterns out of them for analytic outcomes such as extended narratives, categories, themes, assertions, propositions, and/or theories.

6. The main task is to describe and explain the ways people in particular settings come to understand, account for, take action, and otherwise manage their day-to-day situations.

These features may be more relevant for naturalistic, ethnographic studies, but they are configured and used with slight variation in many social research traditions.

FORMULATING RESEARCH QUESTIONS

Description and Rationale

Research questions represent the facets of inquiry that the researcher most wants to explore. Research questions may be general or particular, descriptive or explanatory. The formulation of research questions may precede, follow, or happen concurrently with the development of a conceptual framework and/or the chosen methodological approach. They also may be formulated at the outset or later on and may be revised or reformulated during the course of fieldwork.

It is a direct step from a conceptual framework to research questions. If I have a bin labeled "State-Mandated Textbooks," as in Display 2.1, with an arrow from that bin directed toward "The Language Arts Teacher," I am implicitly asking myself some questions about how textbooks influence a teacher's practice (e.g., *In what ways do state-mandated language arts textbooks shape the language arts teacher's curriculum?*). If I have a two-way arrow between "The Language Arts Teacher" and "Students," as in Display 2.2, my question has to do with the reciprocal interrelationship between them and the interpersonal dynamics of education (e.g., *What kinds of teaching-learning methods best prepare students for state-mandated testing in language arts?*).

If my conceptual framework is more constrained, so are my questions. In Display 2.2, the State School Board has little, if any, direct *influence and affect* (our qualitative preference over quantitative research's "cause and effect") on the teacher—even though it was the body that mandated state standards and testing. To the teacher, the *tests* are perceived as the primary influence on her practice, not the personnel or administrative overview of the State School Board. There may be one research question about the board to verify its inconsequential impact, but not much time or effort will be spent in pursuing this minimal factor.

What do these questions do for me? They tell me what I want to know most or first; my collection of data will be more focused. I am also beginning to make some implicit sampling decisions. I will look only at *some* participants in *some* contexts dealing with *some* issues. The questions also begin to point me toward data-gathering methods—observations, interviews, and document collection. Finally, the research questions begin to operationalize the conceptual framework and make the initial theoretical assumptions even more explicit.

A conceptual framework's display shows researchers' preferred bins and relational arrows as they map and carve up social phenomena. They use these explicitly or implicitly to decide which questions are most important and how they should get the answers. We believe that better research happens when you make your framework (and associated choices of research questions, cases, sampling, instrumentation, etc.) explicit, rather than claiming inductive purity.

Example

Our (Miles and Huberman's) school improvement study investigated the dissemination of educational innovations carried out from 1979 to 1983. (Many display examples in this text come from that classic study. More detailed information appears in the first, second, and third editions of this book.) The study was nested in a larger study of school improvement, covering 145 school buildings and nearly 4,000 people throughout the United States involved in the implementation of educational innovations. Joined by two colleagues, Beverly Loy Taylor and Jo Anne Goldberg, we repeatedly visited a stratified sample of 12 field sites across the country throughout the 1979–1980 school year, with follow-up contacts the next year to verify the main findings.

The volume of data collected included 440 interviews, 85 observations, some 259 documents, and 2,713 pages of field notes. We developed a common set of data displays and, for each of the 12 field sites, used them to draw conclusions, resulting in 12 case reports ranging from 70 to 140 pages each, with a common format. Our subsequent cross-case analysis was built from the appropriate sections of the 12 case reports.

A study of this scope necessitated an extensive series of research questions, and we present just one subset of them related to a school's decision to adopt an educational innovation. The procedure we used was to cluster specific research questions under more general ones, as shown in Display 2.5.

DISPLAY 2.5 ● General and Special Research Questions Relating to the Adoption Decision (School Improvement Study)

How was the adoption decision made?

Who was involved (e.g., principal, users, central office people, school board, outside agencies)?

How was the decision made (top-down, persuasive, consultative, collegial-participative, or delegated styles)?

How much priority and centrality did the new program have at the time of the adoption decision?

How much support and commitment was there from administrators?

How important was it for teachers, seen in relation to their routine, "ordinary" activities, and any other innovations that were being contemplated or attempted?

Realistically, how large did it loom in the scheme of things?

Was it a one-time event or one of a series?

What were the components of the original plan for implementation?

These might have included front-end training, monitoring and debugging/troubleshooting unexpected problems, and ongoing support.

How precise and elaborate was this plan?

Were people satisfied with it at the time?

Did it deal with all of the problems anticipated?

Were the requisite conditions for implementation ensured before it began?

These might have included commitment, understanding, materials and equipment, skills, time allocation, and organizational backup.

Were any important conditions seen as missing? Which were most missing?

Source: Miles, M. B., & Huberman, A. M. (1994). *Qualitative data analysis: An expanded sourcebook* (2nd ed.). Thousand Oaks, CA: Sage Publications.

Notice the choices being made within each topic area. For example, in the first two areas, the main things we want to know about the decision to adopt are who was involved, how the decision was actually made, and how important this project was relative to others. All of the questions seem to be functional, rather than theoretical or descriptive—they have to do with getting something done. When such a research question gets operationalized, an attempt will be made to determine whether these conditions were present or absent at the various field sites and whether that made any difference in the execution of the project. This is an example of how research questions feed directly into data collection and thus analysis.

Research Question Advice

1. Even if you are in a highly inductive mode, it is a good idea to start with some general research questions. They allow you to get clear about what, in the general domain, is of most interest. They make the implicit explicit, without necessarily freezing or limiting your vision.

2. Formulating more than a dozen or so overarching research questions is looking for trouble. You can easily lose the forest for the trees and fragment the collection of data. Having a large number of questions makes it harder to see emergent links across different parts of the database and to integrate findings. A solution to research question proliferation for a small-scale study is the use of one major question with no more than five related subquestions for clarity and specificity. Studies with larger magnitude (e.g., multiple-case or longitudinal) can generate more research questions.

3. It is sometimes easier to develop a conceptual framework *after* you've made a list of research questions. You look at the list for common themes, common concepts, implicit or explicit relationships, and so on, and then begin to map out the underlying framework joining these pieces. Some researchers operate best in this mode.

4. Once the list of research questions is generated and honed, look it over to ensure that each question is, in fact, researchable. Delete or revise those questions that you or your participants have no real means of answering, or you of measuring (qualitatively or quantitatively).

5. In a multiple-case study, be sure all fieldworkers understand each question and see its importance. Multiple-case studies have to be more explicit, so that several researchers can be aligned as they collect information in the field. Unclear questions or different understandings can make for incomparable data across cases.

6. Keep the research questions in hand and review them during fieldwork. This closeness will focus data collection and analysis. You will think twice before noting down what participants have for lunch or where they park their cars. Unless something has an obvious, direct, or potentially important link to a research question, it should not be entered into your field notes.

DEFINING THE CASE

Description and Rationale

Qualitative researchers often struggle with questions of "what my case is" and "where my case leaves off." Abstractly, we can define a *case* as a phenomenon of some sort occurring in a bounded context. The case is, in effect, your unit of analysis. Studies may be of just one case or of several. Display 2.6 shows this graphically: There is a focus or "heart" of the study, and a somewhat indeterminate boundary defines the edge of the case: what will not be studied.

Examples

What are some examples of cases? Sometimes the "phenomenon" may be an *individual* in a defined context, as suggested by Displays 2.1 and 2.2: a language arts teacher and her series of classes with junior-level high school students during an 18-week spring semester—the same semester her students will take a state-mandated standardized "high-stakes" test in language arts. Note that the

DISPLAY 2.6 ● The Case as the Unit of Analysis

Boundary

(Setting, Concepts, Sampling, etc.)

Focus

Source: Miles, M. B., & Huberman, A. M. (1994). *Qualitative data analysis: An expanded sourcebook* (2nd ed.). Thousand Oaks, CA: Sage Publications.

"heart" here is the teacher. The boundary defines her students and school site as the major contexts. The researcher will not, for example, interview the teacher's mother or visit the child care facility where the teacher leaves her own child during workdays.

The bounding is also by *time*: No information will be gathered after the spring semester ends in 18 weeks and the standardized test scores have been reported. We can also expect that the boundary will be defined further by *sampling*, which we'll discuss later. For example, this researcher will not be interviewing the school guidance counselor, only the principal and, if pertinent, other language arts teachers.

A case may also be defined by

1. a *role* (school principal, CEO, nurse supervisor);

2. a *small group* (African American men in an inner-city neighborhood, a college-level rock band, a breast cancer survivor support group);

3. an *organization* (a nursery school, a software engineering company, the American Sociological Association);

4. *space and environment* (a mall for adolescents to "hang out," visitors at the Vietnam Veterans Memorial Mall in Washington DC, nighttime foot traffic along the Las Vegas strip);

5. a *community or settlement* (the French Quarter of New Orleans, a village in Tanzania, the Tenderloin District of San Francisco);

6. *episodes or encounters* (voting for the first time, a "one-night stand," bullying incidents on an elementary school playground);

7. an *event* (a search committee meeting, a high school graduation ceremony, New Year's Eve in New York City's Times Square);

8. a *period of time* (a day in the life of a firefighter, spring break, how customers use their time between ordering food from a server and having it delivered to their table);

9. a *process* (grocery shopping and meal preparation, organizing and managing an international conference, the adoption and implementation of an innovational education program in a school district);

10. a *culture or subculture* (African American women in academia, Los Angeles drag queens, "skater dudes"); or

11. a *nation* (Greece during the period of its 21st-century economic crisis, America during the 2018 midterm election cycle).

Single cases are the stuff of much qualitative research and can be very vivid and illuminating, especially if they are chosen to be "critical," "extreme," or "revelatory," as Yin (2018, p. 24) suggests. But the cases may not be monolithic; cases may have subcases embedded within them. A case study of a school will contain cases of specific classrooms; a case study of a hospital ward may have cases of specific medical personnel–patient relationships within it.

We suggest that multiple cases offer the researcher an even deeper understanding of the processes and outcomes of cases, the chance to test (not just develop) hypotheses, and a good picture of locally grounded causation. The question of just which cases to include in a sample is discussed below.

A comment on notation: We sometimes prefer—and use here and there in this book—the word *site* because it reminds us that a "case" always occurs in a specified social and physical *setting*; we cannot study individual cases devoid of their site-specific context in the way a quantitative researcher often does.

Case Advice

1. Define the case as early as you can during a study. Given a starting conceptual framework and research questions, it pays to get a bit stern about who and what you are defining as a case; that will help clarify further both the framework and the questions.

2. Start intuitively but remember the focus and build outward. Think of whom and what you will *not* be studying as a way to firm up the boundaries.

3. Attend to several dimensions of the case: its *conceptual* nature, its *social size*, its *physical* location, and its *temporal* extent.

4. Remember that sampling will define the case(s) further.

SAMPLING: BOUNDING THE COLLECTION OF DATA

Description and Rationale

Sampling involves decisions not only about which people to observe and/or interview but also about settings, events, and social processes. Qualitative studies call for continual refocusing and redrawing of study parameters during fieldwork, but some initial selection still is required. A conceptual framework and research questions can help set the foci and boundaries for sampling decisions.

Sampling may look easy, but settings have subsettings (schools have classrooms, classrooms have cliques, cliques have individuals), so deciding where to look is not easy. Within any case, social phenomena proliferate (science lessons, teachers' questioning techniques, student unruliness, use of innovations); they, too, must be sampled. But as much as you might want to, you cannot study everyone everywhere doing everything. Your choices—whom to look at or talk with, where, when, about what, and why—place limits on the conclusions you can draw and on how confident you and others feel about them. Sampling is crucial for later analysis, so how do we manage it all? We discuss some general principles and suggest useful references for detailed help.

Key Features of Qualitative Sampling

Qualitative researchers usually work with small samples of people, nested in their context and studied in-depth—unlike quantitative researchers, who aim for larger numbers of context-stripped cases and seek statistical significance.

Sampling in qualitative research involves two actions that sometimes pull in different directions. First, you need to set *boundaries*: to define aspects of your case(s) that you can study within the limits of your time and budget, that connect directly to your research questions, and that probably will include examples of what you want to study. Second, at the same time, you need to create a conceptual *frame* to help you uncover, confirm, or qualify the basic processes or concepts that undergird your study. Display 2.2 suggests that the frame of this study is primarily about the pressures and consequences of state-mandated testing on one language arts teacher and her students.

Qualitative samples tend to be *purposive* rather than random. Samples in qualitative studies are usually not wholly prespecified but can evolve once fieldwork begins. The initial choices of participants lead you to similar and different ones, observing one class of events invites comparison with another, and understanding one key relationship in the setting reveals facets to be studied in others. This is conceptually driven *sequential* sampling.

Qualitative sampling is sometimes *theory driven*, either "up front" or progressively, as in a grounded theory mode. Suppose that you were studying how adolescents develop friendships and that you could only manage to look at one high school. At first, that seems very limited. But if you chose a site according to relevant theory, you might choose one that has a wide range and diversity of students in terms of gender, race/ethnicity, socioeconomic class, sexual orientation, religious background, and so on. This will enable you to test the theory that friendships become more selective—that is, discriminating—when multiple choices are available to adolescents.

You would sample *within* each class (freshman, sophomore, junior, senior) for certain developmentally expected processes such as clique formation, orientation of the newcomer, use of technology for friendship maintenance, and so on. You might also find that certain events, such as lunchtime and organized extracurricular sports and arts activities, are unusually rich with socialization actions, and then you would sample more carefully for these. Sampling both within and across cases puts flesh on the bones of general concepts and their relationships. We can see generic processes; our generalizations are not to "all adolescents" but to existing or new theories of how friendship development works.

General Sampling Strategies

Erickson (1986) suggests a generic, funneling sampling sequence, working from the outside in to the core of a setting. For example, in studying schools, he would begin with the school community (census data, a walk around the neighborhood) and then enter the school and the classroom, staying several days to get a sense of the frequency and occurrence of different events. From there, the focus would tighten: specific events, times, and locations. Periodically, however, Erickson would follow lines of influence into the surrounding environment to test the typicality of what was found in a given classroom and to get a better fix on external influences and determinants.

There is a wide range of sampling strategies available to qualitative researchers within a complex case or across cases (Patton, 2008, 2015). They can be selected ahead of time or can evolve during early data collection. It is impossible to prescribe which sampling strategies go best with each type of study, for there are too many unique conditions within each project (specific research questions, specific sites and cases, etc.). But you should be able to provide to your readers justification for why you selected certain types of sampling over others.

Random sampling is a gold standard of quantitative research but is used quite minimally in qualitative research because random sampling can sometimes deal you a nebulous hand. Our sampling tends to be more *strategic* and *purposive* because we are focusing on a case's unique contexts. Admittedly, there are times when we select a case to study because it is accessible to us geographically and immediately—a form of *convenience* sampling.

How do sampling strategies affect analysis? *Maximum variation sampling*, for example, involves looking for outlier cases to see whether the main patterns still hold, while *homogeneous sampling* focuses on people with similar demographic or social characteristics. The *critical case* is the instance that supports or exemplifies the main findings. Searching deliberately for *confirming and disconfirming cases, extreme or deviant cases,* and *typical cases* serves to increase confidence in analytic conclusions. Some strategies benefit inductive, theory-building analysis (e.g., *opportunistic* or *snowball sampling*). *Politically important cases* are salient participants who may need to be included (or excluded) because they connect with politically sensitive issues anticipated in the analysis.

Other strategies can be used for selection of participants prior to data collection. For example, Goetz and LeCompte (1984) offer (a) *comprehensive sampling*—examining every case, instance, or element in a given population; (b) *quota selection*—identifying the major subgroups and then taking an arbitrary number from each; (c) *reputational case selection*—instances chosen on the recommendation of an expert or key participant; and (d) *comparable case selection*—selecting individuals, sites, and groups on the same relevant characteristics over time (a replication strategy). Most of these strategies will increase confidence in analytic findings on the grounds of representativeness.

The sampling strategies we've been discussing can be applied both within and across multiple cases. Let's turn to some of the core issues in each of these domains.

Within-Case Sampling

A qualitative case may range widely in definition from individuals to roles, groups, organizations, processes, and cultures. But even when the case is an individual, the qualitative researcher has many within-case sampling decisions: Which *activities, processes, events, times, locations,* and *role partners* will I sample?

Within-case sampling is almost always *nested*—for example, studying children within classrooms within schools within neighborhoods, with regular movement up and down that ladder. For a cardiovascular bypass patient, we might want to sample his or her diet and exercise activities; the processes of understanding, taking in, and acting on medical advice; events such as admission and discharge interviews; time periods, including prehospitalization, hospitalization, and posthospitalization (once every 2 weeks); locations, including the recovery room, the ward, and the patient's home; and role partners, including the patient's physician, ward nurses, dietitian, and spouse.

A second major point is that such sampling should be *theoretically* driven—whether the theory is prespecified or emerges as you go, as in traditional grounded theory's "theoretical sampling." Choices of participants, episodes, and interactions should be driven by a conceptual question, not by a concern for representativeness. To get to the concept, such as *negotiation*, we need to see different instances of it at different moments in different places with different people. The prime concern is with the *conditions* under which the concept or theory operates, not with the generalization of the findings to other populations.

The third point is that within-case sampling has an *iterative* or "rolling" quality, working in progressive waves as the study progresses. Sampling is investigative; we observe, talk to people, and examine artifacts and documents. That leads us to new samples of participants and observations, new documents. At each step along the evidential trail, we are making sampling decisions to clarify the main patterns, see contrasts, identify exceptions or discrepant instances, and uncover negative instances—where the pattern does not hold. Our analytic conclusions depend deeply on the within-case sampling choices we made.

So, within-case sampling helps us see a local configuration in some depth. What can additional cases do for us, and how do we create a sample of cases?

Multiple-Case Sampling

Multiple-case sampling adds *confidence* to findings. By looking at a range of similar and contrasting cases, we can understand a single-case finding, grounding it by specifying *how* and *where* and, if possible, *why* it carries on as it does. We can strengthen the precision, validity, stability, and trustworthiness of the findings. In other words, we are following a *replication* strategy (Yin, 2018). If a finding holds in one setting and, given its profile, also holds in a comparable setting but does not in a contrasting case, the finding is more robust.

With multiple-case studies, does the issue of *generalizability* change? Essentially, no. We are generalizing from one case to the next on the basis of a match to the underlying theory, not to a larger universe. The choice of cases usually is made on *conceptual* grounds, not on representative grounds. The cases often are arrayed on a continuum (e.g., highly gifted to underachieving pupils), with few exemplars of each, or they are contrasted (e.g., assertive and passive adolescents). Other, unique properties may be added (e.g., some assertive adolescents are from cities, some from rural areas). Because case study researchers examine intact settings in such minute detail, they know all too well that each setting has a few properties it shares with *many* others, some properties it shares with *some* others, and some properties it shares with *no* others. Nevertheless, multiple-case sampling gives us confidence that our emerging theory is transferable, because we have seen it work out—or not work out—in predictable ways across different cases.

How many cases should a multiple-case study have? This question is not answerable on statistical grounds, of course. We have to deal with the issue conceptually: How many cases, and in what kind of sampling frame, would give us confidence in our analytic generalizations? It also depends on how rich and complex the within-case sampling is. With high complexity, a study with more than 10 cases or so can become unwieldy. There are too many data to scan visually and too many permutations to account for. And the problems of practical and intellectual coordination among multiple researchers get very large once you are a staff of more than five people. Still, we've seen multiple-case studies in the 20s and 30s; the price is usually thinner data. If we were forced to recommend a specific number, we would suggest five or six richly researched cases as a minimum for multiple-case sampling adequacy. (We have read outstanding qualitative studies that compared just two, three, and four cases, but their authors did not assert any generalizability.)

Questions of practicality also face us. There is a finite amount of time, with variable access to different participants and events, and an abundance of logistical problems. Being selective calls for some restraint in the classes of data you go after. Here we might suggest some guidelines. For example, useful data would (a) identify *new leads* of importance, (b) *extend* the area of information, (c) *relate* or bridge the already existing elements, (d) reinforce the main *trends*, (e) account for *other information* already in hand, (f) exemplify or provide more evidence for an *important theme*, and (g) *qualify or refute* existing information.

Key processes can be identified at the outset or gradually—often via pattern codes, analytic memos, and interim summaries (to be described in later chapters). Being explicit about processes and collecting comparable data on them will foster cross-case comparability and give you easier access to the core underlying concepts as you get deeper into data collection.

Sampling Advice

1. If you're new to qualitative research, rest assured that there is never enough time to do any study. It is probably a good idea to start with a fallback sample of participants and subsettings: the things you have to cover in light of what you know at that point. That sample will change later, but less than you may think.

2. Just thinking in sampling-frame terms is good for your study's health. If you are talking with one kind of participant, you need to consider why this kind of participant is important and, from there, who else should be interviewed or observed.

3. In complex cases, remember that you are sampling people to get at the characteristics of settings, events, and processes. This means watching out for an overreliance on talk or on observation of participants while neglecting sampling for key events, interactions in different settings, and episodes embodying the emerging patterns in the study. The sampling choices at the start of the study may not be the most pertinent or data-rich ones. A systematic review can sharpen the early and later choices.

4. There is a danger of sampling too narrowly. Go to the meatiest, most study-relevant sources. But it is also important to work a bit at the peripheries—to talk to people who are not central to the phenomenon but are neighbors to it, to people no longer actively involved, to dissidents, renegades, and eccentrics. Spending a day in the adjoining village, school, neighborhood, or clinic is also worth the time, even if you don't see the sense at that point. You may learn a lot and obtain contrasting and comparative information that may help you understand the phenomenon at hand by decentering yourself from a particular way of viewing your primary cases.

5. Spend some time checking whether your sampling frame is feasible. Be sure the time is there, the resources are there, the requisite access to people and places is ensured, and the conditions are right for doing a careful job. Plan to study a bit less, rather than more, and "bank" the extra time. If you are done, the time is yours for a wider or deeper pass at the field.

6. Three kinds of instances have great payoff. The first is the apparently "typical" or "representative" instance. If you can find it, try to find another one. The second is the "negative" or "disconfirming" instance; it gives you both the limits of your conclusions and the point of greatest variation. The third is the "exceptional" or "discrepant" instance. This instance will allow you to qualify your findings and to specify the variations or contingencies in the main patterns observed. Going deliberately after negative and atypical instances is also healthy in itself; it may force you to clarify your concepts, and it may tell you that you indeed have sampled too narrowly.

INSTRUMENTATION

Description and Rationale

Instrumentation comprises specific methods for collecting data. They may be focused on qualitatively or quantitatively organized information and may be loosely to tightly structured. Note that the term *instrumentation* may mean little more than some shorthand devices for observing and recording events. But note, too, that even when the instrumentation is an open-ended interview or fieldwork observation, some technical choices must be made: Will notes be taken? Of what sort? Will the transaction be audio- or video-recorded? Transcribed?

Kvale and Brinkmann (2015) point out that during an open-ended interview, some analysis and interpretation occur along the way. The person describing his or her "life world" may discover new relationships and patterns during the interview. The researcher who occasionally summarizes or reflects what has been heard is, in fact, condensing and interpreting the flow of meaning. Data are not being collected but rather coauthored.

We've discussed how conceptual frameworks, research questions, and sampling have a focusing role within a study. They give some direction to the researcher, before and during fieldwork, by clarifying what he or she wants to find out from whom and why. Knowing what you want to find out, at least initially, leads to the question of *how* you will get that information. That question, in turn, later determines the analyses you can conduct. If I want to find out how crime suspects are arrested and booked, I may decide to *interview* the people associated with this activity (police officers, suspects, and attorneys); *observe* bookings; and collect arrest-relevant *documents* (e.g., regulations, interrogation transcripts). If permitted, I may also take digital *photographs or video* of arrests and bookings. But how much of this instrumentation has to be designed prior to going out to the field, and how much structure should such instruments have?

There are several possible answers to how much preplanning and structuring of instrumentation is desirable: "little" (i.e., hardly any prior instrumentation) to "a lot" (of prior instrumentation, well structured) to "it depends" (on the nature of the study). Each view has supporting arguments; let's review them in capsule form (Display 2.7 is a summary of some of the main issues in deciding on the appropriate amount of front-end instrumentation).

DISPLAY 2.7 ● Prior Instrumentation: Key Decision Factors		
Little Prior Instrumentation	**"It Depends"**	**A Lot of Prior Instrumentation**
Rich context description needed		Context less crucial
Concepts inductively grounded in local meanings		Concepts defined ahead by researcher
Exploratory, inductive		Confirmatory, theory-driven
Descriptive intent		Explanatory intent
"Basic" research emphasis		Applied, evaluation or policy emphasis
Single case		Multiple cases
Comparability not too important		Comparability important
Simple, manageable, single-level case		Complex, multilevel, overloading case
Generalizing not a concern		Generalizability/representativeness important
Need to avoid researcher impact		Researcher impact of less concern
Qualitative only, freestanding study		Multimethod study, quantitative included

Source: Miles, M. B., & Huberman, A. M. (1994). *Qualitative data analysis: An expanded sourcebook* (2nd ed.). Thousand Oaks, CA: Sage Publications.

Arguments for Little Prior Instrumentation

1. Predesigned and structured instruments blind the researcher to the site. If the most important phenomena or underlying concepts at work in the field are not collected through the instruments, they will be overlooked or misrepresented.

2. Prior instrumentation is usually stripped of context for purposes of universality, uniformity, and comparability. But qualitative research lives and breathes through seeing site-specific contexts; it is the particularities that produce the generalities, not the reverse.

3. Many qualitative studies involve single cases with few people involved. Who needs standardized questionnaires, observation schedules, or tests—whose usual function is to yield economical, comparable, and parametric distributions for large samples?

4. The lion's share of fieldwork consists of taking field notes; recording events (conversations, meetings); interviewing participants; and examining things (documents, products, artifacts). *Instrumentation* is a misnomer; some orienting questions for observations may be all you need at the start.

Arguments for a Lot of Prior Instrumentation

1. If you know what you are after, there is no reason not to plan in advance how to collect the information.

2. If interview protocols or observation schedules are not focused, too much superfluous information will be collected. An overload of data will compromise the efficiency and power of the analysis.

3. Using the same instruments as in prior studies is an efficient way to converse across studies. Otherwise, the work will be noncomparable, except in a very global way. We need common instruments to construct explanations or predictions, and to make recommendations about practice.

4. A biased or uninformed researcher will ask partial questions, take selective notes, make unreliable observations, and skew information. The data will be invalid and unreliable. Using validated instruments well is the best guarantee of dependable and meaningful findings.

Arguments for "It Depends"

1. If you are running an *exploratory*, largely descriptive study, you do not really know the parameters or dynamics of a social setting. So, heavy initial instrumentation or closed-ended devices are inappropriate. If, however, you are doing a *confirmatory* study, with relatively focused research questions and a well-bounded sample of persons, events, and processes, then well-structured instrument designs are a logical choice. Within a given study, there can be both exploratory and confirmatory aspects that call for differential front-end structure, or there can be exploratory and confirmatory *times*, with exploration often called for at the outset and confirmation near the end.

2. A *single-case* study calls for less front-end preparation than does a *multiple-case* study. The latter is looking forward to cross-case comparison, which requires some standardization of instruments so that findings can be laid side by side in the course of analysis. Similarly, *a freestanding* study has fewer constraints than a *multimethod* study. A *basic* study often needs less advance organizing than an *evaluation* or *policy* study. In the latter cases, the focus is tighter and the instrumentation more closely keyed to the variables of interest.

3. Much depends on the *case definition* and levels of analysis expected. A researcher studying classroom subculture in an elementary school might choose to look intensively in 3 of the building's 35 classrooms and so probably would be right to start with a looser, orienting set of instruments. If, however, an attempt is made to say something about how classroom subculture issues are embedded in the working culture of the school building as a whole, a more standardized, validated instrument—a teacher survey or a group interview protocol— may also be necessary.

Figure out first what kind of study you are doing and what kind of instruments you are likely to need at different moments within that study, and then go to work on the ones needed at the outset. But in all cases, the amount and type of instrumentation should be a function of your conceptual framework, research questions, and sampling criteria. If not, the tail is likely to be wagging the dog, and later analysis will suffer.

Example

We provide an example of how front-end instrument design can be driven in different ways by a study's scope and focus, showing a mix of predesigned and open-ended instrumentation.

Miles and Huberman's school improvement study was a multiple-case ($N = 12$) project, and the phenomenon under investigation was moderately well (but not fully) understood from prior research. Both of these points suggested that some front-end instruments were likely to be called for. Previous empirical research and cognitive and social-psychological theory both led us to the idea that people will adapt or reinvent practices while using them. Thus, one important research question in the study was this: *In which ways did people redefine, reorganize, or reinvent the new program to use it successfully?*

The *sampling* decisions were straightforward. The question addresses teachers in particular, and to get the answer, we had to observe or interview them or, ideally, do both. We sampled events such as the teacher's first encounter with the innovation, and processes such as assessing the innovation's strong and weak points and making changes in it to fit one's practice.

Let's look at the interview component of the *instrumentation*. We developed a semi-structured interview guide (see Display 2.8). Each field researcher was closely familiar with the guide but had the latitude to use a personally congenial way of asking and sequencing the questions and to segment them appropriately for different respondents.

The guide was designed after field work had begun. An initial wave of site visits had been conducted to get a sense of the context, the participants, and how the school improvement process seemed to be working locally. From that knowledge, we went for a deeper and broader understanding. The interviewer begins by taking the participant back to the time just before he or she was to use the innovation with students, asking for detailed context—what was happening, who the colleagues were, and what feelings they had.

Questions 33 through 36 in Display 2.8 move forward through time, asking how the innovation looked, its ready or unready parts, and what the teacher was doing to prepare for its use. Question 40 comes directly to the research question, assessing the pre-use changes made in the innovation. The probes can be handled in various ways: as aids to help the interviewer flesh out the question, as prompts for items the participant may have overlooked, or as subquestions derived from previous research. Later in the interview, the same question recurs as the interviewer evokes the teacher's retrospective views of early and later use, then moves into the present ("What changes are you making now?") and the future ("What changes are you considering?").

DISPLAY 2.8 ● Excerpts From Interview Guide, School Improvement Study

33. Probably you have a certain idea of how _____ looks to you now, but keep thinking back to how it first looked to you then, just before students came. How did it seem to you then?

    Probes:

    _____ Clearly connected, differentiated vs. unconnected, confusing

    _____ Clear how to start vs. awesome, difficult

    _____ Complex (many parts) vs. simple and straightforward

    _____ Prescriptive and rigid vs. flexible and manipulatable

34. What parts of aspects seemed ready to use, things you thought would work out OK?

35. What parts or aspects seemed not worked out, not ready for use?

36. Could you describe what you actually did during that week or so before you started using _____ with students?

    Probes:

    _____ Reading

    _____ Preparing materials

    _____ Planning

    _____ Talking (with whom, about what)

    _____ Training

. . . .

40. Did you make any changes in the standard format for the program before you started using it with students? What kind of changes with things you thought might not work, things you didn't like, things you couldn't do in this school?

    Probes:

    _____ Things dropped

    _____ Things added, created

    _____ Things revised

Source: Miles, M. B., & Huberman, A. M. (1994). *Qualitative data analysis: An expanded sourcebook* (2nd ed.). Thousand Oaks, CA: Sage Publications.

Instrumentation Advice

1. Simply thinking in instrument design terms from the outset strengthens data collection as you go. If you regularly ask, "Given this research question, how can I get an answer?" it will sharpen *sampling* decisions, help clarify *concepts*, and help set *priorities* for actual data collection. You also will learn the skills of redesigning instrumentation as new questions, new subsamples, and new lines of inquiry develop.

2. People and settings in field studies can be observed more than once. Not everything is riding on the single interview or observation. In qualitative research, there is nearly always a second chance. So, front-end instrumentation can be revised—in fact, should be revised. You learn how to ask a question in the site's terms and to look with new eyes at something that began to emerge during the first visit. Instrumentation can be modified steadily to explore new leads, address a revised research question, or interview a new group of participants.

3. In qualitative research, issues of instrument trustworthiness ride largely on the skills of the researcher. Essentially a *person* is observing, interviewing, and recording, while modifying the observation, interviewing, and recording devices from one field visit to the next. Thus, you need to ask about yourself and your colleagues: How trustworthy is this *person* likely to be as an information-gathering instrument? To us, some markers of a good qualitative researcher-as-instrument are

   a. strong familiarity with the phenomenon and the setting under study;

   b. a multidisciplinary approach, as opposed to a narrow grounding or focus in a single discipline or research methodology;

   c. good investigative skills, the ability to draw people out, and meticulous attention to detail;

   d. being comfortable, resilient, and nonjudgmental with participants in the setting; and

   e. a heightened sense of empathetic engagement, balanced with a heightened sense of objective awareness.

We believe that a savvy researcher with excellent social interaction skills is often the best data collection instrument in a qualitative study: sharper, more attentive, people-friendly, worldly wise, and quicker to home in on core processes and meanings about participants and the case.

LINKING QUALITATIVE AND QUANTITATIVE DATA

We have to face the fact that numbers and words are *both* needed if we are to understand the world. The question is not whether the two sorts of data and their associated methods can be linked during study design but whether it should be done, how it will be done, and for what purposes.

Both types of data can be productive for descriptive, exploratory, inductive, and opening-up purposes. And both can be productive for explanatory, confirmatory, and hypothesis-testing purposes. In multiple-case studies, it is possible to rank cases and to benefit from the availability of nonparametric statistical techniques for contrasting them. When words and numbers are combined with the up-close, deep, credible understanding of complex, real-world contexts that characterize good qualitative studies, we have a very powerful mix.

Looked at the other way, qualitative data can help the quantitative side of a study during design by aiding in conceptual framework development, methodological choice(s), research question design, and instrumentation. They can help during data collection by making access and data collection easier. During analysis, they can help by validating, interpreting, clarifying, and illustrating quantitative findings, as well as through strengthening and revising theory.

There is, of course, a long and well-developed tradition of dealing quantitatively with qualitative data: content analysis, where the issue is one of counting the frequency and sequencing of particular words, phrases, concepts, or visual images found in the data (Neuendorf, 2017). Also note the tradition of using quantitative information in anthropological field work; Bernard (2018) includes a helpful compilation of methods.

Approaches to Mixed Methods Designs

Mixed methods is a genre of inquiry that has been gaining ground in several research circles (Creamer, 2018; Creswell & Plano Clark, 2018). Whether you choose to employ some form of quantitative component in your qualitative study is both an epistemological and a methodological decision that should be driven by your study's needs, not by the assumption that statistics will somehow enhance the rigor and trustworthiness of your study. The reasons cited most often for mixing both genres are to (a) provide analytic texture to your work; (b) compensate for the deficiencies of one genre with the strengths of another; and (c) modify or strengthen the analytic findings when the results of each genre support, corroborate, or contradict each other.

Examples

Analytic Texture

Words alone and numbers alone can each communicate selected facets of experience. But sometimes both, in strategic combination, can add more dimension to the analysis and findings. We offer that when the quantitative accompanies the qualitative, it provides *analytic texture* to a report.

During Miles and Huberman's school improvement study, we gradually became aware of the importance of job mobility and looked at people in our sites who had changed jobs (moving up, out, sideways, or down). It proved helpful to know how many people had moved (75, for 12 sites); how many of these had moved because of their experience with the innovation (83%); and how many were actually upward career moves (35%). Descriptive statistics such as these were useful as data summaries to accompany and support the qualitative findings from interviews.

Quantitizing is the transformation of qualitative data into numeric representations of some kind. We converted some interview data into rating scales or *magnitudes*: the degree of pressure teachers felt to adopt an innovation, their satisfaction with the assistance they received, or the "roughness" or "smoothness" of the implementation. Because our cases were schools, not individuals, this conversion involved examining interviews from different people, checking the degree of agreement, and arriving at a site-level rating. Three- to five-point scales seemed the easiest and most reliable; for example,

- 5 = high, 4 = moderate/high, 3 = moderate, 2 = moderate/low, 1 = low

- 5 = smooth, 4 = mostly smooth, 3 = mixed, 2 = rough, 1 = very rough

In the displays and analysis, we kept the numbers or magnitudes like these closely associated with the words from which we drew the judgment. Many times, a reader has a tacit understanding of what a 2 on a 5-point evaluation scale suggests. In this case, a number succinctly captures the researchers' interpretations of the participants' overall qualitative experiences.

Compensating for Each Genre

Some mixed methodologists disagree whether one paradigm (e.g., the qualitative) compensates for its "deficiencies" with the "strengths" of another paradigm (e.g., the quantitative). Both paradigms are worthy unto themselves as epistemologies and research approaches, and the notion that each one has its own set of deficiencies is a misplaced assumption. Both the quantitative and qualitative bring different gifts to the research enterprise, each one value-adding to the investigation. Nevertheless, a realist perspective must acknowledge that numbers alone do not tell the whole story. And while words alone can spin a glorious narrative, we cannot escape our need to sometimes quantify our experiences with terms such as "most," "few," "excellent," and "only."

McCammon, Saldaña, Hines, and Omasta (2012) received e-mail survey responses from 234 participants about their high school arts experiences. The survey asked for demographic information (e.g., gender, year of high school graduation, state[s] of high school attendance) as well as participants' ratings to a series of prompts (4 = strongly agree, 3 = agree, 2 = disagree, 1 = strongly disagree), and it provided space for an open-ended qualitative commentary to the prompts. The demographic information provided descriptive statistics such as percentages. The ratings provided means and other statistics for various significance tests. The open-ended survey responses were qualitatively coded and analyzed.

The respondents' mean rating to the survey prompt, "My participation in high school speech and/or theatre has affected the adult I am now," was 3.82 (veering toward "strongly agree") out of a possible 4.00. This is an impressive statistic that supports the perceived impact of the subject areas on their former students. But *why* such a high rating? This is where qualitative analysis enters to support and explain the quantitative result. The open-ended follow-up prompt to the survey item was, "In what ways do you think your participation in speech and/or theatre as a high school student has affected the adult you have become?" Respondents' written testimony permitted us to code and categorize their perceptions to learn that the major outcomes of participation in speech and/or theatre are self-confidence, enhanced thinking and work habits, identity formation, and emotional growth.

This mixed methods design also enabled us to compare means between various groupings (e.g., between men and women, between younger and older respondents) and apply a two-tailed t test to discern any significant statistical differences ($p < .05$), followed by a qualitative comparison of codes. After a few initial queries, we observed *paradigmatic corroboration*: In other words, the lower and more significant the p level, the more qualitative differences seemed to appear between groups; conversely, when the p level was moderate or high and thus less significant, the fewer qualitative differences we could detect between the groups. In this case, sequential quantitative and qualitative analyses and findings supported one another.

Strengthening Analytic Findings

A third reason for conducting a mixed methods study is to modify or strengthen the analytic findings when the results of both the qualitative and quantitative components support, corroborate, or contradict each other. Contradictions in findings—the lack of paradigmatic corroboration—do not always suggest faulty instrumentation or noncomparable data sets. Rather, the discrepant results suggest that deeper analytic work and reflection are needed to resolve the inconsistencies in order to make emergent insights on why the variability exists.

Mixed methodologists strongly recommend that final reports graphically illustrate the qualitative and quantitative data collection and analytic trajectories of the study and their integrated blending. Display 2.9 exhibits that model from Jang, McDougall, Pollon, Herbert, and Russell's (2008) study on improving urban schools facing challenging circumstances. Qualitative data collection is mapped in the upper left of the display, quantitative data collection in the upper right, and their mixing in the center bins. A careful read of the bins' contents will show the participant samples, the instrumentation used, and the analytic moves to mix the two data forms. The coauthors explain:

> The results from the parallel analyses of the qualitative and quantitative data were compared together for synthesis through data transformation. The results from the survey data were transformed into narrative descriptions of the nine factors. Although both strands captured some overlapping aspects of school improvement, the results from the qualitative data provided additional information about the characteristics of school improvement. Furthermore, *inconsistencies were also observed*. Whereas the qualitative data indicated

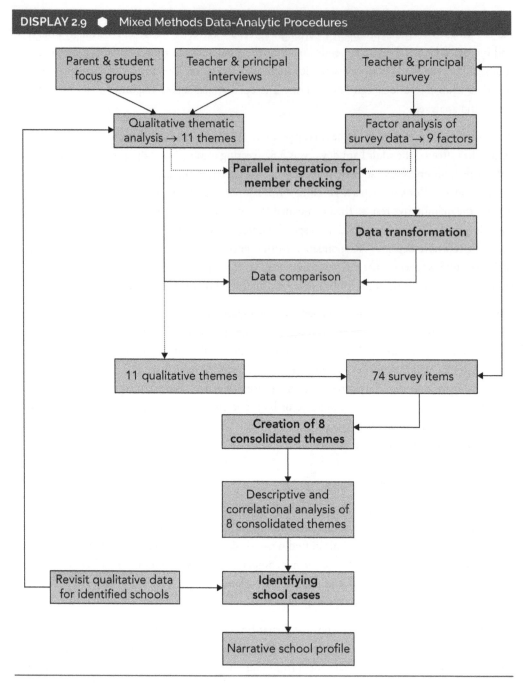

DISPLAY 2.9 ● Mixed Methods Data-Analytic Procedures

Source: Jang et al. (2009), p. 230.

variability in school practice among the schools, the survey data did not show much difference in school staff members' perspectives about school improvement. Therefore, we took integrative analytic approaches using data consolidation and case analytic strategies to gain an in-depth understanding of the causes of these inconsistencies. (Jang et al., 2008, p. 229; emphasis added)

Perhaps the most compelling part of this study is its focus on mixed methodology and the coauthors' analytic journey as they consolidated the themes extracted from each paradigm. Display 2.9 might also serve as inspiration for qualitative research-only studies to display *their* data collection and analytic moves.

Mixed Methods Advice

1. Consider whether your qualitative study can benefit from a quantitative component. Think *purposes* and think ahead: In light of my research questions and the audiences for my study report, will qualitative information be enough or should it be complemented by a numerical data set of some kind?

2. During study design, you are setting up the social system of the project. If you are a lone researcher, can you manage both sorts of information? What technical support might you need? We advise finding and using a mentor who can advise you; critique products; and provide a supportive, different perspective.

3. If you are part of a research team, what will be the consequences of a specific division of labor? In our experience, for example, keeping qualitative and quantitative researchers separate can feed negative comparisons, stereotyping, and sterile arguments about "which data you trust more."

DATA MANAGEMENT ISSUES BEARING ON ANALYSIS

How a qualitative study is managed from Day 1 strongly influences the kinds of analyses that can be done, and how easily. Qualitative studies, especially those done by the lone researcher or the novice graduate student, can be notorious for their vulnerability to poor study management. Kvale and Brinkmann (2015) point out a naive question from a beginner: "How shall I find a method to analyze the 1,000 pages of interview transcripts I have collected?" Their reply is, "Never conduct interview research in such a way that you find yourself in a situation where you ask such a question" (pp. 215–216).

We make no pretense of being exhaustive on issues of study management but want to point to a series of issues with strong implications for analysis. We deal with three topics in turn: data management, the use of computers and software, and staffing/time planning.

Data Management

Typically, large amounts of data come from several sources, cases, or sites, and sometimes include numerical data sets as well. The total collection is termed an *archive*, a *data corpus*, or an assemblage of *empirical materials*. Regardless of what you call them, the main issues are ensuring (a) high-quality, accessible data; (b) documentation of just what analyses have been carried out; and (c) retention of data and associated analyses after the study is complete. Many questions are at hand, but they boil down to these: What do I need to anticipate in the way of data management requirements? How thorough do I need to be? Below we present an ideal wish list of needs to be included in the data that are managed in a project and retained afterwards:

1. Raw material: field notes, digital recordings/photographs, site documents, etc.

2. Partially processed data: write-ups; transcriptions; initial versions; and subsequent corrected, "cleaned," "commented-on" versions

3. Coded data: write-ups with specific codes or themes attached

4. The coding scheme or codebook, in its successive iterations

5. Jottings, analytic memos, or other analytic material; the researcher's reflections on the conceptual meaning of the data

6. Search and retrieval records: information showing which coded units or data segments the researcher looked for during analysis, and the retrieved material; records of links made among segments

7. Data displays: matrices, networks, graphics, etc., used to display retrieved information, along with the associated analytic text; revised versions of these

8. Analysis episodes: documentation of what you did, step by step, to assemble the displays and write the analytic text

9. Report text: successive drafts of what is written on the design, methods, and findings of the study

10. General chronological log or documentation of data collection and analysis work

11. Index of all of the above material

Do you have to set all this up, use it all, and keep it all? No. Will you be better off if you think about these possibilities and their relative importance during the design of the study? Yes. Is it easier to do it with the right software? Yes, two or three times easier, particularly with Microsoft Word and Excel. Some CAQDAS programs (discussed next) automatically generate and store material of this sort as you go along. But you will also need a well-organized physical place for storage and retrieval of raw field notes, audio and related media, edited hard copies, and so on. Preliminary organization is key, yet expect to revise and extend your data management system as you go. Institutional Review Boards (discussed further in Chapter 3) may also impose particular requirements for data management, such as the use of pseudonyms and secure storage, to ensure participant anonymity and confidentiality.

Some researchers prefer to keep each form and unit of data as a separate computer file, but in categorized directory folders. For example, a folder labeled "Interviews" contains the files "Interview 1 - Janice," "Interview 2 - Janice," and so on. Others prefer to label folders by case or site with appropriate subfolders, such as a folder named "Janice Data" with subfolders of "Interviews," "Participant Observation," "Photos," and so on.

Saldaña recommends a single master document for a one-person, short-term, qualitative case study. All the data get placed in one "working" file (with the original and complete data sets in separate backup files) that eventually get condensed and transformed into the final report. Interview excerpts, after condensation, are available as participant quotes for the final report. Related chunks of data get cut-and-pasted together as a form of instantaneous categorization.

Finally, remember that most research data are irreplaceable. If they are inadvertently erased, damaged, stolen, or lost in the cloud, you are out of luck. *Back up all of your work.*

Computer and Software Use

It is taken for granted that you need a good desktop or laptop computer to conduct qualitative research. Handwritten field notes, along with audio or video recordings, must be converted into analyzable text, which then needs to be condensed, displayed, and used to draw and verify conclusions. It's also fair to say that the researcher who does not use software beyond programs such as Microsoft Word will be hampered in comparison with those who do. Below we list some of the most common and frequent tasks qualitative researchers will conduct on a desktop or laptop computer:

1. Making notes in the field

2. Writing up, extending, and revising field notes

3. Transcribing (and in some cases recording) audio- or video-recorded interviews, conversations

4. Coding: attached to segments of text to permit later retrieval

5. Storage: keeping text and other digital materials in an organized database

6. Search and retrieval: locating relevant segments of text and making them available for inspection

7. Data "linking": connecting relevant data segments with each other, forming categories, clusters, or networks of information

8. Analytic memoing: writing reflective commentaries on some aspects of the data as a basis for deeper analysis

9. Content analysis: counting frequencies, sequence, or locations of words and phrases

10. Data display: placing selected data in a condensed, organized format, such as a matrix, network, or graphic

11. Conclusion drawing and verification: aiding the analyst to interpret displayed data and to test or confirm findings

12. Theory building: developing systematic, conceptually coherent explanations of findings; testing hypotheses

13. Graphic mapping: creating diagrams and other displays that depict findings or theories

14. Preparing interim and final reports

"What software is best?" cannot be answered meaningfully. You have to get specific about the kind of database you are building in your project and about the kind of analysis you will be doing. Microsoft Word and Excel (or comparable programs) are bare minimum requirements. Word includes many layout features for text and enables you to easily construct complex tables and matrices for displays. Excel is most useful for unitizing the database in cells, building matrices, and especially for holding qualitative survey data and taking quantitative data through selected statistical calculations and tests—a boon for mixed methods studies (see Display 2.10).

CAQDAS

CAQDAS (Computer Assisted Qualitative Data Analysis Software) consists of specialized programs designed for qualitative database management and for assisting analysis. The software does not analyze data automatically for the researcher. It relies on your use of its programming commands to code, annotate, retrieve, and array the data in different configurations for analytic reflection and discovery.

CAQDAS is first and foremost an excellent way to store and maintain your data corpus, with some programs storing or accessing digital audio and video, and some that can download Internet data such as social media content. Selected programs visually display which code you've assigned to which unit of data through clear, at-a-glance graphics. Their search and retrieval functions permit rapid access of codes and associated data to construct categories or themes and allow you to test your hunches, hypotheses, and queries; they also keep records of these operations for analytic documentation.

DISPLAY 2.10 ⬤ An Excel Spreadsheet With Qualitative and Quantitative Data

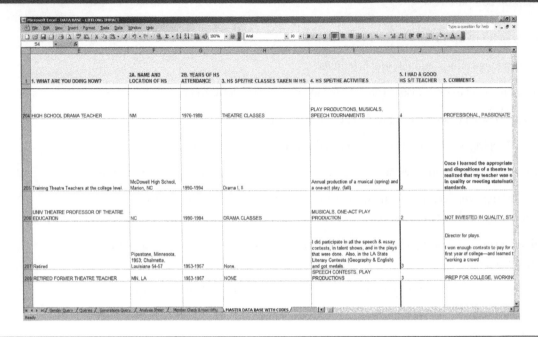

Some programs also feature quantitative/statistical capabilities for mixed methods studies, and more sophisticated CAQDAS packages can construct, with researcher input, semantic networks or other displays with nodes and lines that suggest interrelationships between data chunks or categories. Display 2.11 shows the categories of New Zealand's tourism products (e.g., Natural Resources, Historical and Cultural Resources) as perceived by Chinese tourists (Sun, Ryan, & Pan, 2015, p. 549). The

DISPLAY 2.11 ⬤ Network View Produced by ATLAS.ti

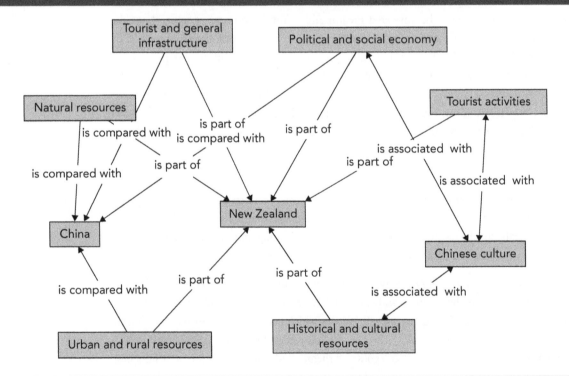

Source: Sun, Ryan, & Pan (2015), p. 549.

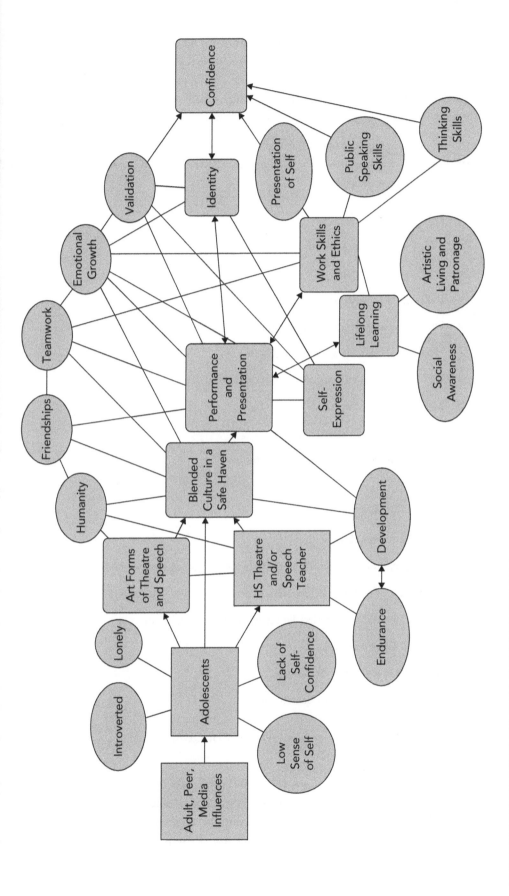

Source: McCammon, L., Saldaña, J., Hines, A., & Omasta, M. (2012). Lifelong impact: Adult perceptions of their high school speech and/or theatre participation. Youth Theatre Journal 26(1), 2–25.

CAQDAS software ATLAS.ti enables researchers to insert not just labels for bins but labels for links ("is part of," "is associated with," "is compared with") for enhanced network analysis.

Saldaña has found the CAQDAS modeling features for network display drawing most helpful and much easier to use than the time-consuming artwork features of text-based programs. Display 2.12 (from McCammon et al., 2012, p. 14) illustrates a complex model of interacting variables leading to participant confidence from participating in high school speech and theatre classes and activities. The model was originally drawn with NVivo 8 software.

There are multiple software options available, varying in complexity, cost, and available functions. These programs' websites provide online tutorials or demonstration software/manual downloads of their most current versions:

- AQUAD: www.aquad.de/en
- ATLAS.ti: www.atlasti.com
- CAT: cat.texifter.com
- Dedoose: www.dedoose.com
- DiscoverText: www.discovertext.com
- HyperRESEARCH: www.researchware.com
- INTERACT: www.mangold-international.com
- MAXQDA: www.maxqda.com
- NVivo: www.qsrinternational.com
- Q-Notes: https://wwwn.cdc.gov/qnotes/
- QDA Miner: www.provalisresearch.com
- Qualrus: www.qualrus.com
- Quirkos: www.quirkos.com
- Studiocode (for video data materials): https://vosaic.com/products/studiocode
- Transana (for audio and video data materials): www.transana.com
- V-Note (for audio and video data materials): www.v-note.org
- WebQDA: www.webqda.net
- Weft QDA: www.pressure.to/qda/
- WordStat: www.provalisresearch.com

Selected CAQDAS programs, such as CAT and Weft QDA, are free of charge but do not provide supplemental technical support.

Online-only programs like TagCrowd (tagcrowd.com), WordItOut (worditout.com), and Wordle (www.wordle.net) enable you to cut-and-paste large amounts of text into a field. The online software then analyzes its word count frequencies and displays the results in a randomized "cloud" design with the more frequent words in a larger font size. These programs employ only basic content-analytic functions yet display results in intriguing visual arrays for analytic reflection. Baral and Pokharel (2017) analyzed the contents of the S&P 500 companies' mission, vision, and values statements to measure the extent to which they reflect the concept of sustainability. Display 2.13 exhibits the 30 most frequently used words in those three separate statements as word clouds, which served as an analytic heuristic before more complex statistical applications were applied.

We do not recommend one software program over others, and you may find that the scope of your study is so small that a CAQDAS program may not even be needed. But this software is indispensable for longitudinal, large-scale, or multiple-case studies and studies with digital photographs, video data, and Internet-downloaded materials. You should select one that seems compatible with your research needs and personal ways of working, or one that permits multiple-user access for team research projects.

Work initially at a level of computer literacy that is comfortable for you, technically speaking, and extend your understanding with the help of friends whose computer skills are stronger than yours. Although manuals and tutorials supplied with programs can help, the best way to learn a new program is to use it on real tasks with a mentor for consultation. Allow time in your study design for learning new software.

There is ongoing debate within the field about the utility of these software programs for data analysis. No single software program can do everything well. You may end up with several programs (e.g., Word, Excel, and Quirkos; see Display 2.14), each with specific strengths, rather than with one all-purpose package. Transana (see Display 2.15), for example, is indispensable for video data and conversation analysis with the Jefferson notation system. Some CAQDAS programs include wonderful features to support analyses, but there is a steep learning curve for most programs. Invest your time

DISPLAY 2.13 ⬡ Word Clouds of Top 30 Most Frequent Words in the Mission (top), Vision (middle), and Values (bottom) Statements of the S&P 500 Companies

Source: Baral & Pokharel (2017), p. 127.

DISPLAY 2.14 ⬡ A Screenshot of Quirkos CAQDAS Software

Source: Courtesy of Daniel Turner, Quirkos Software; www.quirkos.com.

DISPLAY 2.15 ● A Screenshot of Transana CAQDAS Software

Source: Courtesy of David K. Woods, Transana; www.transana.com.

wisely; spend it more on analyzing data and not on figuring out a software program's operations and syntax. Think critically about what you need as your projects and research career evolve.

CAQDAS is a fast-moving field. Expect the information here to become outdated as new programs are created and updated versions appear. Refer to the appendix for recommended titles in print to supplement the use of basic text programs. We purposely decline to recommend certain software programs over others. To do so would be unfair to the developers, and our personal preferences may not be yours. More about CAQDAS will be discussed throughout later chapters.

Staffing and Time Planning

Qualitative studies are chronically labor intensive, but the details are rarely provided. Here, too, we rely on our experience and that of colleagues.

Who will do the work, and how much time will it take? These innocent questions mask more complexity than you often expect. We've said that lone researchers, new or experienced, should find a critical friend, partner, mentor, or colleague who can supply alternative perspectives, support, and protection from bias. In studies that have more than one staff member, there will always be a diversity of experiences, backgrounds, and skills.

That complexity means that the social system of the project needs attention; it will not develop automatically. It is crucial to build strong relationships with research partners or within larger staffs. We've found it useful, for example, to devote plenty of early time to work on core issues (the conceptual framework, research questions, sampling) and to more general maintenance issues such as hopes for and worries about the project, reports of "what else is happening in my life," and procedural guidelines for joint work. Research teams are not built in a day. Take time deliberately for startup of the relationship between you and your research partner or the functioning of the research team.

One other rule of thumb we've found useful: Avoid sharp senior-junior divisions of labor, such as having juniors do the field work and the seniors do the analysis and writing. Senior people need to be directly involved in data collection in order to have a concrete feel for what the field setting is like. You cannot be a principal investigator in a field study without spending time in the field. Junior people will function poorly as "hired hands." Both need to be actively and mutually engaged in thinking about the project and the meaning of emergent findings.

At the start, people rarely have all the skills they need for a study. Allow for learning time on issues such as fluency with new software, use of a new coding method, or drawing data displays. The time estimates we use look something like this: For each day of field work, expect to spend

- 2 or 3 days processing field notes (writing them up, correcting, etc.); if audio or video recordings are being transcribed, the multiple may run from 3 to 5 days, depending on the recording length, fineness of detail, the transcriber's familiarity with the content, and available time;

- 3 to 5 days coding (depending on the fineness and complexity of the evolving scheme); and

- 2 or 3 days completing displays (depending on the number and type of displays).

These are rough estimates for a single case. For a multiple-case study, (a) multiply by the number of cases, (b) consider what cross-case analyses will be carried out and what the within-case and cross-case reports will look like, and (c) make a total-days estimation.

CLOSURE AND TRANSITION

We've looked at substantive moves that focus on the collection of data and condensing it. These moves include systematic *conceptual frameworks* of variables or concepts and their interrelationships, *research questions* that further define the inquiry, bounding the core and parameters of a study through *case definition*, planning for within-case and multiple-case *sampling*, and creating *instrumentation*. All of these moves serve to both constrain and support analysis. Such choices depend on not only your preferred research style but also the study's topic and goals, available theory, and the researcher's familiarity with the settings being studied.

Added design issues that make a big difference in analysis include how qualitative data may be linked with *quantitative information* from the same setting, and a series of nuts-and-bolts management issues. Careful decisions about which *computer software* to use for what purposes need to be made. A systematic plan for *data management*—storage and retrieval of everything from data to final study reports—is equally important. Building good colleague and staff *relationships* is essential, as is initial and recurring *time* planning.

In the next chapter, we examine the more human dimensions of field work and analysis through the perspectives of the participants and our ethical obligations to them.

ETHICAL ISSUES IN ANALYSIS

CHAPTER SUMMARY

This chapter surveys ethical matters and dilemmas that may be faced by researchers during field work and data analysis. Questions are posed to consider issues such as participant consent, benefits, risk, confidentiality, and data ownership.

CONTENTS

Introduction

Agreements With Study Participants

    Agreement Advice

Ethical Issues

    Worthiness of the Project

    Competence

    Informed Consent

    Benefits, Costs, and Reciprocity

    Harm and Risk

Honesty and Trust

Privacy, Confidentiality, and Anonymity

Intervention and Advocacy

Research Integrity and Quality

Ownership of Data and Conclusions

Use and Misuse of Results

Ethical Conflicts and Dilemmas

Closure and Transition

INTRODUCTION

We cannot focus only on the quality of the knowledge we are producing, as if its truth were all that counts. We must also consider the potential "wrongness" of our actions as qualitative researchers in relation to the people whose lives we are studying, our colleagues, and those who sponsor our work. All researchers must be guided by the classic principle of humane conduct: *First, do no harm.*

Any responsible qualitative researcher ponders moral and ethical questions such as the following: Am I exploiting people with my research? Do the respondents have a right to see my report? What good is anonymity if people and their colleagues can easily recognize themselves in my report? When they do, might it hurt or damage them in some way? What do I do if I observe harmful actions during my field work? Who owns the data, and who owns the report?

We cannot begin to deal with all ethical issues in research, but we do hope to cut across some of the major problems involved and raise as much ethical consciousness as we can. In this chapter, we describe agreements with participants and specific issues that often arise in qualitative research, exploring their implications for analysis.

AGREEMENTS WITH STUDY PARTICIPANTS

Study participants and researchers need to reach some explicit agreements in writing about shared expectations to ensure safe, fair treatment and to maintain and improve the quality of the project. Are we contemplating an equal-status, *polyvocal* model, in which researchers and participants jointly tell their stories? Or are we heading for a *collaborative* or *participatory action research* model, in which researchers join forces with people facing a problem in their community to help them study and resolve it? Or will it be a more *traditional* model that differentiates researchers from participants, on whom the research is conducted? The first two models imply more shared control over the design and conduct of the project than does the last.

Whatever the basic relationship, some matters need to be clarified with participants at the outset. It's important to remember that these matters may not be fully understood on both sides until the study unfolds. Below are some of the issues that might be considered as an initial set of expectations, though many different agreements can be reached:

1. How much time and effort will be involved for participants?

2. What kind of data collection is involved (e.g., observation, interviewing, journal writing)?

3. Is participation voluntary?

4. Is withdrawing from a study an option?

5. Who will design and steer the study?

6. Will participants' privacy, anonymity, and confidentiality be maintained?

7. Who will produce the descriptive and explanatory products?

8. Will participants get to review and critique interim and final products?

9. What intrinsic or extrinsic benefits will accrue to both participants and researchers?

An individual, group, or organization not assured in advance of anonymity and confidentiality in study reports may provide biased data (self-censored, defensive, or rosy) if it is believed that an accurate, identifiable account would jeopardize some interest. Plus, anonymity of individuals is difficult or impossible to assure when a case study of a group or organization is read by its members. (An alternative agreement is to use real names from the outset; under these circumstances, individuals only provide information they regard as public or nondamaging. This, too, has its conclusion-narrowing aspects.)

A typical agreement is that researchers will produce the products of the study. This agreement rests on the traditional assumption that well-prepared researchers will get good data and will draw well-founded conclusions. In some models, however, expertise resides in participants as much as in researchers. The collaborative or participatory action research model implies that participant expertise is developed through the researcher's facilitation during the process—for example, in community-based projects. In either case, issues of "goodness of analysis" are just as pressing as in the traditional model (see Chapter 11).

Study products are sometimes fed back to participants as a way of providing member checks on the accuracy of descriptions, explanations, and interpretations. Agreements can vary: Does an individual see material about his or her case before others do? Can an individual or group censor or veto material, or even block publication? Or is the agreement only that errors of fact will be corrected and alternative interpretations will be included in footnotes? Such agreements can improve the quality of both the data and the final conclusions, but they also can result in truncated or distorted conclusions if someone has been given, and exercises, the right of censorship.

Researchers usually benefit from their studies through insights, recognition, promotion, new grants, and consulting. Participants' benefits are often posed quite vaguely at the start: "the chance to reflect," "clarifying ideas," "learning what others are doing," "benefits to your field." Advance agreements that mention assistance (as in collaborative research), consultation or training, joint authorship, or shared royalties as expected benefits may improve the quality of the data and the conclusions. If the benefits do not materialize, data and conclusion quality may suffer.

Agreement Advice

We offer these general pieces of advice on agreements with study participants:

1. Researchers held to their Institutional Review Board (IRB) regulations may have specific forms and requirements imposed on them that affect researcher–participant relationships, agreements, and data collection protocols. See Display 3.1 for a sample informed consent letter typically required by IRBs.

2. Be clear in your mind what you want your agreement with participants to be like. Commit it to paper as a vehicle for discussion with them while negotiating entry and access. Once the agreement is clear, a copy of a summary of the study's design and its ground rules is helpful for a study that has multiple participants.

3. Incorporate in data collection plans an explicit procedure for logging participants' understanding (or misunderstanding) of agreements, including any threats to data or conclusion quality that you see.

DISPLAY 3.1 ⬥ Sample Informed Consent Letter

INFORMED CONSENT

Patient Perspectives of Type 2 Diabetes

Introduction and Purpose: Dr. Xan Escobar, a faculty member in the College of Public Health at State University, is conducting a research study to find out more about what people with Type 2 diabetes think about the disease and public reactions to it. We are inviting you to participate in the study because you indicated to your doctor that you would be interested in participating in a study of this nature. There will be approximately 100 total participants in this research. Gabrielle Anderson will be serving as a student researcher on this study under Dr. Escobar's supervision.

Procedures: If you agree to be in this research study, you will first be asked to complete a survey with basic demographic and health-related questions; this survey will take approximately 15 minutes to complete. You will next be asked to participate in an individual interview with a member of the research team; this interview will take approximately 30 minutes to complete.

(Continued)

(Continued)

Risks: There is minimal risk in participating in this research. However, there is a potential risk for loss of confidentiality, but we will take steps to minimize these risks. You will be assigned a random identification number if you participate in the study, and after your interview is transcribed, only this identifier (not your name) will be associated with your responses. Your name and individual responses will never be shared with anyone outside the research team.

Benefits: By better understanding how people with Type 2 diabetes learned about their condition and how people without the disease perceive it, we hope to create better materials for a public diabetes awareness campaign that will promote understanding of the disease and prompt those diagnosed with the disease to seek more effective treatment sooner after diagnosis.

Explanation and offer to answer questions: Through this letter, the researchers have explained this research study to you. If you have other questions or research-related problems, you may reach Gabrielle Anderson at ganderson@xsu.ed (555) 555-8328 or Dr. Escobar at (555) 555-2469 or xescobar@xsu.ed.

Voluntary nature of participation and right to withdraw without consequence: Participation in this study is entirely voluntary. You may refuse to participate in this research without recourse. Should you withdraw from participation, you will not complete any additional surveys or interviews. Any data previously collected prior to such withdrawal will be destroyed. Withdrawing from the study will not cause any consequence or loss of benefits.

Confidentiality: Research records will be kept confidential, consistent with federal and state regulations. Only the researchers will have access to the data, which will be stored in password-protected files on password-protected computers to maintain confidentiality. To protect your privacy, personal, identifiable information will be removed from study documents and replaced with a study identifier. All identifying information will be stored separately from data and will be destroyed upon completion of data analysis.

IRB approval statement: The Institutional Review Board for the protection of human participants at State University has approved this research study. If you have any questions or concerns about your rights or a research-related injury and would like to contact someone other than the research team, you may contact the IRB Director at (555) 555-2325 or irb@xsu.ed to obtain information or to offer input.

Copy of consent: You have been given two copies of this document. Please sign both copies. Keep one copy for your files and return the second to us.

Investigator statement: "I certify that the research study has been explained to the participant through this letter, including the nature and purpose and the possible risks and benefits associated with taking part in this research study. The participant can contact the researchers with any questions about the study at (555) 555-2469."

_____		_____	
Xan Escobar, Ph.D.	Date	Gabrielle Anderson	Date
Principal Investigator		Student Researcher	
(555) 555-2469		(555) 555-8328	
xescobar@xsu.ed		ganderson@xsu.ed	

Participant signature: By signing below, I agree to participate in this study.

_____   _____   _____/_____/_____

Printed Name   Signature   Date

Source: Saldaña & Omasta (2018), pp. 204–205.

ETHICAL ISSUES

Most research-oriented professions have well-defined codes of ethics, which include guidelines ranging from human participants' rights to inappropriate forms of researcher–participant relationships. Organizations subject to an IRB or comparable overseeing agency also mandate guidelines for securing permissions, maintaining confidentiality, working with minors, and other legal matters. But fieldwork and its accompanying dilemmas are often quite unpredictable and site-specific. Plus, research questions, instrumentation, and sampling all may evolve over the course of a qualitative study, making the IRB's requirements for these details to be precisely specified *before* a study begins nearly impossible to comply with. Nevertheless, some planning and forethought are necessary for study approval. An IRB application composed simultaneously during the research design stage is a wise course of action.

We now outline some specific ethical matters and issues for reflection.

Worthiness of the Project

Ask yourself: Is my contemplated study worth doing? Will it contribute in some significant way to a domain broader than my funding, my publication opportunities, and my career? And is it congruent with values important to me?

Implications for Analysis

In general, a study that is only opportunistic, without a larger significance or real meaning to you, is likely to be pursued in a shallow way, with less care devoted to design, data collection, and analysis. The report will be written to "look good" rather than to be right. Initial conclusions may not be questioned; follow-up analyses with rival hypotheses may be rare. There's nothing wrong with taking on a commissioned research project for personal income. But if you slant your findings to accommodate and please your funders, you become complicit and dishonest.

Competence

Ask yourself: Do I (and my colleagues) have the expertise to carry out a study of good quality? Or (because researchers, both novice and experienced ones, are always exploring things new to them) am I prepared to study and be trained and supervised? Is such help available?

Implications for Analysis

Unacknowledged (or not understood) incompetence is, we think, responsible for a certain pattern of analytic weakness in qualitative studies: accumulating large amounts of poorly collected, unanalyzed data and drawing superficial and hasty conclusions as deadlines loom. This picture often occurs when lone researchers fail to seek help from friends, colleagues, or mentors. Graduate students often understand their own inexperience but sometimes cannot get support and help from their teachers or dissertation supervisors. That is research malpractice.

Informed Consent

Ask yourself: Do the people I am studying have full information about what the study will involve? Is their consent to participate freely given—fully voluntary and uncoerced? Does a hierarchy of consent (e.g., children, parents, teachers, administrators) affect such decisions?

IRB regulations are strict but thorough when it comes to recruiting voluntary participants, informing them about the study's goals, and assuring them of their rights throughout the project. Research with minors or other vulnerable populations (e.g., prisoners, pregnant women) includes additional guidelines for permissions processes, such as securing parental consent and children's assent.

Be an open book with your project; this will help develop a sense of trust between you and the setting's individuals. Also, acknowledge that participants are doing the researcher a great favor by volunteering to be part of the study. Respect their gifts of time, insight, and privacy, for the root meaning of "data" is not something that is collected but something that is *given*. If children and adolescents are part of the mix, they too have a say in the matter. There are only extremely rare occasions when covert research and deceit are necessary for the integrity of a research project's goals (e.g., investigating the social processes of humans engaged in illegal activity). If you have something to hide from participants, it better be for good reason.

Implications for Analysis

Weak consent usually leads to poor data. Respondents will try to protect themselves in a mistrusted relationship or one formed with the researcher by superiors only. Ambiguity about later stages of analysis also can be damaging to study quality and to the interests of people in the case. If you plan to use "member checks" to verify or deepen conclusions, that expectation and specific procedures need to be clear as the study proceeds. Securing a participant's permission is not a single hurdle to be jumped; dialogue and ongoing renegotiation are needed throughout the study.

Benefits, Costs, and Reciprocity

Ask yourself: What do participants have to invest in time, energy, or financial resources? What will each party in the study gain from having taken part? Is the balance equitable?

As we suggested earlier, researchers are often "paid" in one way or another. They usually enjoy their work and learn from it; they may get a dissertation out of it; and their papers, articles, and books not only contribute to their fields but also can bring them recognition, royalties, new funding, and career advancement.

Study participants have a somewhat different set of benefits: They get to be listened to, they may gain insight or learning, they may improve their personal practice, a program or policy they are involved with may be strengthened, and they may get help in taking effective action on some recurring problem. But study participants rarely share in publication, and they usually don't become famous. Most don't get paid for their research contributions.

The question of costs and who bears them is important. The researcher's time is repaid—usually not fully—in cash or a class grade or dissertation approval. Research participants normally must take time from or beyond whatever else they are doing and are usually not recompensed. A participating site may well have added costs (e.g., for teacher substitutes).

Implications for Analysis

Study participants' concern about the inequity of benefits and costs serves to jeopardize access and thin out data. But we are always moved and amazed when people do keep talking to us thoughtfully, inviting us into their lives day after day, when the benefits to them seem so slim, so intangible, and often so delayed.

Researchers vary in their perspectives about monetarily compensating their participants (e.g., offering a gift card or a token $20.00 for each hour of interview time). Some feel that the offer of money may unduly influence participants' responses to become more favorable and positive than they really think. Other researchers feel that working-class professionals, such as teachers and social workers, deserve some type of financial compensation for their valuable time and opinions. This is an issue to be resolved by each individual researcher and his or her particular project's budget.

Researchers traffic in *understanding*. Most study participants are preoccupied with *action*—how to work and live better. It can be argued that if you approach your analytic work with a deeper sense of its action implications, your understanding will be deeper—and the benefits to participants more equitable.

Harm and Risk

Ask yourself: What might this study do to hurt the people involved? How likely is it that such harm will occur?

Harm to participants can come in many varieties: from blows to self-esteem or "looking bad" to others; to threats to one's interests, position, or advancement in the organization; to loss of funding for a program, and so on, up to being sued or arrested. The information from a qualitative study is never value-free, and it may have negative consequences.

Harm cuts both ways. We like the story told by a *New York Times* reporter who asked a drug dealer if he really felt comfortable about talking frankly. The dealer said cheerfully, "Sure. If I don't like what you write, I'll kill you." As researchers, we have occasionally been threatened with litigation and with warnings to intervene with our funding agency when a draft report was seen as threatening a key interest.

Sieber (1992) points out that it's important to think of varying vulnerability to harm. More vulnerable persons and institutions include those who are publicly visible, lack resources or autonomy, are stigmatized, are weakened or institutionalized, cannot speak for themselves, are involved in illegal acts, or are too closely associated with those studied.

Setting risk levels for potential harm is very difficult—perhaps impossible—in qualitative studies. It's wise to assume that the chances of some type of harm are better than others and to consider in advance ways of reducing that likelihood.

Implications for Analysis

As with inequitable benefits and costs, if harm is expected, access and data quality may suffer. The prospect of immediately impending harm—which well may occur when reports are made to local participants, sponsors, or funding agencies—can lead to pressure on you to revise or delete conclusions or to self-censor them in advance.

Honesty and Trust

Ask yourself: What's my relationship with the people I'm studying? Am I telling the truth? Do we trust each other?

Most qualitative researchers are unlikely to lie, cheat, or steal in the course of their work. But broken promises are not unknown. And some researchers have reported deceiving respondents about the true nature of the inquiry (as in some participant observation studies such as Humphreys' [1970] classic study of homosexuals, where he posed as a "watch queen" lookout outside public toilets).

Typically, dishonesty is subtler. The fieldworker may project a "fake persona" (the friendly listener or the would-be insider) to gain knowledge or access. At some levels, as van Maanen (1979) notes, whenever the fieldworker works to "penetrate fronts," symbolic violence is being done: "People are, to a degree, coaxed, persuaded, pushed, pressured, and sometimes almost blackmailed into providing information to the researcher that they might otherwise prefer to shield" (p. 545). There are always individually drawn moral limits to this violence: A researcher may decide not to push on a delicate matter, or to leave an embarrassing scene. Nevertheless, the question of just how coercive and unauthentic relationships with respondents are cannot be ignored.

Implications for Analysis

If people feel betrayed by you when they read a report, it becomes almost impossible for them to accept it as a reasonable interpretation of what happened because of their natural defensiveness when "the truth hurts," as it well may, and their feelings of anger at having been misled. Deceptiveness and broken promises—especially if benefits and costs have been inequitable or harm has occurred—will make any continuation of the inquiry problematic. We will have wronged not only our respondents but also our colleagues.

We will not pretend to have any easy or foolproof answers for this slippery category of ethical dilemmas. All we can pass along is some classic advice: When in doubt, tell the truth.

Privacy, Confidentiality, and Anonymity

Ask yourself: In what ways will the study intrude or come closer to people than they want? How will information be guarded? How identifiable are the individuals and organizations studied?

Sieber (1992) makes these helpful distinctions among three terms, which often are confused or used interchangeably in research practice:

- *Privacy:* control over others' access to oneself and associated information or preservation of boundaries against giving protected information or receiving unwanted information

- *Confidentiality:* agreements with a person or organization about what will be done (and may not be done) with their data—may include legal constraints

- *Anonymity:* lack of identifiers, information that would indicate which individuals or organizations provided which data

As Sieber notes, issues of privacy are often subtle and misunderstood by the researcher, surfacing only when there are unexpected reluctances, an outpouring of information beyond what the person meant to say, or a confidence overheard by others. Privacy is, in part, about secrecy.

Confidentiality and anonymity are usually promised—sometimes very superficially—in initial agreements with respondents. For example, unless the researcher explains very clearly what a feedback case will look like, people may not realize that they will *not* be anonymous at all to other people within the setting who read the case.

Issues of privacy, confidentiality, and anonymity take a completely new turn when visual media such as digital photos and video are used in data collection and reporting. Individuals and groups still need to have control over how they are depicted, and can resist privacy invasions (e.g., by vetoing specific pictures or sequences), but the possibility of anonymity is almost surely gone, even with facial-blur effects.

Implications for Analysis

When you realize that privacy has been threatened, new analytic moves (e.g., data from other sources) may be needed to protect data quality. If privacy has, in fact, been breached, questions of the report's impact when it is fed back to respondents become central; can the information involved be connected with an identifiable person?

Using member checks to verify or extend interpretations and conclusions helps with anonymity problems, particularly if you begin with the most vulnerable respondents before moving in a wider circle; they usually (though not always) can spot information that would identify them and thus threaten their interests.

The basic problem of identifiability when the case is a complex site must be considered before and during report preparation. Local people nearly always can tell (or will assume) who is being depicted. You may need to err on the side of protecting anonymity, if it has been promised, and rely on dialogue and negotiation for corrective action before the report is finalized.

Explicit confidentiality agreements about where raw data and analyses will be stored, and who will have access to them, probably enhance data quality by increasing trust. However, courts have not normally treated social science researchers' data as a legally privileged communication. If a case is brought to litigation, your documents and other data could become nonconfidential evidence.

Intervention and Advocacy

Ask yourself: What do I do when I see harmful, illegal, or wrongful behavior on the part of others during a study? Should I speak for anyone's interests besides my own? If so, whose interests do I advocate?

Take, for example, the vivid instance of police brutality witnessed by van Maanen (1983) and written up in his field notes. Although he did not assist the police, he did not protest or intervene either. He thus protected the police by default and avoided supporting the victim. Later, in a suit brought by police officers against a newspaper, van Maanen opted to protect the interests of the patrolmen by refusing to release his field notes.

Ethical choices are not always so dramatic, but they are still there when we see ineffective teachers, medical malpractice, abused children, or evidence of misspent funds—and do or don't report them. Ethical choices are also present when we study people who are breaking the law as we study them: drug dealers and users, corrupt agency heads, violent gang members, embezzlers, and so on. It is important to know more about deviance; but are we somehow condoning it by our neutral, noncondemning presence?

Implications for Analysis

A situation in which you have "dirty hands"—cannot evade doing wrong to one party or another—is personally anguishing. And no matter how it is resolved, it skews your understanding and personal values system. If you decide to withhold knowledge or to not intervene in favor of continued access, then not only your public reports but also your conceptualization and explanatory theories may become lopsided.

Research Integrity and Quality

Ask yourself: Is my study being conducted carefully, thoughtfully, and correctly in terms of some reasonable set of standards or established practices?

"On-the-job training" for a student of qualitative research is part of the learning curve; there will be some expected stumbling and gaffes along the way. But a student's teacher/supervisor should ensure that there has been sufficient preparation for independent field work, and constant communication and monitoring throughout the process to better guarantee a quality experience for all concerned.

As for the findings, if we provide a set of conclusions based on sloppy (or even fraudulent) work and claim their validity, then we are being dishonest with our sponsors, colleagues, supervisors, participants, and anyone else who reads and trusts our reports. Outright scientific fraud is rare, but it does occur when the stakes are high (funding, primacy of discovery, career advancement). It would be naive to expect that a qualitative study could never be faked.

Far more common, as noted in Adler's (1991) report of a conference on integrity in behavioral science research, is "poor science": sloppy data recording; insufficient, selective, or misleading reporting of findings; unwillingness to share or retain data; undisclosed conflicts of interest; and inappropriate citation.

Implications for Analysis

In Chapter 11, we will acknowledge the difficulties of assessing the quality of qualitative studies and suggest a series of tactics for enhancing the goodness of any particular study: its confirmability, dependability, credibility, and potential transferability to other settings. A student should run his or her data and analyses in progress past a supervisor, mentor, or peers for periodic "reality checks."

The practical implication here is that if you have not attended to the issue of goodness criteria in your study, you are on shaky intellectual ground. It is not just that we must somehow please our critical colleague audiences; the deeper issue is avoiding self-delusion. After that, we can turn to the task of being honest with our readers about how we did the study and what worried us about its quality.

As for fraud, the truth eventually will come out, though it may take as long as the decades before Cyril Burt's famous results on the intelligence similarity of separated twins were detected as faked. We should concentrate on not lying to *ourselves*.

Ownership of Data and Conclusions

Ask yourself: Who owns my field notes, transcripts, and analyses: me, my organization, my participants, or my funders? And once my reports are written, who controls their distribution?

The issue of confidentiality requires being clear about who can have access to the data. Most researchers consider their data and analyses as belonging to them and, in the absence of some form of litigation, consider themselves to be responsible for preserving anonymity; safeguarding their confidentiality; and making the data available to others for auditing, re-analyses, secondary analyses, and replications.

But the issues here are not that simple. For example, the Freedom of Information Act in the United States permits public access to field work data from federally funded projects. IRBs may require that a project's data records be destroyed/erased within a specified period of time. Also, there is still no definitive guidance for the research use of Internet-sourced data such as social media posts on Twitter, Facebook, and publicly accessible blogs.

The control of report diffusion is also a crucial issue. Some participants may vehemently object to an unpublished report's depiction of them and threaten to block its publication through legal means. Funding agencies, too, may exert this right. At an annual meeting of the American Educational Research Association, there were at least two instances of a government agency refusing to allow a public report of completed research: In one, it appeared that the agency saw the release of the findings as politically unwise; in the other, the agency's "internal review had not been completed."

Implications for Analysis

Make certain that all ownership agreements are specified in writing before data are collected. There are potential risks to respondents if the data fall into the wrong hands, so you need to think carefully about how others can access your database and how confidentiality and anonymity can be maintained. Check carefully for any copyright statements or terms of service guidelines connected with Internet-sourced data.

In our experience, nothing seems to hit a researcher harder than the realization that some person, group, or organization may block the dissemination of months or years of research effort. Freedom of scholarly inquiry is a strong value, as are the values of career advancement, recognition, and funding. You need to be clear about the political context of your work and to guard against agreeing too easily to others' veto efforts or to altering important substantive aspects as a way of ensuring publication or continued funding.

Use and Misuse of Results

Ask yourself: Do I have an obligation to help my findings to be used appropriately? What if they are used harmfully or wrongly? Who am I trying to help, specifically? Do I have the right to change my participants' values, attitudes, and beliefs? Is consciousness raising without action support enough?

Examples of misuse of study findings are not hard to find. Findings may be misinterpreted (deliberately or not) and used to support wrong policies (e.g., student test score differences as a justification for tracking or segregation). Or the findings, correctly understood, can be used by organizations the researcher deplores (e.g., by conservative political action committees). We may have discovered something that the participants may not realize (e.g., a program that has adverse rather than positive effects) and attempt to "change the system," when the system feels that it's not our place or right to interfere with its established ways of working. A participant may share an opinion or perspective that you find disturbing during an interview, and you may be tempted to debate the issue rather than to listen and learn more. Knowledge is not exactly power. Rather, the use of our knowledge raises our awareness of—and enmeshes us in—the power relationships in the world we have been studying.

Implications for Analysis

On any given project, it probably pays to be as clear as possible from the start just how committed you are to supporting the use of your findings (and/or to warding off misuse from various quarters). Check your findings regularly with the people you're researching to discuss the broader implications and ramifications. Accept the fact that not everyone thinks and feels the same way as you and that you have an obligation in your analysis to acknowledge the multiple perspectives you encounter. Your write-up should also clearly specify how you envision your findings being used by others, especially for policy and practice.

ETHICAL CONFLICTS AND DILEMMAS

The infamous long-term study of syphilis patients begun in 1932 at the Tuskegee Institute exemplifies the dilemma of *scientific understanding versus individual rights*, which in this case was resolved in a particularly inhumane and destructive way. The scientific purpose was understanding the long-term course of syphilis, and it was given priority. African American men in the study were left without treatment and were not informed of the availability of penicillin (in 1943) as an effective treatment. The study was not terminated until 1972, by which time most of the participants had died. A positive outcome of this atrocity was the composition of ethical principles and guidelines for research involving human participants—The Belmont Report. At a less tragic level, this dilemma appears in studies where we do not intervene in harmful situations for fear of jeopardizing our access (and thus perhaps our future scientific understanding).

The more typical qualitative research experience is also full of dilemmas. For example, there is often a conflict between the demands of *validity versus avoiding harm*. One of us once studied a school where the new principal, a bit shaky on the job, received regular consultation from an experienced ex-principal—who was called by some staff members "the principal's babysitter." During feedback of a report draft, several respondents said, "You don't need to put that in," acknowledging tacitly that it would damage the principal's self-esteem.

There is also the dilemma of *help giving versus confidentiality*. It's ordinarily quite difficult to assist or get assistance for a respondent you have discovered to be in need (let's say, a new teacher who is floundering unassisted in the classroom) without breaching the agreement that no one else will have access to what the person told you. This also illustrates the conflict of *naturalistic observation versus researcher intervention*. If the ethnographic goal is to study other people's lives as they are lived every day, will the researcher's spontaneous yet well-intentioned actions to assist participants with their problems "skew" the data and thus the analysis and thereby the final report?

This overview of conflicts and dilemmas is illustrative; it certainly is not exhaustive. And more often than not, multiple dilemmas will be in play. If ethical issues and their resolutions were clear-cut, life would be simple. But we have to keep thinking and talking about ethical dilemmas, weighing how we and our respondents are choosing one side or the other.

Ethics Advice

We offer these final pieces of advice on ethics in qualitative studies:

1. *Anticipation:* Most of the specific issues raised earlier can benefit from advance thinking during the early stages of project design. Do not delude yourself that they can be pre-resolved, but thinking them through—perhaps running through the issues as a sort of checklist—can help you avoid problems later.

2. *Third parties:* Because ethical issues often tend to be masked by our taken-for-granted assumptions, values, attitudes, and beliefs, engaging a trusted third party can be very helpful in bringing them to our attention. Such a person can raise unheeded issues, suggest alternate viewpoints, help surface tacit assumptions, be an advocate for respondents, or serve as a mediator between participants and researchers when there are unresolved problems.

3. *Regular checking and renegotiation:* The evolution of any qualitative study normally involves some twists and turns that no one fully anticipated, even with the best of goodwill. Initial agreements and working procedures almost always need updates. In our experience, agreement revision is quite typical as issues of feedback, member checks, and reporting come into focus. It's useful from the start to create the expectation that agreements may need renegotiation and that "recheck" meetings can be called at any point by either researchers or participants.

CLOSURE AND TRANSITION

We've examined a series of specific ethical issues, ranging from early matters, to those occurring as a project develops, and those that are prominent later. All have implications for analysis, the quality of findings, and our reportage. Dealing with ethical issues effectively involves heightened awareness, a willingness to renegotiate, and a sensitive moral compass rather than the application of foolproof rules.

In the next chapter, we present some fundamental principles of qualitative data analysis before venturing into methods of display in Part Two.

FUNDAMENTALS OF QUALITATIVE DATA ANALYSIS

CHAPTER SUMMARY

This chapter reviews fundamental approaches to qualitative data analysis with a particular focus on coding data segments for category, theme, and pattern development. Other analytic strategies include jottings, memos, and the formulation of assertions and propositions. Within-case and cross-case analysis are then compared for their unique advantages and contributions to the research enterprise.

CONTENTS

INTRODUCTION

In this chapter, we describe fundamental methods for qualitative data analysis while data collection progresses. They help organize data for later, deeper analyses, such as those using the displays described in Chapters 5 through 10. The appendix provides recommended titles for additional analytic guidance.

Some qualitative researchers put primary energy into data collection for weeks, months, or even years and then retire from the field to "work over their notes." We believe this is a big mistake. It rules out the possibility of collecting new data to fill in gaps or to test new hypotheses that emerge during analysis. It discourages the formulation of rival hypotheses that question a fieldworker's routine assumptions. And it makes analysis into a giant, sometimes overwhelming task that frustrates the researcher and reduces the quality of the work produced.

We strongly advise analysis concurrent with data collection (see Display 1.1). It helps the fieldworker cycle back and forth between thinking about the existing data and generating strategies for collecting new, often better, data. It makes analysis an ongoing, lively enterprise that contributes to the energizing process of field work. Furthermore, early analysis permits the production of interim reports required in most evaluation and policy studies.

For the methods in this and following chapters, we assume that the fieldworker has collected information in the form of handwritten or typed field notes, audio or video recordings of interviews or other events in the field setting, and documents or other print/digital artifacts. We further assume that the basic, raw data (scribbled field notes, interview recordings) must be processed before they are available for analysis. Expanded field note write-ups, interview transcripts, and so on can be read easily, edited for accuracy, commented on, coded, and analyzed using several of the methods we later describe.

We begin with First Cycle *coding*, then second cycle or *pattern codes*, and the process of deriving even more general themes through *jottings* and *analytic memoing*. We then discuss *assertion and proposition development*, and conclude this chapter with a section on *within-case* and *cross-case analysis*. Our presentation here addresses only the fundamentals of analysis; Chapters 5 through 10 include additional methods and specific examples.

FIRST CYCLE CODES AND CODING

Description

Codes are labels that assign symbolic meaning to the descriptive or inferential information compiled during a study. Codes usually are attached to data "chunks" or units of varying size and can take the form of a straightforward, descriptive label or a more evocative and complex one (e.g., a concept, value, or metaphor). Saldaña (2016) defines a code as

> most often a word or short phrase that symbolically assigns a summative, salient, essence-capturing, and/or evocative attribute for a portion of language-based or visual data. The data can consist of interview transcripts, participant observation field notes, journals, documents, open-ended survey responses, drawings, artifacts, photographs, video, Internet sites, e-mail correspondence, academic and fictional literature, and so on. The portion of data coded during First Cycle coding processes can range in magnitude from a single word to a full paragraph, an entire page of text or a stream of moving images. In second cycle coding processes, the portions coded can be the exact same units, longer passages of text, analytic memos about the data, and even a reconfiguration of the codes themselves developed thus far. Charmaz (2001) describes coding as the "critical link" between data collection and their explanation of meaning. . . .
>
> In qualitative data analysis, a code is a researcher-generated construct that symbolizes or "translates" data (Vogt, Vogt, Gardner, & Haeffele, 2014, p. 13) and thus attributes interpreted meaning to each individual datum for later purposes of pattern detection, categorization, assertion or proposition development, theory building, and other analytic processes. Just as a title represents and captures a book, film, or poem's primary content and essence, so does a code represent and capture a datum's primary content and essence. (p. 4)

Some research methodologists believe that coding is merely technical, preparatory work for higher level thinking about the study. But we believe that coding is deep reflection about and, thus, deep interpretation of the data's meanings. In other words, coding *is* analysis.

Codes are primarily, but not exclusively, used to retrieve and categorize similar data units so the researcher can quickly find, pull out, and cluster the segments relating to a particular research question, hypothesis, concept, or theme. Clustering and the display of condensed units then set the stage for further analysis and drawing conclusions.

For example, let's assume you were interested, as we were in the school improvement study, in the reasons why a new educational practice is adopted. You might begin by asking participants why they or others decided to try the practice. A piece of the formatted field notes might look like this:

> I asked the principal what the need for the new program was, and he responded that the students coming into the 9th grade were two years below grade level and that the old curriculum was ineffective. Through testing [the Nelson Reading Test] it was determined that students were growing academically only 5 or 6 months during the 10-month school year.

Assuming that you found it possible to apply a single summarizing notation or code to this unit, it might be MOTIVATION FOR ADOPTION (other codes could be applicable). That code would appear capitalized in the right-hand margin beside the segment (the left-hand margin might be used for a *jotting*, explained later):

[1] I asked the principal what the need for the new program was, and he responded that the students coming into the 9th grade were two years below grade level and that the old curriculum was ineffective. Through testing [the Nelson Reading Test] it was determined that students were growing academically only 5 or 6 months during the 10-month school year.	[1] MOTIVATION FOR ADOPTION

Other units of field notes or interview transcripts that also relate to MOTIVATION FOR ADOPTION would receive the same code.

Coding is a *heuristic*—a method of discovery. You determine the code for a unit of data by careful reading and reflection on its core content or meaning. This gives you intimate, interpretive familiarity with every datum in the corpus.

Rationale

As soon as the field researcher begins to compile information, challenges appear. A big one comes from the multiplicity of data sources and forms. Some information comes from structured or informal observations. More, if not most, comes from interviews. There are also everyday or special documents, archival records, and physical artifacts. In some studies, there can be information from questionnaires and surveys, photographs, videos, or statistical records.

All of this information piles up exponentially. In the early stages of a study, most of it looks promising. But if you don't know what matters more, everything matters. You may never have the time to condense and order, much less to analyze and write up, all of this material. That's why we think conceptual frameworks and research questions are the best defense against overload. They also reflect a point we made earlier: that data collection is inescapably a *selective* process and that you cannot and do not "get it all," even though you might think you can.

You may need roughly three to five times as much time for processing and ordering the data as the time you needed to collect them. Just one substantive week at a field site often can result in something like hundreds of pages of typed-up field notes, interview transcripts, documents, and ancillary materials. Not everything in a database has to be coded—just those units that relate directly to answering the research questions of interest, and those units that merit a place in the condensed empirical materials for their emergent importance to the study. Codes are *prompts* or *triggers* for deeper reflection on the data's meanings. Coding is thus a *data condensation* task that enables you to retrieve the most meaningful material, assemble units of data that go together, and further condense the bulk into readily analyzable units.

Codes are first assigned to data units in order to detect recurring *patterns*. From these patterns, similar codes are clustered together to create a smaller number of categories, themes, or *Pattern Codes*. The categories' interrelationships with each other are then constructed to develop higher level analytic meanings for assertion, proposition, hypothesis, and/or theory development.

FIRST CYCLE CODING EXAMPLES

Saldaña (2016) divides coding into two major stages: First Cycle and Second Cycle coding. First Cycle coding methods are codes initially assigned to the data units. Second Cycle coding methods generally work with the resulting First Cycle codes themselves.

First Cycle coding methods include over 25 different approaches, each one with a particular function or purpose. You do not need to stick with just one approach for your coding efforts; some of these can be compatibly "mixed and matched" as needed. Below is a review of some of the most pertinent ones that apply to the particular analytic approaches profiled in this book. See Saldaña's (2016) *The Coding Manual for Qualitative Researchers* for a fuller description of each method.

Newcomers to coding can get easily overwhelmed by the numerous approaches available to them. It can even induce a sense of analytic paralysis: "I don't know which coding method to use!" Each profile below includes a few recommendations for when a particular coding method may be appropriate for your particular data, research goals, and methodological approach. Qualitative inquiry defies standardization, and that includes algorithmic prescriptions for codes and coding. You (in consultation with a peer or mentor) are the best judge for which method(s) is/are appropriate for your unique study.

First, there are four *Elemental Methods* that serve as foundation approaches to coding: Descriptive, In Vivo, Process, and Concept Coding.

Descriptive Coding

A descriptive code assigns labels to data that summarize in a word or short phrase—most often as a noun—the basic topic of a passage of qualitative data. These eventually provide an inventory of topics for indexing and categorizing, which is especially helpful for ethnographies and studies with a wide variety of data forms (field notes, documents, artifacts, etc.). Descriptive codes are perhaps more appropriate for social environments and settings rather than interviews. An example comes from field notes about a lower-middle-class neighborhood:

[1] As I walked toward the school, there was a 7-11 convenience store 1 block away, next to a small professional office building: an optometrist, podiatrist, and other medical/health-related clinics. Directly across the street was an empty lot, but next to that stood a Burger King restaurant.	[1] BUSINESSES

An analyst would extract all passages coded BUSINESSES from various field notes to compose a more detailed inventory of the case and to construct a narrative describing the business climate in the area.

In Vivo Coding

This is one of the most well-known qualitative coding methods. In Vivo Coding uses words or short phrases from the participant's own language in the data record as codes. It may include folk or indigenous terms of a particular culture, subculture, or microculture to suggest the existence of the group's cultural categories (e.g., in a hospital, you may hear unique terms such as "code blue," "sharps," and "scripts"). Phrases that are used repeatedly by participants are good leads; they often point to regularities or patterns in the setting.

In Vivo Coding is appropriate for virtually all qualitative studies, but particularly for beginning qualitative researchers learning how to code data, and studies that prioritize and honor the participant's voice. In Vivo Codes are placed in quotation marks to differentiate them from researcher-generated codes. Examples below are taken from a coded interview transcript about an adolescent girl's experiences with school:

I [1] hated school last year. Freshman year, it was awful, I hated it. And [2] this year's a lot better actually. I, um, don't know why. I guess, over the summer I kind of [3] stopped caring about what other people thought and cared more about, just, I don't know.	[1] "HATED SCHOOL" [2] "THIS YEAR'S A LOT BETTER" [3] "STOPPED CARING"

Process Coding

This coding method uses gerunds ("-ing" words) exclusively to connote observable and conceptual action in the data. Processes also imply actions intertwined with the dynamics of time, such as things that emerge, change, occur in particular sequences, or become strategically implemented. Process Coding is appropriate for virtually all qualitative studies, but particularly for grounded theory research that extracts participant action/interaction and consequences. An example comes from an interview transcript about an adolescent girl explaining how rumors get spread:

Well, that's one problem, that [my school is] pretty small, so [1] if you say one thing to one person, and they decide to tell two people, then those two people tell two people, and in one period everybody else knows. [2] Everybody in the entire school knows that you said whatever it was.	[1] SPREADING RUMORS [2] KNOWING WHAT YOU SAID

Concept Coding

Concept Codes assign meso- or macrolevels of meaning to data or to data analytic work in progress (e.g., a series of codes or categories). A concept is a word or short phrase that symbolically represents a suggested meaning broader than a single item or action—a "bigger picture" beyond the tangible and apparent. A concept suggests an idea rather than an object or observable behavior. For example, a clock is something you can touch and see as it changes minute to minute, but its conceptual attribution is *time*. One can see and touch a church building, but not the concepts of *spirituality* or *religion*. Note that these concepts are nouns.

Concepts also refer to processes such as *surviving* or *coping*. Conceptual processes consist of smaller observable actions that add up to a bigger and broader scheme. For example, I can spend an afternoon at a shopping mall window shopping, buying things, and eating lunch at a food court, but the overall concept is *consuming*. Visiting Starbucks five mornings a week, for some, is not just for purchasing and drinking coffee (the observable actions), but for *performing a morning ritual, maintaining a workday habit*, or *feeding an addiction*. Note that these concept phrases begin with gerunds ("-ing" words) to describe broader processes at work.

Concept Codes tend to be applied to larger units or stanzas of data—an analytic "lumping" task that harmonizes with the bigger picture suggested by a concept. Concept Coding is an appropriate method when the analyst wishes to transcend the local and particular of the study to more abstract or generalizable contexts. The method bypasses the detail and nuance of other coding methods to transcend the particular participants of your fieldwork and to progress toward the *ideas* suggested by the study.

Concept Coding is illustrated here as a stand-alone method, but it is worth noting that most First Cycle methods such as Process, Values, and Holistic Coding can utilize codes that are conceptual in nature. A series or categorized collection of First Cycle codes can be condensed even further into a Concept Code.

Below is an example of an Irishman speaking to an American tourist about his perceptions of America. Note that the Concept Code attached to the datum is an evocative choice and, in part, employs an In Vivo Code:

[1] What I love about America is the excess. You know, I'll walk into a coffee shop here [in Ireland] and all there'll be is milk. I go into a coffee shop in America, and there's 1%, 2%, skim milk, whole milk, half and half, you know? And the highways! There's two lanes at most here goin' one way, and over there you've got five, six lanes of highway all goin' in the same direction. We just don't have the cars or the land for that much highway. And the malls—you'll never see things like that over here. It's usually one shop at a time, but there you've got it all under one roof. Big stores, too, big stores.

[1] AMERICAN "EXCESS"

Next, there are three *Affective Methods* that tap into the more subjective experiences we encounter with our participants: Emotion, Values, and Evaluation Coding.

Emotion Coding

Perhaps obviously, this method labels the emotions recalled and/or experienced by the participant, or inferred by the researcher about the participant. Emotion Coding is particularly appropriate for studies that explore intrapersonal and interpersonal participant experiences and actions. It also provides insight into the participants' perspectives, worldviews, and life conditions. Note that a participant himself or herself may sometimes label the emotion, and thus, it should be In Vivo Coded in quotation marks. An example comes from an interview transcript about a middle-aged man complaining about one of his work colleagues:

[1] I just hated it when he got awarded with the honor. [2] I mean, we're praising mediocrity now. Never mind that what you've accomplished isn't worth squat, it's all about who you know in the good ol' boys network.

[1] "HATED IT"
[2] BITTERNESS

Values Coding

This is the application of three different types of related codes onto qualitative data that reflect a participant's values, attitudes, and beliefs, representing his or her perspectives or worldview. A value (V:) is the importance we attribute to ourselves, another person, a thing, or an idea. An attitude (A:) is the way we think and feel about ourselves, another person, a thing, or an idea. A belief (B:) is part of a system that includes values and attitudes, plus personal knowledge, experiences, opinions, prejudices, morals, and other interpretive perceptions of the social world. Values Coding is appropriate for studies that explore cultural values, identity, intrapersonal and interpersonal participant experiences and actions in case studies, appreciative inquiry, oral history, and critical ethnography. An example comes from an interview transcript about a female university student discussing her political beliefs:

[1] Government regulation of women's health issues has gotten out of hand. It's not about "protecting" us, it's about their need to control and dominate women [2] through covert religious ideology. White Christian men are deciding what's law and what's moral and what's, how it's supposed to be. [3] They can say, "It's *not* a war on women" all they want, but trust me—it's a war on women.

[1] B: GOVERNMENT CONTROL

[2] B: COVERT RELIGIOUS MOTIVES
[3] A: MISOGYNIST MOTIVES

Evaluation Coding

This method applies primarily nonquantitative codes onto qualitative data that assign judgments about the merit, worth, or significance of programs or policy. Evaluation Coding is appropriate for policy, critical, action, organizational, and evaluation studies, particularly across multiple cases and extended periods of time. Selected coding methods profiled thus far, such as Descriptive or In Vivo Codes, can be applied to or supplement Evaluation Coding, but the methods are customized for specific studies. A + symbol before a code tags it as a positive evaluation. Second-order codes that follow a primary code and a colon are called Subcodes (discussed later). An example comes from an interview transcript about an elementary school teacher assessing an artist-in-residency program:

[1] The artist-in-residency program was pretty successful this year. [2] The arts agency did a great job at selecting qualified candidates this time around. [3] We were pretty impressed at how they integrated math and geometry with art-making without the teachers telling them to. I think they knew the score and that it was pretty important that they cover those subject areas. And they did it in a way that made it [4] interesting for the kids. For the teachers, too! We learned some things that we can integrate into our own curriculum next year.	[1] + RESIDENCY: "SUCCESSFUL" [2] + CANDIDATES: QUALIFIED [3] + CURRICULUM: INTEGRATION [4] + CURRICULUM: "INTERESTING"

One *Literary and Language Method*, Dramaturgical Coding, explores human action, reaction, and interaction through strategic analysis of people's motives.

Dramaturgical Coding

This method applies the terms and conventions of character, play script, and production analysis onto qualitative data. For character, these terms include items such as participant

- objectives (OBJ)
- conflicts (CON)
- tactics (TAC)
- attitudes (ATT)
- emotions (EMO)
- subtexts (SUB)

Dramaturgical Coding is appropriate for exploring intrapersonal and interpersonal participant experiences and actions in case studies, power relationships, and the processes of human motives and agency. An example comes from an interview transcript about a community college instructor's dilemmas with her unit's budget cuts:

[1] There was a lot of pressure this year to "do more with less." And that always [2] frustrates me, because you don't "do more with less"—you do *less with less*. So [3] if they're expecting me to do more with less money and less resources, they're not	[1] CON: LESS RESOURCES [2] EMO: FRUSTRATION [3] TAC: RESISTANCE

going to get it. And it's not because I'm being snotty or passive-aggressive about this; [4] it's simply that you can't squeeze blood out of a turnip. There's only so much you can do with what you have. [5] And yes, I'm spending some of my own money this year on classroom supplies because we don't have enough to last us through the end of the year. [6] That's just the way it is these days.	[4] ATT: LIMITATIONS [5] TAC: SACRIFICING [6] ATT: ACCEPTING "THE WAY IT IS"

Three *Exploratory Methods*—Holistic, Provisional, and Hypothesis Coding—make preliminary or global coding assignments, based on what the researcher deductively assumes may be present in the data before they are analyzed.

Holistic Coding

This method applies a single code to a large unit of data in the corpus, rather than detailed coding, to capture a sense of the overall contents and the possible categories that may develop. Holistic Coding is often a preparatory approach to a unit of data before a more detailed coding or categorization process through First or Second Cycle methods. The coded unit can be as small as one-half a page in length, to as large as an entire completed study. Holistic Coding is most applicable when the researcher has a general idea of what to investigate in the data. An example comes from field notes by a researcher observing how new, tenure-track faculty become oriented to academia:

[1] The chair of the committee debated whether to start on time or to wait for latecomers to join the meeting. "We all made the effort to be here at 8:00 a.m., so let's start," he said. The network meeting began with obligatory self-introductions of the 6 people seated around a large table designed to hold 12. Most attendees were newcomers to academia at the assistant professor or faculty associate level, primarily from midwest and east coast institutions. Each one appeared to be in his or her late 20s or early 30s. "You're the new guard of the college," said the chair, "and we're here to find ways to network and support each other as you begin your teaching careers."	[1] THE "NEW GUARD"

Provisional Coding

This approach begins with an a priori or "start" list of researcher-generated codes, based on what preparatory investigation suggests might appear in the data before they are collected and analyzed. Provisional Codes can be revised, modified, deleted, or expanded to include new codes. This method is appropriate for qualitative studies that build on or corroborate previous research and investigations. For example, a researcher about to interview people who successfully quit smoking may develop the following Provisional Codes of smoking cessation methods beforehand:

PRESCRIPTION MEDICATION

NICOTINE PATCHES

NICOTINE GUM/LOZENGES

ELECTRONIC CIGARETTES

PROFESSIONAL COUNSELING

PEER SUPPORT SYSTEM

"COLD TURKEY"

Hypothesis Coding

This is the application of a researcher-generated, predetermined list of codes onto qualitative data specifically to assess a researcher-generated hypothesis. The codes are developed from a theory/prediction about what will be found in the data before they have been collected or analyzed. Statistical applications, if needed, can range from simple frequency counts to more complex multivariate analyses. This method is appropriate for hypothesis testing, content analysis, and analytic induction of the qualitative data set, particularly the search for rules, causes, and explanations in the data.

Hypothesis Coding also can be applied midway or later in a qualitative study's data collection or analysis to confirm or disconfirm any assertions, propositions, or theories developed thus far. For example, it is hypothesized that the responses to a particular question about language issues in the United States will generate one of four answers (and thus coded responses) from participants:

RIGHT = We have the right to speak whatever language we want in America

SAME = We need to speak the same language in America: English

MORE = We need to know how to speak more than one language

NR = No Response or "I don't know"

Two *Procedural Methods* utilize specific rather than open-ended ways of coding data: Protocol and Causation Coding.

Protocol Coding

This is the coding of qualitative data according to a preestablished, recommended, standardized, or prescribed system. The generally comprehensive list of codes and categories provided to the researcher are applied after his or her own data collection. Some protocols also recommend specific qualitative (and quantitative) data analytic techniques with the coded data. Protocol Coding is appropriate for qualitative studies in disciplines with previously developed and field-tested coding systems. It can also be used to code data collected across multiple sites for cross-case comparison. For example, a selected list of codes from a protocol used to determine causes of family violence include the following:

ALCOH = alcoholism or drinking

DRUG = drug use

EDUC = lack of education

MONEY = lack of money or financial problems

Causation Coding

This method extracts attributions or causal beliefs from participant data about not just how but why particular outcomes came about. The analyst searches for combinations of *antecedent conditions* influenced and affected by certain *mediating variables* that lead toward certain *outcome* pathways, and attempts to map a three-part process as a CODE 1 → CODE 2 → CODE 3 sequence.

Causation Coding is appropriate for discerning motives, belief systems, worldviews, processes, recent histories, interrelationships, and the complexity of influences and affects on human actions and phenomena. This method may serve grounded theorists in searches for causes, conditions, contexts, and consequences. It is also appropriate for evaluating the efficacy of a particular program, or as preparatory work before diagramming or modeling a process through visual means such as decision modeling and cognitive networks. For example, a survey respondent describes in writing what challenges she faced when she took speech classes in high school. The + symbol refers to a combination of conditions, variables, or outcomes that are mentioned by the participant as connected parts of the causation sequence; the → symbol means "leads to":

[1] Without a doubt, it was a fear of speaking in front of others. My ultimate career as an adult was in the field of journalism. Early fears I had about approaching strangers and speaking in front of a group of people were overcome due to involvement in speaking events. As I mentioned above, I think speech class and the events that I participated in due to taking that class, probably led directly to my choosing journalism as a career. My success in the field of journalism would have never come about without those speech classes in high school.	[1] "FEAR OF SPEAKING" → SPEAKING EVENTS + SPEECH CLASS → JOURNALISM CAREER + SUCCESS

Four *Grammatical Methods* play a role in the mechanics of coding: Attribute Coding, Magnitude Coding, Subcoding, and Simultaneous Coding.

Attribute Coding

This method is the notation of basic descriptive information such as the field work setting, participant characteristics or demographics, data format, and other variables of interest for qualitative and some applications of quantitative analysis. This is appropriate for virtually all qualitative studies, but particularly for those with multiple participants and sites, cross-case studies, and studies with a wide variety of data forms. Attribute Coding provides essential participant information for future management, reference, and contexts for analysis and interpretation. Examples from a data set about an educational study include the following:

CASE: Martinez School

PARTICIPANT: Nancy (pseudonym)

INTERVIEW: 2 of 5

INTERVIEW TOPICS:

    Evaluation of School Day

    Salary Issues

    Principal–Teacher Relationship

    Upcoming Extracurricular Activities

    Upcoming Fundraising Project

Magnitude Coding

Magnitudes consist of supplemental alphanumeric or symbolic codes or Subcodes to existing coded data or a category to indicate their intensity, frequency, direction, presence, or evaluative content. Magnitude Codes can be qualitative, quantitative, and/or nominal indicators to enhance description. They are most appropriate for mixed methods and qualitative studies in education, social science, and health care disciplines that also support quantitative measures as evidence of outcomes. Examples used in the school improvement study include the following:

MAJOR

MODERATE

MINOR

√√ = Yes, clearly

√ = Possibly, in part

0 = No

++ = Very effective

+ = Effective

± = Mixed

We argue that although words may be more unwieldy than numbers, they render more meaning than numbers alone and should be hung on to throughout data analysis. Converting words into numbers and then tossing away the words gets a researcher into all kinds of trouble. You are assuming that the chief property of the words is that there are more of some than of others. Focusing solely on numbers and quantities shifts attention from substance to arithmetic, throwing out the whole notion of their qualities or essential characteristics. A solution to this problem, as we will see in later sections and displays, is to keep words and any associated magnitudes (LOW, EFFECTIVE, √) *together* throughout the analysis.

Subcoding

A Subcode is a second-order tag assigned after a primary code to detail or enrich the entry. The method is appropriate for virtually all qualitative studies, but particularly for ethnographies and content analyses, studies with multiple participants and sites, and studies with a wide variety of data forms. Subcoding is also appropriate when general code entries will later require more extensive indexing, categorizing, and subcategorizing into hierarchies or taxonomies, or for nuanced qualitative data analysis. It can be employed after an initial yet general coding scheme has been applied and the researcher realizes that the classification scheme may have been too broad, or added to primary codes if particular qualities or interrelationships emerge. This example comes from a set of field notes describing a school's facilities:

[1] The school's multipurpose room functions as a cafeteria, auditorium, assembly space, meeting space, and study hall. Its portable tables with attached seating fold up easily for somewhat quick transformation and cleaning of the space. [2] The adjoining media center houses books, a computer lab with 26 stations, study "nooks" for small groups, and various tables and chairs. A large screen and LCD projector suspended from the ceiling make the space look like a private movie theater.	[1] SCHOOL - MULTIPURPOSE SPACE [2] SCHOOL - MEDIA CENTER

Simultaneous Coding

This is the application of two or more different codes to a single qualitative datum, or the overlapped occurrence of two or more codes applied to sequential units of qualitative data. The method is appropriate when the data's content suggests multiple meanings (e.g., descriptively and inferentially) that necessitate and justify more than one code. Simultaneous Coding should be used sparingly, however; too many codes suggest a vague handle on the research questions and study's purpose. An example of the method comes from field notes about an organizational study of a community theatre program:

[1 & 2] The board of directors struggled with ways to keep the community theatre program going for another full season. It had been a staple in the area for almost 40 years, but now faced (like many comparable programs) the end of its existence. Less financial contributions and lower box office revenue had put the theatre severely in the red. Long-time volunteers and members were thinking with their hearts more than with their heads as they claimed that the "traditions" of this program could not be ended. The board felt otherwise, for none of its members wanted the liability of debt.	[1] FINANCIAL LOSS [2] END OF TRADITION

One stand-alone method, *Themeing the Data*, elaborates on what may be perceived as the terse shorthand of codes and coding.

Themeing the Data

In addition to codes, extended thematic phrases can be applied to units of data. Themeing is perhaps most applicable to phenomenology, but the method also lends itself to the analysis of qualitative data for comparison to comparably themed quantitative data for mixed methods studies.

Overall, a theme is an *extended phrase* or *sentence* that identifies what a unit of data is *about* and/or what it *means*. To Rubin and Rubin (2012), themes are statements *qua* (in the role of) ideas presented by participants during interviews that summarize what is going on, explain what is happening, or suggest why something is done the way it is (p. 118). It is important to note that coding and themeing are not either/or procedures. Analysts, if they wish, can code their data first, cluster the codes according to commonality, and construct an extended thematic statement rather than a short category label from the assemblage.

In the interview transcript below, a health care researcher examines the concept of "recovery" by assigning extended phrases or brief sentences to portions of the participant's story about a knee injury.

[1] I injured my right knee in a sports accident in college. It was just a bunch of guys playing football, not a college team or anything. But I squatted down as I was running and I guess I twisted my leg in a direction it wasn't supposed to go and it just hurt like hell. The pain was in the back of my knee, here. [2] I went to the emergency room, had to be on crutches for a few weeks, it hurt like a bitch but eventually healed up. [3] But I've still got a scar or something inside me, a friend told me it was a flap of some kind inside me, that can go out of whack if I move my leg the wrong way. And if it does, my knee freezes up, it locks, and I have to bend it back in place carefully by twisting my leg this way. [4] It's a pain to be so careful with how I move now because it can go out on me unexpectedly.	[1] INJURY FROM UNNATURAL BODY MOVEMENT [2] RECOVERY IS PAINFUL BUT EVENTUAL [3] RECOVERY LEAVES INTERNAL SCARS [4] RECOVERY MEANS ATTENTIVE CAUTION

CODING CRAFT AND DESIGN

Before we proceed to Second Cycle Coding, we need to discuss a few technical matters related to the craft and design of codes and coding.

Levels of Coding Detail

How detailed should coding be? That depends on the study and your goals. More typically, codes get applied to larger units—sentences, monothematic "chunks" of sentences in interview transcripts, or full paragraphs in written-up field notes. If you are coding by hand on hard copies of data and the margins get piled up with multiple codes, you are in for heavy sledding when the codes need to be clustered for Second Cycle Pattern Coding. This problem is not critical when data have been coded with CAQDAS (Computer Assisted Qualitative Data Analysis Software), or even with Microsoft Office programs like Word and Excel (see Display 2.10).

Finally, not every portion of the field notes or interview transcripts must be coded. There are things such as trivial, irrelevant data. Most field notes and selected portions of transcripts usually contain much dross—material unrelated to the research questions, either prespecified or emerging. And, if done carefully, coding of later material can be more sparing.

A Priori Codes

One method of creating codes is developing a provisional "start list" of codes prior to field work—*deductive* or a priori coding. The list comes from the literature review, conceptual framework, list of research questions, hypotheses, problem areas, and/or key variables that the researcher brings to the study.

In our (Miles and Huberman) school improvement study, for example, we conceptualized the innovation process, in part, as one of RECIPROCAL TRANSFORMATIONS. Teachers change the characteristics of new practices. Those practices, in turn, change the teachers and modify working arrangements in the classroom, which, in turn, influence how much of the innovation can be used, and so on.

We began with a master code—TRANSFORMATION or TRANS for short—to indicate the transformational process we had hypothesized, plus some Subcodes—TRANS-USER, TRANS-CLASS (classroom changes), TRANS-ORG (organizational changes), TRANS-INN (changes in the innovation)—to mark off segments of data in each class of variables. The list was held lightly, applied to the first sets of field notes, and then examined closely for fit and utility. Quite a few codes were revised, but the conceptual orientation seemed to bear real fruit—to fit and account well for what we saw and heard.

A start list can have from a dozen or so up to 50 codes; that number can be kept surprisingly well in the analyst's memory without constant reference to the full list—*if* the list has a clear structure and rationale. It is a good idea to get that list on a single sheet for easy reference. Most CAQDAS programs can retain these Provisional Codes before data are entered into their programs.

Still other codes emerge progressively during data collection—*inductive* coding. These are better grounded empirically and are especially satisfying to the researcher who has uncovered an important local factor. They also satisfy other readers, who can see that the researcher is open to what the site has to say rather than determined to force-fit the data into preexisting codes. Most field researchers, no matter how conceptually oriented, will recognize when an a priori coding system is ill molded to the data or when a rival perspective looks more promising.

Revising Codes

For all approaches to coding, several codes will change and evolve as field experience continues. Researchers with start lists know that codes will change; there is more going on out there than our initial frames have dreamed of, and few field researchers are foolish enough to avoid looking for these things.

Some codes do not work; others decay. No field material fits them, or the way they slice up the phenomenon is not the way the phenomenon appears empirically. This issue calls for doing away with the code or changing its type (e.g., transforming a noun-based Descriptive Code such as COUNSELING CENTER into an action-oriented Process Code such as REHABILITATING CLIENTS). Other codes flourish, sometimes too much so. Too many segments get the same code, thus creating the familiar problem of bulk. This problem calls for breaking down codes into Subcodes.

With manual coding, revision is tedious: Every unit you have coded before has to be relabeled. But the search-and-replace facility of your text-based software and most CAQDAS programs can accomplish this easily.

STRUCTURE AND UNITY IN CODE LISTS

Whether codes are created and revised early or late is less important than whether they have some conceptual and structural unity. Codes should relate to one another in coherent, study-important ways; they should be part of a unified structure. Incrementally adding, removing, or reconfiguring codes is certainly permissible, so long as some sense of "belonging" is maintained.

Display 4.1 exhibits the coding system developed by Westerman, Cobham, and McDermott (2017) for their *Qualitative Health Research* article, "Trauma-Focused Cognitive Behavior Therapy: Narratives of Children and Adolescents." Young people with PTSD after a local flood disaster were interviewed by therapists. The transcripts were coded using concepts from the professional literature and the researchers' emergent design, which resulted in three primary categories with their related codes. The co-authors explain that

> The three concepts of *coherence*, *elaboration*, and *evaluation* formed a functional matrix with which to describe the patterns within the stories. *Coherence* was divided into structure (beginnings, sequences, and endings), orientation (time, place, and persons), and normative referents. *Elaboration* was divided into description (sensory and kinesthetic information), emotion, and sense of self. *Evaluation* was divided into causality, insight, and integration. (Westerman, Cobham, & McDermott, 2017, p. 228; emphasis added)

DISPLAY 4.1 ● Details of the Coding System

Coherence: General

A coherent narrative is one that can be understood within an exchange

Coherence: Structure

How beginnings are constructed

The sequencing of information

How endings are constructed

(Continued)

(Continued)

Coherence: Orientation

An awareness of time, setting, and persons

Coherence: Normative

The cultural context evident within the story

Elaboration: General

The complexity of detail in the stories (stories may be sparse or complex)

The amount of detail may indicate accessibility, or avoidance, of memories

Elaboration: Description

Includes sensory details (sight, sound, touch, taste, smell, kinesthetic)

Elaboration: Emotion

The level of articulation of emotional domains

Intensity of expressed emotion

Both internal feelings and awareness of the feelings of others

Elaboration: Sense of self

The use of words that indicate thinking, knowing, remembering, intentions, perspective taking or positioning, relatedness, and values

Evaluation: Causality

Explanations, links between information, and plausibility

May relate to action, emotion, cognitions, or social relationships

Evaluation: Insight

Self-reflectivity and criticality

Flexibility and a tolerance of contradictions and uncertainties

Immediate lessons or global understanding that are gained from the traumatic experience

Evaluation: Integration

Meaning making in sense of self and identity in relation to information, agency, and predictive ability

Source: Westerman, Cobham, & McDermott (2017), p. 229.

The co-authors sought a balance between simple and more complex coding systems that had been developed in the narrative psychology literature. With this elegant coding system, the research team was able to provide a concrete data example for each code, which included the percentage of stories that were assigned the code.

There is a "good fit" between the data and the emergent codes, but also between and among the categories and codes themselves in Display 4.1. Their efficacy was also noted by the coauthors, who concluded, "The coding system developed for this study elicited a wealth of information about the changes that occurred within the trauma narratives as therapy progressed. Our results suggest that narratives within this clinical intervention do have the potential to yield useful and specific information about change processes for clinicians" (p. 230).

An operative coding scheme is not simply a list or index of disjointed descriptors but rather a conceptual web, including larger meanings and their constitutive characteristics. CAQDAS is especially helpful in displaying the structure of coding schemes, either in hierarchical or taxonomic form or in a network.

DEFINITIONS OF CODES

Whether codes are prespecified or developed along the way, clear operational definitions are indispensable so they can be applied consistently by a single researcher over time, and multiple researchers will be thinking about the same phenomena as they code. A First Cycle code can consist of a single term—for example, TRANSFORMATION—that can easily suggest different meanings to different analysts. Because codes will drive the retrieval and organization of the data for analysis, they must be precise and their meaning shared among analysts. Defining them helps on both counts.

McHugh, Horner, Colditz, and Wallace (2013) explored through focus group interviews with diverse youth their "Bridges and Barriers: Adolescent Perceptions of Student-Teacher Relationships." This *Urban Education* article features as an appendix a rarely seen abbreviated codebook that includes each code's definition employed for the study's analysis (see Display 4.2).

DISPLAY 4.2 ● Abbreviated Codebook

Barriers

Back-Channel Communication: incident in which two or more people are talking about another; most frequently, topic person is not present (though this may occur), and such communications are inferred by or later related to topic person.

Boundaries: participant expresses that someone is expected to act or speak in some way based on rank, role, or relationship.

Carelessness: instances or occurrences in which the participant or the person about whom the participant is relating failed to adequately take into consideration another person's needs, desires or likes/dislikes; may refer to verbal, physical, engagement, emotive, or relational.

Consequence: a repercussion of a given action, behavior, statement or incidence.

Inattention: instances or occurrences in which the participant or the person about whom the participant is relating failed to adequately attend to another person's actions or communicated thoughts or feelings; may refer to verbal, physical, emotive, or relational.

Stereotype: when a person is presumed to behave, believe, think, or experience some emotion simply because of some external categorization; typified by an intensified, overgeneralized, and frequent reinterpretation of a perceived attribute to an extreme degree and applied regardless of contrary fact/observations.

Unspecified Barriers: processes that act as barriers to a relationship growing closer, but that do not meet the definitional criteria of another specific barrier process.

Bridges

Connecting: participant refers to or describes the process by which someone transitions into "being known" by the participant, or by which the participant is "known" by them; the act of connecting with another person, or growing closer.

Effortful Engagement: an instance in which one person actively and deliberately engages another on an interpersonal level.

Help Seeking: the act of requesting and/or receiving assistance from another person; may be educational, verbal, financial, physical, or advisory; the request for one to enact one's resources for the benefit of another.

Personal Disclosure: participant describes or relates an occurrence in which they either shared something personal with another person, or when another person shared something personal with the participant; may be positive, neutral, expression of uncertainty or vulnerability, or any of these in combination with negative.

Prediction and Interpretation: when a person demonstrates the ability to predict another person's reaction (verbal, active, emotive, etc.) to an action (verbal, active, or emotive) performed by the predictor, and to accurately gauge their intention underlying communication, actions undertaken, etc.

(Continued)

(Continued)

(Understanding) Constraints: temporal, monetary, physical, familial/relational, etc. features of a participant's life which, per participant report, may make connecting to others or completing a given task a more complicated and/or difficult proposition than would otherwise be.

Support

Unspecified Support: the act of providing or sharing emotional assistance, reassurance or bolstering, or other form of support that does not meet the definitional criteria of another specific support process.

Catharsis: mutual emotion sharing or emotional expression between two or more persons.

Companionship: the desire to share time, physical space, or communication with another person, typically in a friendly or emotionally positive manner.

Conflict Resolution: the act between two or more people to work collaboratively on resolving a point of disagreement, conflict, misunderstanding, etc.; primarily verbal, though may incorporate resource allocation.

Empathizing: an attempt to share in or re-create another's emotional experience.

Leniency/Willingness to Work Out Difficulties: the emotional and cognitive intention and commitment to resolving conflicts, differences of opinion, etc., that occur between two or more persons; this implies the intention to apply effort.

Problem Solving: request and/or receipt of assistance from one person by another in dealing with a real or hypothetical problem, conflict, tumultuous situation, or issue; primarily verbal in nature, and tends to be focused on social situations or circumstances.

Protection: the act of buffering or guarding another person; may be verbal (e.g., verbal defense), physical, legal, or emotional/relational.

Resource: various different types or degrees of assistance that one person can or does offer another person; may be financial, emotional, temporal, protective, work/education, etc.

Sharing of Difficulties: discussion of the revelation of personal problems, concerns, or issues to another person; participant may be discloser, or disclosed-to, but specific subject matter regards a negative occurrence in the discloser's life.

Soothing: the desire of a person for the consideration, kind words, or soothing actions of another person; the act of providing the above.

Structural Codes

Teacher Does: incidents in which a participant relates a specific instance or example of behavior that was specifically done by the teacher.

Teacher Does Not: incidents in which a participant relates a specific instance or example of behavior that was specifically NOT done by the teacher; these incidents are most typically paired with a value judgment.

Teacher Should: incidents in which a participant relates a specific instance when they feel that a teacher SHOULD have done something (coded regardless of actual occurrence of the behavior), or example of (potential or actual) teacher behavior that the student relayed feelings (or an affirming value judgment) that such behavior SHOULD happen.

Teacher Should Not: incidents in which a participant relates a specific instance when they feel that a teacher SHOULD NOT have done something (coded regardless of actual occurrence of the behavior), or example of (potential or actual) teacher behavior that the student relayed feelings (or a negative value judgment) that such behavior SHOULD NOT happen.

Source: McHugh, Horner, Colditz, & Wallace (2013), pp. 35–38.

The co-authors detail their meticulous coding procedures and the difficulties they encountered with overlapping codes applied to ever-shifting topics in focus group transcripts (see Chapter 11). Their emergent system eventually honed in on the central purpose of the study, which enabled them to

> deliberately label the perceived effect of the interaction on the closeness of the interpersonal relationship. As such, we were able to explore the driving question in this coding process, "Did the interaction *bridge* the two people to bring them closer together, or did it separate them or create a *barrier* between closeness developing?" (McHugh et al., 2013, p. 18)

The codebook in Display 4.2 is an exemplar of fine-grained, nuanced definitions essential for analyzing complex relationship dynamics in multicultural settings.

Definitions become sharper when two researchers code the same data set and discuss their initial difficulties. A disagreement shows that a definition has to be expanded or otherwise amended. Time spent on this task is not hair-splitting but reaps real rewards by bringing you to a common vision of what the codes mean and which units of data best fit which code.

Team coding not only aids definitional clarity but also is a good reliability check. Do two coders working separately agree on how big a codable block of data is? And do they use roughly the same codes for the same blocks of data? If not, they are headed for different analyses and need to reconcile their differences for more credible and trustworthy findings.

Similarly, each coder is well-advised to code the first dozen pages of field notes, once right away and again (on an uncoded copy) a few days later. How good is the internal consistency? Eventually, intra- and/or intercoder agreement should be within the 85% to 90% range, depending on the size and range of the coding scheme. There are more robust statistical measures of agreement available such as Pearson's r and the Kappa coefficient for those who must provide quantitative evidence to readers. We believe, however, that a simple high percentage of agreement is sufficient for most qualitative studies.

SECOND CYCLE CODING—PATTERN CODES

Description

First Cycle coding is a way to initially summarize segments of data. Pattern Coding, as a Second Cycle method, is a way of grouping those summaries into a smaller number of *categories*, *themes*, or *concepts*. For quantitative researchers, it's an analog to the cluster-analytic and factor-analytic devices used in statistical analysis. Its parallel to grounded theory coding methods is Focused Coding or Axial Coding.

Pattern codes are inferential or explanatory codes, ones that identify a "bigger picture" configuration. They pull together a lot of material from First Cycle coding into more meaningful units of analysis. They are a sort of meta-code.

Applications

For the qualitative analyst, Pattern Coding has four important functions:

1. It condenses large amounts of data/codes into a smaller number of analytic units (e.g., categories, themes, concepts).

2. It gets the researcher into analysis during data collection, so that later fieldwork can be more focused.

3. It helps the researcher elaborate a cognitive network—an evolving, more integrated schema for understanding local incidents and interactions.

4. For multiple-case studies, it lays the groundwork for cross-case analysis by surfacing common themes and directional processes.

These four functions can be clarified as we discuss how Pattern Codes are generated, what they look like, and what the field researcher does with them in the course of data collection.

Examples

Generating Pattern Codes

During initial fieldwork, the researcher is looking for threads that tie together bits of data. For example, if two or three participants say independently that they "resent" a decision made by their boss, we may be on to several different phenomena—a conflict, an organizational climate factor, or a disgruntled subgroup of employees. Any of these interpretations involves chunking and sorting data (Function 1, above). For starters, is there anything else in common between these participants or in the site given for resenting the decision? Is there a different or opposing perspective among participants who are *not* resentful?

These first bits of data and the review of the coded segments being pulled together are leads; they suggest important variables to check out—factors that may account for other local perceptions and behaviors (Function 2, above). Seeing the RESENTMENT data (a First Cycle Emotion Code) in any of these alternative ways also helps the researcher make sense of puzzling or surprising observations. These several bits come together into an initial plot of the terrain (Function 3). Finally, if a colleague in a multi-case study comes across a similar profile of resentment or, alternatively, finds no resentment of decisions at all in a place otherwise similar to the more "resentful" case, we have the first threads of cross-case comparison (Function 4).

Patterning happens quickly because it is the way we instinctively and naturally process information. The danger is getting locked too quickly into naming a pattern, assuming you understand it, and then thrusting the name onto data that fit it poorly. The trick here is to work with loosely held units of meaning, to be ready to unfreeze and reconfigure them as the data shape up otherwise, to subject the most compelling themes to cross-checking, and to lay aside the more tenuous ones until other participants and observations give them better empirical grounding. In a more inductive study, it helps to look for recurring phrases (i.e., In Vivo Codes) or common threads in participants' accounts or, alternatively, for internal differences that you or participants have noted. Typically, those differences will bring forth a higher level commonality.

What Pattern Codes Look Like

Pattern Codes usually consist of four, often interrelated, summarizers:

1. Categories or themes

2. Causes or explanations

3. Relationships among people

4. Concepts or theoretical constructs

Below are some concrete examples of Pattern Codes in capital letters, followed by their brief definitions.

Categories or Themes

RULES: You don't "shop talk" in the staff lounge; the unspoken understanding is that social small talk to decompress is OK; complaining is also acceptable but without generating solutions to problems.

TRAJECTORIES: The metaphor of career "trajectories"—people are using these projects to get away from some jobs and places to other ones.

Causes or Explanations

DYSFUNCTIONAL DIRECTION: Staff perceptions of and interactions with ineffective leadership that influence workplace morale and effectiveness.

BEST PRACTICES: The best projects are ones that put together the best practitioners' tested recipes for success.

Relationships Among People

LEADERS' NETWORK: The unofficial collective of individuals seen as key leaders at their respective sites: A. Becker, P. Harrison, and V. Wales.

NEW GUARD: The new, thirtyish generation of faculty members with an aggressive yet socially conscious edge to them.

Concepts or Theoretical Constructs

BARGAINING: Bargaining or negotiating, most often covertly, seems to be the way decisions get made; a conflict model is a more plausible account of how actions get initiated, rather than through cooperative teamwork.

SURVIVAL: A defeatist, mostly negative attitude that suggests one is working on a day-to-day basis with minimal resources and support to accomplish much against sometimes overwhelming odds.

Pattern codes can emerge from repeatedly observed routines, rituals, rules, roles, and relationships; local meanings and explanations; commonsense explanations and more conceptual ones; inferential clusters and "metaphorical" ones; and single-case and cross-case observations.

Using Pattern Codes in Analysis

It may be useful at some point to "map" the Pattern Codes—that is, to lay out the component codes that got you the pattern—along with segments from the field notes. It helps to do it visually, in a network display, seeing how the components interconnect. The mapping is a new take on your conceptual framework. Although it is not hard to do this by hand, mapping by computer and CAQDAS has some powerful advantages and does this well.

Next, the most promising codes to emerge from this exercise are written up in the form of an analytic memo (discussed later) that expands on the significance of the code. This process helps the writer become less fuzzy about the emergent category, theme, concept, and so on, and gets cross-case and higher level analytic energy flowing.

Usually, a Pattern Code does not get discounted, but rather gets *qualified*: The conditions under which it holds are specified. For example, the RULE of "no 'shop talk' in the lounge" can be bent in cases of conflict, crisis, or socializing of new members. This clarification provides more precise parameters for the pattern and strengthens its validity.

If a general Pattern Code (such as RULES) is used a good deal, it is helpful to create Subcodes that explain the content and enable easy retrieval:

RULES-INDIVIDUAL: Rules about individual participant behavior

RULES-PUBLIC: Rules about behavior in public settings

RULES-WORK: Rules that specify how formal work tasks are to be carried out

Finally, Pattern Codes get checked out in the next wave of data collection. This is largely an inferential process. The analyst tries out the code on a new participant or during an observation in a similar setting; engages in **if-then** tactics (if the pattern holds, other things will happen or won't happen); or checks out a **rival explanation**.

(The **boldface** terms refer to specific tactics of drawing and verifying conclusions, which are discussed in detail in Chapter 11. We use this convention as a way of pointing to tactics as they occur in later chapters.) See Saldaña (2016) for additional Second Cycle coding methods, particularly those designed for grounded theory and longitudinal studies.

FROM CODES TO PATTERNS

Your initial or First Cycle coding of data generates an array of individual codes associated with their respective data units. Let's take a look at a fictional and extended example of how First Cycle codes transform into Second Cycle Pattern Codes and then get inserted into three display forms: matrices, networks, and graphics.

A selected series of codes related to the first month of withdrawal symptoms described by a participant voluntarily participating in a smoking cessation treatment program, in random order and with their First Cycle code types indicated, are as follows:

1. ANXIETY [Emotion Code]

2. NERVOUSNESS [Emotion Code]

3. "HURT SOMEONE BAD" [In Vivo Code/Emotion Code]

4. RESTLESSNESS [Emotion Code]

5. DEEP BREATHING [Process Code]

6. THROAT BURNING [Process Code]

7. "FELT LIKE CRYING" [In Vivo Code/Emotion Code/Process Code]

8. ANGRY [Emotion Code]

9. "EATING A LOT MORE" [In Vivo Code/Process Code]

10. WANDERING AROUND [Process Code]

11. HABITUAL MOVEMENTS [Descriptive Code]

12. MEMORIES OF SMOKING [Descriptive Code]

13. SMELLING NEW THINGS [Process Code]

There are several ways to approach the categorizing or patterning of these 13 codes. One possible way is to pattern them by code type, such as the following:

- **EMOTIONS** (ANXIETY, NERVOUSNESS, "HURT SOMEONE BAD," RESTLESSNESS, "FELT LIKE CRYING," ANGRY)

- **PROCESSES** (DEEP BREATHING, THROAT BURNING, "FELT LIKE CRYING," "EATING A LOT MORE," WANDERING AROUND, SMELLING NEW THINGS)

- **DESCRIPTORS** (HABITUAL MOVEMENTS, MEMORIES OF SMOKING)

Since negative and strong emotions seem to play a critical role in withdrawal symptoms from smoking, EMOTIONS as a Pattern Code choice makes sense. One can even enhance the code further with the adjective NEGATIVE EMOTIONS.

The PROCESSES and DESCRIPTORS labels, however, seem to lack the "oomph" needed for a Pattern Code. Recall that Pattern Codes usually consist of four, often interrelated, summarizers: categories or themes, causes or explanations, relationships among people, and concepts or theoretical constructs. There are several ways of recategorizing the remaining codes, first by reassembling them into particular clusters because they seem to go together. The analyst proposes the following:

- **Cluster 1**: DEEP BREATHING, THROAT BURNING, "EATING A LOT MORE," SMELLING NEW THINGS
- **Cluster 2**: WANDERING AROUND, HABITUAL MOVEMENTS
- **Cluster 3**: "FELT LIKE CRYING," MEMORIES OF SMOKING

First, what do the four codes in Cluster 1 have in common? They seem to be all upper body functions: respiratory, sensory, and digestive. The analyst reflects on what the four codes have in common; they seem to have a PHYSICAL CHANGES theme that unifies them, and thus get that Pattern Code assigned to them.

The codes of Cluster 2 (WANDERING AROUND, HABITUAL MOVEMENTS) seem to evoke a metaphoric RESTLESS JOURNEY of some sort. Cluster 3's codes ("FELT LIKE CRYING," MEMORIES OF SMOKING) suggest a conceptual Pattern Code of REGRETFUL LOSS. Where did the Pattern Code labels of RESTLESS JOURNEY and REGRETFUL LOSS come from? They came from researcher reflection on what their constituent codes seemed to have in common.

Notice that these four Pattern Codes—NEGATIVE EMOTIONS, PHYSICAL CHANGES, RESTLESS JOURNEY, and REGRETFUL LOSS—are one person's analytic proposals. Other researchers reflecting on and clustering the First Cycle codes might have developed different Pattern Codes altogether. Thus, an important principle to note here is that Pattern Coding—indeed, *all* coding—is not a precise science; it's primarily an interpretive act.

The researcher can now use these four Pattern Codes in various ways, according to the needs of the study. Basic narrative description is one approach; visual displays such as matrices, networks, and graphics are another primary way of analyzing data for fresh perspectives.

Narrative Description

The researcher can compose a section that identifies and elaborates on the Pattern Code, weaving its component First Cycle codes into the narrative and supporting it with field note data:

> Smoking withdrawal symptoms during Month 1 include a *restless journey* for the individual: "I found myself just wandering around the house, just walking from room to room because I couldn't smoke, so I didn't know what to do with myself." The ex-smoker also continues to replicate habitual movements related to smoking, such as reaching for a cigarette pack in a shirt pocket, or leaving an indoor office to go outside to smoke. These physical actions interrelate with, and may even be caused by, several of the *negative emotions* induced by nicotine withdrawal: anxiety, nervousness, and restlessness.

In this case, the storyline function of narrative enables the researcher to outline the plot points of human action and how participants (or "characters") changed throughout the course of the study. Prosaic representation and presentation of our findings are essential ways to communicate to readers how the social action we witnessed and synthesized unfolded and flowed through time. But matrices, networks, and graphics are other ways of representing and presenting those observations.

Matrix Display

Matrix displays will be discussed more fully in the next six chapters, but they are briefly described here for illustrative purposes. Matrix displays chart or table the data—including codes—for analytic purposes. They organize the vast array of condensed material into an at-a-glance format for reflection, verification, conclusion drawing, and other analytic acts.

DISPLAY 4.3 ● Matrix of Smoking Cessation Patterns at Months 1 and 6		
Initiating Smoking Cessation Patterns	Month 1	Month 6
NEGATIVE EMOTIONS	Anxious, nervous, angry, aggressive	Occasionally anxious
PHYSICAL CHANGES	Gained 5 pounds, felt "burning" sensation in throat and lungs	On weight loss program after gaining 20 pounds, heightened sense of smell
RESTLESS JOURNEY	Wandering and habitual movements	Habitual movements
REGRETFUL LOSS	"Felt like crying," hyper-conscious of cessation	Nostalgic for smoking, "hangs around" smokers

Suppose that the smoking cessation study was interested in how withdrawal symptoms change across *time*. Display 4.3 charts a participant's data at 1 month and 6 months after quitting. The Pattern Codes are placed in one column, and related First Cycle codes or other data summarizers are placed in the respective columns. A simple matrix such as this enables you—and a reader of your report—to take in the salient findings of your analysis. For example, in the NEGATIVE EMOTIONS row, you can see that such phenomena decrease across a 6-month period, but *anxiety* is still present, albeit in milder form. Each cell of this matrix does not have to include the kitchen sink of withdrawal symptoms, only some of the most relevant exemplars from coding and analysis.

Network Display

This particular withdrawal symptom example describes a *process*, and thus a network of how things act or transform across time (or other aspects such as relationship dynamics or organizational patterns) can be mapped (see Display 4.4). The codes in matrix cells now become possible labels for bins. Lines and arrows indicate connections and flows between the clusters of action they represent.

The analyst has shown how the Pattern Code REGRETFUL LOSS and its constituent codes of "FELT LIKE CRYING" and MEMORIES OF SMOKING have changed from Month 1 through Month 6. Follow-up interviews with the participant suggested that the impulse to cry transformed through time into mild anxiety, while the deeply embedded memories of years of smoking changed into nostalgic reflection on past habits. An interesting track, however, appeared in the interview with the participant 6 months after he quit smoking:

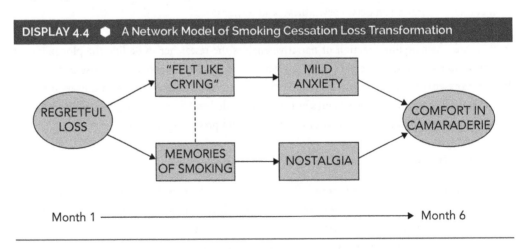

DISPLAY 4.4 ● A Network Model of Smoking Cessation Loss Transformation

It's still hard, but I find myself hanging around smokers on campus whenever I can, just to smell the cigarette smoke as I smoke on my electronic cigarette. It's comforting just to hang around with smokers even though I don't smoke any more. I still feel like I'm connected to smoking in some way. And I can talk to them about my new habit and stuff. We're still partners in crime.

This interview excerpt, combined with other related coded units of data, led the analyst to compose the evolutionary Month 6 Pattern Code COMFORT IN CAMARADERIE. The participant's ever-present mild anxiety becomes alleviated when he "hangs with" current smokers; his nostalgia for a former habit can be fed by physically placing himself among those who currently smoke. But don't let the elegance and symmetry of the Display 4.4 network fool you into thinking that social life is always linear, balanced, and smooth flowing, and that it can be reduced to a few key variables.

Graphic Display

A graphic display utilizes artistic principles to convey what words alone cannot. The researcher literally *renders* an account through line, shape, mass, color, and other design elements to evoke within its viewers an impressionistic yet research-based summary of the research story. Pie charts and bar graphs are some of the most well-known forms of graphic quantitative data display. But qualitative researchers have at their disposal more innovative forms and formats (discussed further in Chapter 5).

For the smoking cessation data, imagine if we asked the participant himself to *draw* what his emotional states were like at Month 1 and later at Month 6. This form of arts-based inquiry, shown in Display 4.5, displays an aggressive and heavy use of diagonal lines (as smoke) emerging from a broken cigarette in Month 1, while Month 6 displays a snuffed cigarette butt sticking out of an ashtray with a small curve of wistful smoke emanating from it. Interpreting the drawing, in consultation with the participant, the smoker no longer smokes at Month 6, yet the images of a cigarette and smoke are still present. He no longer engages in the habit, but the memories of it still remain in his mind. In contrast with Month 1, the anxiety is lessened; nostalgia has taken its place. "MONTH 1" is written in/with an angry hand; "MONTH 6" appears more controlled and relaxed.

DISPLAY 4.5 ◗ Arts-Based Graphic Representation of Smoking Cessation at Months 1 and 6

These simple examples of representing smoking cessation were intended to illustrate how Pattern Codes can become grist for narratives, matrices, networks, and graphics, to be more fully explicated in Chapters 5 through 10.

Coding Advice

Coding is not just something you do to "get the data ready" for analysis; rather, as we have said several times, it is a form of early and continuing analysis that drives ongoing data collection. It typically leads to a reshaping of your perspective and instrumentation for the next round.

Every project needs a systematic way to store coded field data and a way to retrieve them easily during analysis. Three-ring notebooks, file folders, half-sheets of paper, index cards, sticky notes, and summaries on poster-size paper taped to a wall are "old school" but time-honored methods for qualitative data analysis. Yet, as we note, good computer software is far ahead of them when it comes to data organization and management.

Perhaps the more important point is this: The ultimate power of field research lies in the researcher's emerging map of what is happening and why. So, any method that will force more differentiation and integration of that map, while remaining flexible, is a good idea. Coding, working through iterative cycles of induction and deduction to power the analysis, can accomplish these goals.

But coding can tire you; it often feels longer than it really is. So, it helps to intersperse coding with jottings and analytic memos.

JOTTINGS

Think of a jotting (Emerson, Fretz, & Shaw, 2011) as an "analytic sticky note"—a piece of writing that could literally fit onto the space of a small square piece of paper. Adobe's PDF document reader has this function; Microsoft Word's "New Comment" feature is an equivalent. CAQDAS programs enable the user to insert "annotations" or "comments" that can be attached to particular units of data. If you're working on hard copy, you could use actual sticky notes, but these can get easily detached if you're not careful. Handwriting notes in the margins will suffice and, in a text file, a separate paragraph (in a different font or color to distinguish it from the rest of the data) will serve for jottings.

So, what is a jotting and what goes into it? A jotting holds the researcher's fleeting and emergent reflections and commentary on issues that emerge during field work and especially data analysis. As you work on a project, reflections of several sorts typically swim into awareness. For example, consider the following:

- Subtextual inferences on the meaning of what a key participant was "really" saying during an exchange that seemed somehow important

- Personal reactions to some participants' remarks or actions

- What the relationship with participants feels like

- Doubts about the quality of some of the data

- Second thoughts about some of the interview questions and observation protocols

- A mental note to pursue an issue further in the next contact

- Cross-reference to material in another part of the data set

- Elaboration or clarification of a prior incident or event that now seems of possible significance

When something like any of these examples arises, it's useful to jot your mental note directly into field notes or somewhere else in the data corpus. It may or may not be fodder for a deeper analytic memo (discussed later), but at least it's in print. One convention is to distinguish the remark with italics to signal that it is of a different order from the data it comments on. Here's a field note example with a jotting:

> The administrative assistant speaks in a sincere voice over the phone: "Well, thank you so much for your help, I really appreciate it. Good-bye." Then she slams the handset into the carriage. *I find it almost amusing to hear the juxtaposition of a "professionally nice" voice followed by a hard, hang-up slam of the phone. She's probably masking a lot of on-the-job tension or frustration.*

Remarks such as these add substantial meaning to the analysis and perhaps even the write-up.

Jottings can strengthen coding by pointing to deeper or underlying issues that deserve analytic attention. Coding, as we have noted, can become tedious if you treat yourself as a sort of machine scanning the pages methodically, picking out small segments of data and assigning labels to them. The sensation of being bored is usually a signal that you have ceased to think. One way of retaining mindfulness in coding is occasional jotting (see Display 4.6 for jottings on a Word document through its New Comment function).

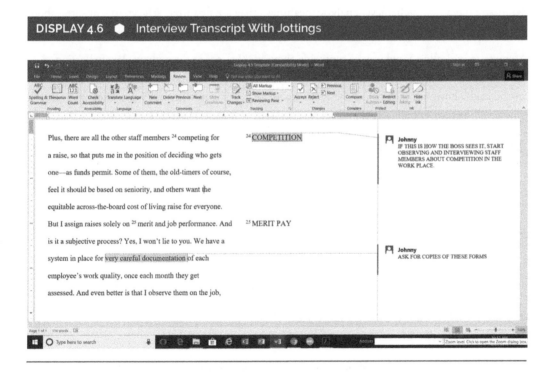

DISPLAY 4.6 ⬡ Interview Transcript With Jottings

As coding proceeds, if you are alert about what you are doing, ideas and reactions to the meaning of what you are seeing will well up steadily. These ideas are important; they suggest new interpretations, leads, and connections with other parts of the data; and they usually point toward questions and issues to look into during the next wave of data collection and to ways of elaborating some of these ideas. These marginal remarks also point to important issues that a given code may be missing or blurring, suggesting revisions to the coding scheme.

Jottings in the form of reflective remarks can be added while you are writing or expanding on raw field notes. You are simultaneously aware of events in the site and of your own feelings, reactions, insights, and interpretations. Bogdan and Biklen (2007) call these sections "Observer's Comments" or, in field notes, "OCs." These can be separated from the main field notes through a different font style and/or indent:

The committee chair recommended that they take a ten-minute break, but Carla recommended that they continue. "We've got just three more evaluations to get through, we can do that in half an hour." The chair noted, "Well, one of them's going to take a while to get through," so it would be best to come back to the task refreshed and alert.

OC: *The chair gave his reason with a matter-of-fact tone of voice, but one could sense that there were a lot of sticky issues to get through with the one new candidate. Carla seems oblivious to the political infighting I've observed at other meetings, and I feel the rest of the committee wants her to stay that way.*

Marginal notes can be perceived as important "bread crumbs" that are dropped to the ground for later collection by the analyst for expansion through memoing, discussed next.

ANALYTIC MEMOING

Description and Rationale

An analytic memo is a brief or extended narrative that documents the researcher's reflections and thinking processes about the data. These are not just descriptive summaries of data but attempts to synthesize them into higher level analytic meanings. They are first draft self-reports, of sorts, about the study's phenomena and serve as the basis for more expanded and final reports.

Memos are typically a rapid way of capturing thoughts that occur throughout data collection, data condensation, data display, conclusion drawing, conclusion verification, and final reporting. Later in the study, however, memos can be more elaborate, especially when they piece together several strands of the data or look across multiple measures of a concept.

Saldaña (2016) notes that analytic memos can be developed along the following topics:

- A descriptive summary of the data
- How you personally relate to the participants and/or the phenomenon
- The participants' actions, reactions, and interactions
- The participants' routines, rituals, rules, roles, and relationships
- What you find intriguing, surprising, or disturbing (Sunstein & Chiseri-Strater, 2012)
- Your code choices and their operational definitions
- Emergent patterns, categories, themes, concepts, and assertions
- The possible networks and processes (links, connections, overlaps, flows) among the codes, patterns, categories, themes, concepts, and assertions
- An emergent or related existent theory
- Any problems with the study
- Any personal or ethical dilemmas with the study
- Future directions for the study
- The analytic memos generated thus far (metamemos)
- Tentative answers to your study's research questions
- Passage drafts for the final report for the study

Analytic memos don't just report data; they tie together different pieces of data into a recognizable cluster, often to show that those data are instances of a general concept. Analytic memos can also go well beyond codes and their relationships to any aspect of the study—personal, methodological, and substantive. Memo writing often provides sharp, sunlit moments of clarity or insight—little conceptual epiphanies. They are one of the most useful and powerful sense-making tools at hand.

Examples

Analytic memos should be dated for reference to the analytic history and progress of your study, titled with its memo type (e.g., CODE DEFINITION, ASSERTION, THEORY, ETHICS) and subtitled with its more specific content (e.g., WHAT CASES HAVE IN COMMON, PARTICIPANT LEERINESS, AGENDA FOR NEXT SITE VISIT). Most CAQDAS programs can create and maintain memos (also called "comments" or "annotations" in selected programs), but they can also be kept as a running diary of sorts in a separate research journal. It is recommended that analytic memos not be embedded within field notes, transcripts, or other data but be kept as a separate document.

Here are a few examples of analytic memos from McCammon et al.'s (2012) "Lifelong Impact" study, which surveyed adults about their high school arts education experiences. This first memo documents a pattern observed by the analyst after the codes had been arranged to contrast the younger respondents with older ones:

January 17, 2011

PATTERN: INTRINSIC AND EXTRINSIC

One of the most striking contrasts between survey respondents who graduated in the 2000s and in the 1950s–1970s is what they seem to value about the experiences. More recent graduates wrote about those intangible, intrinsic outcomes such as "camaraderie," "self-discovery," and identity, while the older generations put more stock into awards, specific roles they played, and what they've accomplished over their life course. I wonder if just being recently graduated from high school means that the memories are fresher about those internal experiences, and so it's going to be more in your head. As someone who's from the older generation, I know that I myself put a lot of stock into my own legacy, those tangible things that are evidence of what I've accomplished.

Ironically, I would have thought the older generations would have been more reflective and internal about those memories, more nostalgic, while the younger "me" generation would have valued awards, letter jackets, etc. Maybe it has something to do with human development—when you're in your late teens and early twenties, you're still trying to figure out "Who am I?" So, you're still looking within and exploring what's really important to you.

Below is an example of how a rough analytic memo eventually transformed into a finished narrative for a final report. First, the memo:

November 2, 2010

METAMEMO: ANTHROPOLOGICAL METAPHORS

It's interesting to see how this study has ties to the social sciences, and how the psychological, sociological, and anthropological disciplines have lenses to offer to the analysis. As for the anthropological, I was struck by a recent reading that used the phrase "the mastery of sacred texts" as a condition for growing up and becoming part of the culture. In theatre and speech, the mastery of sacred texts is memorizing the script—becoming "one" with the play and taking deep ownership of a character. Theatre and religion have been long explored for their parallels, but I don't think the "rite of passage" theme through performance has been tackled (but check Victor Turner's writings on this just to be sure).

After reviewing the memos to date on major categories, labels such as "community," "tribe," and "family" appear frequently (though theatre people themselves are more likely to use the term "ensemble"—occupational term, I guess). Even better is when respondents told stories about feeling "lost" in performance—a kind of journey taken to achieve spiritual knowledge. The journeys of these participants are both internal and actual (out-of-town speech tournaments, especially)—getting lost to find yourself, leaving home to compete and either win or lose, but coming back stronger than when you left.

And now, these paragraphs from the unpublished technical report illustrate how the ideas from the memo were adapted and woven into the analytic portions of the text:

> From social science perspectives (Lancy, Bock, & Gaskins, 2010), there is public expectation and prejudice, if not stigma, toward those who participate in theatre. Adolescent outcasts find their niche among a community tribe of like-minded kin. In these demarcated spaces of classrooms and performance venues, there are operant local school and national cultures of high school educational theatre programs. The adolescent cultural member assumes and adopts the ethos—the values, attitudes, and beliefs—of the social environment in which he/she participates, but with the prerequisite that the young person feels a sense of belonging in that culture. Cognitive maps for survival and safety, emotional and moral socialization, plus individual personality formation occur in these safe spaces through observation, interaction, and challenge. The rote learning and memorization of play scripts and speeches is comparable to the mastery of "sacred texts," valued as "acts of piety, discipline, personal transformation, and cultural preservation" (p. 212). These literal and community narratives contribute to identity, belonging, and expression.
>
> The inherent demands of theatre and speech accelerate adult preparedness. There is high risk for high status. Achievement through awards, placements, and competitions harkens back to initiation rituals and rites of passage to progress toward a higher level of adulthood. Travel to another world, such as the spiritual one of performance and the spatial one of an out of town speech tournament, is comparable to the classic hero's journey in which trial must precede triumph in order to return to the tribe stronger than before. (McCammon & Saldaña, 2011, p. 103)

Memoing Advice

Here we draw on the recommendations of grounded theory's creators, Barney Glaser and Anselm Strauss, and Strauss's later collaborator, Juliet Corbin. Our advice is an amalgam of their experiences and ours. Also see Saldaña (2016) for an extended chapter on analytic memo writing:

1. When an idea strikes, stop whatever else you are doing and write the memo. Don't worry about prose elegance or even grammar. Include your musings of all sorts, even the fuzzy and foggy ones. Give yourself the freedom to think; don't self-censor.

2. Memoing should begin as soon as the first field data start coming in and usually should continue right up to production of the final report. Just as codes should stabilize

reasonably well by one-half or two-thirds of the way through data collection, the ideas raised in memos usually will start settling down then or shortly afterward, as the analyst approaches what grounded theorists call "saturation" (no significantly new explanations for data). Memoing also contributes strongly to the development/revision of the coding system.

3. Keep memos sortable; caption them by basic content. Like coded data, memos can be stored and retrieved using a wide variety of methods.

4. Once again, memos are about *ideas*. Simply summarizing or recounting data examples is not enough.

ON VISUAL DATA

There is much now in qualitative inquiry about the analysis of visual materials, especially since accessible and ubiquitous digital tools enable researchers to document field work with ease, and the availability and amount of Internet resources proliferate daily. Good ethnographers have always documented the visual elements of social life in one way or another. It's just that the media we have nowadays permit us to archive the visual *as* images rather than just through descriptive and evocative writing. And when both text and image work together in integrated concert, as we promote through data display, the result is a more coherent whole (Ledin & Machin, 2018, p. 29).

Analyzing the visual has its own unique repertoire of methods, and we do not have the space to outline them here in detail. We do, however, advocate that interpretation of what we see as still visual documentation—in a magazine, on a website, as a digital photograph, and so on—is more of a holistic, interpretive venture rather than a systematic one. Analytic memoing of your impressions about the frozen, captured image is a more appropriate form of exploration than detailed breakdowns of components such as color, angle, and composition.

But moving images and lengthier passages of television, film, YouTube clips, and other digital streams are more complex and might rely on more traditional content analytic methods such as counts and categories for nuanced analysis. We muse, however, that the analysis of moving images is not all that different from the observation and analysis of real life in real time in real field settings. One advantage of video is that researchers have the opportunity to replay slices of life repeatedly to discern more nuance and patterns of human action such as gaze, touch, gesture, posture, and spatial positioning (Rapley, 2018, p. 69).

Paradoxically, "a picture is worth a thousand words" must contend with "images don't speak for themselves." You as the researcher must interpret the visual and determine whether the task merits analytic methods and strategies not applicable to language-based data. To us, the visual has *always* been a vital part of fieldwork investigation. It is simply the forms and formats—the representation and presentation—of visual data that have evolved over these decades.

As an example, ethnographer and visual artist Paul J. Mack photographed street scenes from urban and inner-city areas. Display 4.7 exhibits a digital photo taken of a residential area situated in the west side of Chicago. Saldaña and Omasta (2018, Chapter 3) offer several guidelines for the analysis of visual materials, ranging from inference-making of the values, attitudes, and beliefs suggested by an image, to a breakdown of its manifest and latent contents, to an analysis of an image's symbols and evocation.

DISPLAY 4.7 ◆ A Residential Exterior From the West Side of Chicago, 2018

Source: © 2018, Paul J. Mack; original in color.

A content analysis of Display 4.7 might first begin with a bullet-pointed list of specific and related elements:

- A recycling trash container filled with gardening and lawn care tools

- Plywood, warped boards stacked along a wooden staircase guard railing in slight disrepair

- A child's red wagon with a missing wheel and handle, propped on its side next to a large trash can (which has the missing wagon wheel and presumably the handle on top)

- A rusty gutter and drain pipe (which leads to a newer drain pipe section at ground level)

- Cracks, holes, missing sections, discoloration, occasional vegetation, minimal patched repairs on the building's exterior concrete surface

- Older air conditioning window unit and new DIRECTV satellite dish protruding from the building

- Utility connections (cable, satellite, telephone, electricity) visible on building exterior

- Left side residence's doors and window frames in varied stages of decay; right side residence's window frames not as decayed

- Porch/landing area of one residence contains a barbeque, a rectangular folding table, one folding chair, two green metalwork chairs, two plastic buckets, one trash can, one patio umbrella

- Etc.

With this narrative documentation of the visual, the researcher now expands on the image through *inferences*, *interpretations*, and *implications* of the image through analytic memoing:

August 18, 2018

INTRIGUING: ADDITIVE EVOLUTION

I am struck by the age and weather-beaten decay of the structure and its miscellaneous debris collected in its small yards, juxtaposed with three "modern" conveniences: a barbeque pit, an air conditioning window unit, and a DIRECTV satellite dish. A late-19th-/early-20th-century dwelling is occasionally punctuated with 20th- and 21st-century technology and wiring. Old-world electric/gas lamps are juxtaposed with modern security lights. The hardness of gray concrete is juxtaposed with natural greenery, forcibly growing where it probably shouldn't.

I sense that the debris in this yard is not collected carelessly and haphazardly out of negligence, but stored purposefully for future needs of some kind: salvageable wood for building materials, miscellaneous metal and plastic pieces for contingency repairs or repurposing. I smile at the use of the blue recycling trash can for the storage of tools rather than for its intended purpose. Things at this dwelling are not recycled for the good of the environment, but for the good of these residents' immediate and possible future needs.

Without knowing anything about the people who populate these residences, I infer that at least one of them has younger children, and that there is either low-wage employment, freelance work (e.g., landscaping/lawn care), and/or state/federal assistance. It may be a rental property, owned and operated by an exploitative landlord.

Some social artifacts evolve additively rather than renewably or transformatively. Over time, this entire structure seems *pieced* rather than *integrated* with technology as it has been developed. Its debris, like the repurposed recycling bin, consists not of unattended discards but purposely stored materials for future additive piecing as needed.

Analyzing the visual can range from systematic methods for content analysis, discursive readings for critical analysis, inferential readings for interpretative analysis, and so on (see Richardson, Pickus, & Parks, 2017, for an exemplar). There are several diverse approaches that require visual analysis to have its own methods books devoted exclusively to the subject. We will address the visual in later chapters, but we offer only a small slice of what is possible here. Refer to the appendix for excellent resources available for supplemental guidance.

HYPOTHESES, ASSERTIONS, AND PROPOSITIONS

Coding triggers analytic thought, and jotting and memoing capture the thoughts of the analyst "writing out loud," so to say. But as a study proceeds, there is a greater need to formalize the researcher's thinking into a more condensed and coherent set of explanations. One way to do that is to generate *assertions* and *propositions*, statements that reflect the summative findings and conclusions of the study, both of which can be tested as *hypotheses* before formalization. It will make more sense if we discuss the outcomes before we discuss how to develop them.

To us, an *assertion* is a declarative statement of summative synthesis, supported by confirming evidence from the data, and revised when disconfirming evidence or discrepant cases require modification of the assertion (e.g., "The workers at Adco Incorporated were not self-motivated to achieve excellence"). A *proposition* is a statement that puts forth a conditional event—an if-then or why-because proposal that gets closer to prediction or theory (e.g., "When employees work in a dysfunctional environment, their individual workplace skills may decay from lack of motivation to achieve excellence").

Assertions and propositions are ways of condensing and synthesizing a vast number of individual analytic observations. They are like "bullet points" of major patterns, themes, trends, and findings that you feel you can confidently put forth about your study. These points can range from descriptive, broad brushstroke facts (e.g., "Overall, the children seemed engaged with the new, experimental learning program") to higher level interpretations about the meanings of the study (e.g., "Experimental learning programs can be high-risk ventures for educators already demoralized by low public opinion of their status and efficacy").

As an example, Kell (1990) conducted a multiple-case study of the effects of computers on classroom instruction. At the first analytic meeting, field researchers recorded their case-specific assertions and propositions, keyed to the research questions. The statements then were clustered thematically, and evidence was sifted for each case. In this study, *the propositions took the form of emerging hypotheses*—that is, statements to be tested by the data. Here are two illustrations from project data charts:

- Teachers' preferences for different software programs are greatly influenced by their theoretical orientations to reading—that is, phonics or whole-language.

- Individualized learning and self-direction, as well as cooperation and peer teaching, are promoted through computer use, and some transfer of these learning styles to other class activities may occur.

The degree of support for the hypothesis/proposition in each case was then rated as "strong," "qualified," "neutral," or "contradictory."

After the next wave of data collection, which attended to missing data, the propositions *qua* [in the role of] hypotheses were revisited. For a matrix with rows showing each teacher at each site, column entries included data that supported the hypothesis/proposition and data that did not. As it turned out, the second hypothesis/proposition (above) was not supported. At the end, the hypotheses/propositions were tested further with other data sources, and cases that did not fit the patterns were reexamined carefully.

Although this illustration describes proposition generation in the later stages of a study, it can be used productively much earlier—even after the first round of site visits. Keep a running list of bullet-pointed assertions and propositions as a study progresses—that is, hypotheses—and revise them as field work continues and evidence appears that confirms and/or disconfirms them. These statements in progress can also be used as a guide for next-step analysis and further data collection. Eventually, organize the bullet points into a sequential outline format and/or narrative that tells the story of your analysis.

Display 4.8 illustrates the process of moving from a hypothesis to an assertion or proposition. If the data support or confirm the hypothesis, the statement moves forward as a trustworthy finding. But if the data disconfirm the hypothesis, the statement is revised until the data support its "truth value." Also, to clarify the sometimes muddied terminology, a dashed arrow is drawn from the proposition bin to the assertion bin. This is because all propositions are also assertions, but not all assertions are propositions.

DISPLAY 4.8 ● **The Hypothesis Process**

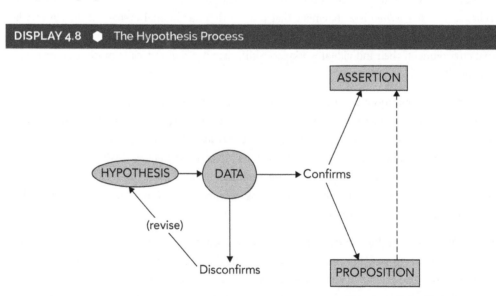

WITHIN-CASE AND CROSS-CASE ANALYSIS

A primary goal of within-case analysis is to describe, understand, and explain what has happened in a single, bounded context—the "case" or site. That is the task of the traditional ethnographic researcher, whose effort is to emerge with a well-grounded sense of local reality, whether the focus is on an individual, a family, a classroom, a school, a tribe, a formal organization, a community, or even a culture as a whole.

Many researchers have leaned toward multiple individual cases (e.g., teachers, alcoholics, middle managers, battered women, taxi drivers). And during the past few decades, there's been a substantial growth in studies of complex settings using multi-case designs, often with mixed methods approaches and multiple research team members (Creswell & Plano-Clark, 2018).

One advantage of studying cross-case or multiple cases is to increase generalizability, reassuring yourself that the events and processes in one well-described setting are not wholly idiosyncratic. At a deeper level, the purpose is to see processes and outcomes across many cases, to understand how they are qualified by local conditions, and thus to develop more sophisticated descriptions and more powerful explanations.

But developing a good cross-case analysis or synthesis is not a simple matter. Alcoholic A turns out to be quite different in personality dynamics from Alcoholic B and can't be easily compared, as Denzin (1993) eloquently shows us. Or suppose, for example, you have developed a good causal network explaining processes in a particular case. If you have a dozen such cases, just adding up separate variables, as in a quantitative survey approach, will destroy the local web of causality and result only in a smoothed-down set of generalizations that may not apply to any specific case in the set—let alone others. Each case must be understood on its own terms, yet we hunger for the understanding that comparative analysis can bring.

Purposes of Cross-Case Analysis

One reason to conduct a cross-case analysis is to enhance *generalizability or transferability to other contexts*. Although it's argued that this goal is sometimes inappropriate for qualitative studies, the question does not go away. We would like to know something about the relevance or applicability of our findings to other similar settings, to transcend the particular in order to understand the general. Multiple cases, adequately sampled (Are they typical? Are they diverse? Are they unusually effective or ineffective?) and analyzed carefully, can help us answer the question, Do these findings apply beyond one specific case?

A second, more fundamental reason for cross-case analysis is to deepen *understanding and explanation*. Multiple cases help the researcher find negative cases to strengthen a theory, built through examination of similarities and differences across cases. That process is much quicker and easier with multiple cases than with a single case. Multiple cases not only pin down the specific conditions under which a finding will occur but also help us form the more general categories of how those conditions may be related.

A Key Distinction: Variables Versus Cases

Our search for helpful cross-case analysis methods will be aided if we clarify two basically different approaches to inquiry.

Ragin (1987) emphasizes that a *case-oriented approach* considers the case as a whole entity, looking at configurations, associations, causes, and effects *within* the case—and only then turns to comparative analysis of a (usually limited) number of cases. We would look for underlying similarities and constant associations, compare cases with different outcomes, and begin to form more general explanations.

The *variable-oriented approach* is conceptual and theory-centered from the start, casting a wide net over a (usually large) number of cases. The "building blocks" are variables and their interrelationships, rather than cases. So the details of any specific case recede behind the broad patterns found across a wide variety of cases, and little explicit case-to-case comparison is done.

As an example, *a case-oriented approach* would consist of looking at about five different families to observe how particular couples and single parents raise their children. Each parent would be interviewed to get his or her own family background, education, and so on, in addition to particular circumstances, such as ages of all family members, income, work and child care schedules, and so on. These various and richly detailed family biographical profiles would then be compared for analysis.

A *variable-oriented approach* would consist of looking at 50 families representing a diverse sample of structures (two parent, single parent, gay couple, one stepparent and one biological parent, foster parents, etc.) to observe and interview them about a predetermined set of variables included under the main category of "parent–child communication" (e.g., informal dinner conversations, directions and instructions, discipline matters, problem solving, mentorship for "growing up," bedtime stories, tone of voice, etc.).

Each approach has pluses and minuses. Variable-oriented analysis with 50 families is good for finding probabilistic relationships among variables in a large population, but it is poor at handling the complexities of dealing with multiple subsamples; its findings are often very general, even vacuous. Case-oriented analysis with five families is good at finding specific, concrete, historically grounded patterns common to small sets of cases, but its findings often remain particularistic and ill-suited to generalizability.

The implication is not that one or the other approach is better for qualitative data analysis. Rather, the issue is one of making deliberate choices, alternating and/or combining or integrating methods as a study proceeds. The forthcoming methods and display chapters will show how we can focus on either variables or cases or both simultaneously as analytic needs arise.

Strategies for Cross-Case Analysis

How do qualitative researchers proceed when it comes to analyzing data from multiple cases? Here we outline several approaches (and consult the methods profiles in later chapters for more information). The goal here is to show what choices can be made as you approach the question of cross-case analysis.

Displays can help you summarize and compare findings within (and across) cases, but they also can be straitjackets. They may force the data into shapes that are superficially comparable across cases, but you actually may be comparing intrinsically different things on dimensions that turn out to be trivial. As a general rule of thumb, if the formats of within-case displays for a cross-case study are comparable, the work of the cross-case analyst is much easier.

Case-Oriented Strategies

Yin (2018) advocates a *replication* strategy: One case is studied in depth, then successive cases are examined to see whether the pattern found matches that in previous cases. It's also useful to examine cases where the pattern is expected on a theoretical basis to be weaker or absent.

Denzin (2001) approaches the problem through *multiple exemplars*. The issue is not so much "analysis" as interpretive *synthesis*. After deconstructing prior conceptions of a particular phenomenon (e.g., the alcoholic self), you collect multiple instances (cases) and then bracket or isolate the relevant data passages, inspecting them carefully for essential elements or components. The elements are then rebuilt into an ordered whole and put back into the natural social context.

Many researchers approach cross-case comparison by forming *types* or *families*. You inspect cases in a set to see whether they fall into clusters or groups that share certain patterns or configurations. Sometimes, the clusters can be ordered or sorted along some dimensions. For example, Morse and Bottorff (1992) found that 61 lactating mothers fell into four groups: those who could express milk, those who could not, those who perceived it as easy, and those who perceived it as a hassle. The meaning of the experience was fundamentally different for each type of mother.

Researchers usually assume that the cases at hand are more or less comparable, structured in similar ways. *Metasummary, metasynthesis,* and *meta-ethnography* (Major & Savin-Baden, 2010; Noblit & Hare, 1988; Sandelowski & Barroso, 2007) make no such assumptions. These approaches systematically *synthesize* interpretations across two or more cases, even if they were conducted by different researchers with different assumptions and different participant types.

Variable-Oriented Strategies

Researchers often look for *themes* that cut across cases. Hlava and Elfers (2014) examined "The Lived Experience of Gratitude" across a diverse range of 51 individuals as a phenomenological study. The overarching concept of gratitude consists of several variables that the co-researchers discerned from interviews with their participants. Hlava and Elfers first explain their data-analytic process of how they progressed from codes to themes:

> The coding cycles used an In Vivo method to preserve verbatim statements of participants, thus allowing the lived experience of gratitude to be expressed in its own terms. The First Cycle of coding employed descriptive methods to identify all statements relevant to sensory and somatic experience. The second iteration of coding used a structural method to label and organize statements by content. . . . Finally, a thematic approach was used to frame the presentation of the lived experience of gratitude. . . . Emphasis was placed on identifying experiences common to all participants, as well as features unique to individuals. (p. 438)

Just some of the themes related to gratitude developed by the co-researchers include

- Gratitude as self–other relatedness

- Sensations in the heart and chest/warmth

- Thankfulness and appreciation

- Comfort, security, acceptance

In phenomenological studies, researchers interview participants in order to compile cross-case meanings. This is not to neglect the primacy or dignity of each individual's story, but to consolidate their experiences to discern their common or most frequent constituent elements (i.e., variables).

Mixed Strategies

It's possible, and usually desirable, to combine or integrate case-oriented and variable-oriented approaches. At a number of points in the forthcoming methods and display chapters, we suggest a strategy that might be called *stacking comparable cases*. You write up each of a series of cases, using a more or less standard set of variables (with leeway for uniqueness as it emerges). Then, you use matrices and other displays to analyze each case in depth. After each case is well understood (the cross-cutting variables may evolve and change during this process), you stack the case-level displays in a "meta-matrix" (which has columns and subcolumns, rows and subrows), which is then further condensed, permitting systematic comparison.

An example of a mixed strategy is Rosen et al. (2016), who examined legal records from highly adjudicated court cases to find and describe the acute precipitants for physical elder abuse. The *cases* were legal records from 87 successfully prosecuted physical elder abuse cases from 2003 to 2015 in an urban district attorney's files. The *variable* examined was the triggers that led to physical violence (see Display 4.9). The co-researchers employed a cross-case content analysis where each research team member

> made determinations of categories for the acute precipitants by organizing and corroborating them with the rest of the team. These categories were discussed by the entire team at several meetings, and we combined categories that were similar and eliminated those without significant support in the transcripts. We developed consensus around 10 categories of acute precipitants using this process. After finalizing categories, the narratives of each case were reviewed to identify whether each of the acute precipitant categories was present. This was also completed with consensus. (Rosen et al., 2016, p. 5)

DISPLAY 4.9 ● Categories of Acute Precipitants of Physical Elder Abuse

Acute Precipitant	Description/Examples
Threat or concern that the victim would involve the authorities	• Victim threatening to call the police and/or reminding abuser about order of protection
Disputes over minor household issues	• Arguments about moving another person's possessions, closing a door loudly, or leaving the television on • Abuser unwilling to contribute to housework despite financial dependence on victim
Confrontation about financial exploitation/demanding money	• Victim refusing or unable to provide support or continue long-time support
Dispute over theft/destruction of property	• Confrontation about victim's missing property • Destruction of victim's property as part of escalating confrontation
Victim attempting to prevent the perpetrator from entering or demanding that he or she leave	• Abuser uses force to attempt to enter the victim's home • Abuser uses keys to enter without the victim's permission and then refuses to leave
Issues with multigenerational child rearing	• Conflicts between grandparents and parents about appropriate child care strategies • Issues of custody and parental access to children that involve grandparents • Arguments between teenage children and a custodial grandparent about household rules and the child's behavior that escalates to assault by the teenager
Conflict about the abuser's substance abuse	• Victim confronting the abuser about ongoing substance use • Victim trying to stop substance use or prevent access to alcohol and/or drugs
Victim threatening or attempting to leave/escape	• Victim trying to leave during an argument, often attempting to de-escalate
Presence during/intervention in ongoing family violence	• Victim present during intimate partner abuse or child abuse and injured by accident • Victim attempting to intervene
Conflict about romantic relationship	• Abuser's suspicion of infidelity • Threat by victim to end the relationship

Source: Rosen et al. (2016), p. 7.

CLOSURE AND TRANSITION

We resonate with qualitative methodologist Robert E. Stake (1995), who muses, "Good research is not about good methods as much as it is about good thinking" (p. 19). Good thinking means to look for and find patterns in the data. Good thinking means to construct substantial categories or themes from an array of codes. Good thinking means to transcend the localness of a particular case to find its generalizability and transferability to other contexts. Research methods are excellent tools, but they are only as good as the craftsperson who uses them.

This chapter provided an overview of analysis fundamentals for and with qualitative data. Yet it does not presume to be the definitive guide; see the appendix for a list of additional resources. These are foundation methods for the more display-oriented strategies that now follow in Part Two.

DISPLAYING
THE DATA

PART II

DESIGNING MATRIX, NETWORK, AND GRAPHIC DISPLAYS

CHAPTER SUMMARY

This chapter provides fundamental principles for the design and content of three analytic display methods: matrices, networks, and graphics. These methods condense the major data and findings in progress from a study to further analyze and/or to represent and present the conclusions.

CONTENTS

INTRODUCTION

Rapley (2018) muses, "We think in generalities but we live in detail" (p. 118). Lengthy, uncondensed text in the form of interview transcripts, field notes, documents, and so on is cumbersome because it is dispersed over many pages and is not easy to see as a whole. It is sequential rather than simultaneous, making it difficult to look at two or three variables at once. Comparing several extended texts carefully is very difficult. It is usually poorly ordered, can get very bulky, and can make us feel monotonously overloaded. The same objections apply with even stronger force for readers of our final reports. They need, if not deserve, a concise delivery of what we analyzed. And in this highly visual culture, showing rather than telling can make a more effective and memorable impact on our audiences.

A major purpose of this text is to encourage the creation and dissemination of matrix, network, and graphic displays for qualitative data. The central argument of this book is, *You know what you display*. Credible and trustworthy analysis requires, and is driven by, displays that are focused enough to permit a viewing of a full data set in the same location and are arranged systematically to answer the research questions at hand. A "full data set" does not, of course, mean the complete corpus of interview transcripts, field notes, documents, and so on. Rather, the condensed, distilled data presented are drawn from the full range of persons, events, and processes under study.

The idea of display is central to this book. By *display* we mean a visual format that presents information systematically (and sometimes evocatively), so the user can draw conclusions and take needed action. Although such displays may sometimes be busy, they will never be monotonous. Most important, the chances of drawing and verifying conclusions are much greater than for extended text, because the display is arranged coherently to permit careful comparisons, detection of differences, noting of patterns and themes, seeing trends, and so on.

Quantitative researchers have software packages that can develop publishable tables, graphs, and charts. Qualitative researchers have CAQDAS programs for our unique approaches to data analysis. And even basic Microsoft Office programs such as Word and Excel are sufficient for most matrix, network, and basic graphic displays. But the qualitative analyst has to handcraft appropriate data display formats because each project is unique. As yet, there are few familiar, agreed-on data setups among qualitative researchers, so each analyst has to adapt those of others or invent new ones. The display ideas we offer in this book are nothing more than that—*ideas*, not prescriptions or standards, for qualitative data display.

Not everyone loves matrix, network, and graphic displays—and not everyone thinks visually. But displaying your condensed data in a systematic way has immense consequences for your understanding. It requires you to think about your research questions and what portions of your data are needed to answer them; it requires you to make full analyses, ignoring no relevant information; and it focuses and organizes your information coherently. These advantages are repeated when you include displays in a final report; the reader can re-create your intellectual journey with some confidence.

DISPLAY FORMAT OPTIONS

Deciding on and generating the format for displaying qualitative data are important first steps. Your template is a visual outline, of sorts, for the data and/or findings to be filled in. Formats can be as varied as the imagination of the analyst, but the ones described in this book tend to fall into three major families:

1. *Matrices*, with defined rows and columns

2. *Networks*, a series of nodes or bins with links (lines and arrows) between them

3. *Graphics*, consisting of a wide array of other visual devices in various forms and formats

Data entries, however, are multiform: short blocks of text, quotes, phrases, variable labels, ratings, abbreviations, codes, categories, themes, concepts, bullet pointed lists, symbolic figures, labeled lines (dashed or solid), arrows (one way or two way), and so on.

The display format and content of the entries will depend on what you are trying to understand: a general situation, detailed chronologies, the actions of people in different roles, the interaction and interplay of variables, and so on. In other words, form follows function: Formats must always be driven by the research questions involved and your developing concepts. Formatting determines which variables will be analyzed in which ways. If a variable isn't included in the format, it won't get compared with another variable.

And it depends on how far along you are in the study and what has priority right now. The need might be for "eyeballing" (i.e., systematically browsing through) data in an exploratory way. Or it could be for carrying out detailed analyses; for setting up data to use in another, more differentiated display; for combining parallel data for a single case; for combining data from several cases; or for reporting findings. A good format will allow all of these uses to some degree but inevitably will do some well and others less well.

Let's examine the three major families of displays with examples and illustrations.

Matrices

A matrix (used interchangeably with *table*) is essentially the "intersection" of two lists, set up as rows and columns. Let's take a look at a sample format, explaining and labeling it as we go.

Display 5.1, originally drawn with Microsoft Word software, is aimed at understanding the effects of *assistance* supplied to a school site—the Masepa Case—by various sources. This was part of Miles and Huberman's school improvement study that observed how a new project innovation was implemented. The matrix format calls for the researcher to address five related variables, distinguish two of them according to time, pool responses, align some responses along an evaluative scale, and explain the response pattern for each type of assistance source. Here, condensed information from 30 pages of field notes has been packed into a single page.

Note that the data are abstractions: There are no quotes, and generalizations and other inferential remarks appear in the last two columns. The *Longer-Run Consequences* and *Researcher Explanations* are not direct condensations of participants' remarks or researchers' observations. Rather, for any given consequence, such as the one in the top row ("users are helped administratively and substantively, feel obliged to do ECRI [Exemplary Center for Reading Instruction] with minor adaptations"), the researcher has looked at the data segments in the three preceding columns, checked to see whether they covary in some patterned way, and drawn a second-order generalization. In this case (see first row—*Building Administration*) themes such as "eases schedules"; "consults, offers solutions"; "relieves pressure, encourages"; "helps early implementation"; and the *Users' Assessment* of generally positive magnitude codes all suggested the reception of help and a sense of user obligation for reasonably faithful implementation. A similar process of inductive inference occurs under *Researcher Explanations*.

Overall, the matrix is a tabular format that collects and arranges data for easy viewing in one place, permits detailed analysis, and sets the stage for later cross-case analysis with other comparable cases or sites. As chapters progress, you'll learn how matrices can *order* data by case or time, and can arrange and stack a matrix's cells in such a way to create *meta-matrices*, which contain multiple rows within a single row and/or multiple columns within a single column.

Formatting the Matrix Template

Since matrices are more text-heavy than networks and graphics, we need to discuss some matters related to matrix formatting and data entry.

DISPLAY 5.1 ● Effects Matrix: Assistance Location and Types (Masepa Case)

Location	User's Assessment	Types Provided	Short-Run Effects (User's 'State')	Longer-Run Consequences	Researcher Explanations
Building Administration	++ ++ − +	1. authorizes changes 2. eases schedules 3. controls fidelity 4. consults, offers solutions	1. relieves pressure, encourages 2. helps early implementation 3. feeling policed 4. feeling backed-up, substantially helped	users are helped administratively and substantively, feel obliged to do ECRI with minor adaptations	administration, authority, servicing, availability, and flexibility lead to sustained, faithful implementation model
Central Office Administration	+ ++	1. promotes ECRI 2. answers building administration, trainers' requests	1. pressures non-users 2. building administrators have material, administrative support	program is perceived as supported, assisted, 'protected' by central office	central office able to push program and answer requests, yet not perceived as main actor by users
Helping Teacher	++ + ++ ++ ±	1. provides materials 2. demonstrates, models 3. answers requests 4. encourages 5. circulates, controls	1. reduces effort, increases repertoire 2. trains, facilitates use 3. problems solved rapidly 4. maintains level of effort 5. ambivalent: helped yet coerced	new, experienced users receive systematic instruction, follow-up, materials; stay with program and are careful about making changes in it	personalized in-service mechanism, with both training and assistance, allows for mastery and spread of ECRI in 'faithful' format
User-Helping Teacher Meetings	++ + + +	1. comparing practices with others 2. debugging, complaining 3. learning about new parts 4. encouragement	1. encourages, regulates 2. cathartic, solves short-run problems 3. expands repertoire 4. gets through rough moments	creates reference group, gives users a voice, solves ongoing problems, and lowers anxiety	multi-purpose forum which consolidates use and users, defuses opposition
Teacher-Users in Other Schools: Target Schools	+ + +	1. sharing materials 2. exchanging tips, solutions 3. comparing, encouraging	1. increases stock 2. new ideas, practices; problems solved 3. motivates, stimulates	increases commitment, regulates use (decreases deviance)	additional source of assistance, which increases as number of users grows
Trainers in Target School, Other School	++ ++ + +	1. tips for presentations 2. solution to short-term problems 3. encourages 4. serves as successful model	1. facilitates practice 2. helps expand beyond core format 3. maintains effort 4. stimulates	reliable, unthreatening backup provided in school	elaborate and effective lateral network: trainers seen as peers

Legend
++ = very effective
+ = effective
± = mixed effective
− = ineffective

Source: Miles, M. B., & Huberman, A. M. (1994). *Qualitative data analysis: An expanded sourcebook* (2nd ed.). Thousand Oaks, CA: Sage Publications.

There are no fixed canons for constructing a matrix. Rather, matrix construction is a creative yet systematic task that furthers your understanding of the substance and meaning of your database, even before you begin entering information. Thus, the issue is not whether you are building a "correct" matrix but whether it is a *helpful* one that will give you reasonable answers to the questions you are asking, or suggest promising new ways to lay out the data to get answers. At a deeper level, the message of this book is not "use these matrices," but *"think display."* Adapt and invent formats that will serve you best.

We offer some friendly advice rather than harsh prescriptions for building the templates, outlines, and frameworks of matrix displays:

1. Look at your *research question(s) and key variables* and think of the data that are or will be available.

2. Get a *colleague to look at your initial format* to help you detect the assumptions you are making, and to suggest alternative ways to display your data.

3. Set up the matrix template by using a *text program* (Word tables), *database management program* (Excel spreadsheet), or *CAQDAS software*, but don't discount using pencil and paper first. Try to make the display completely readable on your monitor screen or on one printed sheet of paper. You have to be able to see it all at once.

4. Don't try to include more than a dozen or so *variables in rows or columns*; five or six is more manageable.

5. The simplest matrices are organized in two dimensions. You have a choice to move to more complexity if the data demand it by creating *partitions* for *meta-matrices*—rows within a row and/or columns within a column (to be illustrated in forthcoming chapters).

6. If the matrix is an ordered one, expect to *transpose rows and columns* for a while until you have a satisfactory version. Most text-based software, database management, and CAQDAS programs can do this quite easily.

7. Always stay open to the idea of *adding new rows or columns*, even late in your analysis operations.

8. Keep *rows and columns fine grained* enough to accommodate meaningful differentiations in the data, but not so fine as to bury you under indiscriminate detail.

9. Keep in mind that any particular research question may require a *series of displays*; for example, an initial partially ordered descriptive matrix may lead to a small summary table and then to a network display. Think ahead to this possibility but allow new matrix forms to emerge as the analysis proceeds.

Creating matrix templates is usually a matter of a few minutes; revising them as the early items of data are entered is also quick work. Virtually all programs can enable reformatting as data are entered and coded. The time taken to enter data into a display actually depends on the following: (a) the number of variables or dimensions in the display, (b) the number of respondents and cases, and (c) the kind and number of transformations made.

Which types of row and column headings (or network and graphic labels) are possible? The set is almost infinite, ranging from cases to variables, and from themes to concepts. To illustrate, here is just a sample of types adapted from Gobo and Molle (2017), Lofland, Snow, Anderson, and Lofland (2006), and Bogdan and Biklen (2007). For concreteness, we use examples from health care settings:

Individuals:	Jane Hughes, RN, Dr. Luis Garcia
Roles:	patients, nurses, doctors, administrators
Relationships and groups:	patient–spouse, nurse–resident, intensive care unit staff, accounting department, surgical team
Settings within sites:	operating room, emergency room, cafeteria
Sites as wholes:	Good Samaritan Hospital, downtown health maintenance organization, free clinic
Specific actions (what people do and say):	diagnostic questions, answers, listening, information giving, blood draws, comforting
Events (marked-off happenings or occurrences):	admission, operation, discharge
Activities (regularly occurring, connected sets of actions):	grand rounds, lab tests, billing
Strategies (activities aimed toward some goal):	rehabilitation plan, nutrition counseling, radiation treatment
Meanings and perspectives (how people construe events):	patient and physician views of an HIV-positive diagnosis, the experience of labor and childbirth
Attitudes, values, and beliefs:	resentment toward physician seniority, pro-choice versus pro-life, patient anxiety
Emotions and states:	staff morale, patient fear, critical condition, denial of impending death
Processes (ongoing flows, phases, stages, cycles, changes over time):	wound healing, convalescence, triage, decision making, social support, bereavement

You always have choices about the level and type of data to be entered. For example, you can include the following:

Direct quotes, extracts from written-up field notes:	"Surgeons are basically macho types—the best ones, I mean. They have to be, but they can't help it."
Summaries, paraphrases, or abstracts:	Patient advocate seems increasingly distrusted. Rules for residents' time use largely ignored.
Researcher explanations:	Patient uncertainty about diagnosis is a function of life-threatening conditions and use of denial as a buffer.
Ratings or summarized judgments:	Risk reduction behavior after cardiovascular bypass: worse, no change, improved, much improved.

Combinations of the above:

Risk reduction: improved. Diet ("I even tried broccoli."); some exercise (walks 20–30 minutes daily); and smoking (reduced, is considering nicotine patch).

Networks

Conceptual framework design in Chapter 2 illustrated several network arrays to describe the process of research in action (see Displays 2.2, 2.3, and 2.4). In this and in following chapters, a network is a collection of *nodes* or bins connected by *links* or lines that display streams of participant actions, events, and processes. Networks lend themselves well to a case-oriented approach that re-creates the "plot" or storyline of events over time, as well as showing complex interrelationships between variables. They give us the kinds of narratives that tend to get chopped up analytically in matrices. They are very helpful when you want to focus on multiple variables at the same time for readily analyzable information at a glance.

Display 5.2 is a network model from McCammon et al.'s (2012) study of how high school speech classes influenced and affected adolescents and their adulthood after graduation. The network is an outline of "plot points" for an accompanying research narrative.

The proverb of this research story—the theory—suggested by the oval nodes is as follows: When *Adolescents* enroll in high school *Speech Classes*, they gain *Confidence* as an *Adolescent & Adult*. But that storyline is too thin and needs to be fleshed out through an analytic narrative. The rectangular nodes attached to *Speech Classes* indicate that the classroom content must be led by a teacher who provides *Good Coaching*. Students must also feel that they are part of a classroom community through a *Sense of Belonging*.

Not all but some students from those classes participated in extracurricular speech tournaments or forensic *Competitions* (debate, extemporaneous speaking, oral interpretation of literature, etc.). Thus, a separate trajectory or stream is drawn. Respondents testified that participation in these events

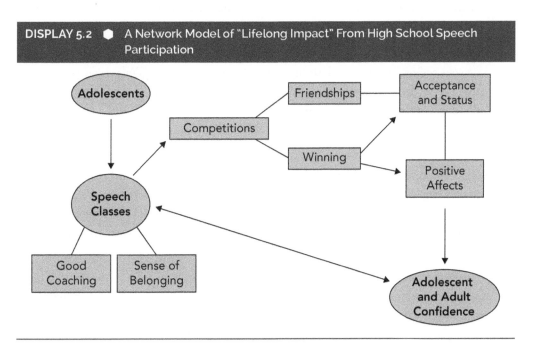

DISPLAY 5.2 ●   A Network Model of "Lifelong Impact" From High School Speech Participation

Source: Saldaña, J. (2016). *The coding manual for qualitative researchers* (3rd ed.). Thousand Oaks, CA: Sage Publications.

developed *Friendships*, a sense of *Acceptance & Status*, and thus *Positive Affects*, but especially for those who reached the achievement of *Winning* at these competitive events. Regardless of whether one won or not, the respondents' stated outcome was *Confidence*—both as an *Adolescent* and later as an *Adult*.

The bidirectional arrow between *Speech Classes* and *Adolescent & Adult Confidence* suggests a cyclical or interactive effect: The more speech classes you took, the more confident you became; the more confident you became, the more likely you continued participating in speech classes and competitions.

Networks are also effective heuristics for higher level analyses such as mapping social processes, discerning causation, analyzing longitudinal trends, and developing hypotheses and theories. They are not any easier or harder to construct than matrices—both display forms take comparable amounts of time and thought to design and assemble. Selected CAQDAS programs, however, can greatly assist with complex network construction (see Displays 2.11 and 2.12).

We offer some friendly advice for network display construction:

1. Create your initial network design with pencil and paper, or use index cards or sticky notes that can be arranged and rearranged on a table, to explore the bins' best placement. Then, transfer the more finalized design into a software program.

2. Go beyond "is related to" thinking when a line is connected between one bin and another. Think of the *type* of relationship the line represents. In addition to "is related to," consider if the line suggests "must be present with," "is a subset of," "happens simultaneously with," and so on.

3. Likewise, go beyond "leads to" thinking when an arrow is connected between one bin and another. Think of the *type of action* intended by the arrow. Aside from "leads to," consider if the arrow suggests "influences and affects," "generates," "is necessary for," "is a consequence of," and so on.

4. Consider how rich text, colors, fonts, shapes, spacing, and line/arrow widths can make a network display more dynamic and better represent the phenomenon.

5. Selected CAQDAS programs can assist with modeling the emerging network display, based on your coding and other analytic input. Employ one of these programs if you anticipate that a complex network of variables, categories, themes, and so on may be needed to illustrate the results of your analysis.

Graphics

Any research-informed visual design that is not a matrix or network is considered a graphic. Creativity is certainly employed when developing any visual display, but creativity is most necessary for the artistic rendering of the research story through graphic representation and presentation. It is an act of imaginative data condensation and analysis that, at its best, evokes from its reader an at-a-glance understanding of the entire study.

Since the possibilities for graphic designs are virtually limitless, we offer in this section just a few quick examples from various studies to illustrate just a small slice of classic and innovative design approaches available. Some are adapted from the canon of quantitative research displays, others from traditional forms of modeling, and a few from the creative prowess of their researcher/designers.

The *pie chart* is one of the most well-known graphics. Display 5.3 represents the percentages of three main categories of coded data from focus group interview transcripts. Santiago-Brown, Jerran, Metcalfe, and Collins (2015) collected data from farmers on their perceptions of the economic, environmental, and social sustainability of their grape vineyards. Though quantitative in function, the pie chart serves the qualitative researcher as a heuristic for assessing proportion, variability, priority, and magnitude in the data.

Display 5.4, from the same study as Display 5.3, shows another classic model under "A," the *Venn diagram*. The Venn diagram illustrates the conceptual overlay and integration of selected variables. In Display 5.4A, the three categories of vineyard sustainability are conventionally perceived as overlapping states. But in this representation, they read as static states rather than dynamic processes, which the co-researchers found to be more likely. Under Display 5.4B, a *cycle diagram*, sustainability is re-envisioned by the research team as a more active, reactive, and interactive enterprise:

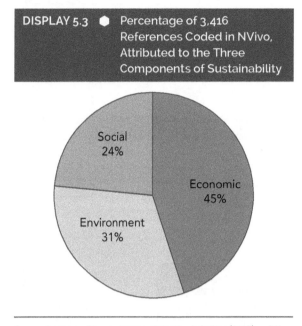

DISPLAY 5.3 ● Percentage of 3,416 References Coded in NVivo, Attributed to the Three Components of Sustainability

Source: Santiago–Brown, Jerran, Metcalfe, & Collins (2015), p. 241.

Trade-offs over time promote continuous tension between the economic, social, and environmental components. Moreover, these three components often overlap and an objective categorization of specific variables in each one of these three components seems to be context dependent. . . . In this way, sustainability should be redefined as follows: "The continuous pursuit of equilibrium between economic, social and environmental variables, and their trade-offs over time." (Santiago-Brown et al., 2015, p. 246)

DISPLAY 5.4 ● A Sustainability Definition: (A) Classic Triple Bottom-Line Approach and (B) Proposed Representation Emphasizing Time and Trade–Offs

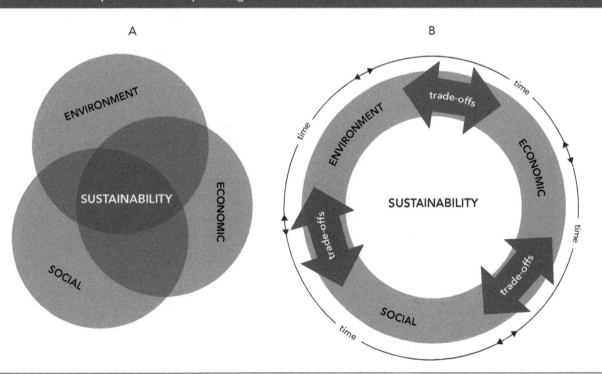

Source: Santiago–Brown, Jerran, Metcalfe, & Collins (2015), p. 246.

Variations of Venn diagrams and cycle diagrams are available to qualitative researchers. Display 5.5 illustrates a *nested model* from Casey's (2017) content analysis of 43 women's written accounts of incarceration. The themes and subthemes developed from the data are listed within the diagram and appropriately placed within the design to suggest their interrelationship.

DISPLAY 5.5   ⬡   Impact of Correctional Environment Upon Individual Women

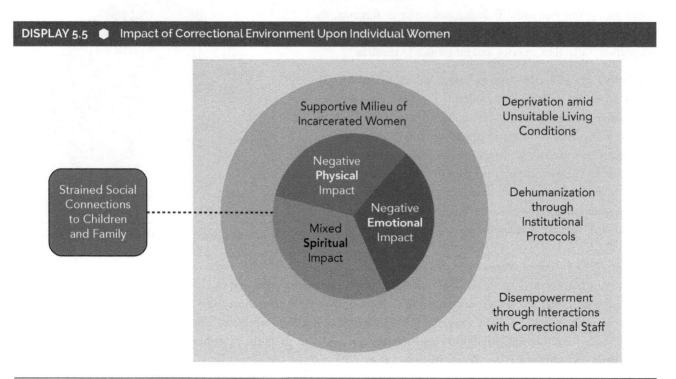

Source: Casey (2017), p. 5.

Display 5.6 is another cycle diagram but, like Display 5.5, exhibits the analytic themes and subthemes for at-a-glance reference. Cloyes, Rosenkranz, Wold, Berry, and Supiano (2014) explored the growing need for end-of-life care through prison inmate volunteer programs. From their particular study,

> These 3 overarching themes—constructing self as a hospice volunteer, constructing self in relation to others through hospice service, and constructing collective identity as a community that cares for its most vulnerable members—point toward a larger process that unfolds in relation to the volunteers' hospice caregiving experience. In their roles and activities as peer care volunteers, inmate volunteers' process of identification begins with constructing (or reconstructing) self-identity then, as volunteers become more patient and program oriented, their expressions of self-identity shift toward self-in-relation to others, and then self as understood as part of a collective identity built on the values and ethics of hospice. [Display 5.6] represents this process in connection with data-based themes that comprise them. (p. 746)

Another traditional display is the *conceptual web*, somewhat comparable in appearance to a network but intended to illustrate a concept's constituent elements. Display 5.7, from Saldaña and Mallette's (2017) multilayered analysis of a Donald Trump 2015 campaign speech, examined six facets of his narrative using the SPELIT Environmental Analysis Matrix. SPELIT is an acronym for the social, political, economic, legal, intercultural, and technological environments of a culture. The analysts determined that "fabrication" was the central driver of the presidential candidate's ethos or values system, and the display exhibits each SPELIT category as an element of that ethos.

DISPLAY 5.6 ● Transformative Process of Prison Inmate Hospice Volunteer Service

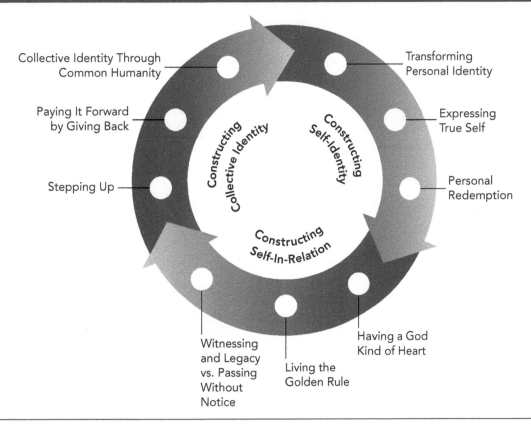

Source: Cloyes, Rosenkranz, Wold, Berry, & Supiano (2014), p. 739.

DISPLAY 5.7 ● Axial Coding of the Six Primary SPELIT Environments of Donald Trump's Campaign Speech

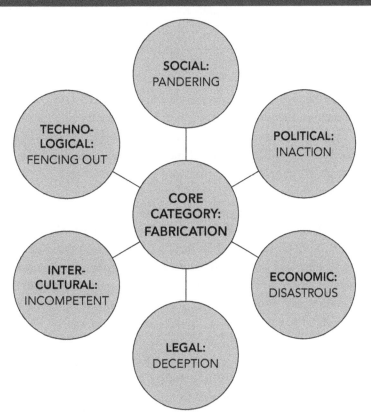

Source: Saldaña & Mallette (2017), p. 166.

Display 5.8 is another conceptual web, but this one incorporates the design structure of a Venn diagram to illustrate in a more integrated fashion the systems thinking of middle school leaders observed by Shaked and Schechter (2017). "In line with the holistic essence of the systems-thinking perspective, these four characteristics should not be viewed as a linear series but as overlapping, interconnected, and interrelated capacities" (p. 712).

DISPLAY 5.8 ● Characteristics of Systems Thinking Among Middle School Leaders

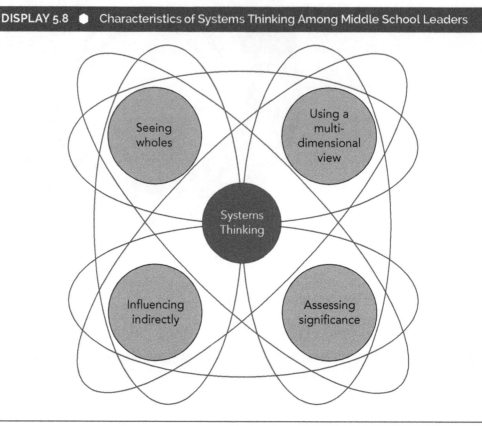

Source: Shaked & Schechter (2017), p. 712.

The final example is a *trajectory* graphic in Display 5.9. Scales et al. (2018) conducted a longitudinal multi-case study to investigate how four novice teachers learned to use professional judgment in their literacy instruction. Rather than displaying their results as a linear model across time, the trajectory design illustrates the holistic, interwoven, and spiraled nature of beginning teacher development. The co-researchers explain:

> Beliefs are woven throughout the journey of learning to use professional judgment, where beliefs are continually influenced by experiences provided during coursework (candidates); the school context, including mentorship from the cooperating teacher (student teacher); and the school context with influence from teaching peers (novice teacher) and regulatory expectations. Furthermore, the trajectory illustrates how interactions along the journey may contribute to someone positioned as and/or the positioning of someone as a teacher. (Scales et al., 2018, p. 18)

Many other examples of graphics can be culled from the academic literature, and a few more examples will be shown in later chapters. We offer graphics as a viable display option when a matrix or network does not seem to capture the findings in progress, or when a more creative way

DISPLAY 5.9 ● Trajectory of Learning to Use Professional Judgment

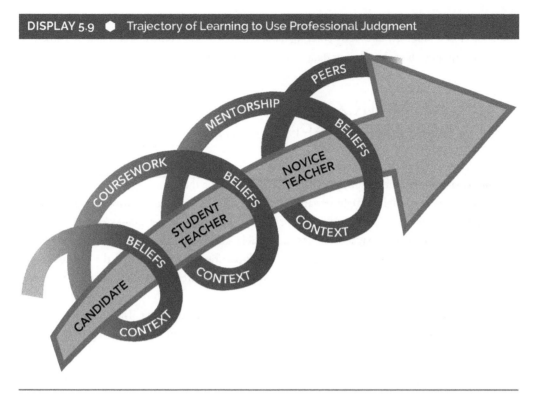

Source: Scales et al. (2018), p. 17.

of representing the study's analysis is needed. See Knowlton and Phillips (2013) for a diverse collection of logic model graphic designs; Evergreen (2018) for expert guidance on the creation and effects of visual design for research; Infogram for online design tools (https://infogram.com/); and the online Periodic Table of Visualization Methods for additional ideas (http://www.visual-literacy.org/periodic_table/periodic_table.html).

TIMING OF DISPLAY DESIGN

When should display formats be generated? Analytic displays can be developed before, during, or after data collection. They can provide preliminary findings about what is happening in the case and suggest leads toward new data. Later, as fuller, more complete descriptions are in hand, these displays can supply the basic material for higher level explanations—that is, plausible reasons for why things are happening as they are.

If the format is at hand during data collection, it helps save energy by encouraging focus: You know what information you will be needing. But there are some cautions here. First, qualitative data evolve; later accounts round out, qualify, put in perspective, and disqualify earlier ones. Analysts scout around, sleuth, and take second and third looks. So, there are risks in entering the data into a set format too soon.

Furthermore, for any given research question or issue, you can develop many different displays (literally dozens) using the same set of variables. Each display makes somewhat different assumptions; each has trade-offs among advantages and costs. Another caution is that display formats nearly always evolve, too. The later ones are more data sensitive than the earlier ones, as things become clearer.

So our general advice is to generate rough formats early during data collection and revise them to a firmer state closer to the end of data collection, when they can be grounded more contextually and empirically. Expect to make several passes or iterations before the first format of the display is working right. Test a proposed format by entering data. Unworkable or confusing formats, or those that do not incorporate all of the relevant data, will show themselves rapidly.

ENTERING MATRIX, NETWORK, AND GRAPHIC DATA

Generally, the choice of data for display entry must be driven by the particular row and column headings involved, your definitions of network nodes and links, or the necessary concepts for a graphic design. But these seemingly straightforward tasks are critical issues in qualitative data analysis. *The conclusions drawn from a display can never be better than the quality of the data entered.* A completed matrix, network, or graphic may look coherent, plausible, and fascinating, but if the data were poorly collected in the first place or were entered in a hasty, ill-partitioned, or vague way, the conclusions are suspect. We offer the following guidelines for data entry into the three display formats we've addressed:

1. A display includes only a very small percentage of the available data. There is always a great deal of *selection and condensation* from the mass of data. You are not throwing away your field notes—you can always refer back to the full material.

2. Be clear about the *forms and types of data or analytic outcomes* you want to enter: direct quotes, ratings, codes, categories, themes, concepts, and so on.

3. Use codes and software *search functions* to locate key material. Entering these data is much easier with text-based software, database management, or a CAQDAS program having multiple windows; they permit you to retrieve coded units to one window or region and to select/edit/condense them on another.

4. *Don't lock up your format* until later in the process. Entering data tests the adequacy, realism, and helpfulness of the display format. Keep revising it as needed.

5. Be open to using *numbers*, *direct quantities*, *or judgments* in the form of ratings, scales, or magnitude codes when applicable to the study.

6. Get a *colleague to review* your display, along with your rationale and written-up field notes, to check the procedural adequacy of your work. Such audits are time-consuming, but used selectively, they are an important check on the confirmability of the procedures you used.

MAKING INFERENCES AND DRAWING CONCLUSIONS FROM MATRIX, NETWORK, AND GRAPHIC DISPLAYS

The test of any display is what it helps you understand and how trustworthy that understanding is. In the next five chapters, there will be many specific tactics for conclusion drawing and verification through the use of **boldface**. Each has its specific advantages and pitfalls, which we will discuss in Chapter 11. Here, we offer some preliminary general advice:

1. It's always helpful to *start with a quick scan*—a "squint analysis" or "eyeballing" down columns and across rows, through network pathways, and in graphic visual arrays to see what jumps out. Then, verify, revise, or disconfirm that impression through a more careful review.

2. Any given display will always have *multiple tactics* used on it. The ones we have used most frequently for drawing first conclusions are **noting patterns, themes**; **making contrasts, comparisons**; **clustering**; and **counting**.

3. Displays never speak for themselves—either to you or to the reader; *accompanying text is always needed*. As conclusions form in your mind, always write text explaining them. Make your conclusions explicit. The process of writing inevitably leads to reformulation, added clarity, and ideas for further analysis. Writing is itself a form of analysis.

4. First conclusions drawn from a display almost always need to be *checked against written-up field notes*. If a conclusion does not ring true at the "ground level" when you try it out there, it needs revision. Look at the raw data to guard against this. Even better, check with your research colleagues and the participants themselves, when possible.

5. Any early conclusion typically needs *confirmation, checking, and verification*. The most frequently used tactics we've used are as follows: **following up surprises**, **triangulating**, **making if-then tests**, and **checking out rival explanations**.

6. Be sure your descriptive understanding is *clear at the individual or within-case level first* before you try to understand multiple cross-case patterns.

7. Remember that analysis usually has to *go beyond descriptive summation and reach toward explanation*. Clarify the conceptual implications of your conclusions—that is, how they tie into your or someone else's theory of social action.

Conclusions about data displays normally appear in what we call an analytic text or narrative, found most often in the "Results" section of a journal article. Analytic narrative draws attention to the features of the displayed data and makes sense of them, knitting them together and permitting the analyst to draw conclusions and add interpretations. It also encourages a return to the field notes to consult information not in the display and to add it to the text for further clarity. Since a display does not speak for itself, analytic text does not stand alone without reference to the display.

In fact, the act of writing text as you ruminate over the meaning of a display is itself a focusing and forcing device that propels further analysis and often display revision. Writing does not come after analysis; it *is* analysis, happening as the writer thinks through the meaning of data in the display. Writing is thinking, not the report of thought.

Stay open on the question of whether the display format you use for analysis should be the same display used for final reporting (the answer is often "yes"). Readers can see for themselves how conclusions were drawn, rather than being handed summarized study results to be taken on faith. Sometimes, of course, a display will be used for intermediate, for-the-researcher's-eyes-only purposes and will not necessarily be shown to readers of the final report.

The tradition of presenting basic data is deeply ingrained in reports of quantitative data analysis, so much so that it would be unthinkable for a researcher to present conclusions without statistical data tables or, at least, without reference to working documents containing them. We believe that the same norms should apply to qualitative researchers working within particular traditional genres of inquiry (e.g., ethnography, grounded theory, content analysis, evaluation research, and others). Some data displays should be a normal part of reporting findings and conclusions. In some instances, of course, a summary table may suffice.

We can hardly do better than to quote Tufte (1986), speaking primarily of quantitative work but with relevance for qualitative researchers:

> What we are seeking in graphic and tabular displays of information is the clear portrayal of complexity. Not the complication of the simple; rather the task of the designer is to give visual access to the subtle and the difficult—that is, the revelation of the complex. (p. 80)

But always give elegance a chance. As the classic saying goes, "Things can be complex without being complicated."

THE METHODS PROFILES

In the next five chapters, each method profile will be presented in this format:

- *Description:* The method is briefly described with reference to its accompanying display.

- *Applications:* This section outlines the purposes of the method and its recommended uses for particular research studies or goals.

- *Example:* Studies drawn from the coauthors' previous work and other published sources are used to illustrate the display, its design, and data entry.

- *Analysis:* The discussion shifts to how the assembled data in the matrix, network, or graphic were analyzed and interpreted by the researchers. Recommendations for reader applications are also provided.

- *Notes:* Supplemental or concluding comments about the method are offered.

The profiles vary in length, depending on the complexity of the method. They are grouped into subcategories within each chapter, when appropriate, if they share a common purpose.

We also emphasize here that the names we gave to our methods and displays were for convenient description, not for standardization. Who cares whether it is a "Case-Ordered Descriptive Meta-Matrix" or a "Predictor-Outcome-Consequences Matrix"? The names may sound like jargon, but don't worry about that; the issue is how any given display works and how it can further your *understanding* of the data.

All of the methods and displays can be adapted to meet the needs of any particular study. If they seem too complex, simplify; they can be modified easily for studies where the cases are a few individuals. Not every single method has to be used for every single study. Take only what is useful for your research purposes and goals.

CLOSURE AND TRANSITION

This chapter provides foundations for the next set of chapters—that is, methods of displaying and analyzing qualitative data through five modalities: exploring, describing, ordering, explaining, and predicting. You're encouraged to read Chapters 6 through 10 in order, for the techniques of one strategy are generally used in the next.

METHODS OF EXPLORING

CHAPTER SUMMARY

This chapter profiles methods of displaying data to provide initial compilations for analytic exploration. They are methods of documenting field work in progress, exploring salient variables as they emerge, and preparing preliminary outlines for the emerging reports.

CONTENTS

INTRODUCTION

Virtually everything about a research study can be exploratory in one way or another, from initial conceptualization to final write-up. But *exploratory* in this chapter refers to methods that are documentary and provisional in their analyses—first-draft attempts, if you will, at making sense of qualitative data. Exploratory displays are not necessarily developed for final publication. They are intended as heuristics for the researcher to analyze data in progress. In the exploratory mode, it's as if we are trying to solve an unstated or ambiguous problem, which has to be framed and reframed as we go.

Exploring Field Work in Progress consists of methods to keep the researcher from getting overwhelmed by the voluminous accumulation of qualitative data. They are ways of staying ahead of the game through occasional summary and synthesis. *Exploring Variables* looks at those constituent elements of the data corpus to examine their properties, dimensions, and overall qualities. And *Exploring Reports in Progress* shows how the write-up builds over time and contributes to further studies.

EXPLORING FIELD WORK IN PROGRESS

The *Data Accounting Log* is a record-keeping tool for the types and quantity of data collected. A *Contact Summary Form* is a one-page form that logs a field site visit's most salient data. The *Case Analysis Meeting* systematically documents a research team's discussion about a study to date. The *Interim Case Summary* is a provisional draft of the study's field work and its major findings to date. The *Partially Ordered Meta-Matrix* is a first-draft assemblage of the most relevant data from a multi-case study into a composite display.

Data Accounting Log

Description

A data accounting log is a management method that documents on a single form when and what types of data have been collected from specific participants and sites. The analyst enters in each cell when a set of data is in hand, plus any supplemental notes (see Display 6.1).

Applications

A data accounting log is highly recommended for all qualitative studies as good record keeping and management, particularly for those projects with large numbers of participants or sites and various instrumentation. This method may look laborious but it pays handsome rewards. In field research, you lose sight all too quickly of how much—and what kinds of—data have been collected from different participants. Because these data are often corroborative—verifying an explanation given by others, testing an emerging hypothesis or conclusion—they are the evidential bricks on which an analysis can be built.

Example

Display 6.1 illustrates a small-scale study's data accounting log, noting the key participants in column headings and data forms in rows. Dates, supplemental notes, and researcher-generated confirmation marks have been entered for at-a-glance documentation of the corpus. Excel software was used for constructing the display.

Analysis

A scan of the form shows both the data collection in progress and, toward a study's end, the completed corpus record. Reflection on the log might suggest additional forms of data needed or that could be collected. A copy of the data accounting log can be attached to a Contact Summary Form (profiled next) and used in planning the next steps in data collection. The log can also serve as an auditor's reference or as an appendix to a technical report or thesis/dissertation.

Notes

You can make a data accounting log as detailed as you need it to be. Cells can be devoted to confirming whether different participants from several cross-case sites have been asked the same particular

DISPLAY 6.1 ● Data Accounting Log

	Carol (Teacher)	Tom (Student)	LeAnn (Principal)	Elana (Counselor)	Marci (Adm Asst)	Jake (Father)	Liz (Mother)
INTERVIEW 1	05/04/2012	05/08/2012	05/15/2012	05/17/2012	05/23/2012	05/09/2012	05/09/2012
INTERVIEW 2	05/14/2012	05/17/2012	X	inquire if a follow-up interview is possible	X	was asked but declined a 2nd interview	11/5/2012—phone interview
INTERVIEW 3	05/31/2012	X	X	X	X	X	X
PARTICIPANT OBS. 1	04/26/2012	04/26/2012	N/A	N/A	N/A	N/A	N/A
PARTICIPANT OBS. 2	4/27/2012—date of key incident	4/27/2012—date of key incident	N/A	N/A	N/A	N/A	N/A
PARTICIPANT OBS. 3	04/30/2012	04/30/2012	N/A	N/A	N/A	N/A	N/A
PARTICIPANT OBS. 4	05/01/2012	absent	N/A	N/A	N/A	N/A	N/A
PARTICIPANT OBS. 5	05/02/2012	05/02/2012	N/A	N/A	N/A	N/A	N/A
DOCUMENTS							
Lesson Plans	√	N/A	N/A	N/A	N/A	N/A	N/A
Referral Files	√—for Tom	√—has copy	√—has copy	see for access	see for access	has copy	has copy
OTHER							
Student Assignments	√—for all students	√	N/A	N/A	N/A	N/A	has copy of Tom's assignment
Standardized Test Scores	N/A	√	N/A	see for access	see for access	N/A	N/A
Transcripts	N/A	√	N/A	see for access	see for access	N/A	N/A

interview question from a protocol or whether the researcher has collected sufficient forms of data to help answer a particular set of research questions.

Contact Summary Form

Description

A contact summary form is a one-page document with some focusing or summarizing questions about a particular field contact. The fieldworker reviews the written-up field notes and answers each question briefly to develop an overall summary of the main points in the contact (see Display 6.2).

DISPLAY 6.2 ●   Contact Summary Form: Illustration (Excerpts)

Contact type: Site: <u>Tindale</u>
   Visit   <u>X   </u>   Contact date: <u>11/28-29/79</u>
   Phone   <u>   </u>   Today's date: <u>12/28/79</u>
            (with whom)   Written by: BLT

1. <u>What were the main issues or themes that struck you in this contact?</u>

   Interplay between highly prescriptive, "teacher-proof" curriculum that is top-down imposed and the actual writing of the curriculum by the teachers themselves.

   Split between the "watchdogs" (administrators) and the "house masters" (dept. chairs & teachers) vis a vis job foci.

   District curric. coord'r as decision maker are school's acceptance of research relationship.

2. <u>Summarize the information you got (or failed to get) on each of the target questions you had for this contact.</u>

Question	Information
History of dev. of innov'n	Conceptualized by Curric. Coord'r, English Chairman & Assoc. Chairman; written by teachers in summer; revised by teachers following summer with field testing data
School's org'l structure	Principal & admin'rs responsible for discipline; dept chairs are educ'l leaders
Demographics	Racial conflicts in late 60's; 60% black stud. pop.; heavy emphasis on discipline & on keeping out non-district students slipping in from Chicago
Teacher response to innov'n	Rigid, structured, etc. at first; now, they say they like it/NEEDS EXPLORATION
Research access	Very good; only restriction: teachers not required to cooperate

3. <u>Anything else that struck you as salient, interesting, illuminating or important in this contact?</u>

   Thoroughness of the innv'n's development and training.

   Its embeddedness in the district's curriculum as planned and executed by the district curriculum coordinator.

   The initial resistance to its high prescriptiveness (as reported by users) as contrasted with their current acceptance and approval of it (again, as reported by users).

4. <u>What new (or remaining) target questions do you have in considering the next contact with this site?</u>

   How do users really perceive the innov'n? If they do indeed embrace it, what accounts for the change from early resistance?

   Nature and amount of networking among users of innov'n.

Information on "stubborn" math teachers whose ideas weren't heard initially—who are they? Situation particulars? Resolution?

Follow-up on English teacher Reilly's "fall from the chairmanship."

Follow a team through a day of rotation, planning, etc.

CONCERN: The consequences of eating school cafeteria food two days per week for the next four or five months . . .

Source: Miles, M. B., & Huberman, A. M. (1994). *Qualitative data analysis: An expanded sourcebook* (2nd ed.). Thousand Oaks, CA: Sage Publications.

Applications

After a field contact (from one to several days) and the production of write-ups, there is often a need to pause and ponder: What were the main concepts, themes, issues, and questions that I saw and heard during this contact? Without such reflection, it is easy to get lost in a welter of detail.

The contact summary form is a rapid, practical way to do first-run data condensation without losing any of the basic information to which it refers. It captures thoughtful impressions and reflections and makes them available for further reflection and analysis not only by the fieldworker but also by other team members.

Example

First, be clear about what you or your research team members need to know now about a particular field contact, with a write-up that may later run to dozens of pages. Which questions will get to the essence of the data set? Here are some possibilities:

- What people, events, or situations were involved?

- What were the main themes or issues in the contact?

- What was intriguing, surprising, or disturbing? (Sunstein & Chiseri-Strater, 2012)

- Which research questions and which variables in the initial framework did the contact bear on most centrally?

- What new assertions, propositions, hypotheses, or speculations about the field situations were suggested by the contact?

- Where should the fieldworker place the most energy during the next contact, and what kinds of information should be sought?

Questions should be arranged on a single sheet of paper (or within the one-page space limit of a text-based program), with room for the fieldworker's answers. Identifying information on the case, the particular contact, the fieldworker, and the date should be indicated as well.

The data on a contact summary form are essentially phrases or sentences that the fieldworker considers to be an answer to the form's questions after the complete write-up of the contact has been reviewed and corrected. At this point, you have a perspective that combines immediacy with a reflective overview of what went on in the contact. You can include your own reflective remarks, as well as questions to be answered, during the next contact. Waiting until a contact's full data have been coded thoroughly and fully is probably too late.

Display 6.2 shows excerpts from an example. Note that Questions 2 and 4 of this form indicate that the fieldworker started with a focused set of "target questions." Those are useful when your time is limited. Information on each question is summarized, and new target questions are posed for the next visit. Some of these questions come from the study's research questions ("How do users really perceive the innovation?"), and some are provoked by data collected during the visit (e.g., "Follow-up on English teacher Reilly's 'fall from the chairmanship.'").

Analysis

The filled-out contact summary form can be used in several ways:

- To guide planning for the next contact

- To reorient yourself to the contact when returning to the write-up

- To help with coordination when more than one fieldworker is involved in the study

- To help with further data analysis—that is, the summary forms for a number of contacts can themselves be coded and analyzed

- To suggest new or revised codes

All of these uses are easier if the forms have been entered into a database. It is also helpful to digitally cut and paste a copy of the completed contact summary form before the first page of the write-up, so it's close to the data it summarizes. We encourage doing write-ups no later than the day after a field contact.

Contact summary forms also can be used in a more systematic way by applying codes or keywords to them. An excerpted illustration appears in Display 6.3. Here, the analyst had a list of codes (called Themes/Aspects) that were applied to the Salient Points selected from the write-up. New codes were also generated.

DISPLAY 6.3 ⬡ Contact Summary Form: Illustration With Themes/Aspects (Excerpts)

CONTACT SUMMARY

Type of contact: Mtg.   <u>Principals</u>   <u>Ken's office</u>   <u>4/2/76</u>   SITE <u>Westgate</u>
                                 Who, what group   place   date

                  Phone _____   _____   _____   Coder <u>MM</u>
                                 With whom, by whom   place   date   Date coded <u>4/18/76</u>

                  Inf. Int. _____   _____   _____
                                 With whom, by whom   place   date

1. Pick out the most salient points in the contact. Number in order on this sheet and note page number on which point appears. Number point in text of write-up. Attach theme or aspect to each point in CAPITALS. Invent themes where no existing ones apply and asterisk those. Comment may also be included in double parentheses.

Page	Salient Points	Themes/Aspects
1	1. Staff decisions have to be made by April 30.	STAFF
1	2. Teachers will have to go out of their present grade-level assignment when they transfer.	STAFF/RESOURCE MGMT.
2	3. Teachers vary in their willingness to integrate special ed kids into their classrooms—some teachers are "a pain in the elbow."	*RESISTANCE

Page	Salient Points	Themes/Aspects
2	4. Ken points out that tentative teacher assignment lists got leaked from the previous meeting (implicity deplores this).	INTERNAL COMMUNIC.
2	5. Ken says, "Teachers act as if they had the right to decide who should be transferred." (would make outcry)	POWER DISTRIB.
2	6. Tacit/explicit decision: "It's our decision to make." (voiced by Ken, agreed by Ed)	POWER DISTRIB/ CONFLICT MGMT.
2	7. Principals and Ken, John, and Walker agree that Ms. Epstein is "bitch."	*STEREOTYPING
2	8. Ken decides not to tell teachers ahead of time (now) about transfers ("because then we'd have a fait accompli").	PLAN FOR PLANNING/ TIME MGMT

Source: Miles, M. B., & Huberman, A. M. (1994). *Qualitative data analysis: An expanded sourcebook* (2nd ed.). Thousand Oaks, CA: Sage Publications.

Notes

Keep contact summary forms simple. You need an instrument that makes it easy to do a rapid retrieval and synthesis of what the contact was all about. Focus on the primary concepts, questions, and issues.

Case Analysis Meeting

Description

At a case analysis meeting, the fieldworker most conversant with a case meets with one or more people—a critical friend, a colleague, a dissertation chair, or coresearchers—to summarize the current status of the case. The meeting is guided by a series of prepared questions, and notes are taken on answers to the questions as the meeting progresses. Case analysis meetings can also focus on a single theme in one case, or treat such a theme across several cases (see Display 6.4).

DISPLAY 6.4 ● Case Analysis Meeting Form

Case Analysis Meeting Form   Date _____   Case _____

Recorder _____   Meeting Attendance _____

1. MAIN THEMES, IMPRESSIONS, SUMMARY STATEMENTS about what is going on in the case. Comments about the general state of the planning/implementation system.

2. EXPLANATIONS, SPECULATIONS, HYPOTHESES, PROPOSITIONS, ASSERTIONS about what is going in the case.

3. ALTERNATIVE INTERPRETATIONS, EXPLANATIONS, DISAGREEMENTS about what is going on in the case.

4. NEXT STEPS FOR DATA COLLECTION: follow-up questions, specific actions, general directions field work should take.

5. Implications for REVISION, UPDATING OF CODING SCHEME.

Source: Miles, M. B., & Huberman, A. M. (1994). *Qualitative data analysis: An expanded sourcebook* (2nd ed.). Thousand Oaks, CA: Sage Publications.

Applications

In any study that has multiple cases, the meaning of what is happening in each case tends increasingly to get lost in the welter of field work, coding, and other preliminary analyses. A lone researcher or a research staff can understand quickly and economically what is happening in a case, keep themselves current, and develop coherent concepts to guide later analysis through case analysis meetings and summaries.

Case analysis meetings are good devices for rapid retrieval of impressions and "headnotes," and for forming preliminary descriptive and inferential generalizations. The back and forth interaction among colleagues helps keep the fieldworker honest. Even so, care should be taken not to get locked into premature generalizations. The themes and suggestions from case analysis meetings should always be checked against events in the case, as noted in carefully coded write-ups of field notes.

If the group is larger than three people, it will help to have someone chairing it as well as recording it.

Example

Our (Miles and Huberman) study of the creation of new schools included multiple sites. We wanted to keep as current as we could on events in the planning and implementation of each new school. We were also seeking explanations and hypotheses—and we were feeling strongly that our too-complex, unhelpful coding scheme needed to be revised.

We settled on the idea of a case analysis meeting that would be held for each of the six sites in rotation. To help focus the meeting, a note-taking form was needed, which appears in compressed form in Display 6.4. This particular example was focused on a complex case—a school—that we were following over time, but it can be adapted easily if the case is an individual or a small group.

In using the form, the meeting can begin profitably with the most involved fieldworkers launching a discussion of Item 1, Main Themes, Impressions, Summary Statements. Others ask questions for clarification. The recorder follows the discussion, taking notes (either by hand or on a laptop) under that heading and asking for further clarification if needed.

Often the discussion will jump forward to later questions (e.g., a theme suggests an interpretation), and the recorder should enter those data under appropriate headings. Points or items under each heading should be numbered to mark them off and aid reference to them during discussion. If the group does not move gradually to later questions, the recorder should ask them to do so. The recorder should also summarize the notes from time to time to ensure that the discussion is being represented accurately.

Analysis

Photocopies of the notes are made for everyone, or digital copies are e-mailed to the team; they can be reviewed at the end of the meeting. Specific plans can be made (to revise codes, how to collect new data of a certain sort), although such review and planning can be done afterward, too. Display 6.5 presents some excerpts from a filled-out case analysis form for our new schools study.

In this display, we can see that a main theme was the researcher's effort to describe (Item 1) and then understand (Item 2) why early implementation of the open-space teaching was going relatively smoothly even though the advance preparation had been poor. The hypotheses and hunches in Item 2 (e.g., the "retreatability" concept, the principal–teacher relationship, or teacher professionalization) led to additional data collection plans in Item 4 (e.g., teacher interviews), as do the alternative, rival hypotheses suggested in Item 3. The notes from case analysis meetings, as well as guiding specific next steps in data collection, can be revisited after the next round or two of data collection for confirmation/disconfirmation.

DISPLAY 6.5 ● Case Analysis Form: Exhibit With Data

1. MAIN THEMES, IMPRESSIONS, SUMMARY STATEMENTS about what is going on in the site.

    1. Ed (principal) efficient "technical" manager, not dealing with social system; doesn't think about it. When Ken (asst. supt.) pointed out need for Ed to work with Janet, a complaining teacher ("treat her with kid gloves . . . good luck."), Ed said, "She'll be the one needing good luck." Not supportive especially: One teacher asked the field-worker for help, seemed reluctant when FW referred her back to Ed.

    2. Implementation of the open space approach is incredibly smooth in light of the minimal advance preparation and training. There is still a "walking on cracked eggs" feeling, though.

    3. Teachers seem cautiously willing to see how it will work out, not directly optimistic. Uncertainty, feeling unprepared. "If it doesn't work out I hope we can undo it" suggests weak commitment; is called "retreatability."

    4. Children relaxed.

    5. Teachers feel principal had no idea of what would be involved, really, in start-up.

    . . . .

2. EXPLANATIONS, SPECULATIONS, HYPOTHESES, PROPOSITIONS, ASSERTIONS about what is going on in the site.

    1. Ed's "efficiency" emphasis helps smoothness.

    2. People know who to go to for support.

    3. Many teachers were students of asst. supt. and trust him.

    4. Things aren't being imposed by outsiders.

    5. Teacher attitudes may be related to the "retreatability" concept.

    6. Principal knew teachers well enough to compose workable teams to implement the open space concept. Also sent complaining teachers to another school.

    7. Principal respects the teachers—even though during the administrative planning they were treated like cattle.

3. ALTERNATIVE EXPLANATIONS, MINORITY REPORTS, DISAGREEMENTS about what is going on in the site.

    1. Perhaps the teachers' considerable past experience and training, their professionalization makes for a smooth implementation.

    2. The size of Ed's faculty has doubled; there are many strangers. That may be increasing the uncertainty as much as the lack of preparation.

    . . . .

4. NEXT STEPS FOR DATA COLLECTION: follow-up questions, specific actions, general directions field work should take.

    1. Ask Ed about Janet, how she's adjusting. Get to know her.

    2. Need time to talk with teachers, not just observe the start-up. Teachers are probably bothered more than their "professional" surface behavior shows.

    3. Will or can Ken give the teachers technical help?

    4. What happened in yesterday's faculty meeting?

    5. We should do a careful retrieval interview with Ken and Ed about the summer work, planning decisions, etc. that preceded the start-up.

    6. Ask key people: What are your hopes for the way the school will be by Christmas? by June? What indicators would they use for good teacher collaboration? humanization of teaching?

    . . . .

5. Implications for REVISION, UPDATING OF CODING SCHEME.

    1. Consider a code for *support.*

    2. Something on teacher *commitment or ownership* of the innovation.

    3. Use a pattern for the "retreatability" idea, which seems quite key.

    4. Our codes on "planning-implementation linkage" are too complicated; need to simplify them considerably.

    . . . .

Source: Miles, M. B., & Huberman, A. M. (1994). *Qualitative data analysis: An expanded sourcebook* (2nd ed.). Thousand Oaks, CA: Sage Publications.

Don't let a fieldworker's generalization or impression go unquestioned or unillustrated. The meeting allows people to entertain opposing views. The tone should be not one of arguing but one of friendly skepticism and efforts at concreteness and shared clarity. A balance should be maintained between getting reasonable consensus and testing alternative, rival hypotheses. Summarize frequently to check understandings.

A case analysis meeting longer than 90 minutes or so begins to lose focus and productivity. The frequency of such meetings depends on factors such as the number of people and cases involved and the frequency of case contacts. The rule of thumb is this: Don't let a large amount of case data pile up before holding an analysis meeting. In our school improvement project, we found it useful to hold short case analysis meetings after each site visit (which usually had occupied 2 or 3 days and accumulated plenty of information).

The summaries drawn from case analysis meetings can themselves be coded and drawn on for analysis. Display 6.6 shows how this process can work.

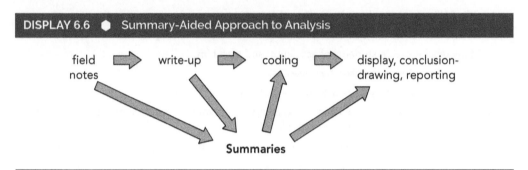

DISPLAY 6.6 ● Summary-Aided Approach to Analysis

field notes ⇨ write-up ⇨ coding ⇨ display, conclusion-drawing, reporting

Summaries

Source: Miles, M. B., & Huberman, A. M. (1994). *Qualitative data analysis: An expanded sourcebook* (2nd ed.). Thousand Oaks, CA: Sage Publications.

Notes

The specific research questions for a study may also generate additional substantive issues that can go on the case analysis meeting form (e.g., What are the current outcomes of the innovation? How politically stable is the program?). Other general questions can be generated to guide case analysis meetings, such as the following:

- What is intriguing, surprising, or disturbing about recent case events?
- What is our rapport with various people in key roles?
- What additional analyses do we need of existing data to understand the case better?
- What is definitely not true of the case at this point?
- What probably will happen over the next few days/weeks in the case?

Interim Case Summary

Description

The interim case summary is a provisional product of varying length (five or more pages, depending on the scope of the study) that is the first attempt to derive a coherent, overall account of the case—a synthesis of what the researcher knows about the case and what may remain to be explored. It presents (a) a review of findings, (b) a careful look at the quality of data supporting them, and (c) the agenda for the next waves of data collection (see Display 6.7 for a summary outline).

DISPLAY 6.7 ● Interim Case Summary Outline: Illustration

Table of Contents

A. The Site

  1. Geography, setting

  2. Demographics of community and district

  3. Organization chart (showing key actors and their relationships)

B. Brief Chronology

  1. Adoption (includes brief description of the innovation)

  2. Planning (anything postadoption and pre-actual use with pupils)

  3. Implementation up to present

C. Current Status of Research Questions

  1. The innovation (deal with all subquestions; summarize what is currently known / if unknown, say so / if puzzles, describe them)

  2. The school as social organization, preimplementation

  3. The adoption decision

  4. Site dynamics during implementation/transformation

  5. New configurations/outcomes

  6. Role of external and internal assistance

   (CONCLUDE THIS SECTION WITH A LIST OF UNCERTAINTIES/PUZZLES)

D. Causal Network

  1. Graphic network of variables, at this site, seen as affecting outcomes (draws on pattern codes)

  2. Discussion of network, including ties to other previous conceptual/empirical work on dissemination that seems especially salient or relevant

E. Brief Methodological Notes (how analysis was done, problems encountered, etc.; confidence in results, suggestions for next summary, etc.)

Source: Miles, M. B., & Huberman, A. M. (1994). *Qualitative data analysis: An expanded sourcebook* (2nd ed.). Thousand Oaks, CA: Sage Publications.

The interim case summary forces the researcher to digest the materials in hand, formulate a clearer sense of the case, and self-critique the adequacy of the data that have been collected. This process leads to next-step data collection, planning, and usually reformulation of codes and further analysis plans.

Applications

Typically, interim data examination is done on the run or is done for some subsets of data but not for others. You need an integrative exercise that obliges you to audit what is known and how well it is known—to collate the main findings to date; estimate the confidence held in those findings; and list gaps, puzzles, and data that still need to be collected. The interim case summary serves these purposes.

Whether the researcher is working alone, with occasional advisory colleague contact, or has colleagues working on other parallel cases, the interim case summary is helpful. Exchanging interim summaries with colleagues keeps them up to date. And the exchange is a good occasion to subject your emerging concepts or recurrent themes to a critical review. Blind spots are usually obvious to a second reader.

Exchanging and discussing interim summaries also helps cross-case analysis. Research team members can better align their visions, argue on the basis of shared and documented instances, and resolve fuzzy or shadowy issues that need clarification for the study as a whole to move forward. Team discussion may also yield emergent explanatory variables that can be checked out rather than generated post hoc.

Strategically, the best time to compose an interim case summary is about a third of the way into field work, when there are initial data to report and enough time left to atone for the gaps or weaknesses the summary has revealed. This exercise also helps you address more long-range substantive questions such as the following: What patterns and themes seem to be emerging? What is really going on in the case so far? What's the big picture?

Example

Display 6.7 presents the table of contents given to each researcher in Miles and Huberman's school improvement study as an outline for the interim case summary. Note that common formatting like this will enable cross-case comparability—which may suggest promising avenues for other analysts for their next site visits and will certainly dredge up themes and concepts that exist in more than one case.

Whether the codes have been derived directly from the research questions or evolved during early exploratory work and are more distantly connected, it makes sense to scan the write-ups, looking for the primary codes of interest, jotting down notes as you go, and then writing the summary. This process will go quite rapidly if your database is in computer files rather than only on hard copy; you can search for coded units, see them in context, and switch to another file to write up the themes you see emerging. Some analysts prefer to reread the write-ups carefully and then tackle all the research questions in one fell swoop. They then use pattern codes to pull together material for the summary.

Analysis

Interim summaries come in all shapes and sizes. The best ones are shapely and small—something on the order of 5 to 10 pages. Summaries also can be more specialized. For example, rather than collating material for both individual research questions and overarching themes, you might do two consecutive summaries, one reviewing the research questions and, a month or so later, another tackling the larger issues that, by then, should have become clearer.

In a multi-case study, be sure to allow time for individual researchers to study and discuss one another's summaries. These are usually focused and informed interactions springing from a common exercise, and they are typically more intellectual—and therefore more mind-expanding—than logistically oriented staff meetings. Discussion of interim summaries is a fertile, risk-free arena for individual researchers to try out their sense of how the data—theirs and others'—are coming together, and to get the analytic juices flowing.

Very brief summaries also can be produced rapidly by one fieldworker interviewing another fieldworker for an hour using a standard set of questions such as, "How would you characterize the principal's interactions with people?" "What do you think of first when someone says _____ School?" This method helps the fieldworker be integrative by pulling together impressions of the case and core themes that begin to appear.

The most difficult part seems to be accepting the fact that interim summaries are *interim*—and likely to be incomplete, rapidly written, and fragmented. To do them well would require upwards of a week, which is too much time proportionate to the yield. Do them rapidly, and then think about them with your colleagues.

Notes

Customize the Interim Case Summary form to your specific study. Let your central and related research questions guide the form's table of contents.

Partially Ordered Meta-Matrix

Description

Meta-matrices (matrices with rows and subrows, and/or columns and subcolumns) are master charts assembling descriptive data from each of several cases into a standard format. It stacks up all the single-case displays onto one large chart. The basic principle is *inclusion* of all relevant, condensed data (see Display 6.8).

DISPLAY 6.8 ● Case-Level Display for Partially Ordered Meta-Matrix (Format)				
Users	Feelings/ Concerns	How Innovation Looked	What Was User Doing Most?	Problems
1.				
2.				
3.				
4.				
5., etc.				

Source: Miles, M. B., & Huberman, A. M. (1994). *Qualitative data analysis: An expanded sourcebook* (2nd ed.). Thousand Oaks, CA: Sage Publications.

From there, you usually move to *partition* the data further (divide it in new ways), and *cluster* data that fall together so that contrasts between sets of cases on variables of interest can become clearer. These partitioned and clustered meta-matrices are progressively more refined, usually requiring further transformations of case-level data into short quotes, summarizing phrases, ratings, and/or symbols (see Displays 6.9 and 6.11 for examples).

Applications

Cross-case analysis multiplies the data set by the number of single cases. If each case produces several hundred pages of field notes and ancillary material, no matter how well you understand things at the case level, you are faced with overload and unmanageability when you try to draw meaningful cross-case conclusions deeper than similarities and differences. Cross-case data need to be made comparable via common codes, common displays of commonly coded data segments, and common reporting formats for each case.

As with a single case, it's useful to start with displays that have some—but not too much—internal order. A meta-matrix is the first exploratory deep dive into cross-case analysis to see what the general territory looks like. It's also a critical one, because it will collapse the cross-case data set into partitions and clusters that may be used for subsequent analyses. Refinements in the clustering and grouping of data may be made later, but for now, you are making a commitment to a certain way of summarizing and looking at what's there, making sense of it, and trying to work out the next most likely analytic steps (which may include meta-matrices that are ordered conceptually according to key variables; by cases—such as strong to weak on some variable; or by time—such as early to late).

Example

Cross-case analysis first depends on coherent within-case information. In the example shown here, the analyst was trying to answer several questions about the experience of teachers using a new educational practice. They are as follows:

- How did it look to the user?

- What was the user doing?

- Which feelings and concerns were paramount?

- Which problems were looming large?

- How did all of this work over a long period of time?

The empty case-level display might look like Display 6.8.

You then sort the condensed case data into analytic categories, user by user, in separate but commonly formatted matrices, one per case. Display 6.9 shows the display with data entered for one case, Lido School, for one time period.

Cell entries are short phrases condensing coded units from the case data. Some selection and grouping have been done, too. The analyst has selected feelings, problems, and so on according to some

DISPLAY 6.9 ◆ Case-Level Display for Partially Ordered Meta-Matrix: Users' Second Year of Implementation at Lido				
User	**Feelings/Concerns**	**How Innovation Looked**	**What Was User Doing Most?**	**Problems**
Vance	More comfortable with style of teaching and with having kids outside	Still useful, giving good direction & helpful ideas, activities	Working through materials Giving, participating in env'l educ workshops Working with community Off-campus site work	Time too limited for tasks to be done
Drew	Concern with growing number of non-achievers in forestry/ecology class	Too discovery-oriented for kids without biology basics; lecture style more appropriate	Adapting materials & lessons to growing non-achiever population Off-campus site work	Dealing with more non-achievers successfully
Carroll	Excitement with new activities, expanding science program	Same as first year	Working with community Giving, participating in env'l educ workshops Off-campus site work	Over-extended activity commitment

Source: Miles, M. B., & Huberman, A. M. (1994). *Qualitative data analysis: An expanded sourcebook* (2nd ed.). Thousand Oaks, CA: Sage Publications.

explicit decision rules and has clustered discrete but similar items (e.g., under Problems in the far right column, the presence of several overloading tasks equals the problem of too limited time).

Now that each cell entry includes several words/phrases, the next task is to condense these even further. You now have N case-level displays—comparable with ones entered in Display 6.9. If there are no more than a dozen cases or so, and if the displays are no more complex than these examples, the data can probably all go into one composite partially ordered meta-matrix.

The partially ordered meta-matrix will be simply a stack of the case-level charts. For example, the first two columns would appear as shown in Display 6.10. Table construction and data entry will be relatively easy with appropriate software.

DISPLAY 6.10 ⬡ Partially Ordered Meta-Matrix: Users' Feelings/Concerns and Other Variables (Format)		
Sites/Users	**Feelings/Concerns**	**. . .**
Lido School		
1.		
2.		
3.		
Masepa School		
1.		
2.		
3., etc.		

Source: Miles, M. B., & Huberman, A. M. (1994). *Qualitative data analysis: An expanded sourcebook* (2nd ed.). Thousand Oaks, CA: Sage Publications.

Usually, you need to distill case-level cell entries somewhat as the work proceeds. Thus, for example, the filled-in chart for Lido School in Display 6.9 might appear as in Display 6.11, which shows that we are down to fewer, case-typifying words and some symbols.

Feelings/Concerns have been dichotomized with positive and negative magnitude codes, and each entry has a type of feeling or concern set at about a middle range of abstraction (e.g., "comfortable," with a qualification), and often a short, category-grounding phrase (e.g., "underachievers assigned") to keep the analyst aware of what specifically was going on at this particular site.

DISPLAY 6.11 ⬡ Partially Ordered Meta-Matrix: Users' Feelings/Concerns and Other Variables (Lido Data)	
Sites/Users	**Feelings/Concerns**
Lido School	
1. Vance	+ Comfortable with new style, norms (lower control)
2. Drew	– Shift in target public (underachievers assigned)
3. Carroll	+ New, expanding (program, activities)

Source: Miles, M. B., & Huberman, A. M. (1994). *Qualitative data analysis: An expanded sourcebook* (2nd ed.). Thousand Oaks, CA: Sage Publications.

The meta-matrix has assembled and pruned down multiple tables into one big one that has considerably condensed the original data. It lets you see all of the data in one large place. Include "just enough" words, phrases, and symbols that make summative sense to you and that prompt your ability to recall the most important features about each particular case.

Analysis

From now on, the matrices and analyses will depend more on what the data have to say and on the kinds of relationships you are most interested in. Indeed, variations of and additions to your original meta-matrices are possible. Reformatting and resorting the cells will enable you to employ the tactics of **partitioning** and **clustering** (see Chapter 11) to determine whether new analytic observations can be constructed.

Display 6.12, for example, sorts the data by the Type of Concern across each Year. This matrix enables you to scan the cells for two sets of things: trends—concerns that change or remain constant through time—and types of concerns. Thus, the new display **partitions** the data (in this case, by time and concerns) by **clustering** the data (into different types of concerns). You may discover, for example, that types of concerns cluster into two major forms: individual and institutional. And you may also discover that there were more institutional than individual concerns during later implementation (tactic: **making if-then tests**).

DISPLAY 6.12 ● Time-Ordered Meta-Matrix (Format)				
Type of Concern	**Year 1**	**Year 2**	**Year 3**	**Year 4**
1.				
2.				
3., etc.				

Source: Miles, M. B., & Huberman, A. M. (1994). *Qualitative data analysis: An expanded sourcebook* (2nd ed.). Thousand Oaks, CA: Sage Publications.

As a next step, you could create a summary table (see Display 6.13) of individual and institutional concerns (**partitioning** the data according to some predefined variables) and see at which of the 12 cases they were considered to be primary during later implementation. During this process, you can do some empirical **clustering** within each of the two broad categories ("relational problems," "motivational problems," etc.).

Here is much useful descriptive information. For example, some school cases have multiple troubles (e.g., Banestown, Perry-Parkdale); others only one kind (Masepa); and 2 sites of the 12 have escaped unscathed (tactic: **counting**). Also, it looks as if individual concerns are mostly nontechnical, and institutional concerns emphasize continuation (lower priority, poor functioning, delivering on promises) (tactic: **noting patterns, themes**). Such a finding leads you back to other parts of the cross-case chart to test hunches (**making if-then tests**). In this case, the hunch might be that projects with high technical mastery have just as many institutional concerns as those that do not.

Word tables, Excel database management, and CAQDAS applications can speed the mechanics of basic meta-matrix assembly and the processes of clustering and partitioning. But there is no real way to shortcut the *thinking* time needed. The process of understanding a cross-case data set, even for a few variables, is one of making gradual sense. It cannot be hurried.

DISPLAY 6.13 ● Summary Table: Individual and Institutional Concerns During Later Implementation

Type of Concern/Item	School Sites at Which Item Mentioned
Individual Concerns	
Relational problems—friction among project staff	Banestown, Perry-Parkdale
Motivational problems (discouragement, "distaste" for the practice)	Calston, Lido, Masepa, Dun Hollow, Proville, Tindale
Stamina, exhaustion, excessive demands of the project	Masepa, Carson, Plummet
Institutional Concerns	
Lower institutional or district-level priority of project (with attendant lessening of rewards)	Lido, Plummet
Poor overall functioning (project as a whole, or a component)	Perry-Parkdale, Dun Hollow, Proville
Resistance, obstruction, lack of support by other staff not on project	Banestown, Perry-Parkdale, Carson
Worry whether project will "deliver" on its promises or objectives	Banestown
Continuation the following year(s)	Banestown, Calston, Lido, Perry-Parkdale, Plummet

Source: Miles, M. B., & Huberman, A. M. (1994). *Qualitative data analysis: An expanded sourcebook* (2nd ed.). Thousand Oaks, CA: Sage Publications.

Notes

Don't impose conceptual, chronological, or other shapes too quickly for a meta-matrix. If your cases are less complex than ours, so will your meta-matrices be. It usually takes several alternative cuts before a workable and productive set of partitions and/or clusters emerges. For more on **partitioning** and **clustering**, see Chapter 11.

EXPLORING VARIABLES

The *Code Frequency Table* provides a descriptive statistical account of the number and type of codes generated from data analysis. A *Checklist Matrix* explores the multiple dynamics of one key variable. A *Content-Analytic Summary Table* is a multi-case display about a variable or dimension of interest. A *Contrast Table* highlights the variability of a dimension to see its extreme ranges. And the *Two-Variable Case-Ordered Matrix* simultaneously explores how multiple variables relate to a selected number of cases.

Code Frequency Table

Description

A code frequency table lists the numbers or percentages of codes derived from initial analysis to examine their distribution. These codes also may be appropriately clustered to examine their category distribution (see Display 6.14).

DISPLAY 6.14 ● Summary of Memorable Messages of Social Support	
Type of Support	**Frequency**
Informational support	
Guide performance	23
Identify means of success	20
Address autonomy	5
Esteem support	
Emphasize capabilities to succeed	17
Recognize intangible qualities	7
Reinforce relationships with teammates	5
Emotional support	
Support well-being	15
Praise athletes	12
Assist in performance	11
Deal with poor performances	8

Source: Cranmer, Anzur, & Sollitto (2017), p. 611.

Applications

Code frequency tables provide a tally of the most and least frequent codes that have been applied to qualitative data units. It is a method of assessing the magnitude of some codes (and thus variables) over others, and to begin a hierarchical, taxonomic, or categorical arrangement of the codes for an organizational display and reflection for further analysis. It can also initiate the development of Pattern Codes from the assembled array of First Cycle codes.

Example

Cranmer, Anzur, and Sollitto (2017) administered open-ended surveys to over 100 former high school athletes to assess the memorable messages of social support respondents received from their head coaches. Previous research and the conceptual framework for the study suggested that coaches communicate three general types of message-based support to their students: *informational, esteem*, and *emotional*. Thus, the specific codes generated from analysis were clustered under these three main categories, as seen in Display 6.14.

Analysis

The display is a results table, and it offered the coresearchers an overview of how the coded data were distributed among respondents. Most important, it provided the narrative outline for descriptions about the *types* of responses and their interplay within each category. The coresearchers conclude that

> the qualitative approach utilized within this study adds nuance to scholarly understanding of coach support. In particular, this study distinguishes between the different types of social support, which provide a more detailed understanding of which types of messages provide advice or information, build confidence in self-worth or abilities, or demonstrate concern or empathy. (Cranmer et al., 2017, p. 617)

An alternative graphic design possibility for code frequencies is *code landscaping* (Saldaña, 2016). Word clouds (see Display 2.13) arrange the most frequent words or phrases from a text in a larger font size than the others. As the frequency of particular words or phrases decreases, so does their size. But word clouds create random rather than ordered arrangements. Code landscaping, a manual operation by the analyst, organizes the various-sized codes into an outline format.

Display 6.15 illustrates an organized array of codes assigned to portions of qualitative survey responses that asked 234 participants, "My participation in high school speech and/or theatre has affected the adult I am now. In what ways do you think your participation in speech and/or theatre as a high school student has affected the adult you have become?" (McCammon & Saldaña, 2011; McCammon et al., 2012). Notice how font size is used to convey the frequency of codes and thus their magnitude. The font size of a code was manually increased once for each time it appeared in the data. The font size for the FRIEND-SHIPS code means that 18 people total mentioned this as an outcome of their high school experiences. The SOCIAL code font size indicates eight responses; INTERACTION WITH PEOPLE seven responses; CONNECTING WITH PEOPLE five responses; and FAMILY RELA-TIONSHIPS one response.

Simple cut-and-paste outlining and indenting on a text editing page organized the major codes and their related subcodes and sub-subcodes further. Words with no indents (FRIENDSHIPS, SOCIAL, and IDENTITY) suggested that these were the major elements for discussion in analytic

| DISPLAY 6.15 ● Code Landscaping of "Lifelong Impact" Survey Responses |

FRIENDSHIPS
SOCIAL
  INTERACTION WITH PEOPLE
    CONNECTING WITH PEOPLE
      FAMILY RELATIONSHIPS
      NETWORKING (WITH OTHER GAY PEOPLE)
      RECREATE COMMUNITY
      TALKATIVE
  HUMAN AWARENESS
    OPEN-MINDEDNESS / TOLERANCE
    CULTURAL AWARENESS
    TRUSTING OTHERS
    LISTENING
  BELONGING
    ACCEPTANCE
IDENTITY
  DISCOVERY OF TALENTS / STRENGTHS
    ENTERTAINING
  SENSE OF PURPOSE / FOCUS
    WISH FULFILLMENT
    WHAT MATTERS
    BELIEF SYSTEMS
  EMPATHY
    EMOTIONAL INTELLIGENCE / GROUNDING
      HAPPINESS
        PASSION
        JOY
        HAVE FUN
        SENSE OF HUMOR
        PRIDE
        LOVABLE
  SELF-ESTEEM / SELF-WORTH
    "HIGHS"
    "ALIVE AS A HUMAN BEING"
    MOTIVATING FOR LIFE / ADVENTURE
    SECURITY
  SELF-AWARENESS
    MATURITY / CHARACTER
      FACE SITUATIONS
      CHALLENGING SELF
      RESILIENCY
      VULNERABILITY
    BODY AWARENESS
      RELAXATION
NO CHANGE

Source: Saldaña (2016), p. 224.

memos and the final report. The indented words and phrases under them enabled the writer to "flesh out" the meanings of the primary codes further with detail and nuance. The code landscape graphic serves as a thumbnail sketch for the analytic write-up.

Notes

Numeric frequency is not necessarily and not always an indicator of qualitative significance. But **counting** is a legitimate heuristic/tactic for exploring whether there *may* be some hierarchical or proportionate importance of some kind in coded data.

Checklist Matrix

Description

A checklist matrix is a format for analyzing field data on a major variable or general domain of interest. The basic principle is that the matrix includes several components of a single, coherent variable, though it does not necessarily order the components (see Display 6.16).

Applications

Checklist matrices are good when you are exploring a new domain. If you have some rough ideas about a key variable and some components of it, you can begin and then amplify the display as you learn more.

DISPLAY 6.16 ●	Checklist Matrix: Conditions Supporting Preparedness at Smithson School, Banestown Case	
	Presence of Supporting Conditions	
Condition	**For Users**	**For Administrators**
Commitment	Strong—"wanted to make it work."	Weak at building level. Prime movers in central office committed; others not.
Understanding	"Basic" ("felt I could do it, but I just wasn't sure how.") for teacher. Absent for aide ("didn't understand how we were going to get all this.")	Absent at building level and among staff. Basic for 2 prime movers ("got all the help we needed from developer.") Absent for other central office staff.
Materials	Inadequate: ordered late, puzzling ("different from anything I ever used"), discarded.	N.A.
Front-end training	"Sketchy" for teacher ("it all happened so quickly"); no demo class. None for aide ("totally unprepared. I had to learn along with the children.")	Prime movers in central office had training at developer site; none for others.
Skills	Weak-adequate for teacher. "None" for aide.	One prime mover (Robeson) skilled in substance; others unskilled.
Ongoing in-service	None, except for monthly committee meeting; no substitute funds.	None
Planning, coordination time	None: both users on other tasks during day; lab tightly scheduled, no free time.	None
Provisions for debugging	None systematized: spontaneous work done by users during summer.	None
School admin. support	Adequate	N.A.
Central admin. support	Very strong on part of prime movers.	Building admin, only acting on basis of central office commitment.
Relevant prior experience	Strong and useful in both cases: had done individualized instruction, worked with low achievers. But aide no diagnostic experience.	Present and useful in central office, esp. Robeson (specialist).

Source: Miles, M. B., & Huberman, A. M. (1994). *Qualitative data analysis: An expanded sourcebook* (2nd ed.). Thousand Oaks, CA: Sage Publications.

Sometimes qualitative researchers may need to collect comparable data from all key participants and enter them in a prespecified format. This may happen in the following situations:

- When the variable is conceptually important to the study

- When the variable can be unbundled easily into distinct components or indicators

- When you need the variable to support your findings (e.g., as a good outcome measure)

- When the study has multiple cases requiring comparability of formatting and measurement

- When you want to relate field data to survey measures of the same variable (e.g., for a mixed methods study)

A checklist format makes data collection more systematic, enables verification, encourages comparability, and even permits simple quantification when appropriate. Checklist matrices can be formatted through programs such as Word tables and Excel, or through comparable CAQDAS features.

Example

In our (Miles and Huberman) school improvement study, "preparedness" was tied to implementation success in our conceptual framework and had strong backing in the literature. It also made good common sense that people do better on those things for which they are prepared. Empirical studies had broken down preparedness to distinct components that correlated well with good project execution. In short, the variable had a lot going for it. In addition, we were studying 12 cases and needed parallel measures. We also wanted to link our findings with a large survey that had a preparedness section in its questionnaire.

We did have some doubts about the variable, though. We wondered whether the preparedness → good execution logic was too mechanistic. For example, a highly experienced user could look well prepared, even though the technical training itself may have been dismal. And we believed that many unpredictable school-level factors could well affect project execution. So, a largely individual and technical factor such as preparedness could hardly account by itself for varying degrees of successful use of the new practice. We needed a display to help us sort out these matters.

The two major research questions for this study were as follows:

1. What were the components of the original plan for implementation? (e.g., front-end training, monitoring and debugging/troubleshooting unexpected problems, ongoing support)

2. Were the requisite conditions for implementation assured before it began? (e.g., commitment, understanding, materials and equipment, skills, time allocation, organizational backup)

Display 6.16 is a checklist for assessing "preparedness" prior to executing a new practice. In this case, the innovation was a remedial lab program in reading being used for the first time by a teacher and an aide. The *rows* are drawn from the various components of the implementation plan and the supporting conditions mentioned in the research questions. There is no effort to sort or order the components at this point. But we believed that preparedness might well differ for users of the new program and administrators, so the *columns* reflect that distinction. The matrix is thus partially ordered by *role*.

The cell entries include summary phrases, direct quotes, and an overall *adequacy judgment* of the condition by the analyst—evaluative words that ranged in magnitude:

- Absent/none

- Weak

- Inadequate

- Sketchy

- Basic

- Adequate

- Present

- Strong

- Very strong

The participant quotes help both justify and illuminate the rating (i.e., the magnitude codes).

For a checklist matrix, the analyst reviews relevant sections of the write-ups, retrieves material by codes, forms a general judgment or rating (if needed) of the level of adequacy of the component at hand, and locates relevant and supporting quotes.

The quotes and the ratings are kept together in the cell. The idea here is that ratings only tell you how much there is of something, not what that something *means*. Brief quotes are enough to communicate and help another analyst judge, by going back to the write-ups, whether the rating is justified or not. Keep quotes and ratings together in the matrix so that their compatibility can be assessed.

Analysis

Now, we scan down the columns of the Display 6.16 matrix and form a general idea of the level of preparedness for different components. The analytic tactic here is one of **noting patterns, themes** (see Chapter 11), not simply "adding up" judgments. For example, after eyeballing the data, the analyst wrote, in part: "The image is one of solid commitment and administrative support (except for the building principal), but minimal adequacy in requisite skills and understanding of the practice, and absence of forward-looking mechanisms for training, debugging or planning."

But the display suggests a new question: What's going on here? The central office administrators were committed and had more basic understanding of the program than the users (tactic: **making comparisons**). Why didn't they help? The analyst went back to field notes and noted,

> For Mrs. Baeurs [the administratively oriented, less skilled prime mover], all the lab teachers required were the provision of materials and initial training. . . . The teachers, she reasoned, had already done individualized work with children "so they didn't really have to do any kind of mind change." . . . At one point, however, she says, "I don't know. Maybe we got into it too fast."
>
> Even Mrs. Robeson, the reading specialist, acknowledged that the teachers "didn't think they were ready," but saw few ways in which initial preparation could have been better. She also played down the size of the needed changes in teachers.

Thus, the analyst found more information: The weak, hasty training and support came because *distant administrators minimized the actual needs of new users*. Administrators emphasized funds and materials, but teachers had more doubts about whether there was motivation to achieve project purposes.

That finding, in turn, helped the analyst realize that a major missing row in the matrix was *support of other classroom teachers*, whose lack of commitment to and understanding of the lab program led to poor coordination, skepticism, and disgruntlement that was offset only partly by their personal liking for the lab teacher and aide.

Overall, checklist matrices are effective for the systematic collection and rating of, and rumination over, a particular significant chunk of related data.

Notes

Any given research question and set of variables can have many different displays. Each has advantages and limitations. For example, Display 6.17 Checklist Matrix on Preparedness (Alternative Format 1) recasts Display 6.16 by transposing rows and columns so we can easily follow the responses of a specific *individual* across all conditions, rather than having to lump them in one cell as in Display 6.16. Also, the analyst has clustered the conditions into two general domains: Psychosocial Conditions and the Implementation Plan. That clustering permits comparing these more easily.

DISPLAY 6.17 ● Checklist Matrix on Preparedness (Alternative Format 1)												
	Psychosocial Conditions						Implementation Plan					
	Relevant Prior Experience	Commitment	Understanding	Skills	School Admin. Support	Central Admin. Support	Materials	Front-End Training	Ongoing In-Service	Planning, Coordination Time	Etc.	
Users 1 2												
Building Administrator (Principal) 1 2												
Central Office Administrator 1 2												
Other Central Office Staff												

Source: Miles, M. B., & Huberman, A. M. (1994). *Qualitative data analysis: An expanded sourcebook* (2nd ed.). Thousand Oaks, CA: Sage Publications.

Display 6.18 Checklist Matrix on Preparedness (Alternative Format 2) takes a different cut. The cell entries here are the names of Conditions, together with the *N* of Users and Administrators reporting. But note that we now have lost the data for individuals that appeared in Display 6.17. It is also much harder to track the status of any particular condition.

Display 6.19 Checklist Matrix on Preparedness (Alternative Format 3), a third possibility, de-emphasizes the differentiation among administrators and users and takes a decisive turn toward the *dynamics of conditions*—how and why they are important. We have retained the idea

DISPLAY 6.18 ⬡ Checklist Matrix on Preparedness (Alternative Format 2)

Conditions	Users	Administrators
Missing		
Weak		
Adequate		
Strong		

Source: Miles, M. B., & Huberman, A. M. (1994). *Qualitative data analysis: An expanded sourcebook* (2nd ed.). Thousand Oaks, CA: Sage Publications.

DISPLAY 6.19 ⬡ Checklist Matrix on Preparedness (Alternative Format 3)

Conditions	Examples[a]	How Important[b]	Why Important[c]
Commitment			
Understanding			
Materials			
Training			
etc.			

[a]Specific illustrations, marked with A or U for administrator or user, respectively.
[b]Rating: very, quite, somewhat, or not important.
[c]Explanations of reasons for importance of condition, given by respondent (A or U) or researcher (R).

Source: Miles, M. B., & Huberman, A. M. (1994). *Qualitative data analysis: An expanded sourcebook* (2nd ed.). Thousand Oaks, CA: Sage Publications.

of specific examples, but we have lost identifiable individuals and the capacity to make easy comparisons between users and administrators.

Do not close up too rapidly on a display format, especially since the cut-and-paste functions of text-based software enable multiple variations. Try several iterations; get colleagues' ideas and reactions. Especially for exploratory work, it pays to have a column headed "Remarks," where relevant commentary of any sort can be included to aid understanding.

Content-Analytic Summary Table

Description

A content-analytic summary table is a meta-matrix display that batches or brings together all related and pertinent data from multiple cases into a single form for initial or exploratory analysis. Each cell of the meta-matrix specifies the dimensions you are interested in (see Display 6.20).

Applications

One of the first tasks in moving from a single-case to a cross-case analysis is determining how many cases share similar characteristics. Quite simply, you take the original matrix used for the single cases and generate a meta-matrix that contains all of the condensed data. When the same characteristic appears in more than one case, this can be noted numerically next to the characteristic (e.g., "Shift in student input (5)" means that this observation occurred at five different sites).

DISPLAY 6.20 ● Content-Analytic Summary Table: The Content of Organization Changes				
	Transitory Changes		Durable Changes	
Type of Change	Within the Innovation	In the Organization	Within the Innovation	In the Organization
Structural	Addition of project directors Evolving departments Creation and dropping of advisory committee	Change in locus of control, funding, and supervision	Shift in student input (5) Reorganization: more department interdependence Advisory committee Team teaching	Innovation itself (5): remedial lab, alt. school work experience program, English curriculum, accountability system None (5) Scheduling (4) Expansion of innovation to new users (3) Space for program (2) Creation of coordinator role Creation of management committee Creation of in-service committee Summer-school version of program added Increased team teaching Creation of helping teacher role
Procedural	Active, coercive student recruiting Leadership providing support (emotional, material) Leader "consultation" with teachers Non-users help users with testing Aides, parents help with instruction Increased community contact	Innovation lapsed, is discontinued Field testing of materials Teachers exchange books Other instruction displaced	Tighter supervision, control (2) Student "batching" Routinization of forms/procedures Charismatic leader more distant Fewer staff meetings Reduced student time in program Staff reassignment Selective use of materials	Innovation itself (5): pupil screening, referral/intake, teaming, pullout procedures More paperwork (2) Added student transportation (2) Teacher load reduction Freeing time: substitutes, early dismissal Dropping letter grades More coordination among teachers More teacher discussion of individual students Loss of teacher control over student assignment
Climate	Conflict (4): in teams between users, users-aides, departments More cohesiveness (2), pioneer spirit, esprit User resentment (2) Tension, fear, mistrust	User-non-user conflict (2) User resentment of remedial lab Ambiguity about management committee Expectations for more upward influence, violated, lower morale Resistance by principals, then support	Discouragement, burnout, loss of interest (3) Collaborative, help-giving climate (2) Cohesiveness (2) Less cohesiveness Overload Development of friendships/enmities	Resentment re. paperwork (2) Wariness about innovation More openness to innovation Norm change: flexibility, colleague-ship, el.-sec. interaction None: climate still good None: climate still bad More administrative awareness of the innovation

*Each item represents a change occurring at one site. Changes occurring in more than one site have numbers appended.

Source: Miles, M. B., & Huberman, A. M. (1994). *Qualitative data analysis: An expanded sourcebook* (2nd ed.). Thousand Oaks, CA: Sage Publications.

Sometimes you may want to focus primarily on the *content* of your observations entered in a meta-matrix, without reference to which specific cases it came from. This sort of data entry deliberately drops the case identification of data to see the main trends across the cases. The aim is to be more conceptual rather than site specific.

For initial descriptive matrices, which are often large and complex because of the need to "get it all in," use content-analytic summary tables to clarify your understanding. Then, check back with the larger matrix to make sure you have not oversimplified or distorted your conclusions.

Example

Display 6.20 is an example of a content-analytic summary table from the school improvement study. We (Miles and Huberman) wanted to document two types of changes we observed: transitory and durable. We subdivided each type of change further into two more forms: those seen within the innovation itself and those seen in the organization as a whole.

We subdivided our observations of transitory and durable changes even further into three types of change in rows: structural, procedural, and climate (referring to the social and emotional dynamics of the participants). Each cell contains relevant characteristics we observed at various school sites that were documented in our team's field notes.

Analysis

You can see at a glance the multiple-case activity in any one of the cells by noting the numbers in parentheses. You can also tell how many kinds of organizational changes are within any one type by noting the number of entries in a cell.

For example, transitory changes in structure within the innovation (upper left cell) are not frequent and occur in no more than one case, while transitory climate changes within the innovation (two cells down) are more diverse and show recurrence across several cases (tactics: **making contrasts, comparisons; counting**).

But the picture is somewhat different for durable changes. It looks as if durable changes in the organization (upper cell at far right) are numerous and occurred at multiple sites. A simple eyeballing of the matrix suggests that there are many more durable than transitory changes.

This initial, exploratory assemblage of data helps you understand the structure of the data across all cases at a single glance. It suggests which characteristics, variables, interrelationships, and/or trends may be interesting for analytic follow-up.

Notes

You may, of course, attach initials or a code of some type to, or use a colored font for, each data bit in the matrix that identifies the specific case or site it came from. This will allow you to track or get back to a particular case if you wish for reference and follow-up.

Contrast Table

Description

A contrast table deliberately brings together a representative range—extremes, exemplars, and/or outliers—from cases into one table to explore selected variables of interest among them (see Display 6.21).

DISPLAY 6.21 ● Contrast Table: Summary of Contextual Factors Shaping Political Styles			
Factor	Liberal Arts College	Research University	Regional Public University
Strength of student social ties to campus at large	High	Medium	Low
Description of external campus boundaries	Rigid and enclosed	Semipermeable	Rigid and permeable
Description of internal organizational boundaries	Minimal and nonexclusive	Differentiated and exclusive	Minimal and nonexclusive
Organizational role for members	Contributing to diversity on campus	Family away from home/ identity	Instrumental connections
Political style	Deliberative politics as campus ethos	Politics as a divisive boundary between organizations	Issue-oriented and contentious politics
Latino politics inhabited through . . .	Political talk and event planning	Political talk and event planning exclusively by one organization	Protest

Source: Reyes (2015), p. 307.

Applications

When you're trying to understand the meaning of a general variable, perhaps an important outcome for a study, and how it plays itself out across different cases, the contrast table is a useful exploratory device. It enables you to scan just a few of what may be many cases by examining a sample of the range. Sometimes, juxtaposing the positive with the negative, or the excelling with the failing, generates analytic insights not possible from seeing a wide variable range or a large continuum of cases.

It is important to note that you have to read through all or most cases before you know which cases are representative exemplars of the range. This process also helps you locate their attributes.

Example

Reyes (2015) conducted 60 in-depth interviews and 20 months of ethnographic fieldwork with six Latino student organizations at a liberal arts college, a research university, and a regional public university. Her conceptual framework posited that, to comply with the ideals of multiculturalism and diversity, "postsecondary institutions incorporate Latino students into distinct campus cultures. These cultures influence how students interact with one another, the university community at large, and communities outside of campus, ultimately shaping how students inhabit Latino politics" (p. 302).

Reyes employed a contrast table to log her condensed observations from three different higher education institutions. The first column of Factors in Display 6.21 consists of "contextual factors that influenced Latino students' relationships to the broader campus community and the meaning systems they used to interpret these relationships" in order to examine how these factors "produced a particular organizational culture for Latino student groups that led them to inhabit Latino politics differently" (p. 307). The "Strength of student social ties to campus at large" row contains three magnitude codes: high, medium, and low; the remaining rows include her summarized descriptors of the three college/university settings' factors.

Analysis

The cell entries of Display 6.21 provide the range of observations across three different higher education cases. Each column's six particular factors provide the outline for the researcher's analytic narrative for each site. Reyes concluded that students "expressed unique styles of political expression as they inhabited Latino ethnic politics within the organizational culture of their [particular] schools" (p. 314). As the contrast table suggests,

> Through interactions with the broader campus culture and within Latino organizations, students learn distinct modes of political action to pursue their interests. Students at the wealthiest institution in my study, LAC [Liberal Arts College], learned to express their concerns through deliberation and collegial discourse. Latino students at RU [Research University] focused on divisive interorganizational dynamics, and RPU [Regional Public University] students expressed their concerns through contentious protest. Students were concerned with similar issues regarding Latino politics—namely, education equity and immigration policy—but through interactive processes on campus, they developed different repertoires and cultural styles to communicate those concerns. (pp. 315–316)

By exhibiting unique information about anywhere from two to five cases representing a spectrum of differences, the analyst can explore their particular qualities through comparison but especially through contrast. It is through differences that we come to understand the properties and dimensions of variables, factors, states, and so on. Contrast tables can also be used to display information about *individuals* in addition to sites and larger cases.

Contrast tables often point toward useful variables for a predictor-outcome-consequences matrix (see Chapter 10). For example, based on the findings in Display 6.21, we might hypothesize that a *different* liberal arts college, research university, and regional public university with comparable student demographics might exhibit the same factorial observations listed in the display's respective cells. A new set of representative cases in a new contrast table configuration may confirm this.

Notes

The contrast table brings together a selected and/or extreme range of multiple cases for exploratory analysis. Do not rely solely on this sample as representative of other comparable cases in your study.

Two-Variable Case-Ordered Matrix

Description

A two-variable case-ordered matrix generally orders cases carefully by rows on a well-known variable, then by columns that can include several aspects of a less well-known variable(s) to explore possible interrelationships (see Display 6.22).

Applications

There are times when one portion of a research puzzle has been completed, but another portion still remains a mystery. Or there are times when several cases have been initially grouped together according to some commonality but now need further analysis to see if even more commonalities exist among and between them. A two-variable case-ordered matrix can help with these two particular research needs. This method is also very useful in studying the possible interrelationships between two variables, but where the direction of causation is unknown or ambiguous.

DISPLAY 6.22 ⬡ Two-Variable Case-Ordered Matrix: Relationships Between User Practice Stabilization and Local Continuation

Extent of practice stabilization/Cases	1. End of project year	2. Users' attitudes to continuation*	3. Likelihood of continued use* (Same level or better)	4. Prime factors contributing to high/low likelihood of continuation
High Stabilization				
ASTORIA (E)	1	Positive	High	Project mandated Heavy local transformation for good fit
TINDALE (L)	3	Mostly positive	High	Local mandate well enforced Procedures codified User satisfaction
Moderate-High Stabilization				
CALSTON (E)	2	Mixed*	Low	Budget crisis—staff cuts, reassignments
PERRY-PARKDALE (E)	3	Mostly positive	Uncertain	Staff turnover Uncertain funding
LIDO (E)	4	Mixed⁺	Uncertain	Lower administrative support Lower priority (new facility now available) Users' discouragement
Moderate Stabilization				
BURTON (E)	1	Positive	High	Parts of project written into curriculum Heavy local transformation, good user fit
BANESTOWN (E)	2	Positive	Uncertain	Budget crisis Staff reduced, reassigned
MASEPA (E)	3	Mixed	High	Project mandated Strong logistical support Improved pupil performance
CARSON (L)	3	Mostly positive	High	Procedures codified, routinized Project mandated Widespread local support
PLUMMET (L)	4	Positive	Uncertain	Likely staff turnover Lower district support
Low Stabilization				
DUN HOLLOW (L)	3	Negative	Low	User + principal dissatisfaction No strong local advocate
PROVILLE (L)	4	Negative	Nil	Other central office priorities; no advocate Project discontinued User and principal dissatisfaction

*Researcher assessment, usually pooled from interview data and case report tables

⁺Some wanting to continue, others not

(E) = externally developed innovation

(L) = locally developed innovation

Source: Miles, M. B., & Huberman, A. M. (1994). *Qualitative data analysis: An expanded sourcebook* (2nd ed.). Thousand Oaks, CA: Sage Publications.

Example

Display 6.22 illustrates 12 school cases that have been vertically classified by row according to researcher-perceived practice stabilization, ranging from high, moderate-high, moderate, to low. The rows include the variable that was already investigated and "set"; the columns reflect the variables yet to be explored.

Columns 2 and 3 include additional magnitude codes (positive, mixed, high, uncertain, etc.) attributed to the cases, with column 4 listing primary factors that may contribute to the school's likelihood of program continuance. The analyst wanted to know how "users' attitudes" and the "likelihood of continued use" may interrelate with the "prime factors."

Analysis

This display proved very rich. The analyst scanned the matrix and developed the following excerpted assertions and propositions based on tactical observations:

> Column 2 tells us that in 7 of the 12 cases, users wanted—mostly or unequivocally—to continue (tactic: **counting**). But at only 4 of these sites were their wishes likely to be fulfilled. So, positive user attitudes may enhance but do not deliver a high likelihood of continuation (tactic: **noting relations between variables**). On the other hand, users *not* liking the innovation look like a slightly better predictor. Still, it seems that teacher preferences are not decisive, at least when it comes to insuring continued use at a site.
>
> In the meatiest column, 4, the prime factors are listed in roughly estimated order of magnitude. They come directly from users' responses, pooled. Looking at *uncertain* continuation sites, it seems that we can expect less continuation when most of the people doing it or administering it do not like it, when other key actors do not support it, or when there is heavy external turbulence. If we look for one overarching contributor, it would clearly be lack of sustained *administrator support*, as seen explicitly and through the medium of budget cuts (tactic: **factoring**).

As part of the exploratory process, this analysis also suggested some next steps: a need to unpack the various causes of stabilization more clearly and to analyze the dynamics of the institutionalization process—the next issue beyond simple "continuation."

Notes

The cut-and-paste functions of software enable you to easily explore various orders and configurations of rows and columns. If something does not strike you analytically after reviewing your initial two-variable case-ordered matrix, try a different configuration of rows or columns to see if the new arrangement generates additional connections and insights.

EXPLORING REPORTS IN PROGRESS

The *Prestructured Case* is a template for successive drafts of a report. *Sequential Analyses* show how successive studies build on previous ones to develop cumulative findings.

Prestructured Case

Description

Assuming that the researcher has established an explicit conceptual framework, a rather precise set of research questions, and a clearly defined sampling plan, the prestructured case begins with a case outline, developed *before* any data are collected. The outline will later include detailed data displays, as well as narrative sections accompanying them. The outline is, in effect, a shell for the data to come. Over several rounds of field visits, the researcher fills in successive drafts of the case, revising steadily. The final version of the case is ready shortly after the last field visit (see Display 6.23).

DISPLAY 6.23 ◆ Prestructured Case Outline: Abbreviated Version

A. Beginning note: case methods and data

   I. The context:

      a. The school: an overview
      b. The community context
      c. The school district
      d. The state context (SEA and legislature)
      e. The school: a more detailed picture
      f. Preconditions for change

   II. The improvement program as planned: an overview

   III. Why this program

   IV. The story of planning and implementation

      a. Chronology
      b. The process of planning and implementation
      c. The problems
      d. The assistance provided

         1. Sources, types, and adequacy
         2. Why this assistance?

      e. How problems were dealt with

         1. Managing and coping strategies
         2. Why these strategies?

   V. The program implementation effort

      a. Overall program extent and quality
      b. Prospects for the future
      c. Why implementation occurred as it did

   VI. The results
      a. Interim results
      b. Long-term results

   VII. Why these results?

   VIII. Lessons for improving the urban high school

Source: Miles, M. B., & Huberman, A. M. (1994). *Qualitative data analysis: An expanded sourcebook* (2nd ed.). Thousand Oaks, CA: Sage Publications.

Applications

We've alluded often to the problem of data overload in qualitative studies, which is exacerbated by the time required for processing field notes and for coding. In a study where time is limited and research questions are well specified, the prestructured case is a way to focus and streamline data collection and analyses that are "quick and clean" and will more likely provide trustworthy results. These methods take on more importance in multiple-case studies, where comparability across cases is critical for warranted conclusions.

Example

In a study of reform processes in six urban high schools carried out by a staff of five researchers (Louis & Miles, 1990), the team developed a detailed conceptual framework and a set of 14 detailed research questions, such as the following:

- What barriers, problems, and dilemmas were encountered during planning/initiation and implementation of the school improvement project?

- What management and coping strategies were employed to deal with the barriers/problems/dilemmas?

With the research questions in hand, you can put together a clearly specified outline. Display 6.23 shows an abbreviated form of the one used in the study, with an eye toward a 40-page write-up of the case. The aim is to drive the data collection by the anticipated product (Miles, 1990). That is, the fieldworker, knowing what the final write-up has to look like, collects the data needed to fill the shell. Specific data displays (matrices, networks, graphics) are also formatted in advance.

Because time normally is limited when this method is used, it helps to do advance planning for within-case sampling. For example, for the study's two research questions above, we wanted a good sample of the following:

- *Key actors:* people in coordinative positions

- *Key events:* meetings where problem solving and coordination occur

- *Core processes:* problems encountered during initiation, as well as early and later implementation, and coping strategies from a wide range of affected roles (teachers, building administrators, and central office personnel)

Analysis

With the outline clearly in mind, the researcher begins the first round of data collection. The raw field notes are coded without being transformed into write-ups. The researcher reviews the coded field notes, enters data directly into displays, and writes accompanying analytic text—that is, the tentative conclusions drawn from the displayed data. There will be instances of missing or unclear data, and of unanswered research questions; these provide the targets for the next round of data collection. Early versions of the case outline can be limited to descriptive material, "reflective remarks," and a subsection on "puzzles and unanswered questions" in each chapter of the case.

This procedure is iterated until data collection and the completed case are done. Thus, the processes of data collection, analysis, and report writing are condensed into one evolving procedure. With some experience, the researcher has a constant sense of being on top of the data and remains open to checking and extending findings. Feedback from study participants can be sought and incorporated along the way to verify and revise preliminary conclusions.

Display 6.24 shows how this analytic sequence differs from a more traditional one. Both are iterative, but the field work in the prestructured case is driven by the outline, as well as the emerging conclusions, and the report draft itself.

Notes

This method should not be used by inexperienced fieldworkers or by those unfamiliar with the type of setting being studied. Nor should it be used if the conceptual framework and research questions

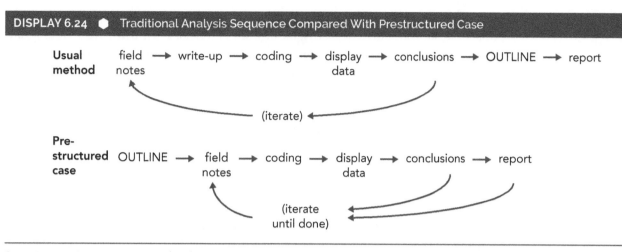

DISPLAY 6.24 ● Traditional Analysis Sequence Compared With Prestructured Case

Usual method field notes → write-up → coding → display data → conclusions → OUTLINE → report

(iterate)

Pre-structured case OUTLINE → field notes → coding → display data → conclusions → report

(iterate until done)

Source: Miles, M. B., & Huberman, A. M. (1994). *Qualitative data analysis: An expanded sourcebook* (2nd ed.). Thousand Oaks, CA: Sage Publications.

are not well spelled out. The prestructured case method can steer the researcher toward early—maybe too early—conclusion drawing.

For experienced, knowledgeable researchers, we advise corrective tactics such as the following: (a) using a pair of researchers for case development to ward off potential difficulties discussed above; (b) ensuring wide data sampling from a range of participants and settings; and (c) **triangulating** (see Chapter 11) with different data collection methods, theories, or respondents.

Sequential Analyses

Description

A sequential analysis is not necessarily a specific set of methods, but an intentional iteration of additional data collection and *reanalysis* to ensure a more robust set of findings, and/or to build on the first cycle of interim findings for future research. Each wave of data collection leads to progressively more "big picture" clustering and analysis.

Applications

A single interim analysis is rarely "enough." The first interim analysis should not only point to improved data collection but also lead to successively deeper, fuller waves of analysis by swinging back to coding, memoing, and assertion and proposition development as more detailed, better quality data become available, and your cognitive network of the case gets richer and more nuanced.

It's easy to fall into the trap of premature closure, a feeling of "rightness" that is grounded falsely—especially because early data collection is usually partial, flawed, and simplistic in some important respects. A good interim analysis is one that helps us reorient our view of the case. And any interim analysis should be the first of several. Their strength is their exploratory, summarizing, and sense-making character. Their potential weaknesses are superficiality, premature closure, and faulty data. These weaknesses may be avoided through intelligent critique from skeptical colleagues, feeding back into subsequent waves of data collection.

Example

McVea (2001) and a team of research colleagues conducted a series of separate qualitative studies over a 4-year period that examined adolescent tobacco use. Each annual study not only informed but also provided additional research questions for the next year's project. Their first exploratory study investigated teenage smoking at one particular high school site. McVea reported that "despite the presence of written tobacco policies, the high school was not a 'safe haven' from smoking pressures. . . . The results from our first study raised an interesting question: Why didn't schools enforce their no smoking policies?" (n.p.). The research team's next annual project explored that question.

Analysis

McVea and colleagues' second study was driven by the most puzzling observation generated from the first study's fieldwork: Why didn't schools enforce their no smoking policies? The team interviewed adolescents and adults and reported:

> We discovered that administrators found rules difficult to enforce because of the large number of smokers, and the significant resources required to police their behavior. Teachers were concerned that students driving off campus to smoke caused them to miss class, and they feared punitive penalties caused more harm than tobacco use. Students interpreted the lack of enforcement as evidence that the faculty "didn't care" about smoking. Smoking students even commented about how the ability to smoke at school with friends contributed to their habit. (n.p.)

Armed with these findings, the third and next set of annual studies explored how smoking cessation programs could be implemented with teenagers. The research team discovered that peer relationships and influence play a strong role in whether an adolescent could or would stop smoking. Each year's study informed the next and enabled richer analyses and evaluation, plus constructive strategies for positive action and outcomes.

The example above was a broad brushstroke case of sequential analysis. As another and more specific example, a Belgian study of primary health care (Schillemans et al., n.d.) focused on treatment of victims of incest. The researchers began with a group of 10 to 15 medical practitioners, meeting in a weekly "exploration group" for 2 years. Here are their successive analytic steps:

1. Review the material from the first patient case (videotapes, documents, notes).

2. Generate a first batch of codes from the case review, such as "fear of the dark," "speech difficulties," "aversion to sexuality."

3. Add more clinical codes from the specialized literature, such as "boundary between man and woman" and "violence."

4. Examine further cases and develop more codes through analytic induction.

5. Develop a key hypothesis (e.g., that incest victims have weakly developed boundaries).

6. Verify the hypothesis through interviews with several patients from the original set.

7. Integrate these findings with the existing empirical and conceptual literature (e.g., on dissociated personalities).

8. Extend the findings to a new sample (screening new cases for instances of incest) and a new analytic cycle.

Each step was a funnel for gathering more data on fewer, but progressively more vital, dimensions in the data set.

Overall, sequential analyses value-add to the cumulative and final written product. The procedure lends more confidence to the researcher's findings in progress and provides dimensionality to the data corpus, thus better guaranteeing a richer analysis of details, nuances, and complexities.

Notes

See "Elaborative Coding" and "Longitudinal Coding" in Saldaña (2016) for additional methods of how sequential studies build on previous ones and inform the next series.

CLOSURE AND TRANSITION

These exploratory methods are offered as initial ways of documenting and reassembling salient data into various display formats for the emergent enterprise that is qualitative inquiry. These methods alone, with a little bit of fine-tuning on your part, may even suffice for your particular research goals. They are offered as "first-draft" heuristics for extracting what is important, synthesizing and summarizing the most important details, reorganizing data to construct meaningful patterns from them, and laying the groundwork for more in-depth analyses.

The next chapter, Methods of Describing, will present displays that more firmly rather than provisionally document the data. They are intended to provide, like Methods of Exploring, foundations for richer analysis such as ordering, explaining, and predicting.

METHODS OF DESCRIBING

CHAPTER SUMMARY

This chapter illustrates methods for organizing condensed qualitative data, from highly systematic to artistically rendered ways, for purposes of descriptive documentation. The descriptive profiles focus on describing participants, variability, and social action.

CONTENTS

INTRODUCTION

Wolcott (1994) advocates that description is qualitative representation that helps the reader see what you saw and hear what you heard. A solid, descriptive foundation of your data enables higher level analysis and interpretation. Usually, it is hard to explain the "hows" and "whys" of something satisfactorily until you understand just *what* that something is.

You begin with a text, trying out codes on it, then moving to identify patterns, categories, or themes, to develop assertions and propositions, to test hypotheses, and then to integrate the data into an explanatory framework—that is, theory. In this sense, we can speak of data transformation as information that is condensed, clustered, sorted, and linked over time. The researcher typically moves through a series of analysis episodes that condenses more and more data into a more and more coherent understanding of *what*—building a solid foundation for later analyzing how and why (Wolcott, 1994).

Describing Participants looks at the relationship dynamics of the people you study. *Describing Variability* charts the spectrum and landscape of what we're finding in the field. And *Describing Action* documents the experiences and processes of our participants from systematic to artistically rendered ways.

DESCRIBING PARTICIPANTS

The *Demographics and Attributes Table* assembles pertinent descriptive participant information. A *Role-Ordered Matrix* charts the essential characteristics relevant to the study about various participants. A *Context Chart* illustrates the hierarchies and interrelationships within, between, and among the participants. And a *Positionality Graphic* illustrates the participants' "place" in social or conceptual space.

Demographics and Attributes Table

Description

A demographics and attributes table lists salient research-related descriptors of participants' social categories such as age/grade level, gender, socioeconomic status, race/ethnicity, sexual orientation, educational attainment, and other categories considered relevant to the study (see Display 7.1).

DISPLAY 7.1 ⬡ Participant Family Profiles					
Case Number	Participant Relationships	Age	Post-Katrina Employment Status	Emic Racial Identifiers	Emic Social Class Identifiers
1	Fiancées	Male – 38 Female – 26	Male – Part-time Female – Unemployed	Male – "Creole-American"/"White" Female – "White"	"Poor Working Class"
2	Married couple	Male – 43 Female – 44	Male & Female – Unemployed	Male & Female – "African American"	"The Blessed – but Poor – Class"
3	Boyfriend/girlfriend	Male – 20 Female – 26	Male – Part-time Female – Part-time	Male & Female – "White"	"Lower Class"
4	"Best friend roommates"	Male – 33 Female – 39	Male – Unemployed Female – Full-time	Male & Female – "White"	Male – "Low Class" Female – "Doing Good Class"
5	Married couple	Male – 35 Female – 36	Male & Female – Full-time	Male & Female – "Caucasian"	"Middle Class"
6	Aunt and niece	Aunt – 55 Niece – 34	Aunt & Niece – Full-time	Aunt & Niece – "Black"	"Working Lower Middle Class"
7	Married couple	Male – 55 Female – 45	Male – Unemployed Female – Full-time	Male – "Black-Korean"/"Black" Female – "American"/"Black"	"Low Class"

Source: Godwin, Foster, & Keefe (2013), p. 18.

Applications

Virtually all studies with multiple participants and/or sites benefit from a tabular display of participant demographics and attributes. It exhibits an at-a-glance assessment of social representation in the project and permits the addition of columns and/or rows of participant-related data such as key quotes, researcher-assigned magnitude codes or brief narratives, and other study-related data.

Example

Godwin, Foster, and Keefe (2013) interviewed seven families living in the metropolitan New Orleans area after the August 2005 Hurricane Katrina disaster in the region. The coresearchers focused on marginalized family systems and how social class may have influenced the family's recovery process. Previous research indicated a strong relationship between socioeconomic status and postdisaster stress levels, but "researchers have yet to examine the way in which this hurricane has impacted family systems, the impact for those families beyond the initial postdisaster time frame, or the way in which social class status has shaped family meaning making in recovery" (p. 16).

The coresearchers assembled a family profiles table, and Display 7.1 contains not only traditional descriptive information such as relationship status, gender, age, and employment status, but also emic racial and social class identifiers provided by the participants themselves.

Analysis

Godwin et al. (2013) adopted a constructivist, "emancipatory paradigm" as part of their conceptual framework for the study. Rather than applying standardized sociological terminology to describe the participants' race and class (e.g., African American, lower middle class), the coresearchers asked participants to describe their own (emic) perceptions of these social constructs ("Creole-American," "The Blessed—but Poor—Class"). "By listening with a careful ear to the words that participants use to describe their unique but connected unfolding narratives, professionals working with families impacted by natural disasters can reconceptualize the way in which treatment methodologies can be applied" (p. 16). The coresearchers also coded the interview data using In Vivo themes ("Money Is Useless in a City Under Water," "Working Our Tails Off to Get What We Need") to keep their analysis embedded in the participants' worldview.

Demographics and attributes tables should not just describe but *inform* the analysis. The table includes, of course, what might be considered conventional entries (age, gender, etc.) for documentation purposes. But eyeballing the table's entries with data unique to the particular study can extend the researcher's inference-making. There may be, for example, relationships between participants' ages and the types of responses they provided, or subtle differences between men's and women's data, meriting further analysis.

Notes

Descriptive statistics can also be applied to demographic and attribute tables to include data such as mean age; percentages of respondents in selected categories; and inclusion/exclusion indicators, ratings, and magnitude codes (e.g., "yes," "no," "high," "low," "4," "2"). Bringing words and numbers together in a single table enriches the data array and interpretations.

Role-Ordered Matrix

Description

A role-ordered matrix sorts data in its rows and columns that have been gathered from or about a certain set of "role occupants"—data reflecting their views. The display systematically permits comparisons across roles on issues of interest to a study, and tests whether people in the same role see issues in comparable ways (see Display 7.2).

DISPLAY 7.2 ● Role-Ordered Matrix: First Reactions to the Innovation

TEACHERS	Salient Characteristics	Size Up	Anticipated Classroom or Organizational Changes @	Fit With Previous Style or Organizational Setting @@
+ REILLY 4th year	Highly structured	Little latitude	DK-1	DK-3
+ KENNEDY 4th year	Frightening format Overload of objectives Reams of handouts	Difficult, complicated No latitude	Teaming (loss of independence) No Scope Magazine use	Poor; user felt she would be locked into structure and others' schedules
+ FARR 1st year	Skill-oriented, organized Activities well planned Pre- & posttesting good	Simple, clear Easy to use & understand	Less freedom to change direction	Fairly good; user views self as structured, organized
+ ROGERS 2nd year	Prescriptive Rigid	Confusing Simplistic content	Working with basic students for 1st time	Composition assignments fit well; grammar, etc. simple-minded
+ FLEMING 4th year	Prescriptive Use of media Teaming Heavy monitoring	Many materials Very complex, not quite clear	Working w/ other Ts Mastering all materials	DK-2
* BENNING 1st year	Objectives too broad Good content	Similar to prev. school's program, easy to use	Break down objectives Add games, activities Give objectives to kids	Close fit, when anticipated changes made
* THATCHER 2nd year	(wrote science curriculum) Skill-oriented Reading emphasis	Too detailed	DK-1	Fair; reading was new; fewer labs
# WOJICK 1st year	Variety of modes (workbooks, worksheets, computer terminals)	Easy to use; level & format right	DK-1	DK-2
# MUSKIE 2nd year	Computer terminals Short worksheets	1st 1/2 flawed; 2nd 1/2 on target Good variety	DK-1	DK-1

	Salient Characteristics	Size Up	Anticipated Classroom or Organizational Changes @	Fit With Previous Style or Organizational Setting @@
DEPT. CHAIRS VAN RUNKEL Science Chrmn	Science content revision Reading reinforcement Flexibility in activities	Questioned content reorg'n would it fit together?	None—same teachers, using new curriculum	Good fit: Program replaced old curriculum
MANNHOELLER English Chrmn	Orderly curriculum w/ horizontal, vertical org'n Reinforcement of 3 strands	Concept is right Depends on being used as it's set up	DK-1	Good fit: Program designed in part to fill basic English course slot
PRINCIPAL MCCARTHY Tindale East	DK-2	DK-2	DK-2	Good fit: Order is maintained; no special requirements
CENTRAL OFFICE CROWDEN Dir of Curriculum	3 strands of level I Sequential, comprehensive Reinforcement	Works if followed Any teacher can use successfully	None—program designed to fit structure	Close fit: same staff, teachers wrote curriculum, same auth. structure
MANN Superintendent	DK-2	DK-2	DK-1	Good fit: Program is a successful curriculum revision effort in district

+ = English teacher
* = science teacher
# = math teacher
DK = Don't know
DK-1 = question not asked of informant
DK-2 = asked, but not answered (strayed from question, didn't know answer)
DK-3 = ambiguous answer
@ Classroom changes question asked of teachers; organizational one asked of others.
@@ Personal style fit question asked of teachers; organizational fit question asked of others.

Source: Miles, M. B., & Huberman, A. M. (1994). *Qualitative data analysis: An expanded sourcebook* (2nd ed.). Thousand Oaks, CA: Sage Publications.

Applications

People who live in groups and organizations and social scientists who study them know that how you see life depends, in part, on your role. A *role* is a complex amalgam of expectations and actions that make up what you do, and should do, as a certain type of actor in a setting—a family, a classroom, a committee, a hospital, a police department, or a multinational corporation.

A role-ordered matrix groups, summarizes, and compares different people's role perceptions about selected topics or issues that enable the researcher to compare and contrast those perceptions. For example, mothers tend to see the world differently than fathers. Bosses tend not to see the frustrations faced by workers, partly because they are distant from them. We each experience the world differently, and a role-ordered matrix is just one way of documenting those varied experiences.

Example

We (Miles and Huberman) draw on our school improvement study for an example. The innovation involved is an intensive remedial high school program emphasizing reading in the subjects of English, science, and math. The question of interest is, "How do people react to an innovation when they first encounter it?" This general question can be unbundled into several subquestions, such as the following:

- Which aspects of the innovation are salient/stand out in people's minds?

- How do people size up the innovation in relation to its eventual implementation?

- What changes—at the classroom or organizational level—do people think the innovation will require?

- How good a fit is the innovation to people's previous classroom styles, or to previous organizational working arrangements?

Keeping in mind that we want to see answers to these questions broken out by different roles, we can consider which roles—for example, teachers, department chairs, principals, and central office personnel—could be expected to attend to the innovation and could provide meaningful reactions to it. The matrix rows could be roles, but if we want to make within-role comparisons, the rows should probably be *persons*, clustered into *role domains*. It might be good, too, to order the roles according to how far they are from the actual locus of the innovation—from teachers to central office administrators. The columns can be devoted to the research subquestions. Display 7.2 shows what this approach looks like.

The data entered in each cell is a brief summary of what the analyst found for each respondent. There are also "DK" ("don't know") entries where data are missing because the relevant question was never asked of that person, was asked but not answered, or was answered ambiguously.

Analysis

Now, we can begin looking down columns of the matrix, both within and across roles, to see what is happening. Scanning the first two columns (Salient Characteristics and Size Up) shows us that many teachers—notably in English—see the new remedial program as *prescriptive*, with little latitude given for adaptation (tactics: **counting** and **making comparisons**). And the teachers who see the innovation as prescriptive are also those who have used it the longest, suggesting that prescriptiveness was highest when the program was first introduced (tactic: **noting relations between**

variables). A number of teachers also mention *complexity* (but note that first-year users are more likely to see the program as simple and easy to use, suggesting program stabilization).

When we drop down to department chairs and central office administrators, the picture is somewhat different. They are more likely to take the "big picture" view, emphasizing the "curriculum," "strands," and the like. Although they, too, emphasize prescriptiveness ("Depends on being used as it's set up" or "Works if followed"), they either do not give clear answers on the issue of complexity or (as in the case of the curriculum director, a major advocate of the program) say that "any teacher can use [it] successfully." But teachers, faced with an initially demanding, rigid program, are not so sure, it seems (tactic: **making comparisons**).

Moving to the third column (Anticipated Classroom or Organizational Changes) of Display 7.2, we can see role-perspective differences. Two teachers mention teaming as an anticipated change, one that curtailed their freedom and made them accountable to peers' schedules and working styles. Administrators considered the teaming necessary to implement the program's several strands, and as a way of helping weaker teachers do better through learning from stronger ones. Even so, they do not consider it a salient change, saying either that no organizational changes are required ("the program is designed to fit the structure") or that they do not know whether organizational changes were anticipated.

Finally, if we continue the **making comparisons** tactic, the fourth column (Fit With Previous Style or Organizational Setting) shows a range of "personal fit" for different teachers, depending on their views of the content, their own styles, and the organizational issues involved. The administrators, however, uniformly emphasize good fit at the organizational level, stressing the appropriateness of the curriculum and its fit into the existing structure.

In short, a matrix of this sort lets us see how perspectives differ according *to role*, as well as *within role*. In this case, users from the English department who came in at the onset of the program had an initially tougher time than later users or than math and science users. A within-role analysis, moving across rows, shows that the superintendent and principal know very little about the innovation. Looking vertically, we can see that department chairs' views are much more like those of central office administrators than those of teachers.

Clarify the list of roles you consider to be most relevant to the issue at hand. Differentiate the matrix by subroles (e.g., teachers of math or science) if relevant. If your case is an individual, role-ordered matrices may well be helpful in showing how role partners view or interact with the person at the center of your case.

Notes

Indicate clearly when data are missing, unclear, or not asked for in the first place, and return to field notes or collect additional data to test emerging conclusions. Role-ordered matrices, because of our prior experience with role differences, can lend themselves to too-quick conclusion drawing. Ask for an audit of your analysis from a colleague (see Chapter 11).

Context Chart

Description

A context chart is a network, mapping in graphic form the interrelationships among the roles and groups (and, if appropriate, organizations) that make up the contexts of individual actions (see Display 7.3).

DISPLAY 7.3 ● Context Chart for Tindale East High School and District

STUDENTS IN PROGRAM

Legend

+ ± 0   within boxes: attitude to the innovation

+ ± 0   between boxes: character of the relationship

       high influence over adoption/implementation

*

Ⓘ   innovation advocate or champion

DK   unknown to analyst

Source: Miles, M. B., & Huberman, A. M. (1994). *Qualitative data analysis: An expanded sourcebook* (2nd ed.). Thousand Oaks, CA: Sage Publications.

Applications

A context chart maps the social contexts of individual actors and actions economically without getting overwhelmed with detail. Context charts work particularly well when your case is an individual—they show you the real richness of a person's life setting.

Most people do their daily work in organizations of some kind: They have superiors, peers, and subordinates; their work is defined in a role-specialized way; and they have different relationships with different people in other roles in their social vicinity. But you are not simply drawing a standard organizational chart; you are mapping salient properties of the social context. Also, your chart will not be exhaustive or complete. It is a collection of organizational fragments or excerpts. (In Display 7.3, custodians, administrative assistants, and the immediate subordinates of most of the school district office personnel are excluded.) Context charts also can be drawn for people in families or in informal groups or communities.

A person's actions have to be understood in their specific contexts—that is, immediately relevant aspects of the situation (where the person is physically, who else is involved, what the recent history of the contact is, etc.), as well as the relevant aspects of the social system in which the person appears (a classroom, a school, a department, a company, a family, a hospital ward, or a local community). Focusing solely on individual actions without attending to their contexts runs the risk of misunderstanding the meanings of events. Contexts drive the way we understand those meanings.

Example

Networks ought to reflect the core characteristics of organizations: authority/hierarchy and division of labor. So, it ought to show who has formal authority over whom and what the role names are. But those things don't tell us very much. We should also know about the *quality* of the working *relationships* between people in different roles.

We (Miles and Huberman) constructed a network display that showed us who advocated an educational innovation, who was actually using the innovation, and people's attitudes toward it. Display 7.3 was created after a fieldworker made a first visit to Tindale East, a high school involved in implementing a new reading program. The analyst selected out the roles and groups that were most critical for understanding the context. District office roles are above, school roles below. The network is thus partially ordered by roles and authority level.

For each individual, we have a name; age (a feature the analyst thought was important in understanding working relationships and career aspirations); a job title; whether the individual was a user of the innovation or not; and his or her attitude toward the innovation, which was represented through magnitude codes:

+ = positive

± = ambivalent

0 = neutral

Special symbols (such as *) were applied when the individual was an innovation advocate or influenced implementation strongly. The relationships between individuals were also characterized (positive, ambivalent, and neutral). Once past the upper echelons, the display simply counts individuals without giving detail.

To get the data, the analyst consulted field notes, available organization charts, and documents. The "innovation advocate" and "high influence" ratings were given only if there was at least one confirmation and no disconfirmations. If there was ambiguous or unknown information, we entered "DK" ("don't know").

Analysis

After a context chart has been constructed, the researcher reviews the hierarchies, flows, and magnitudes entered, in combination with field notes, to develop an analytic memo or narrative that tells the relationship story thus far. An analytic excerpt about Display 7.3 reads as follows:

> Looking at lines of authority, we can see that only one central office person (Crowden) has direct authority over department chairs as they work on the innovation. Crowden is not only an advocate but also has high influence over implementation, and seems to have a license from the superintendent to do this.
>
> The department chairs, it appears, have three other "masters," depending on the immediate issue involved (discipline, teacher evaluation, scheduling). Because, in this case, the innovation does involve scheduling problems, it's of interest that V. Havelock is not only an advocate but has actually used the innovation and is positive toward it. We might draw the inference that Crowden serves as a general pusher, using central office authority, and V. Havelock aids directly with implementation issues; the field notes support this.
>
> Note, too, that Principal McCarthy (a) is not accountable to the superintendent for curriculum issues and (b) has a good relationship with V. Havelock. Perhaps McCarthy gets his main information about the innovation from Havelock and thus judges it positively.

So, the chart shown in Display 7.3 helps us place the actions of individuals (e.g., Crowden, V. Havelock) in context to understand their meaning. For example, when Crowden, discussing the innovation, says, "It is not to be violated; its implementation is not based on the whim of a teacher at any moment in class," the chart helps us understand that this prescriptive stance is backed up with direct authority over department chairs for curriculum issues.

The symbols employed for Display 7.3 were Miles and Huberman's original magnitude codes, but you are not bound to using them. Context charts can employ other visual devices to enhance analysis. For example, dashed lines can be used to show informal influence, while thick lines suggest strong influence. Font size can be used to represent power dynamics—for example, names in a larger or bolded font have more authority than names in a smaller font. Circles can be drawn enclosing informal small groups and subcultures. And for an organizational context that seems to change a lot over time, revised context charts can be drawn for comparison across time.

Notes

Use context charts early during fieldwork to summarize your first understandings and to locate questions for next-step data collection. Keep the study's main research questions in mind, and design the context chart to display the information most relevant to them. Keep your first context charts simple; they can be embroidered as you continue field work.

Positionality Graphic

Description

A positionality graphic illustrates participants or cases in appropriate spatial relationships according to researcher-established criteria or conditions. It is a qualitatively derived sociogram, of sorts, that maps inferred locations or positions within a specified domain(s) of interest (see Display 7.4).

Applications

Networks can, to a large degree, illustrate case relationships and the magnitude of variables through some creative design choices and strategic layout on the part of the researcher. But there are times

DISPLAY 7.4 ◑ Predominant Response Types of Cases

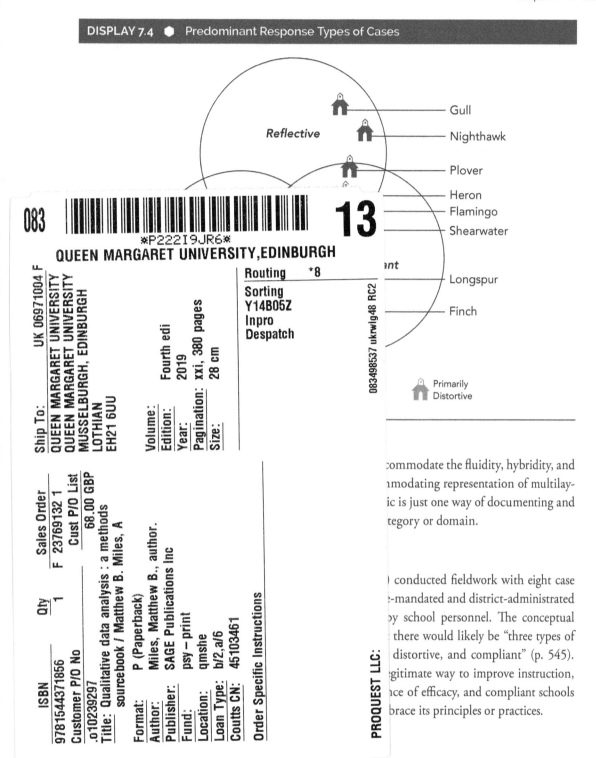

Reflective

Gull

Nighthawk

Plover

Heron
Flamingo
Shearwater

Longspur

Finch

Primarily
Distortive

...commodate the fluidity, hybridity, and ...mmodating representation of multilay-...ic is just one way of documenting and ...tegory or domain.

...) conducted fieldwork with eight case ...e-mandated and district-administered ...by school personnel. The conceptual ...there would likely be "three types of ...distortive, and compliant" (p. 545). ...gitimate way to improve instruction, ...ce of efficacy, and compliant schools ...brace its principles or practices.

The coresearchers utilized various matrices and meta-matrices described in this sourcebook for their within-case and cross-case data analyses of the eight schools, but the two-dimensional format and boundaries of individual cells could not accommodate a unique finding:

> While we began analysis by conceptualizing responses along a continuum, our analyses demonstrated that schools, individuals, and even statements might demonstrate more than one response type. As opposed to mutually exclusive categories, these responses often overlapped and many schools exhibited more than one type, for example, demonstrating a degree of reflection while utilizing some distortive practices. (Marsh et al., 2017, p. 549)

Thus, the positionality graphic of Display 7.4 shows the coresearchers' approximate placement of the eight schools within the Venn diagram of the three policy response types. They also added a third "dimension" to the graphic by using three shades of gray to further illustrate which schools fell within which response areas.

Positionality graphics require two things: participants or cases, and a domain(s) of interest—the geographic or conceptual space or spaces where the cases reside. Relationships between and among the cases can also be plotted using spatial scale—that is, how close or how far they are from one another, and how embedded or how peripheral they are from/within the domain. Unlike formal sociograms, which rely on statistical operations to plot case and variable relationships, positionality graphics model the qualitative researcher's visual interpretation of the human landscape based on field note data.

Notes

Use positionality graphics after constructing or in conjunction with a Role-Ordered Matrix or Context Chart (in this chapter) to add dimension to the data.

DESCRIBING VARIABILITY

A *Concept Table* shows the variability or range of a central concept in a study. A *Conceptually Clustered Matrix* charts participants' varying perspectives about selected concepts. A *Folk Taxonomy* systematically charts the unique ways in which participants organize and categorize their worlds. And a *Thematic Array* graphically illustrates the major findings of a study.

Concept Table

Description

A concept table includes data that highlight the variable properties and/or dimensions of one key concept (or variable, category, theme, etc.) of interest from a study (see Display 7.5).

Applications

Concept tables are particularly valuable for qualitative surveys, grounded theory, and phenomenological studies since they enable an analyst to focus on one core item of interest (a key concept, major variable, core category, central phenomenon, etc.). Traditional grounded theory charges the researcher to examine the *dimensions* or variable ranges of a property, and a concept table assembles that variability for analytic reflection.

Although you may have a general idea in advance about the properties and dimensions of some major variable, such as "lifelong impact," such conceptual variables do not usually become clear until real case data have been explored in some depth. Cross-case concept tables are an excellent way to bring together and examine a core concept, because the way the variable plays out in different contexts illuminates its nature.

Example

McCammon et al. (2012) surveyed 234 adults by e-mail to gather their perceptions of how their participation in high school theatre and speech programming may have influenced and affected their adult life course trajectories. There were certainly influences on careers, since approximately half of the respondents currently worked in the entertainment industries. The other half pursued careers in fields ranging from business to education to health care but still looked back fondly on their high school theatre and speech activities. The vast majority acknowledged a lifelong impact

DISPLAY 7.5 ● Lifelong Impact: Variability of Influence				
Lifelong Impact	**Supporting Respondent Quotes**	**Gender**	**Class of**	**Occupation**
None	"It really has not changed my adult life at all."	male	1982	Quality Manager for a Manufacturing Company
Little to none	"Although I don't feel like being involved in theatre has changed my life, it definitely changed my high school experience. It was something I worked hard at, enjoyed, and looked forward to."	female	2006	High School English Teacher
Some, in combination	"Any career success I've experienced is largely due to the combination of process thinking developed in engineering school and, more significantly, my theatre, speech and debate experience in high school. I learned to communicate effectively, write well, speak clearly and distinctly, engage and hold an audience with pacing, inflection, movement, etc."	female	1984	Global Leader for Distribution and Sales Force Effectiveness [for a major corporation]
High	"My high school speech coach/drama teacher is one of the main influences in my life. She taught me much and helped me grow in ways that I am profoundly grateful for. Were it not for her guidance, I think my life would probably be much different today."	male	1999	Internet Strategy Consultant
Very high	"Theatre and speech saved mine and my brother's lives."	male	1999	Hollywood Sound Effects and Dialogue Editor

from arts participation during their high school years, yet not everyone testified that the impact was comparable. *Variability* in the amount and quality of lifelong impact was observed, and it needed to be documented and acknowledged for a more credible and trustworthy analysis.

Display 7.5 is a table that includes salient data about the concept *Lifelong Impact*. The variability of the concept is illustrated through five selected respondent quotes, including the participants' genders, graduation years from high school, and current occupations, since these were deemed potentially important variables for later analysis. The researcher-assigned assessments of Lifelong Impact range from "none" ("It really has not changed my adult life at all") to "very high" ("Theatre and speech saved mine and my brother's lives").

Analysis

The concept table is a case study of sorts. It contains representative data about one important element in your study that merits enhanced analysis. The variability of that element challenges the researcher to ponder questions such as the following:

- *Why* does variability exist in these data?

- What specific *conditions* might have influenced the variability?

- In what ways might this variability *influence and affect* other outcomes and consequences?

These questions are particularly important for grounded theory studies.

The following analytic narrative was developed to explain the variability of Lifelong Impact. The final two sentences of the excerpt further down preface the analytic findings to emphasize the *conditionality* of participation in high school speech and theatre programming. The researchers did not want to sweepingly suggest that arts education is a magic bullet for social ills and human development, but that meaningful lifelong impact is contingent on several factors such as an outstanding teacher, challenging classroom content, high expectations of artistic quality, and others:

> These five participant responses highlight the *variability* of lifelong impact. The first and second quotes suggest that high school theatre is not necessarily an epiphanic or life-changing experience for everyone, but it can, as the second quote illustrates, function as an important program for adolescent enrichment and engagement. The third quote suggests theatre and/or speech experiences alone, in and of themselves, cannot be solely credited with generating a successful adult career for those who choose nontheatrical professions. The fourth quote suggests that a teacher in the field can have a significant influence on a student during his adolescent development, which may in turn significantly affect his adult life course. And the fifth quote suggests that the art form, guided by a nurturing teacher, can literally and powerfully influence and even save a human life.
>
> We cannot assert that immersed participation in high school theatre or speech programming will benefit everyone to the same degree as they progress through the adult life course. But survey responses collectively suggest a set of *ideal* conditions to maximize the *potential* of lifelong impact. (adapted from McCammon & Saldaña, 2011, p. 92)

Further analysis revealed that high school graduation year—that is, the respondents' generational cohorts—played a significant role in the way memories were recalled and perceived. Gender and current occupation played a less important role in survey patterns.

Scanning the concept table (and reviewing related portions of the database as needed) enables you to see the range and thus the parameters of your data. This keeps you from constructing too narrow an assertion about your observations and helps you modify your interpretive claims to be more inclusive of the breadth of findings from your data.

Notes

Keep a concept table short and sweet. Its primary goal is to focus on the variability of *one* item of interest in a study through a sample of representative data. See the Role-Ordered Matrix and Conceptually Clustered Matrix displays (in this chapter) for formats that contain much more data for interrelationship analysis.

Conceptually Clustered Matrix

Description

A conceptually clustered matrix has its rows and columns arranged to bring together major roles, research subtopics, variables, concepts, and/or themes for at-a-glance summative documentation and analysis. Deciding what composes a row and column heading can happen in two ways: *deductively*, when the analyst may have some a priori ideas about key concepts, themes, or theories that will be explored in a study; or *inductively*, when, during early analysis, you may find that participants are giving very similar or vastly different responses to questions, or that unexpected variables, concepts, and themes are emerging. The basic principle is conceptual or thematic documentation of data in matrix cells, which may or may not be accompanied with researcher-assigned evaluative descriptors (see Displays 7.6 and 7.7).

DISPLAY 7.6 ● Conceptually Clustered Matrix: Motives and Attitudes (Format)				
	Research Questions			
Participants	**Motives (types)**	**Career Relevance (none/some)**	**Centrality (low/mod /high)**	**Initial Attitudes (fav., neutr., unfav.)**
Users U$_1$				
U$_2$, etc.				
Administrators A$_1$				
A$_2$, etc.				

Source: Miles, M. B., & Huberman, A. M. (1994). *Qualitative data analysis: An expanded sourcebook* (2nd ed.). Thousand Oaks, CA: Sage Publications.

Applications

Many studies are designed to answer a lengthy string of research questions. As a result, doing a separate analysis and case report section for each research question is likely to tire out and confuse both the analyst and reader. One solution is to cluster several research questions so that meaning can be generated more easily. Having all of the data in one surveyable place helps you move quickly and legitimately to a condensed matrix by making sure that all the data fit into a reasonable scheme, and that any evaluations or ratings you make are well-founded.

Conceptually clustered matrices are most helpful when some clear concepts or themes have emerged from initial analysis. They also can be used with less complex cases, such as individuals or small groups.

Example

In our (Miles and Huberman) school improvement study, we had a general question about users' and administrators' *motives* for adopting a new educational practice, and a more specific question about whether these motives were *career centered* (e.g., whether participants thought they could get a promotion or a transfer out of the project). So here we had an a priori idea of a possible relationship between two concepts. Then, during data collection, we saw some inkling of a relationship between the motives questions and two others: a *centrality* question (whether the innovation loomed larger than other tasks in the daily life of a user) and an *attitude* question (whether the participant liked the new practice when first introduced to it). We wondered whether a relationship existed between people's motives and their initial attitudes toward the practice.

The best way to find out would be to *cluster* the responses to these questions. Not only is there a relationship to probe, but there is also a general theme (initial attitudes) and a possibility of handling three research questions and their concepts at the same time.

The conceptually clustered matrix is a format that

- displays all of the relevant responses of all key participants on one page;
- allows an initial comparison between responses and between participants;
- lets us see how the data can be analyzed further (e.g., repartitioned or clustered);
- for multi-case studies, lends itself easily to cross-case analysis; and
- for multi-case studies, provides some preliminary standardization—a set of content-analytic themes that all case analysts will be using.

When you are handling several conceptually or thematically related research questions together, a likely start-up format is a simple participant-by-variable matrix, as shown in Display 7.6. Thus, we have on one page a format that includes all respondents and all responses to the research questions (i.e., the concepts of interest in this study). Note that we have set up comparisons between different kinds of participants (users and administrators), so it is role ordered as well as conceptually ordered. The format also calls for some preliminary sorting or scaling of the responses: types of motive, career relevant or not, degree of centrality, and valence of initial attitudes.

Next, we go back to coded segments of data keyed to the research questions and their suggested concepts. The analyst notes down the *Motives* given by or attributed to a participant and then tries to put a label on the motive. One participant, for example, gave several motives: She heard how good the new practice was (social influence), her principal was "really sold on it" and "wanted it in" (pressure), most other teachers were using it or planned to: "It's what's coming" (conformity), and using the new practice was an occasion to "keep growing" (self-improvement).

Turning to *Career Relevance*, the second concept, the analyst summarizes in a phrase or sentence the relevance of adopting the practice by each participant. The next task is to look for evidence of the *Centrality* of this new practice for people, and what their *Initial Attitudes* seemed to be. For these two columns, the analyst assigns a general rating, backing it with specific quotes. When these data are entered in the matrix, we get something like Display 7.7.

Display 7.7 contains about as many data as a qualitative analyst can handle and a reader can follow. The analyst has ordered participants according to their time of implementation (Early Users, Second Generation, and Recent Users) and their roles (Users and Administrators), and, within the group of users, has included a Nonuser to set up an illustrative contrast between motives for adopting and motives for refusing the new practice.

For cell entries, the analyst condensed the data to four kinds of entries: codes or labels (e.g., self-improvement); quotations; short summary phrases; and ratings (none/some, low/high, and favorable/unfavorable). The labels and ratings set up comparisons between participants and, if needed, between cases. The quotations supply some grounded meaning for the material; they put some flesh on the rating or label and can be extracted easily for use in the analytic text.

The summary phrases explain or qualify a rating, usually where there are no quotations (as in the Career Relevance column). In general, it's a good idea to add a short quote or explanatory phrase beside a label or scale; otherwise the analyst is tempted to work with general categories that lump together responses that really mean different things (as seen in the "high" responses in the Centrality column).

Analysis

Reading across the rows gives the analyst a thumbnail profile of each participant and provides an initial test of the relationship between responses to the different questions (tactic: **noting relations between variables**). For example, L. Bayeis does have career-relevant motives, sees the practice as very important, and is initially favorable. But R. Quint's entries do not follow that pattern; we have to look at more rows.

Reading down the columns uses the tactic of **making comparisons** between the Motives of different users and administrators, as well as comparisons between these groups. It also enables similar comparisons between responses to the Career Relevance, Centrality, and Initial Attitude data.

A scan down the columns of Display 7.7 provides both information and leads for follow-up analyses through **making contrasts/comparisons**. For example, there is some career relevance in adoption for users but practically none for administrators. Centrality is high—almost overwhelming—for users but less so for administrators. Users are less favorable initially than administrators.

DISPLAY 7.7 ● Conceptually Clustered Matrix: Motives and Attitudes of Users, Nonusers, and Administrators at Masepa

		Motives	Career Relevance	Centrality	Initial Attitudes Toward Program
Early Users	R. Quint	Self-improvement: "To get better. I had to change." ... "Maybe I wasn't teaching the best ways." Pressure: "They wanted us to do it." Social influence: "Everybody was saying what Gail's doing is great."	None—improvement of practice	High: "Biggest thing I've ever done that somebody else told me to do."	Neutral: "There wasn't any appeal. They said it worked so I was going to try it."
	L. Bayeis	Observation: Saw G. Norrist do it and "was impressed." Fit to personal style: "I like structure." Practice improvement: "looking around for a different way to teach reading." Novelty: "you get tired of always doing the same old thing."	Vehicle to turnkey trainer role: also became Title I Coordinator	High: "most important thing I've been involved with."	Favorable
Second Generation	F. Morelly	Social influence: heard from several friends about program Opportunity, effort justification: "I took the training for recertification credit. After all that, I had to follow through." Pressure: "He (Weelling) is the reason we do it here. He's so enthusiastic about it."	None—possibly stabilizing her job at the school	High: "This is the only new thing I've done since I've been out of school . . . I had to invest so much."	Neutral, apprehensive
	L. Brent	Social opinion, influence: "I heard how good it was." Pressure: "(Weelling) was really sold on it. They really want it in." Conformity: Most doing it or planning to in the school: "it's what's coming." Self-improvement: occasion to "keep growing."	None, possibly fear	High: "It's been a nightmare."	Unfavorable, once training began
Recent Users	V. Sharpen	Obligation: requirement to obtain teaching post: "I didn't have a choice." Practice improvement: complementing pre-service training	Ticket to teaching job in the district	High: "My first job"	Neutral, apprehensive

(Continued)

	Motives	Career Relevance	Centrality	Initial Attitudes Toward Program
A. Olkin	Social influence: "heard it was good," ... "a good friend liked it." Pressure: "strongly encouraged" by Weelling and Dahloff. Observation, modeling: saw G. Norrist. "She really impressed me."	None: felt obligated by administration	High: "This was really the big one for me."	Neutral mixed feelings
S. Sorels	Observation: "It was so good for my own kids . . . tremendous change in reading, spelling, work habits."	Ticket to full-time teaching position	High: "This was really a big step for me—a big move . . . [nothing else] as high as this in my career."	Favorable: "I was excited about it."
Non-User				
C. Shinder	Relative disadvantage: "My program was better." Poor fit with personal style: "too scholastic, too programmed."	None	N/A	Unfavorable
K. Weelling Principal	Met need: "I was looking for a highly structured, skill-oriented reading program." Novelty, promise of practical improvement: intrigued by reading about mastery learning; wanted to see it in operation.	None at first: later, appreciates the visibility	High: "Largest investment I've ever made."	Neutral, then favorable
Administrators				
J. Dahloff Curriculum Coordinator	Relative advantage, face validity of program: "well organized"; could be used for other subject matters. Social influence: "impressed" that outstanding teachers favored the program. Practice improvement: beginning teachers ill-prepared in reading. "We didn't know what to do with them . . . They just had to learn on the job."	Another in a series of implementations	Moderate: "It was one thing among a lot of things I was working on."	Favorable
W. Paisly Asst. Sup't	Social influence: "talked into it" by J. Dahloff	None	Low: "It was no big deal."	Neutral

Source: Miles, M. B., & Huberman, A.M. (1994). *Qualitative data analysis: An expanded sourcebook* (2nd ed.). Thousand Oaks, CA: Sage Publications.

Looking across rows, we use the tactic of **noting relations between variables** and see that, for two of three career-motivated users, a relationship exists among the variables: High centrality and favorable attitudes are also present. But the opposite pattern (low career relevance, low centrality, and neutral/unfavorable attitudes) does not apply. In fact, it looks as if some people who are neutral would have been favorable were they not so apprehensive about doing well (tactic: **finding mediating variables**).

In sum, a conceptually clustered matrix brings together key data from key participants into a single matrix. The goal is to summarize how things stand with regards to selected variables, concepts, or themes of interest. Avoid using more than five related research questions for a conceptually clustered matrix; otherwise, there will be too many data to see inclusively at one time and too much time spent manipulating blocks of data to find clusters and interrelationships.

Notes

Conceptually clustered matrices need not be organized by persons or roles, as in Display 7.7. More general concepts and themes can be the ordering principle in the rows as well as in the columns. For example, rows can consist of cells broken into *Types of Problems*, with columns divided into various *Forms of Coping Strategies*. Less emphasis is placed on specific cases and people, and more on the conceptual and thematic matters of the study.

Folk Taxonomy

Description

A folk taxonomy is best described by a series of its unique constituent terms explained in a particular order. First, McCurdy, Spradley, and Shandy (2005) call

> categories that categorize other categories *domains* and the words that name them *cover terms*. . . . Taxonomies are simply [hierarchical] lists of different things that are classified together under a domain word by members of a microculture on the basis of some shared certain attributes. (pp. 44–45)

Spradley (1979) further defines a *folk taxonomy* as "a set of categories organized on the basis of a single semantic relationship." The taxonomy "shows the relationships among *all* the folk terms in a domain" (p. 137). A verbatim data record to extract folk terms is necessary for constructing a taxonomy. But when no specific folk terms are generated by participants, the researcher develops his or her own— called *analytic terms*.

Semantic relationships are somewhat akin to "if-then" algorithms and include types such as the following (Spradley, 1979):

Form	Semantic Relationship
1. Strict inclusion	X is a kind of Y
2. Spatial	X is a place in Y, X is a part of Y
3. Cause–effect	X is a result of Y, X is a cause of Y
4. Rationale	X is a reason for doing Y
5. Location for action	X is a place for doing Y

Form	Semantic Relationship
6. Function	X is used for Y
7. Means–end	X is a way to do Y
8. Sequence	X is a step (stage) in Y
9. Attribution	X is an attribute (characteristic) of Y (p. 111)

As an example, "fruit" can be a domain/cover term, with "berries" as one kind of fruit—a semantic relationship of *strict inclusion*: X is a kind of Y. The category of berries continues with its own list, such as strawberries, raspberries, blueberries, blackberries, and so on, but without hierarchy at this level—in other words, a strawberry is not more important or more significant than a blackberry, so it doesn't matter in what order the types of berries are listed. "Apples" are then classified as another kind of fruit, with its list of Granny Smith, Delicious, Honeycrisp, and so on.

In sum, a folk taxonomy is an organized network list of participant- and sometimes researcher-generated terms that are appropriately classified and categorized (see Display 7.8).

DISPLAY 7.8 ◗ A Folk Taxonomy of the Ways Children Oppress Each Other

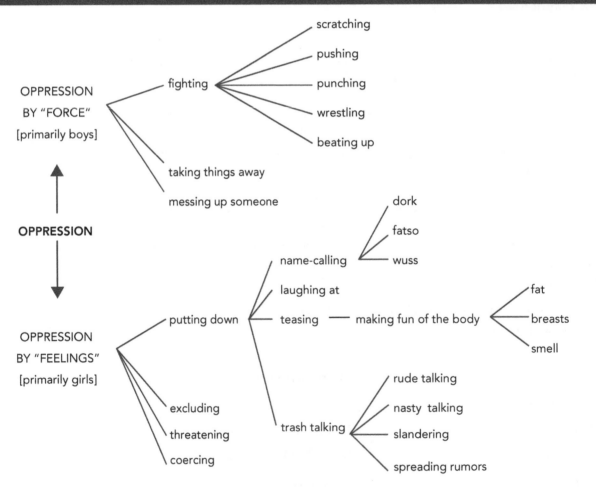

Source: Saldaña, J. (2016). *The coding manual for qualitative researchers* (3rd ed.). Thousand Oaks, CA: Sage Publications.

Applications

Concepts can't always be properly sorted into matrix rows and columns. Sometimes, a network or graphic format is needed, such as a taxonomic diagram, to illustrate the interconnected complexity of social life.

Taxonomies are useful when large or complex sets of unique terms appear in participant data, and researchers' sense of their organization seems necessary to better understand the subculture or microculture's ways of perceiving and living in their immediate social world. Taxonomies also help with classifying and categorizing various related pieces of data—a primary analytic step in synthesizing a massive set of field notes, interview transcripts, and documents. The goal is not to impose some artificial order onto the messiness of everyday living and working, but to bring enhanced cognitive clarity for the analyst's interpretations of the people he or she is learning from and about.

Example

Saldaña (2005) and his research team explored how fourth- and fifth-grade children at one particular elementary school oppress each other. Participant observation, written surveys, and whole-class interviews were prepared for a short-term artists' residency to teach children, through dramatic simulation, how to proactively deal with bullying. The term *oppression* was key to the study, and it was defined for the children. After they grasped its meaning, they offered to the researchers examples of oppression they themselves experienced or witnessed at school and at home:

Fourth-Grade Boy [**group interview**]:	Sometimes when we're playing games and stuff, and this one boy comes over and he says, "Can I play with you guys?", and people say, "No, you're not our kind of people, so you better get out now."
Fifth-Grade Girl [**written survey response**]:	I was made fun of my fatness. I was called fat, huge fatso are you going to have a baby. I was sad all the time. I'm trying to luse wiaght but I just gain, gain and gain. Wiaght. I have not lose eney wight. I have not stoped being appresed.

These children's experiences were examples of the *means-end* semantic relationship: X is a way to do Y, or *excluding* is a way to oppress; *name calling* is a way to oppress. After all of these (often heartwrenching) stories were collected, they were descriptively coded as to the types of oppressive acts they illustrated for further analysis.

Analysis

The proper classification and categorization of individual items for taxonomy development can be conducted through a variety of systematic methods ranging from item-by-item queries with participants, to card and pile sorts, to follow-up interviews (Bernard, 2011; Spradley, 1979, 1980). Which method you choose depends on your own knowledge of the folk terms and their contextual meanings. Most often, intimate familiarity with your data corpus enables you to code and extract these folk terms directly from the database and onto a text-based software page or graphics program. A recommendation is first to cut and paste the array of terms into a traditional outline format, and then to transfer that arrangement into network format with nodes and lines. Most often, nothing more complex than deep reflection and logical reasoning help you figure out how the terms align according to their semantic relationship (X is a kind of Y, X is a way to do Y, etc.).

Display 7.8 (from Saldaña, 2016, p. 185) shows an excerpt from the folk taxonomy constructed to illustrate the ways children oppress each other. Long story short, children themselves told the researchers that oppression was either by "force" or by "feelings," usually enacted by boys and girls, respectively. From these two major categories, forms of physical and verbal oppression were arrayed. Some were folk terms told to us by children (e.g., *fighting*, *scratching*, and *pushing*), while others were researcher-constructed analytic terms that identified the types of oppression children described but had no vocabulary for (e.g., *excluding*, *coercing*, and *slandering*).

As with matrices, eyeballing and scanning the taxonomy may lead to analytic insights or questions for further investigation. For example, the folk term *putting down* has the most complex set of extended nodes and lines, suggesting not only that this type of oppression may be more frequent among older children but also that verbal belittling is potentially more violent than physical harm. For the action research project at the elementary school, these findings suggested that the adult team focus on how to get children to reduce their verbal put-downs and to offer students constructive strategies for coping with verbal abuse from peers.

Note that not everything in this (and possibly any other) taxonomy is perfectly bounded. For example, "taking things away" from someone may be a physical act of "force," but it can eventually lead to victim "feelings" of loss and hurt. There are many shades of grey and exceptions to virtually every rule. The taxonomy is not a perfect model of the ways in which humans classify things in the social world. It is, at best, an analytic heuristic for mapping complexity to grasp at a glance the constituent elements of a culture.

Most CAQDAS programs include graphic capabilities to draw taxonomies. Some programs, such as ATLAS.ti, can "calculate" and display a visual model that illustrates your codes' organizational arrangement based on their frequency and researcher-initiated linkages. CAQDAS programs can also arrange and manage your codes into hierarchies and trees, based on your input.

Notes

Analysts may use the taxonomic method to sort out their own theoretical ideas exclusively—being careful, of course, to call it a researcher rather than a folk taxonomy. This is particularly advised for those employing grounded theory, who might construct a taxonomy composed of their codes: from theoretical, to axial/focused, to in vivo/process/initial codes (see Saldaña, 2016).

Thematic Array

Description

A thematic array graphically illustrates an analysis's major themes (or categories, concepts, assertions, etc.) for at-a-glance review. The arrays can vary from a simple bullet-pointed list to a spray diagram to metaphoric images (see Displays 7.9-7.12).

Applications

Detailed narrative descriptions of our findings are necessary to explain to readers what we discovered about social life from our particular study. But sometimes the prosaic alone cannot inform our audiences of the bigger picture. Extensive analytic description can also overwhelm and become difficult to synthesize and retain in our minds. The thematic array is a visual reference and road map for preliminary review before the reader begins our complex narrative journey. Yet it can also be located toward the end of a report to summarize the analysis just presented. Aside from functioning as a reader's framing device, the thematic array serves as a condensed symbol of the research project's conclusions.

Examples

Rather than showcase just one particular study as an example, we present a gallery of graphics developed by other researchers to exhibit thematic arrays at work. We minimize the discussion of the studies' contents to focus on the display tactics they employed.

Display 7.9 (Steyn, 2015) represents the summative findings of an exploratory case study of a school principal. "This figure shows the necessity of supportive leadership required of the principal; the significance of enhancing collaboration and communication among teachers by removing the isolation among them; and the prerequisite to provide supportive conditions for teacher collaboration" (p. 171). Notice how a simple network diagram with large bins containing major themes, extracted from a narrative analysis of interview transcripts, exhibits both content and process.

Stievano, De Marinis, Russo, Rocco, and Alvaro (2012) analyzed "nurses' professional dignity in their everyday working lives. We explored the factors that affect nursing professional dignity in practice that emerge in relationships with health professionals, among clinical nurses working in hospitals and in community settings in central Italy" (p. 341). One of the primary themes discovered was that nursing professional dignity was perceived by participants as an *achievement*, with selected factors contributing to it. Display 7.10's contents could just as easily have been represented as a bullet-pointed list, but the individual factors with arrows pointing toward the central theme at the top suggest an active, processual dynamic at work. Achievement, as illustrated here, is literally something to work toward and up to.

DISPLAY 7.9 ● A Principal's Experiences and Views on Creating Collaborative Learning Among Teachers

Enhancing Teacher Collaboration In Professional Learning Community Teams

Supportive Leadership

Develop school leadership to ensure teacher collaboration
The principal:
- Is responsible and accountable for teacher collaboration
- Plays a key role to provide cohesion
- Presents the 'big picture' to staff
- Needs to identify the professional needs of teachers/understand their professional responsibilities
- Develops a common goal and language by means of inquiry
- Needs to ensure trust among self and staff members for the sake of effective collaboration

Collaboration and Communication

- Remove isolation between teachers
- Capitalize on the expertise and knowledge of teachers
- Ensure growth opportunities to address shortcomings
- Overcome human nature that hinders collaboration
- Ensure continuity between grades
- Encourage ownership of collaboration
- Use the expertise of staff in collaboration

Supportive Conditions

- Review the current school conditions and make changes
- Identify suitable structures in different grades and on various levels
- Continue to nurture new strategies for teacher collaboration
- Develop collegial relationships among teachers
- Focus teachers on student success
- Be creative in finding appropriate time for staff collaboration

Source: Steyn (2015), p. 171.

DISPLAY 7.10 ● Nursing Professional Dignity Perceived as an Achievement

Source: Stievano et al. (2012), p. 351.

Display 7.11 illustrates another summative graphic of a study's major findings. O'Shaughnessy and Burnes (2016) conducted a

> constructivist grounded theory analysis of 22 in-depth interviews with women early career psychologists [WECP] regarding their experiences of developing a career in psychology. Three primary spheres of influence on career adjustment emerged from the data: identity-based influences, experiential focused influences, and outcome-oriented influences. These major spheres of influence are further refined into themes and subthemes that play a role in the career experiences of women early career psychologists. (p. 786)

In Display 7.11, adjustment, as a *core process*, consists of three categories or *properties* of influence. The *dimensions* (i.e., subthemes) are bullet-pointed next to their spheres of influence. This graphic neatly illustrates a grounded theory model that displays the salient themes extracted from data analysis.

Display 7.12 utilizes a metaphoric image from Weinstein's (2018) study of social media's positive and negative influences on adolescents' affective well-being. "Analyses suggest the relationship between social technology usage and well-being—whether enhanced or degraded—is not confined to an 'either/or' framework: the emotional see-saw of social media use is weighted by both positive and negative influences" (p. 1). The see-saw metaphor, derived from previous research sources, applied readily to Weinstein's data analysis. "Much like a 'see-saw,' well-being involves tilts and shifts based on the dynamic nature of an individual's experiences—including his or her psychological, social, and physical resources and the challenges he or she faces" (p. 4).

Survey and interview data for this mixed methods study generated five dimensions of social media use, located in the center, above the fulcrum of Display 7.12. "Every [adolescent] interviewee's social media experience is characterized by both positive and negative affects across multiple dimensions"

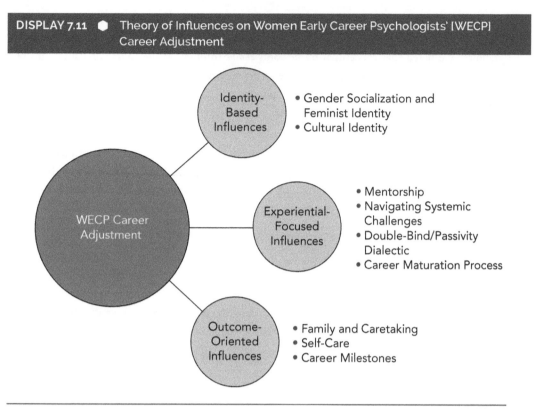

DISPLAY 7.11 ● Theory of Influences on Women Early Career Psychologists' [WECP] Career Adjustment

Source: O'Shaughnessy & Burnes (2016), p. 794.

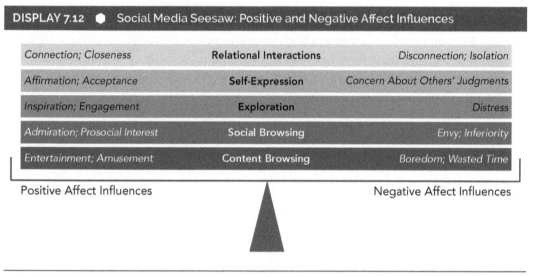

DISPLAY 7.12 ● Social Media Seesaw: Positive and Negative Affect Influences

Source: Weinstein (2018), p. 21.

(p. 13), and the graphic incorporates and extends the see-saw metaphor as a visual representation of participants' fluctuating experiences.

Analysis

These examples portray the summative findings of their respective studies in graphic form. The models are more than descriptive; they are analytic and interpretive (Wolcott, 1994). When category, theme, or concept labels are arranged in diagrammatic spatial relationships with one another, we have displayed our results in dimensioned arrays that tell both a story and its "moral"—that is, the lesson to be learned.

These thematic array examples somewhat resemble the models offered for conceptual framework design in Chapter 2. In a way, conceptual frameworks are the potential origin of these concluding graphics. We noted that conceptual frameworks *evolve* throughout the course of a study. It's possible, then, that the final diagram you create as the research project reaches closure might serve as the condensed visual representation of your findings.

Notes

We have encouraged you to summarize your major findings as narrative assertions, propositions, and other text-based forms. But *think display*. Explore how your major findings and conclusions can be visually represented and presented in elegant graphic forms and formats for reader accessibility.

DESCRIBING ACTION

Vignettes capture significant moments or the action of an extended portion of fieldwork into evocative prose renderings. A *Poetic Display* condenses data into poetic formats for capturing the essences and essentials of meanings. And *Cognitive Networks* diagram an individual's thinking processes as he or she goes through a series of actions.

Vignettes

Description

A vignette is a focused description of a series of events taken to be representative, typical, or emblematic in the case you are studying. It has a narrative, story-like structure that preserves chronological flow and that normally is limited to a brief time span, one or a few key actors, a bounded space, or all three. The vignette can be written solely by the researcher, or collaboratively with research team members and/or research participants. A vignette can range from as short as a single paragraph to as long as a chapter (see the example under "Analysis" further down).

Applications

Vignettes are rich, prosaic renderings of primarily field work observations but can also include adaptations of stories embedded within interview transcripts. Examples are a day in the life of an intensive care unit nurse, the events in a typical college faculty meeting, the story of how a key management decision was reached over a period of several weeks, and the way in which a student solves a particular math problem.

Evocatively written vignettes can be a useful corrective when your data—coded, displayed, and pondered on—somehow lack meaning and contextual richness. Collaboratively written vignettes offer an opportunity to engage study participants actively in producing, reflecting on, and learning from the data.

During early data collection, as a researcher becomes more familiar with how things work in the case at hand, he or she often finds rich pockets of especially representative, meaningful data that can be pulled together in a focused way for interim understanding. Vignettes offer a way to mine such pockets fairly easily. They are also helpful in formulating core issues in a case—that is, your theory of what is happening—for yourself, your study colleagues, and external consumers of interim reports that may be required. They can be embedded usefully in a longer and more formal case report as well.

Example

Saldaña (1997) conducted an ethnography of an inner-city, largely Hispanic, arts magnet school in the Southwest whose theatre program was headed by a novice White female teacher. One of the key themes that emerged from the study was the theatre teacher's unconditional support for her students. Despite the ethnic differences between Nancy, the middle-class White teacher, and her lower-income Hispanic students, a sense of mutual respect was evident in selected interactions.

One of the events observed during the field work period was a school district–wide speech tournament for its junior high school students. Following are excerpts from the raw field notes taken during this off-campus event. They are sketchy, hastily written jottings about a slice of action that happened over no more than 3 minutes of real time:

> Beatriz did a "don't drink and drive" speech. Elian shouted, "You go, Bea!" as she was coming up the stage. Beatriz spoke softly, little inflection. Needed prompting from another Martinez School girl about 4 times. When Beatriz comes back to the row Nancy rubs her shoulder. Beatriz looks hurt yet smiles, and as if she's about to cry.

> *OC: Even though there may not be much competence in comparison to the others, the Martinez School team seems to have a lot of support. Like in* Damn Yankees, *the baseball team may not be good, but they've got "heart."*

These notes do not give the total picture to an outside reader of what the researcher was observing, thinking, and feeling at the time. Thus, a narrative vignette that more fully describes the significance of the event is merited.

Analysis

There are no hard-and-fast guidelines for writing a vignette, though some may prescribe that the content should contain an assertion as a topic sentence, sufficient descriptive detail, analytic commentary, critical or evaluative perspectives, and so forth. But literary writing is a creative enterprise, and the vignette offers the researcher an opportunity to venture away from traditional scholarly discourse and into evocative prose that remains firmly rooted in the data but is not slave to it.

Below is a vignette about the jottings presented in the example above, composed to illustrate why this seemingly small slice of social action held special significance for the researcher and the study's key findings:

> The well-dressed eighth grade persuasive speaker from Canton Junior High spoke with clarity about her topic—adopting shelter animals. She obviously had been coached well to present a polished argument with confidence and volume. After finishing her flawless speech, the hundred or so student and teacher spectators in the auditorium applauded loudly as she stepped off the stage.
>
> The facilitator of the event stood up from the judge's table and spoke to the assembly: "Thank you. Next: Beatriz Guzman from Martinez School."
>
> Beatriz, in her quiet and unassuming way, rose from her chair and scooted across her seated classmates as Elian shouted, "You go, Bea!" Nancy, her coach, smiled as she passed and gave her a "rah-rah" pep-rally gesture. Beatriz, dressed in a pale yellow dress, walked hesitantly toward the stage, obviously nervous, walking up each stair step to the platform with measured care so as not to trip as someone had done earlier.

Beatriz walked to the center of the stage as her student prompter, Maria, took her place below, script in hand, ready to offer Beatriz a line in case she forgot her one-minute memorized persuasive speech (a safety measure permitted by speech tournament rules for young contestants).

Beatriz began and continued to speak softly with a monotonous voice. About four sentences into the speech, she said: "And when people get arrested for drunk driving. . . ." There was a long and uncomfortable pause as Beatriz stared blankly into the darkened auditorium. Nancy looked helplessly at Beatriz and leaned forward in her seat. The student prompter cued, "their lives are. . . ." Beatriz shut her eyes, looked downward briefly, then raised her head and continued: "their lives are ruined forever."

Her speech continued for less than a minute. She needed prompting for forgotten lines three more times. On the final line of her speech, "And that is why people shouldn't drink and drive," Beatriz started leaning toward her right, as if she wanted to quickly finish and run off the stage. When she delivered her final line, the audience clapped politely as they had been instructed to do, with Beatriz's schoolmates cheering and calling out an occasional "Yay!" for her.

Beatriz returned quickly to her seat and sat next to Nancy, both of them silent for a few seconds as the next contestant from another school walked confidently toward the stage. Nancy stretched her arm across Beatriz's shoulder and pulled her student close. Beatriz leaned her head against her teacher's motherly body as Nancy started gently rubbing her student's back. Beatriz smiled through her hurt and looked as if she were about to cry. The two young women sat and said nothing to each other. They really didn't need to say anything at all.

Later that evening, as I reflected on the events of the day, I thought about Beatriz and her deer-in-the-headlights moment on stage—a moment that will probably never be forgotten for the rest of her life—and the reassuring comfort Nancy gave her afterward. It was such a peaceful yet riveting moment for me to observe: a young girl leaning against a young woman in a moment of unconditional support after failure. All I could think of was Nancy's love for her students and the realization that she's just so damn *human*.

Erickson (1986) advocates that writing a vignette after reading through field notes can be a powerful means for surfacing and clarifying your own perspective on what is happening. The method generates "an analytic caricature (of a friendly sort) . . . that highlights the author's interpretive perspective" (p. 150). A well-written vignette as a concrete, focused story will be vivid, compelling, and persuasive to a reader that the researcher has "been there."

If you choose to make your vignettes collaborative constructions with your participants, it helps to meet with several of them to explain the vignette idea. Each person then chooses a situation to be described, makes some notes, and retells or writes an account in everyday language. The researcher reads the typed or transcribed account, makes marginal notes and queries on it, and sends it back to the writer for review. The notes and queries are discussed, and the researcher produces a revised and expanded version, later sent back for further review and discussion. A final version (with pseudonyms replacing real names) then can be circulated to others in the field work setting—an extra benefit in terms of recognition and potential learning for participants.

Notes

The best discussion of this method we have found is in Erickson (1986). Seidman (2013) describes a more extended version called a "profile," a narrative summary using a participant's own words from interview transcripts to describe an experience over an extended time period. Of course, the fields of narrative inquiry, oral history, and autoethnography have developed unique and intriguing methods for extensions of vignette writing. See the appendix for recommended resources in these subject areas.

Poetic Display

Description

Poetic displays arrange carefully selected portions of qualitative data into traditional and variant poetic structures for the evocative representation and presentation of a study, its findings, or a key participant's perspectives (see the display under "Analysis" further down).

Applications

At times, the researcher can feel overwhelmed by the massive amount of detail in a database and needs to grasp its most important or salient contents. One of poetry's unique features is its ability to represent and evoke human experiences in elegant language. Thus, the literary genre can be used as one way to extract core meanings from a large collection of texts.

Poetic displays are arts-based representations and presentations of qualitative data that capture the essence and essentials of the corpus from the researcher's perspective. Their constructions are primarily exploratory for the researcher's use, but a completed poem could be included in a published report if it is of sufficient artistic and scholarly caliber.

A poetic display brings the reader very close to a condensed set of data that forbids superficial attention by the analyst. You have to treat the data set—and the person it came from—seriously, because a poem is something you engage with at a deep level. It is not just a figurative transposition, but an emotional statement as well.

Example

A female principal of an arts magnet school was interviewed about the site's philosophy and mission. Here is just one verbatim excerpt from an hour-long interview about her perceptions of the school and its goals for students:

> It's, um, it's a very different kind of environment because what we're trying to do here is create whole people, give them the opportunity to become lifetime learners, um, to think that learning is joyful, to support them and to, um, be respectful of the backgrounds they bring to us. And that's very different from having a school in which there is a curriculum and these are, these things you have to learn. We haven't been able to find any single thing that people have to learn. You don't have to know the alphabet, you can always just put it down. You don't have to know the multiplication tables, you can carry them in your hip pocket. What you have to learn is attitudes. You know, we want them to have a taste for comprehensive elegance of expression. A love of problem solving. These, these are attitudes, and those are what we're teaching. And we try to teach them very respectfully and joyfully. And that's different—I know it's different.

A poem could (and should) be constructed from the entire interview transcript to holistically capture the principal's major perspectives or some facet that struck the analyst as intriguing. But for illustrative purposes only, a poem will be constructed solely from the transcript excerpt above.

Analysis

Verbatim theatre playwright Anna Deavere Smith attests that people speak in "organic poetry" through their everyday speech. The listener needs to be sharply attuned to a speaker's rhythms, parsing, pausing, and, of course, significant words and passages of text that transcend everyday discourse into insightful and meaningful communication.

The researcher becomes thoroughly familiar with the data corpus and extracts significant and meaningful in vivo words and phrases from the text. In the first sentence of the transcript above, for example, the phrases "whole people" and "lifetime learners" stood out as significant passages that were highlighted. This technique continued with the 170-word transcript.

Selected passages are then reassembled on a separate page to experiment with their arrangement and flow as poetry. Not everything extracted from a database will be needed, and some grammatical leeway may be necessary to change the structure of a word now and then as it gets reformatted into verse.

Eventually, the analyst took what were the selected words and phrases from the 170-word transcript and made artistic choices to compose a 23-word poem that, to him, represents the philosophy, mission, and goals of this particular site—an artistic rendering of an arts-centered school:

> Teach attitudes:
>> Create whole people
>> Lifetime learners
>
> Learn attitudes:
>> A love of problem solving
>> Elegance of expression
>
> Teach and learn:
>> Respectfully
>> Supportively
>> Joyfully

Two points that need to be remembered are that (a) the selection, organization, and presentation of data in a display are decisive analytic actions, and (as in this case) they need to be done in a thoughtful, lucid way; and (b) poetic displays owe as much to art and craft as they do to science. Attend to the poet within you to help find the organic poetry within your participants.

Classic literary poetry can stand on its own, but research as poetry almost always needs some type of introductory framing or supplemental narrative for the reader to contextualize or expand on the artwork. Also acknowledge that poetry has a distinctive set of conventions and traditions, as does academic scholarship. Footnotes and citations of the academic literature have no place in the poem itself; save these, if necessary, for any accompanying prose narrative.

Notes

Do not fall into the epistemological trap of feeling the need to defend or justify your use of poetry as research if you choose to present and publish it. Many practitioners in the field of qualitative inquiry have transcended the outmoded perception of poetry as an "experimental" and "alternative" (i.e., marginalized) form of research, and now see it as a more *progressive* one. But realize that if you do choose to write poetry, it must be artistically sound to make a persuasive case as research representation.

For more on found poetry, poetic structures, and their applications as qualitative research representation and presentation, see Mears (2009) and Prendergast, Leggo, and Sameshima (2009).

Cognitive Networks

Description

A cognitive network displays a person's mental representation of concepts or processes about a particular domain, showing the relationships, flows, and dynamics among them. The visual network helps answer the question, "What may be going through a person's mind as he or she experiences a particular series of actions and/or reflects on an experience?" Descriptive text accompanies the network for explanation (see Display 7.13).

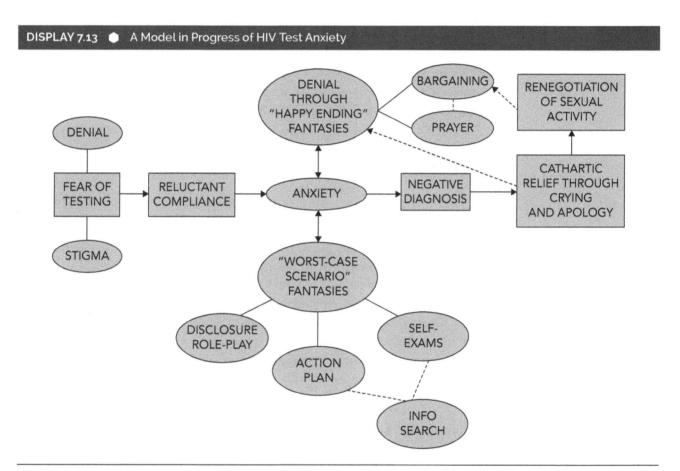

DISPLAY 7.13 ● A Model in Progress of HIV Test Anxiety

Source: Saldaña & Omasta (2018), p. 253.

Applications

There are times when the visual representation of concepts and processes are more effective than narrative alone. If we put stock in the classic folk saying, "A picture is worth a thousand words," then cognitive networks are one way of efficiently and elegantly portraying what may be going through people's minds as they reflect on or undergo an experience.

Many of our examples so far have been complex, multilevel cases. But cases are often focused at the individual level. We need displays that show us the complexity of the person. People's minds—and our theories about them—are not always organized hierarchically, as in folk taxonomies. They can be represented fruitfully in nonhierarchical network form: a collection of nodes attached by links and/or bins extended with arrows.

But qualitative researchers are not mind readers and most likely not neuroscientists, so we can never truly know what's going through someone else's mind. The cognitive network is our best attempt to put into fixed form the dynamic and sometimes idiosyncratic thinking processes of a participant.

Example

Some research studies examine the mundane in humans' lives to understand concepts such as routines, rituals, rules, roles, and relationships—the habits of daily existence (Duhigg, 2012). But there are times when strong emotion-laden and epiphanic experiences interrupt the stability we take for granted.

Display 7.13 illustrates a cognitive network developed by Saldaña for an unpublished pilot study from the late 1990s. The diagram represents the process of gay men reluctantly undergoing an HIV test, waiting for at least 3 days (the average turnaround time during that period), yet receiving negative results.

Three men were interviewed to collect sufficient information to construct a cognitive network of their common, experiential process. In other words, data were solicited to answer the general question, "What may be going through a person's mind as he or she experiences a particular series of actions and/or reflects on an experience?" This includes not just facts but reasoning, memories, and emotions as well. The interview transcripts then become the verbal directions for designing the cognitive network.

Analysis

Drawing and constructing a cognitive network *is* the analysis, for you are trying to visually represent a real-time process. Tools available to you are paper and pencil, "sticky notes" and a wall board, or graphics/modeling software such as that found in most text editing and CAQDAS programs. Whatever method works best for you is fine, so long as you realize that you will be going through several drafts before you feel you've captured the process on paper or on a monitor screen. You'll also discover that alternately drawing a network and writing the accompanying narrative help inform each other. After a draft of a cognitive network, the narrative gets written, which then stimulates a redrafting of the network and clarification of the narrative's details, and so on.

Display 7.13's storyline progresses thusly:

> A participant's FEAR OF TESTING is rooted in two primary causes: fearful DENIAL that one has HIV, and the social STIGMA or shame associated with having the virus. There are multiple factors that motivate different participants to actually take the test (e.g., upon a physician's recommendation, learning that a sex partner has HIV, unusual physical symptoms, needing a "clear conscience," and so on), so they cannot all be graphed at this point. But eventually the participant does consent to the test through RELUCTANT COMPLIANCE for health status awareness.
>
> The primary emotional state while waiting for test results is ANXIETY, and participants experience two vacillating states during this stage of personal intra-action. The first is DENIAL THROUGH "HAPPY ENDING" FANTASIES in which the participant imagines an HIV-negative result, bolstered through BARGAINING with oneself to lead a more cautious sex life in the future and, for others, resorting to PRAYER for divine intervention and good health, even if one is not devoutly religious or a regular worship service attendee.

At the negative end of the experience is mentally enacting "WORST-CASE SCENARIO" FANTASIES in case of HIV-positive results. Several participants imagine DISCLOSURE ROLE-PLAY in which they prepare how they will tell family members, friends, and/or partners about the diagnosis. They also prepare a preliminary ACTION PLAN for personal life choices such as living arrangements and health maintenance. Some will conduct physical SELF-EXAMS, an almost paranoid search for skin blemishes or other markers that might confirm HIV-positive status. These actions are supplemented with a primarily online INFO SEARCH for medical information and stories of those living with HIV.

Eventually, test results are received, and if a NEGATIVE DIAGNOSIS is given by a health professional, several participants share two actions that follow: CATHARTIC RELIEF THROUGH CRYING AND APOLOGY to the doctor or clinician for the reaction. This "dodging a bullet" or "lucky" outcome motivates several participants to reflect on a personal RENEGOTIATION OF SEXUAL ACTIVITY in the future—for example: less-frequent sexual encounters or abstinence, safe sex practices, and so on.

Also notice the dashed arrows between CATHARTIC RELIEF THROUGH CRYING AND APOLOGY and DENIAL THROUGH "HAPPY ENDING" FANTASIES; and between RENEGOTIATION OF SEXUAL ACTIVITY and BARGAINING. Though these connections are not part of the primary linear process through time, the references hark back to previous states in which the "happy ending" is indeed achieved, and the participant now tries to meet the conditions he "bargained" with himself through different and safer sexual behaviors.

[Display 7.13] serves as a graphic outline of the experience of taking and waiting days for HIV test results that end up negative. But as of 2018, results of some HIV tests can be provided almost instantaneously. It would be interesting to determine if these same iterative thought patterns occur within a truncated time frame, or if this model parallels waiting for test results about other severe diseases. (Saldaña & Omasta, 2018, pp. 254–255)

The process described above was the researcher's synthesis and interpretation of what went through three people's minds. But cognitive networks can also be collaboratively constructed between the researcher and participant. The procedure engages the respondent and the researcher in joint work, simultaneously building the display and entering data.

After an initial interview about the experience or process, the researcher transcribes the exchange and extracts key terms, concepts, in vivo codes, and so on. Each one gets written on its own sticky note, and a follow-up networking interview is scheduled with the participant.

At the audio-recorded networking interview, the participant is given the sticky notes and is asked to arrange them on a large poster-size sheet of paper on a wall "in a way that shows how you think about the words." When this task is complete, the researcher asks, "Why are they arranged this way?" The researcher draws lines around concepts that the person says belong together, and evokes a name for the group, which also is written on the display. The question "What relationship is there between _____ and _____?" leads to the person's naming of links between concepts and/or concept groups, and those, too, are written on the display.

During preliminary analysis, the researcher listens to the recording of the network discussion, clarifies any errors, and writes a descriptive text that walks through the complete network. The revised network and narrative are fed back to the respondent to ensure they are an accurate representation of the concept or process.

This version of cognitive networking makes for maximum idiosyncrasy—and complexity—in the results. A simpler version (Morine-Dershimer, 1991) asks the respondent to generate a list of *concepts* related to a major topic. The major topic is placed in the center, and then other concepts are placed around it, with unnamed links radiating out to them, and from them, to other concepts in turn.

Cognitive networks have a way of looking more organized, socially desirable, and systematic than they probably are in the person's mind. Allow for those biases when making analyses and interpretations. Also acknowledge that one person's cognitive network does not necessarily represent others' ways of thinking and acting in comparable situations.

Notes

Cognitive networks also can be drawn from preestablished narratives such as interview transcripts, fiction, or other longer documents. Here, the analyst is interrogating the text rather than the person. You can even use cognitive networking techniques to clarify your own ideas or analytic processes about the meaning of a particular set of data.

CLOSURE AND TRANSITION

These methods for describing social settings and action are documentary processes. They condense a vast array of data into more coherent forms for answering one of the inquiry's most basic questions, "What is happening here?" Sometimes, a research study's goals are focused solely on description, but other goals may include deeper explorations into the "whys" of what humans do.

Exploring and describing are two foundation methods for analyzing qualitative data. In Chapter 8, we will arrange data into more systematic, ordered formats for constructing even more patterns across time, processes, and cases.

METHODS OF ORDERING

CHAPTER SUMMARY

This chapter outlines methods for ordering condensed data according to time, processes, and cases. The ordering provides foundations for determining sequences and hierarchies for further analytic work.

CONTENTS

INTRODUCTION

A third major family of displays *orders* data by time, processes, and cases, preserving chronological flow and permitting a good look at what led to what, and when. Once past initial description, some form of ordering is typically very helpful. Ordering matrices, networks, and graphics by time enables the analysis of phases, stages, cycles, and possibly influences and affects (the preferred terms over the outmoded "cause and effect"), suggesting causation.

Life is chronology; we live in a flow of events. But although we can think of ourselves as being in the midst of a river of events, that metaphor breaks down because the river's flow is not one-dimensional. Some events occur in one domain of life, others elsewhere. Some events are close to us, some distant. Some events are related coherently to other events, and others are adventitious. Distant events can have consequences for close events. And though it may be stating the obvious, events long ago in time have consequences for the present.

As for cases, looking across them deepens our understanding and can increase generalizability. But cross-case analysis is tricky. Simply summarizing superficially across some themes or main variables by itself tells us little. We have to look carefully at the complex configuration of processes within each case and understand the local dynamics before we can begin to see patterning of variables that transcends particular cases. Thus, combining "process" and "variable" approaches is needed for methods of ordering.

Ordering by Time uses chronology as an organizing framework for examining data as they change across time. *Ordering Processes* examines how "big picture" composite journeys can be diagrammed. *Ordering by Cases* hierarchically arranges individuals, groups, and sites according to designated variables of interest.

ORDERING BY TIME

A *Qualitative Timeline* plots a brief history in a linear graphic. An *Event Listing Matrix* documents selected actions during selected periods of time. A *Growth Gradient* illustrates the development of a variable throughout a range of time. And the *Time-Ordered Matrix* shows the concurrent pathways of multiple variables and researcher evaluation notes during selected periods of time.

Qualitative Timeline

Description

A qualitative timeline displays a condensed historic narrative along a linear axis representing time—months, years, ranges, and so on (see Display 8.1).

DISPLAY 8.1 ● River School District [RSD] Timeline Showing 18 Years of Linear Change

1995–1996:
The first teacher RSD grade and attendance computer program was initiated and implemented. Continual updates and changes continued from this point forward.

Late 1990s–2000s:
Various school and district curriculum and education technology application workshops were offered in RSD to help educators learn technology programs.

2007–2008:
Although different schools worked with several types of teacher curriculum web pages, in 2012–2013, the Canvas system became the required teacher web page and communication medium with parents and stakeholders.

2012–2013:
Although curriculum maps were developed collaboratively by some district department committees in the late 1990s to 2000s, teachers were not required to follow them precisely until 2012–2013. The Canvas system became required during this school year.

2013–2014:
Mandatory administrative supervision of teachers for formative and summative evaluations was initiated. Standardized pretests and posttests were implemented for teacher and department accountability.

1995   2000   2005   2010   2015

Source: Allen & Hunsaker (2016), p. 198.

Applications

An at-a-glance graphic of important historic events related to a study helps both the researcher and readers take in the documentary scope of events through time. The brief qualitative entries along a linear axis create a chronological portrait of the cases and salient actions relevant to the study. It provides historic context for readers to absorb how major events unfolded and progressed.

Analytically, the graphic also serves as an outline for extended narrative descriptions that detail the major plot points in a qualitative timeline. It can demarcate events into phases, stages, and/or cycles, especially for longitudinal studies, and include significant epiphanies and turning or reckoning points. Qualitative timelines can initiate researcher reflection on causation (i.e., antecedent conditions, mediating variables, and outcomes) that may be at work (see Chapter 9). Timelines help us see social life as processual action, not just as static snapshots.

Example

Display 8.1 illustrates Allen and Hunsaker's (2016) historic background of a case study, River School District, and its 18 years of "linear change," a process inconducive to administrators and teachers with differing curriculum ideologies:

> In an effort to advance education, River School District [RSD] attempted to improve efficiency using scientifically proven research to implement standardized change. As a consequence of the political sensitivity of this study, an anonymous participant-observer with more than 20 years of experience teaching in RSD provided documented evidence of the linear change efforts. . . . The major areas of change included increased use of computer technology to improve educational efficiency, enhanced accountability through testing, standardized content for each subject area, and improved administrative oversight of teacher classroom performance. (p. 198)

This historic background provides situational context for discussing and analyzing interviews conducted with four veteran teachers currently employed in the district who experienced these changes, and how they adapted their classroom practices and curriculum ideologies through time.

Analysis

After the timeline has been introduced to readers, the co-authors then describe the conflicting ideologies between the district's administrators and the case study teachers:

> With such adjustment processes, RSD attempts at scientific management fall under a scientific or linear curriculum program ideology. Moreover, promoting educational efficiency with management of the four linear changes helps safeguard improvement in student test performance; however, these same changes also have the potential to estrange teachers from their own curriculum creativity and ideological underpinnings, which have proven successful with students in the past. (p. 199)

The report continues with an examination of the four cases' varied curriculum ideologies. The qualitative timeline serves as a port of entry into the study, showing how teachers' ways of working did not always align with their administration's for almost two decades.

Qualitative timelines provide not just historic background and context but also templates for documenting a current study's chronology. The researcher's analytic journey through time can be mapped as well as the participants'. When fieldwork extends across months and sometimes years, it helps to have a one-page visual reference that reminds the researcher of what has happened and how things may be connected. Matrices (discussed next) can include more historic detail to better "connect the dots" of process and causation.

Notes

Keep qualitative timeline entries limited to major events and focused on the research study's primary questions of interest. Explore how the Growth Gradient (discussed later in this chapter) can extend the timeline to another visual dimension for assessing possible change in a key variable.

Event Listing Matrix

Description

An event listing is a matrix that arranges a series of concrete events by chronological time periods, sorting them into several categories (see Display 8.2).

Applications

Qualitative researchers are always interested in events: what they are, when they happened, and what their connections to other events are (or were), to preserve chronology and illuminate the processes occurring. A process, after all, is essentially a string of coherently related events. Typically, these interests lead to the production of an extended narrative arranged in proper time sequence, sometimes peppered with flashbacks, flash-forwards, or flash-sideways.

Narratives are indispensable if we are to understand a complex chronology in its full richness. The problem is that going straight to an extended narrative from written-up field notes runs the risk of telling a story that may be partial, biased, or dead wrong—even though it may look vivid, coherent, and plausible to a reader. The event listing is a good way of guarding against false chronologies. It creates a matrix-based outline for your narrative.

Example

In the school improvement study, we (Miles and Huberman) wanted to display events during the adoption and implementation of an innovation at the school level, showing them by different phases or time periods of the process.

Keeping the classic left-to-right convention for the passage of time, we might make columns of the matrix list successive time periods. These could be defined arbitrarily (e.g., Year 1, Year 2) or more organically by empirically derived phases or stages of the adoption implementation process. Perhaps some events are more critical than others, serving to cause new events, or to move the process forward into a new phase. Rows of the matrix, in this case, deal with the locale of events: state, district, and local levels.

Display 8.2 shows how this technique worked out for a 1970s innovation called SCORE-ON, a laboratory for teaching remedial math and reading skills to children. The time periods (Contextual Press 1976–1978, Emergence of the Problem Oct. 1978, etc.) were initially defined conceptually from a general adoption–implementation model, but labels for each period came from the actual core activities during that period. A new time period was defined when a significant shift in activities occurred. The analyst marked "barometric events" (those that moved the process into the next time period or phase) with an asterisk.

The analyst focused mainly on Smithson School (bottom row) and wanted to have that as the most local of the locales. However, the innovation was also implemented in other schools (next row up). And events could be sorted into district and state/macro levels, which, in turn, influenced the lower levels.

"Score-On" Time Periods

Level	Contextual Press 1976–1978	Emergence of the Problem Oct. 1978	Awareness and Proposal of Solution Nov. 1978	Approval and Preparations Jan.–Feb. 1979	Training and Beginning Operations March–April 1979	Expansion, New Openings Sept. 1979	Budget Reduction, Disruption May 1980
State/Macro	minimal competency levels, testing introduced in state schools			proposal discussed, approval at state level	Smithson middle school teachers, 2 admins, trained at D/D site (4 days, early March)		Reduction in Title I allocations
District	supplemental skills program introduced in reading and math	– alarm at failure rate – internal solutions proposed, found unacceptable	* officials see SCORE-ON at 'awareness fair' – IV-C proposal rapidly drawn up, submitted	* Smithson pupil folders screened – appointments made of Smithson lab teacher and aide	– 30 4th-grade pupils selected for Smithson lab – materials, technical assistance intensified for Smithson lab	– staff active in extending Smithson, launching new labs * funding for all lab staff at Smithson taken over by Title I	* reduction in county, Title I budgets – proposed staff cuts, transfers in elementary schools
Local Schools	pressures begin to raise minimal levels			* continuation for following year planned for 5th grade in 2 middle schools; teachers named	– rooms, staffing completed for middle schools – 2 other elementary schools authorized to implement in the fall	lab opens at Carrington, Banestown Middle modified version opens at Smith Camp, South End	– middle schools unaffected by cuts – threat of discontinuation at Banestown Middle (conflicts)
Smithson School	large numbers of low achievers placed in FACILE classes	* 4th grade teachers report 40 pupils 1–3 grade levels behind – teachers unfavorable to central office proposals	– teachers approve pullout lab formula	– lab teacher and aide replaced; some disgruntlement – lab room created, minimally equipped	– Smithson lab opens (late March) – preparations inadequate, materials not arrived, scheduling difficulties	Smithson expands to 45 pupils in 3rd, 4th grades – new teacher added for morning sessions	* major shifts in lab staffing announced to teachers – program to be cut back, focused on grades 1–3, limited to 1.5 posts

* barometric event

Source: Miles, M. B., & Huberman, A. M. (1994). *Qualitative data analysis: An expanded sourcebook* (2nd ed.). Thousand Oaks, CA: Sage Publications.

An exploratory interview question asked people to describe the history of the innovation ("Can you tell me how SCORE-ON got started in this school?"). Follow-up probes fleshed out the sequence from innovation awareness to adoption, how and by whom key decisions were made, and the reasons involved. The analyst looked at coded field notes (here, the codes are any that include the subcode CHRONOLOGY) and extracted accounts of specific events, such as "4th-grade teachers report 40 pupils 1–3 grade levels behind," or "officials see SCORE-ON at 'awareness fair.'" If at least two people said the event was important, crucial, or "made a big difference" for what happened subsequently, an asterisk was assigned to designate it as a "barometric event."

Analysis

A quick scan across the display shows us that the process of change is strikingly rapid. A problem seen in one elementary school in fall 1978 by the fourth-grade teachers apparently leads to the discovery and introduction of an innovation (SCORE-ON) that was in place in five district schools by fall 1979.

A look at the asterisks helps explain some of the speed: the active involvement of central office officials after they saw the innovation at an awareness fair, leading to justificatory events such as the pupil folder screening, and to specific school-level planning and the appointment of specific teachers to manage the remedial laboratory. State-level competency requirements were the backdrop, and the teachers' report of problems was probably an alarm or trigger that set off actions already fueled by concern at the district level to meet state requirements.

When we note the repercussions of an externally driven budget crisis during the latter school year (September 1979–May 1980), we can infer that the original availability of Title I funds might have played a strong part in the original changes.

These are plausible hunches about the meaning of the data in Display 8.2. To check them out, the analyst could piece together a focused narrative that ties together the different streams into a meaningful account. Here are some excerpts from the focused narrative the analyst produced. They should be read in conjunction with Display 8.2:

> A special impetus was given in the fall of 1978, when the six fourth-grade teachers at Smithson noticed that they had an unusually large cohort (40) of incoming pupils who were one or more grade levels behind in reading achievement. . . . Thirty-eight of these forty had come out of the [existing] FACILE program in the first to third grades. It is not clear how so many of these pupils got to the fourth grade, but no one was surprised. . . .
>
> The teachers were worried that either promoting or retaining so many pupils would cause problems; they were leaning toward retention but feared a massive protest by parents. Essentially, they were covering themselves by announcing early in the year that they had inherited, not created, the problem.

Note several things here: (a) The narrative, which is both straightforwardly descriptive and analytic, helps knit together and flesh out events at different levels of the chart; (b) the analyst can add explanatory conditions or states that show how one event led to another; (c) the return to the field notes often turns up other critical events or supporting information not originally in the display; and (d) the narrative is more understandable when read in conjunction with the display, and vice versa.

When the first version of the display is filled in, start a draft of a focused narrative. That step will require you to return to the field notes as you go. Stay open to the idea of adding new events to the listing or subtracting events that seem trivial or irrelevant.

For a careful reconstruction, the events in a listing can be dated within cells. Time periods can be specified much more narrowly or cover a very brief time span (e.g., 1 hour in a classroom). Events from a listing also can be shown as a network-like flow that includes more general states or conditions such as "lack of enthusiasm" (see Event-State Network later in this chapter). Barometric or significant events in cells can be color coded in red to highlight their importance during at-a-glance review.

The event listing helps ground the analyst's understanding of a complex flow of events, especially for longitudinal qualitative studies, and increases confidence in the associated chronological account. It also lays the basis for the beginnings of a causal analysis: what events led to what further events, and what mechanisms underlay those associations (see Chapter 9).

Notes

Event listings can be limited much more sharply to "critical incidents," defined as important or crucial, and/or limited to an immediate setting or compressed time frame. These matrices can be done at many different levels of detail, but keep the rows to a maximum of five levels, and be sure they represent a meaningfully differentiated set of categories.

Even more selectively, events can be shown as a flow limited to an individual's major events, each demarcated and connected with the causal pushes that may have moved the process from one event to another. Display 8.3 shows a graphic adapted from display work models by Pillet (personal communication, 1983).

The case here is one of Saldaña's (1998, 2003, 2008) longitudinal qualitative studies of a young man from kindergarten through his late 20s. The successive Educational and Occupational experiences are indicated in the left column; at the right, we see the researcher's summary of the Personal major crises and forces moving concurrently throughout the case study's education and work history. The researcher uses this not just as an event listing chronology but as a visual *chronicle* of significant periods and epiphanies from a young life.

Growth Gradient

Description

A growth gradient is a graphic display that illustrates the amounts, levels, or qualities of changes across time through the use of points and links accompanied with text (see Display 8.4).

Applications

Events can sometimes be conceptualized as associated with some underlying variable that changes through time. That variable can serve as the purpose for or central theme of a growth gradient. The illustration provides a long-term picture of a process or a cumulative "connect the dots" map of related events.

A growth gradient tells the story of a variable's journey across time. So it is particularly appropriate for qualitative longitudinal or evaluation studies, ethnographies, and especially for those research projects with a mixed-methods component.

Example

In Display 8.4, we see a simple graphic display designed to show the growth gradient of an innovation's use in one case for our (Miles and Huberman) school improvement study. The graphic is ordered chronologically with five distinct and separated periods. The vertical dimension shows the

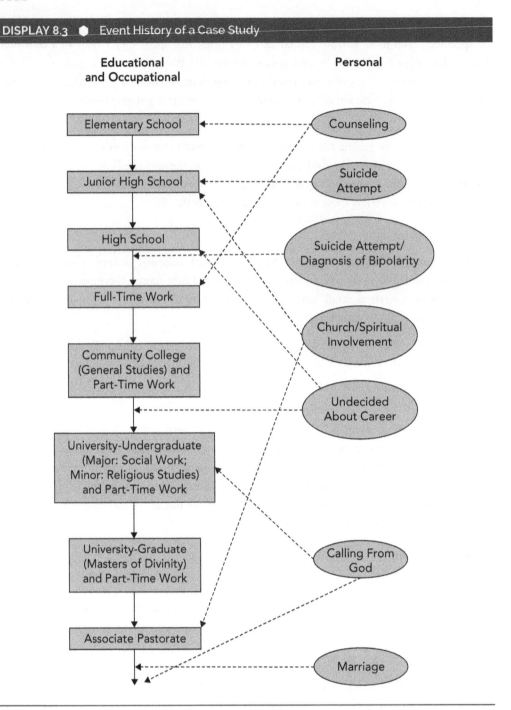

DISPLAY 8.3 ● Event History of a Case Study

number of users, and the horizontal dimension is time. The points or *nodes* are noteworthy events, and the lines or *links* have the implicit meaning "is followed by." Each point is labeled with a more specific month and sometimes a date to mark an event that seemed to the analyst significant to the innovation's implementation and history.

Analysis

Here the analyst is interested in a main variable, *internal diffusion [spread] of an innovation*, defined as growth in the number of teachers using it. That variable is represented in network form as a single line between points. But the analyst has attached various critical events to the line—appointments

Districtwide
Grade
2–8

Extensive

Moderate

Modest

Nil

| Awareness Feb. 75–Aug. 76 | First District Implementation Sept. 76–June 77 | Early Implementation June 77–June 78 | Later Implementation July 78–June 79 | Institutionalization July 79–April 80 |

Feb: 1st Awareness Workshop

April: Commitment from Awareness 1st User

Nov: 1st Turnkey Trainer Trained

June: Helping Teacher Appointed

August: 1st Workshops

Sept 17: Users Start in

Feb: Humphrey Principal and 2 Teachers Trained at D/D Site

March: Visit by D/D

June: 2nd Workshop Series

Sept: Up to 30 Users

June: 3rd Workshop Series

Sept: Up to 36 Users in District; 9/11 in

Humphrey School

April: ECRI Mandated for Grades 3–7

Source: Miles, M. B., & Huberman, A. M. (1994). *Qualitative data analysis: An expanded sourcebook* (2nd ed.). Thousand Oaks, CA: Sage Publications.

of key personnel, training, and the like—that help expand our understanding of the movements of the main variable. You can get a clear idea of the tempo of expansion and can see which events were especially critical (e.g., the first implementation workshops in August 1977). More generally, you can see that workshops appear to be the main mechanism for expanding use of the innovation.

The growth gradient also reveals that it took between 4 and 5 years in the 1970s to achieve "extensive" use of the innovation across various school sites. Some administrators may perceive this as a typical time frame for substantive change to occur and declare the innovation project a success. Other administrators, especially in the fast-paced 21st century, may interpret this as a too slow-moving process that, next time, might be integrated more rapidly into the curriculum through earlier workshop presentations, strategically scheduled right before the school year begins.

Growth gradients can map out not just increases but also decreases, stability, surges, turning points, the erratic, and the idiosyncratic through time (Saldaña, 2003). These patterns are particularly revealing when they seem to emerge gradually or accumulate considerably. You can also map out two or three variables at the same time on a growth gradient, which may reveal some interesting interrelationships and possibly causal factors at work (see Chapter 9).

At least one axis of a growth gradient is time, and the other axis is a range, continuum, or dynamic of some type, be it numbers (1, 2, 3); general amounts (few, some, many); evaluative measures (poor, satisfactory, excellent); frequency (rarely, sometimes, often); direction (negative, neutral, positive); intensity (weak, moderate, strong); position (conservative, moderate, liberal); quality (fractured, ambivalent, unified); and so on. The items you place on nodes in a growth gradient should be related in some way to the primary variable you're examining. The brief event phrases you place on the nodes should be "just enough" to help you properly interpret changes and turning points in the historic timeline.

Notes

Don't be reluctant to use what may seem like a quantitative method with qualitative data. The growth gradient is an effective application for simultaneously assessing long-term quantitative *and* qualitative change. See Belli, Stafford, and Alwin (2009) for calendar and time diary methods for long-term data collection, management, and analysis of qualitative data.

Time-Ordered Matrix

Description

A time-ordered matrix has its columns arranged chronologically by time period to determine when particular phenomena occurred. Row contents depend on what you're studying. This matrix is somewhat comparable with the event listing matrix profiled above, but the time-ordered matrix emphasizes *sequence*, *timing*, and *stability* of processes and experiences (see Display 8.5).

Applications

With qualitative data, you can track sequences, processes, and flows, and are not restricted to "snapshots." The time-ordered matrix displays time-*linked* data referring to phenomena that are bigger than specific events so as to understand (and perhaps later explain) what was happening. Use a descriptive time-ordered matrix like this when your data are fairly complete, to begin developing possible explanations that can be tested by moving back to coded field notes.

Example

In our (Miles and Huberman) 1970s school improvement study, we were concerned with how an innovation changed and transformed across time during several years of implementation. We broke

DISPLAY 8.5 ● Time-Ordered Matrix: Changes in the CARED Innovation (a Work Experience Program)				
		Planning Period Jan.–June 1977	**First Year 1977–1978**	**Second Year 1978–1979**	**Third Year 1979–1980**
Developer Components	Individualization			Some tendency to "batch" students, encourage standard projects, etc.	
	Student responsibility and time use	Added logs/time sheets	Added "accountability" scheme for discipline	Added system of passes for students to leave room	Refusal to accept late work; students were failed
	Direct exposure to work experience				Some tendency to reduce individualization/exploration aspects; more long-term placements; convenience location of jobs
	Program requirements/ curriculum		Added direct instruction on basic skills, separate from job	More competencies required	More competencies and project required
	Learning strategies	Did not include employer seminars; intensified "competencies" experience	Wrote new "competencies" Discarded learning style instrument New basic skills materials	Student learning plan only 1 semester; more basic skills emphasis	Journal more routine communication; less counseling emphasis
	Parental involvement		Parent advisory committee added	Advisory committee mtgs dwindled and stopped	Reduced level of detail in reporting to parents
Other Aspects	Time and credits	Reduced to 4-hr time block; students must take 1 other course			
	Student selection			Moved away from full-random selection to self-selection plus a few random	Lower SES
	Program size		32 students	64 students	70 students, cut to 50 in 2nd semester; 25 for next year (juniors only)

Source: Miles, M. B., & Huberman, A. M. (1994). *Qualitative data analysis: An expanded sourcebook* (2nd ed.). Thousand Oaks, CA: Sage Publications.

down the innovation into specific Developer Components and Other Aspects, using these as rows of the matrix. The columns of the matrix are time periods from early through later use. If a change in a component occurred during the time period, we could enter a short description of the change. A blank cell would mean no change—a nice feature that permits seeing *stability* as well as change.

Display 8.5 shows how this matrix looked. The innovation, CARED, is a work experience program for high school students. The official components were those specified by the original program developer. These Developer Components do not necessarily exhaust important aspects of the innovation, so there are rows for Other Aspects, such as time and credits or student selection. Such aspects usually appear after initial fieldwork and direct experience with the use and meaning of the innovation.

The columns are time periods, starting with the initial planning period (because we expected changes while this relatively demanding and complex innovation was readied for use). The three succeeding school years follow.

In this case, the analyst was looking for changes in the innovation, component by component. Those changes could be found in the coded field notes, where innovation users were asked whether they had made any changes in the innovation's standard format. Follow-up probes asked for parts that had been added, dropped, revised, combined, or selected out for use.

Analysis

Only a few analytic observations culled from the matrix are described below.

Looking across the rows of Display 8.5, you can begin to see drifts or gradual shifts expressing an accumulated tendency underlying specific changes. For example, the row "Program requirements/ curriculum" shows an increasing tendency to make stiffer achievement demands on students (the tactic here is **noting patterns, themes**—see Chapter 11). The component "Student responsibility and time use" suggests that a process of exerting more and more control over student behavior is occurring (the accountability scheme, the system of passes, etc.).

At this point, the analyst can deepen understanding by referring back to other aspects of the field notes, notably what else people said about the changes or reasons for them. In this example, a staff member said, "Your neck is on the block . . . the success and failures of the students rebound [*sic*] directly on you." So, the increased emphasis on control might come from the staff's feelings of vulnerability and mistrust of students (tactic: **noting relations between variables**).

What else is happening? We can note an important structural shift in the second year: moving away from random student selection to self-selection. The field notes showed that this decision was precipitated by principals and counselors, who opposed entry by college-bound students and wanted the program to be a sort of safety valve for poorly performing, alienated students. Thus, the program became a sort of "dumping ground" or "oasis" (tactic: **making metaphors**) for such students. But look at the bottom "Program size" row. Though the program doubles in the second year, it cuts back substantially in the third year. In this case, severe funding problems were beginning to develop (tactic: **finding mediating variables**).

Display 8.5 may be too busy and unfocused for a final report—it is more a for-the-researcher's-eyes-only exhibit than a report of findings. One way of resolving these problems is to condense the matrix even further to (a) verify the tendencies observed in the initial analysis and (b) summarize the core information for the researcher and the reader.

Display 8.5 could be condensed in myriad ways. One approach is to standardize the several drifts by naming them—that is, finding a gerund such as "controlling" or "tightening up" that indicated what was going on when a change was made in the innovation (tactic: **clustering**). The result appears in Display 8.6 as a summary table.

Reading the Tendency column and using the tactic of counting the number of mentions for each theme confirms the accuracy of the initial analysis. The core themes are indeed stiffer achievement

DISPLAY 8.6 ◆ Summary Tables for Verifying and Interpreting a Time-Ordered Matrix: Changes in the CARED Innovation		
Component	**Tendency**	**Significance/Meaning for Site**
Individualization	Standardizing	Undergoes individualization, shows streamlining as response to demandingness
Student responsibility	Controlling, tightening up	Reflects staff feelings of vulnerability, mistrust toward students
Exposure to work	Simplifying, standardizing	Response to demandingness: cutting back on innovativeness of the project
Program requirements	Going academic	Shows vulnerability, marginality of project in the two high schools—again cutting back on innovativeness of CARED
Learning strategies	Going academic, de-individualizing, simplifying, standardizing	More "routinization" overall
Parental involvement	Cutting back, simplifying	Response to demandingness
Time and credits	Cutting back, going academic	Done early: reflects principals' opposition to project, etc.
Student selection	Self-selecting	Project becomes "dumping ground" but also gets stronger endorsement from counselors, principals
Program size	Growing, then dwindling	Reflection of funding problems and possibly of under-endorsement

Source: Miles, M. B., & Huberman, A. M. (1994). *Qualitative data analysis: An expanded sourcebook* (2nd ed.). Thousand Oaks, CA: Sage Publications.

demands ("Going academic"), more control, increased routinization ("Simplifying"), and reduced individualization ("Standardizing"). You might even try for an overarching label to typify the set—something like "Self-protective erosion," thus subsuming particulars into the general—and this labeling can kick off the final analytic text, usable in the report of findings.

A scan of the Significance/Meaning for Site column helps summarize the underlying issues, which we identified as exhaustion, lack of local endorsement, and the discrepancy between the demands of the innovation and the organizational procedures and norms in the immediate environment.

Overall, for time-ordered matrices, be sure the time periods chosen are a good fit for the phenomena under study. They should be fine enough to separate events that you want to keep in sequence, rather than blending them into one big pot. Use Content-Analytic Summary Tables (see Display 6.20) to pull together and look at data from the display if it is too complicated.

Notes

In this profile's example, the time periods were relatively long (a full school year), but depending on the phenomena under study, they could be shorter (semesters, months, weeks, days, hours). The cell entries here were specific *changes*. But you can also enter specific *events* such as decisions, actions, key meetings, or crises.

The rows of this matrix were components or aspects of an innovation. Many other types of rows can be used in a time-ordered matrix: *roles* (principal, teacher, student, parent); *event types* (planned/unplanned, critical actions); *settings* (Classroom 1, Classroom 2, principal's office, central office); or *activity types* (teaching, counseling, formal meetings).

By relabeling the matrix rows, you can examine time-related events or states *across* cases. Data from several cases can be displayed in a way that respects chronology for assessing change (if any) in longitudinal, action, and evaluation studies. For looking at the general flow of events *within* a case, see the methods for an Event Listing Matrix and Event-State Networks in this chapter.

ORDERING PROCESSES

Decision Modeling maps out specific choices and actions we take for a particular process. *Process Mapping* diagrams a flow of action across time and space in graphic form. An *Event-State Network* illustrates how events and their transitional states can be plotted as a flow diagram. And a *Composite Sequence Analysis* integrates multiple participants' journeys into a single diagram.

Decision Modeling

Description

A decision model is a visual network graphic that outlines the thoughts, plans, and choices/decisions made during a flow of actions embedded in a range of conditions (see Display 8.7).

Applications

Sometimes, you want to know how a basic process plays out across an individual or a number of cases and to build a general model of just how it works. One such process is decision making and its related actions by individuals. Decision modeling is either an individual or a collective display of the options available for a particular process and the possible pathways that can be taken—usually but not exclusively—based on "yes" or "no" alternatives.

The method is very useful for making the inexplicit visible and clear and can also be used for recurring decisions involving many people and complex situations (e.g., patient care in an intensive care unit, serving a meal to a large party in a restaurant, dealing with customer complaints). This sort of display lends itself well to improving practice or recasting policy. The model is also effective for diagramming more open-ended participant decision-making processes that will help answer the types of following research questions: How do high school students decide to attend a particular university? What is involved in moving from recreational to addictive drug use?

Example

Even the most seemingly mundane daily life actions contain multiple and sometimes complex decision-making processes based on patterned regularities and occasional contingencies. To put this assertion to the test, Saldaña created a decision model for something he does every day: deciding where to eat dinner. Though the example may seem trivial, the information it contains is of particular interest to the U.S. restaurant industry and its annual sales of nearly 800 billion dollars.

Display 8.7 illustrates the array of minor and major decisions involved with whether to eat at home or to dine out. The initiating action is what he and his partner refer to as their "food mood"—what and thus where they feel like eating. But the final destination—eating at home or dining out—is reached after going through a series of mental decisions and negotiations based on local habits

DISPLAY 8.7 ● A Decision Model for Evening Dinner Choices

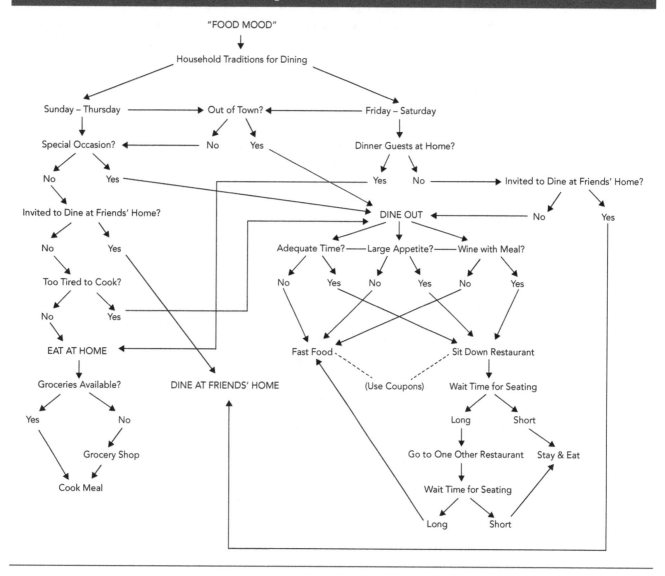

(e.g., dining patterns on selected days of the week); contingencies (e.g., if out of town, if weekend dinner guests are coming to the home); and questions (e.g., is adequate time available?).

Analysis

Display 8.7 was shown to colleagues, who found it clear and self-explanatory. This decision model was created based on personal reflections and recall, but most decision models are generated from interviews with participants explicating a process of some kind, and the various factors that influence and affect their decision making.

After the interview about a process, the researcher reviews the transcript and maps out with pencil and paper the participant's decision-making processes about the topic of interest. The two primary things to remember about a first-draft decision model is to (a) stick with a very focused task—"eating dinner" is a lot simpler to plot than "weekly meal plans"; (b) start with listings of simple decision-making questions and actions that can be furthered through "yes" or "no" or other limited alternatives. You may feel as though this is abhorrently reductive of the richness of what you're trying to model. But this is just a starting point to get you thinking about the *actions* necessary to further *other actions*. And things will get more complex with each additional person you interview about his or her process for eating dinner. New alternatives will enter the picture, and your model will extend beyond "yes" and "no" to reveal Pathway Option 1, Pathway Option 2, Pathway Option 3, and so on (see Display 8.7's links, "Adequate time?", "Large appetite?", and "Wine with meal?").

The procedure for composite decision modeling can be done iteratively: The criteria established by the first person (e.g., Saldaña's model) are used in an interview with a second person, and so on. Repeated interviewing of multiple participants is usually needed, along with attempts to disconfirm the model through feedback and verification, and checking with a new, uninterviewed sample of people. Gradually, a composite decision model for eating dinner is built. Or, a full set of individual decision models like Display 8.7 can be done and then generalized into a composite. The next step is to test the composite model through interviews with new populations, using all of the decision criteria—for example, evening dinner routines of a large family with infant and preschool children, college students on a tight budget, and couples using meal delivery services such as Blue Apron or Grubhub.

Our actions in life are not always a series of strictly "yes" or "no" decisions. There are many times we answer a "yes" or "no" question with "It depends." The decision model approach is stronger on *logical* order, rather than narrative order as such. It strips away nuanced but nonessential information, yet retains the key conditions and specifies contingently the decisions to be made. It's essential to preserve the validity of each separate decision model; each person's path must be represented accurately, even though some more idiosyncratic features may need to be generalized to a more abstract version.

Decision making can be a complex cognitive process, depending on the task at hand, for a flurry of thoughts can race quickly through a person's mind as alternatives beyond "yes" or "no" are considered, benefits to self and others are weighed, moral and ethical soliloquies are pondered, available time and money are calculated, and best- and worst-case outcomes are hypothesized. The decision model attempts to generalize across individuals, but it does not limit itself to generalities. Some models can plot the emotional complexities of and inner motivations for our decision-making dilemmas.

This profile is a gloss of the full procedures and methods, for composite decision modeling is a prescribed process with modest statistical tasks. For more detailed instructions and examples, see Bernard (2011) and Bernard, Wutich, and Ryan (2017).

Notes

The decision model is somewhat comparable to the cognitive network (see Display 7.13). But the decision model focuses on and examines one particular process and its related actions, while the cognitive network attempts to chart more internal, fluid, and open-ended mental experiences.

For a comic yet actual decision model in action, see "The Friendship Algorithm" episode from the popular TV series *The Big Bang Theory*.

Process Mapping

Description

A process map is a drawing, usually freehand, by a participant or researcher that depicts social action in relationship to or as it progresses through time and geographic or conceptual space (see Display 8.8). The process map, if desired, can be formalized with rendering software to give the graphic display a more finished appearance.

DISPLAY 8.8 ● A Process Map of a Chaos Narrative About Cancer

(Some social researchers might refer to this method as "cognitive mapping," but we relabel it *process mapping* in this profile to distinguish it from the more systematic, internal thought processes involved with *cognitive networks* described in Chapter 7; and to emphasize how action in actual or conceptual space/place plays a role in process mapping.)

Applications

The steps or order of a social process can be narratively described in oral or written forms through prosaic, numbered, or bullet pointed formats. This storytelling structure or plot provides a sequential "what happens next?" outline of actions that presents a conventional, linear flow of events. But there are occasions when time or process can interplay closely with space. Human actions—the *what*—always happen somewhere in time, and the *where* often becomes just as important as the *who*, *what* and *when*. In combination, these concepts can often help us answer *how* and *why* questions.

Process mapping utilizes the visual to both support and extend the oral or written narrative. It *shows* rather than tells how events unfold across time and space. Just as software like Google Maps helps us navigate through unknown streets to a needed destination within an estimated time frame, process maps help the researcher navigate an investigative journey through new social phenomena to answer her research questions of interest related to action, time, and place.

Example

Display 8.8 exhibits a five-month trajectory of Saldaña's spring and summer 2018 health issues with a low-grade cancer diagnosis. The visual story begins in the upper left corner with "4.6"—a higher than normal PSA (Prostate-Specific Antigen) level during routine blood work that signaled the possibility of prostate cancer. This moment initiates the process of everything that follows downward on the map.

Major moments or turning points during the time period are depicted within jagged shapes ("4.6," "First Diagnostic Surgery," "Recovery Hell, "Cancer Diagnosis," "Anxiety"), while key players and actions (e.g., "Urologist," "EKG," "Bladder Pain") appear throughout. The downward trajectory to "Recovery Hell" symbolizes a low point or moment during the period. The July 2018 moment of "Anxiety" is not the end of the process, but signals an unknown health-related future, which includes additional surgery, pathology, and treatment.

Analysis

The five-month process or journey of this health-related issue could have been described through prose alone. An arts-based account of this experience through poetic display (see Chapter 7) is yet another alternative. But Display 8.8's irregular lines, shapes, and directions add emphasis to and harmonize with the story's "chaos narrative," as the genre has been labeled.

This autoethnographic rendering, as an example, illustrates how process maps drawn *by* the people we study makes the research enterprise a more participatory one. The participant can be prompted to create a visual display of an experience that unfolds through time and space. The hand drawn display then serves as a stimulus for the researcher's questions to the participant about the process under study. Like visual data analysis of photographs described in Chapter 4, the researcher and participant jointly reflect on and co-construct the *inferences*, *interpretations*, and *implications* of the drawing and thus the phenomenon.

Process maps work effectively when the time span investigated is relatively brief (e.g., ranging from a few hours, days, weeks, or months), and the space/place is limited in area (e.g., accessible within a few hours of time). But process maps can also display the "eventful," such as a family reunion or graduation ceremony, or place emphasis on space over time, such as the activities within a shared dorm room, or the foot traffic within a convenience store retail space. If the participants are up to it, process maps can be drawn for long-term *conceptual ideas* rather than the actual, such as "career," "aging," and "friendship."

Variations of this method also have been used with young people when they were asked to draw elements of their immediate social areas (home, school, neighborhood) as pre-interview framing. Younger children may draw more of a still-life "snapshot" rather than an active map, but with strategic questioning the interviewer can ask the child to elaborate on the drawing's contents and suggested meanings and pathways.

Researchers themselves can also draw process maps as a precursor to matrix or network development, or as a follow-up heuristic after a matrix has been assembled to give the two-dimensional display a more active character. Remember that a process map is an integrated graphic that exhibits social *action* across *time* through a specific or conceptual *space*. Since the goal is to order a sequence of events in graphic form, allow the visual artist in you to go beyond textual narratives and to find symbolic representations to use as vivid illustrations of the phenomena. A process map of a "career" can include simple icons such as a diploma, moving van, desk, paystub, and so on.

The current accessibility and popularity of GIS (geographic information systems) software for qualitative inquiry has generated a heightened interest in place and space in social science research. We have read several studies in which GIS apps enhanced the analysis since location and geography were critical features of the project. But we have also seen a few studies in which GIS was employed for trendiness rather than relevance to the work. If the site(s) you're investigating covers an expansive area (e.g., neighborhoods, districts, cities, regions), then consider how GIS might supplement the research goals of your study.

Notes

Irvine's (2016) study of male and female college students' perceptions of their sexual experiences, with particular attention on the emotional dynamics involved with "the walk of shame" phenomenon, is an excellent example of how the participants we study, rather than the researcher, can create intriguing visual displays that inform a project's analysis, and how space and time work in concert for a qualitative analysis.

Event-State Network

Description

An event-state network is a visual and processual adaptation and representation of an event listing matrix (see Display 8.2). Events are represented as boxes; the sharp edges imply specificity and a narrow time span. States (or conditions) are represented as bubbles; round edges imply more diffuseness, less concreteness, and existence over a longer time. You connect the boxes and bubbles by lines and arrows to show what led to what. States or conditions are not as time-limited as events and often serve as the mediators or links between specific events (see Display 8.9).

Applications

A matrix is a cell-based, linear display that organizes events chronologically. But the tight borders of a matrix do not enable processual illustration of the sometimes multiple and overlapping events happening simultaneously within and driven by specific states and conditions. If life is complex and interconnected, then sometimes our analytic representations and displays need to reflect that complexity and interconnectedness, rather than condense it to more manageable understandings.

An event-state network portrays both the *actions* of participants (as events in boxes) and the *conflicts or rationales* (as states in bubbles) that initiate their actions. The network is thus a heuristic for deducing from data not just *what* happened but the possible motivations for *how* and *why*.

Example

By the time an event listing matrix is generated, you usually have a set of implicit generalizations about why things happened as they did. Event-state networks are a way of making those ideas explicit and verifiable. Display 8.9 shows an excerpt from an event-state network drawn from the data in the event listing matrix in Display 8.2.

Analysis

Once an event listing matrix is done, a network can be generated somewhat quickly. If you wish to work by hand first, write one event per "sticky note," generate state or condition sticky notes as you go, and arrange the emerging network on a large sheet of poster paper, drawing arrows as you go. This method is an especially helpful step toward assessing causal dynamics in a particular case.

DISPLAY 8.9 ● Event–State Network, Banestown Case (Excerpt)

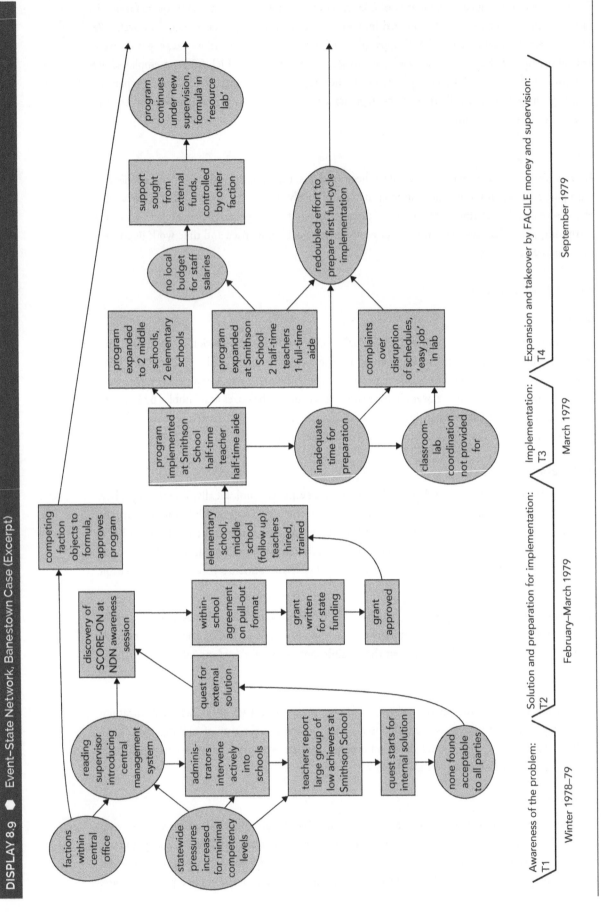

Awareness of the problem:
T1

Winter 1978–79

Solution and preparation for implementation:
T2

February–March 1979

Implementation:
T3

March 1979

Expansion and takeover by FACILE money and supervision:
T4

September 1979

Source: Miles, M. B., & Huberman, A. M. (1994). *Qualitative data analysis: An expanded sourcebook* (2nd ed.). Thousand Oaks, CA: Sage Publications.

To create state or condition sticky notes, (a) recheck the field notes for evidence of the antecedent conditions, mediating variables, and/or outcomes or consequences of specific events; and (b) surface your generalized understandings of what was moving events along in the process you are studying.

A cell-by-cell matrix is not necessarily required preparation for drawing a network, but it greatly helps. In large-scale qualitative studies with a massive database, it is essential to have a firm grasp on the categorical/thematic and processual understandings before tackling a network. In small-scale qualitative studies with a more manageable database, you can experiment with drawing networks *as a way of getting to* categorical/thematic and processual understandings.

Have a colleague examine your network without explanation to see if he or she can follow the processual trail. The audit may also generate valuable discussion for redesigning the drawing. For example, another analyst examined one of Saldaña's diagrams (see Display 2.12) and took issue with how one state led to another. Saldaña agreed and even felt his colleague's suggestion was correct. But the data suggested otherwise; how the researchers felt the process *should* happen was not the way the *participants* said it did. Thus, the participants' version was accepted as final say for the network.

For those who wish to create this type of display with computing software, selected CAQDAS programs such as NVivo permit you to create such networks easily, shifting and changing them as your understanding grows. Word software's Shapes with inserted text are a more accessible option.

Notes

Event-state networks are a visual and processual way to make sense of a text-based event listing matrix. It does not usually help to accompany the network with a long narrative text; the display itself is more economical and illuminating. But a summary set of analytic comments may be useful.

Composite Sequence Analysis

Description

A composite sequence analysis extracts typical stories or scenarios from multiple individual cases to develop a collective network that represents their common and unique features into meaningful sequences and paths (see Display 8.10).

Applications

There are analytic occasions when you need to describe multiple participant journeys through time. These stories can be told through individual narratives and then through a thematically connected one. But the length and number of these individual stories may be too much to grasp in one sitting. A composite sequence display graphically illustrates the participants' collective journey across time (and/or space), while maintaining the tangential and idiosyncratic veer-offs necessary for texture and detail.

Longitudinal research is also interested in demarcated periods of time such as phases, stages, and cycles (Saldaña, 2003). These patterned periodicities provide us with a short- and long-term understanding of how the rhythms of life or work may proceed. We are better prepared for the journey if we know what may lie ahead. Thus, there is predictive utility in composite sequence analysis and display design.

Example

This example comes from Huberman's (1989, 1993) life-cycle study of 160 teachers. Huberman was interested in what he called career trajectories of teachers. He was working from interviews with

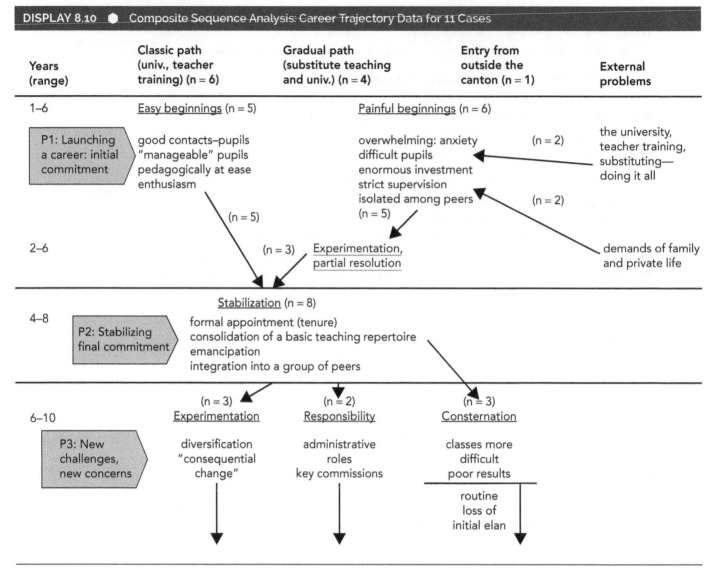

Source: Huberman, A. M. (1989). *The professional life cycle of teachers. Teachers College Record, 97*(1), 31–57.

secondary-level teachers, all of whom had divided their careers into phases or stages. They themselves provided the names or themes for each phase.

First, the material for each case was condensed onto a 25-page protocol, with an identical format for each participant. For each person's career trajectory, the sequence of themes was mapped, with the features of each theme added in. An initial theme labeled "drowning," for example, was often characterized by features such as difficulties with maintaining discipline, exhaustion, unpredictability, feelings of professional inadequacy, overload, and the like.

How could you begin to group the cases, phase by phase, to see any "families" of trajectories? The first step was to group cases *within* phases. The decision rules for grouping cases within a given phase were as follows: (a) The theme itself had to be denotatively or connotatively identical, and (b) at least two features had to be the same. For example, one participant might name a "stabilizing" phase and another a "settling down" phase, while both teachers were at the same point in their sequence and each used two of the same features to describe that phase (e.g., gaining tenure, having a basic instructional repertoire).

Graphically, this procedure amounts to an overlay of individual trajectories, although it is clear that seen up close, each career is qualitatively distinct. But we do get, as Wittgenstein put it so well, "family resemblances," with some intersections, along with their distinctive properties.

Analysis

Let's illustrate these intersections by a look at Display 8.10. It depicts 11 teachers, 1 of 16 subgroups; here we have women with 5 to 10 years of teaching experience at the lower secondary level.

At the left is the range of years of teaching experience within phases and a series of general phases defined by the researchers in light of the phase names given by participants:

P1: Launching a career: initial commitment

P2: Stabilizing: final commitment

P3: New challenges, new concerns

Within each general phase are subgroups. For example, of the 11 women, 5 describe their initial phase in terms of "Easy beginnings" (tactic: **clustering**). The common features are noted under the theme. Six women evoke "Painful beginnings," again with a list of features, and four mention external problems (parallel work at "the university" and "teacher training"; "demands of family and private life"). Through experimentation and trials and errors, these problems are attenuated for three women.

The second phase, *Stabilization*, is common to nearly all. It is, in effect, one of those archetypal stages in the teaching career. Note, however, that $n = 8$, meaning that 3 of the original cohort of 11 have not followed the sequence but rather have taken another path (not shown on the display). In that sense, the sequential analysis gets progressively more stringent. It groups only participants who have attached identical or analogous themes to the same sequence of phases.

Display 8.10 shows a third phase for this cohort, "New challenges," in which the paths diverge still more into three tracks: *Experimentation* (three teachers), *Responsibility* (two teachers), and *Consternation* (three teachers). Once again, these thematic names were provided by the participants.

In this study, the researchers were taking a variable-oriented approach while still trying for a narrative ordering of the data. They were hunting for correspondences across the full set of 160 participants. By reviewing 16 charts like the one just shown, they came out with four modal sequences. The first scenario—the prime sequence in Display 8.10—accounts for 17% of the population and was called "Recovered harmony":

Painful beginnings → Stabilization → Experimentation

Another sequence represents 25% of the sample—by no means the majority, but a strong cluster—a clutch of people describing their career progression in terms of "Reassessment":

Stabilization → Reassessment ⟨ Resolution: "a second wind"
Nonresolution: "The fault of this damned system"

Taken together, the four scenarios located account for 65% of the sample. Much has been lost in the condensation of 25 pages of data to a bare-bones sequence in Display 8.10. But we argue that, in conceptual terms, it is this last scenario-building exercise that tells us most graphically how the case narratives cluster—in this instance, how the teaching career plays out for different subgroups of its members. And we have successfully linked a case-oriented and a variable-oriented approach, protecting case sequences and gaining the conceptual power that cut-across variables can bring.

The most important preparatory work for constructing a composite sequence display is having a solid grasp on how the phases are narratively told, and what researcher- or participant-generated words/phrases best describe and label the phases. This is one of those analytic tasks that asks you to consider what all of the differences—or at least most of them—have in common. You may also discover that working concurrently and back and forth on both the narrative and display will help inform the other's development.

Notes

This method reinforces that network displays can handle narrative complexity more easily than matrices can. For an excellent longitudinal qualitative study that describes five different early career decisions in teaching, see Cochran-Smith et al. (2012).

ORDERING BY CASES

A *Case-Process Comparison* examines two or more cases as they each progress through a series of comparable actions. A *Case-Ordered Descriptive Meta-Matrix* hierarchically organizes cases according to selected criteria to compare common variables or outcomes of interest.

Case-Process Comparison

Description

A case-process comparison graphically illustrates two (or more) cases simultaneously as they each progress through a series of comparable actions. The display highlights the comparability and variability of an ordered process (see Display 8.11).

Applications

We have read several outstanding case study reports in which two individuals or sites were compared and contrasted (e.g., Clark-Ibáñez, 2008; Mages, 2007). The cases' differing processes were narratively described, and quite well. But there are times when a visual graphic can illuminate two individuals' diverse ways of working or living, accompanied with relevant data displayed in a side-by-side format. Their commonalities and differences become more strikingly apparent, and the graphic joins cases *and* the order of a particular shared process through time.

Case-process comparison is useful when two individuals, small groups, or sites are investigated, and a comparable process of some kind is examined. A matrix with step- or time-based cells as columns and participants in rows can certainly fulfill this charge, but a graphic like Display 8.11 is a "sophisticated cartoon strip" of sorts that shows different cases in action through time. It integrates selected principles and elements from the qualitative timeline, time-ordered matrix, decision modeling, and process mapping to display how different people accomplish goals in similar and/or different ways.

Step 1: Situation recognition
Key factors influencing curriculum design

Step 2: Planning steps
Discrete steps taken to plan observed class

Step 3: Artifacts and planned enactment
Artifact developed for class and planned use

Step 4: Actual enactment in the classroom
Classroom observation results

Time

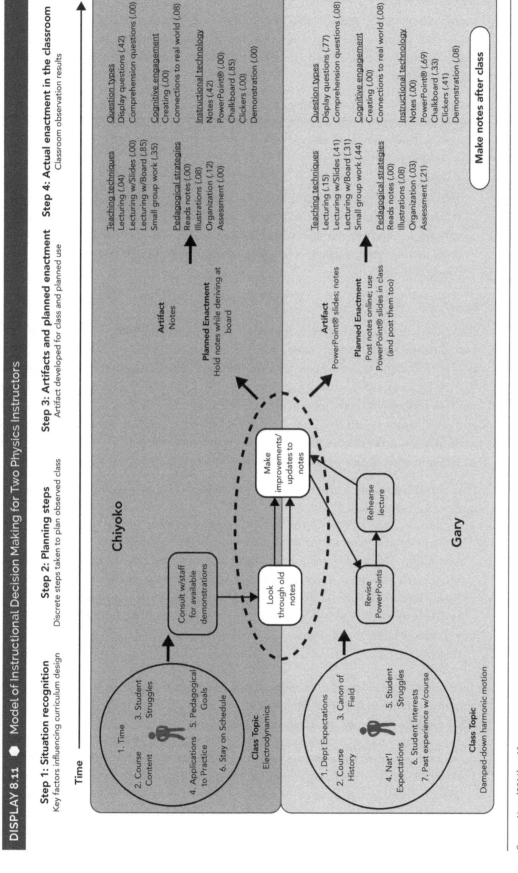

Chiyoko

Class Topic
Electrodynamics

1. Time
2. Course Content
3. Student Struggles
4. Applications to Practice
5. Pedagogical Goals
6. Stay on Schedule

Consult w/staff for available demonstrations

Look through old notes

Make improvements/ updates to notes

Artifact
Notes

Planned Enactment
Hold notes while deriving at board

Teaching techniques
Lecturing (.04)
Lecturing w/Slides (.00)
Lecturing w/Board (.85)
Small group work (.35)

Pedagogical strategies
Reads notes (.00)
Illustrations (.08)
Organization (.12)
Assessment (.00)

Question types
Display questions (.42)
Comprehension questions (.00)

Cognitive engagement
Creating (.00)
Connections to real world (.08)

Instructional technology
Notes (.42)
PowerPoint® (.00)
Chalkboard (.85)
Clickers (.00)
Demonstration (.00)

Gary

Class Topic
Damped-down harmonic motion

1. Dept Expectations
2. Course History
3. Canon of Field
4. Nat'l Expectations
5. Student Struggles
6. Student Interests
7. Past experience w/course

Revise PowerPoints

Rehearse lecture

Artifact
PowerPoint® slides; notes

Planned Enactment
Post notes online; use PowerPoint® slides in class (and post them too)

Teaching techniques
Lecturing (.15)
Lecturing w/Slides (.41)
Lecturing w/Board (.31)
Small group work (.44)

Pedagogical strategies
Reads notes (.00)
Illustrations (.08)
Organization (.03)
Assessment (.21)

Question types
Display questions (.77)
Comprehension questions (.08)

Cognitive engagement
Creating (.00)
Connections to real world (.08)

Instructional technology
Notes (.00)
PowerPoint® (.69)
Chalkboard (.33)
Clickers (.41)
Demonstration (.08)

Make notes after class

Source: Hora (2016), p. 12.

Example

Hora (2016) interviewed 58 university STEM faculty about their curricula and class planning practices in math, biology, chemistry, geology, and physics courses. The primary goal was to examine "how faculty actually plan their courses in real-world settings" (p. 1), meaning, how factors such as course objectives, time, class size, available textbooks, lecture notes, PowerPoint slides, and so on, influenced and affected the "problem space" of instructional preparation and decision making.

Two professors were observed teaching for more in-depth analysis to explore their teaching methods, pedagogical strategies, student-teacher interactions, cognitive engagement, and use of instructional technology. Participant observation of the two instructors, Chiyoko and Gary, followed a particular observation protocol and coding scheme to collect the data:

> The two individuals were selected based on their working in the same discipline, as well as teaching undergraduate courses, thereby holding discipline and teaching assignment constant. . . . The graphics show what I call the "decision chains" that represent the structure and temporal nature of instructional decision making at the individual level. (Hora, 2016, p. 7)

Analysis

Display 8.11 first illustrates process through four "Step" columns. The first, "Situation Recognition," lists the major teaching contexts and influential pedagogical factors for each case, such as "Time," "Course Content," and "Student Struggles" for Chiyoko; and "Dept. Expectations," "Course History," and "Canon of Field" for Gary. Under Step 2, "Planning Steps," both instructors look through and make improvements to their lecture notes, while each case has his or her own class preparation actions. Under Step 3, the cases' teaching artifacts and enactments differ, while Step 4 logs the observer's record of each instructor's pedagogical strategies in percentages according to selected time intervals.

Hora (2016) explains the details of each case presented in the display and offers the following summary for the female teacher:

> In the case of Chiyoko, her personal goal to engage the "middle" group of students who were neither high nor low achievers appeared to have shaped how she designed her classes and selected activities in a way that led to an active and engaging classroom. At the very least, it seems that some consideration of students during the planning process, as is evident in approaches such as backwards design or problem-based learning, contributes to instruction that is well aligned with the interests and aptitudes of a particular group of students. (p. 15)

These two cases are compared and contrasted, and then used to supplement and exemplify the results from the interview analyses with 58 professors. Just some of the key findings from this study and a recommendation for future research are as follows:

> When an instructor walks into a classroom, bringing artifacts such as lecture notes or PowerPoint slides, the learning environment that is subsequently crafted for students is strongly shaped by the nature of these tools. . . . Given the increase in the use of digital technologies for teaching purposes, including learning management systems and online courses, future research should also examine whether these new tools are influencing how instructors think about and conduct their work. (pp. 15–16)

A process map requires three things: action, time, and space. A case-process comparison graphic requires action and time as well, but in this display, space is replaced by *case*—two of them—to reveal both commonalities and differences to inform the analysis. The cases needn't always be people or social settings, however. Perhaps two key variables or concepts' properties and dimensions could be compared. Two different studies' methodologies, contents, and findings could be contrasted.

An *N* of just 2 may seem like too small a sample to some for there to be any utility, much less validity, to the analysis. But a case-process comparison can serve as a detailed subset from a larger corpus that highlights the nuances missing from aggregated, synthesized data. The two cases needn't be outliers or extremes, or lie at polar opposites of a continuum. It is from contrast—subtle as well as stark—that we become aware of just how similar, different, and variable two people really are.

Notes

A case-process comparison graphic, with some creative display arrangement, could be constructed for more than two individuals, small groups, or sites, but we recommend no more than five cases total.

Case-Ordered Descriptive Meta-Matrix

Description

A case-ordered descriptive meta-matrix contains first-level descriptive data from all cases, but the cases are *ordered* (e.g., high, medium, low) according to the main variable being examined (see Displays 8.12 and 8.13).

Applications

Case-ordered displays array data case by case, but the cases are ordered according to some variable of interest so that you can easily see the differences among high, medium, and low cases, for example. It's a powerful way to understand differences across cases to help answer questions such as the following: What are the real patterns of more and less X in the cases? Why do we see more X at one site or case and less of it in another? This makes the method particularly suitable for evaluation and action research studies.

Example

In our (Miles and Huberman) school improvement study, we were interested in a variable we called "student impact." We interviewed not only students themselves but also teachers, parents, administrators, counselors—and had looked at formal evaluation data as well. We wanted to assemble this information in one place and understand the differences among cases that showed high, medium, or low student impact.

Our data focused not only on "direct" student outcomes (e.g., improved reading test scores) but also on what we called "meta-level" or more general outcomes (e.g., increased interest in school activities) and "side effects" (e.g., "zest in experimental program leads to alienation from regular classes"). We also wanted to track both positive and negative effects of the innovation on students.

How can the cases be ordered? You can look at the relevant sections of each case report and note the general level of student impact the writer of the case report had claimed. You place the cases in rough order, and then you reskim the text in each case report to see whether the first impression is justified or whether the ordering should be changed. Some programs aimed high, shooting for everything

DISPLAY 8.12 ● Ordered Meta-Matrix: Format for Student Impact Data					
		Direct effects		Meta-level and side effects	
CASES	Program objectives	Positive	Negative	Positive	Negative
CASE 1 *(highest impact)*					
CASE 2 *(next)*					
Etc.					

Source: Miles, M. B., & Huberman, A. M. (1994). *Qualitative data analysis: An expanded sourcebook* (2nd ed.). Thousand Oaks, CA: Sage Publications.

from student achievement to self-concept, while others were more focused, hoping only, say, for the improvement of reading skills.

That range suggests the usefulness of a format like Display 8.12. The idea here is to show the objectives and to enter data in the form of phrases or sentences in the appropriate cells. This way, we keep more of the raw data, and we can see how outcomes are related to objectives. Our own matrix legend/shorthand to show the data source (i.e., Attribute Codes) was as follows: U for user, A for administrator, E for evaluator, S for student, P for parent, and so on. If the impact was seen as strong, the letter would be underlined; if uncertain, a question mark would be added; if the evidence was conflicting, an X would be added (i.e., Magnitude Codes).

From relevant sections of each case report, we look for coded material on direct and meta-level outcomes and summarize the material in a set of brief sentences or phrases, one for each distinct outcome. We can arrange the data in the Program Objectives and the Direct Outcome columns in parallel fashion to make comparisons easier. Skills and achievement goals might be placed first, followed by affective/attitudinal and other outcomes. Some criteria for a "high" rating are as follows:

1. The program is achieving most of its aims.

2. The program is also achieving other positive meta-level and side effects.

3. These judgments are corroborated, either through repeated responses from one role through cross-role agreement or through evaluation data.

Display 8.13 shows how this sort of data display worked out. The rows show two cases (Perry-Parkdale, Masepa) where student impact was high; two where it was moderate (Carson, Calston); one moderate to low (Dun Hollow); and one low (Burton). (For simplicity, we show an excerpted table, with only 6 of our 12 cases.)

Analysis

At first glance, Display 8.13 looks daunting and overloading. But first try eyeballing or a "squint analysis" by asking where in the table the data look dense or sparse.

Looking across rows, we can see that positive effects are more frequent than negative ones (tactic: **making contrasts, comparisons**). Another squint shows us that cases where many negative effects are noted (e.g., Perry-Parkdale, Masepa) are cases where much is being attempted (in terms of the

Program Objectives column). Apparently, large efforts are more likely to spin off negative effects along with the positive ones (tactic: **noting relations between variables**).

Looking at the two right-hand columns shows significant meta-level and side effects in nearly all cases (tactic: **noting patterns, themes**); in only the lowest impact case (Burton) do we see none at all. Perhaps this pattern means that the claims for meta-level changes in moderate-impact cases are suspect. Maybe so—they are less likely to have repeated mention (underlines) and have fewer instances of multiple-role confirmation (tactic: **using extreme cases**).

To clarify the last two columns: We defined meta-level outcomes as congruent with the program's purposes but affecting more general aspects of students' functioning. Note the reading program at Calston: It led to the direct outcome of improved reading skills, but by providing interesting materials and opportunities for independent student work, it may have induced the meta-level outcome of increased student self-direction. Side effects are more unintended: Note the alienation of Perry-Parkdale students, who liked their program's concreteness and relevance, but thereby came to dislike their regular high school's courses and activities.

During analysis of a case-ordered descriptive meta-matrix, first do a general squint. Where is the matrix dense, where is it empty? Draw conclusions and write them out. Then, look down particular columns, **comparing/contrasting** what things look like for high, medium, and low cases. It may be useful to look at more than one column at a time to **note relations between variables**.

A first-cut case-ordered descriptive meta-matrix can be big. Expect to make several cuts at the format of the matrix before you settle on the one best for your purposes. Recheck the ordering of cases at several points as you proceed; ask a colleague to confirm or argue with your ordering. For less complex databases, it often helps to enter actual direct quotes from case reports, rather than researcher-constructed sentences or phrases. They give an even more direct grounding in the data for the analyst and the reader.

A case-ordered descriptive meta-matrix is usually a fundamental next step in understanding what's going on across cases. Time spent on this is well worth the investment because so much later analysis rests on it.

Notes

Miles and Huberman's classic Display 8.13 employed a legend of single letters and symbols to differentiate between sources and corroboration of data. Today, software such as Word and Excel can color code or use rich text features and varying font sizes to separate different types of data from one another in a matrix and make them much more visually discernible at a glance.

Also remember that rows and columns can be transposed for your analytic goals. It's usually easier to show affects by rows rather than columns, simply because there is more space to insert text there.

CASES	Program Objectives	Direct Outcome — Positive	Direct Outcome — Negative	Meta-Level Outcomes and Side Effects — Positive	Meta-Level Outcomes and Side Effects — Negative
High Impact					
Perry-Parkdale (E)	Basic skills (reading, math, communication, etc.) Life skills (critical thinking, citizenship) Life competencies (credit, health, etc.) Job-finding skills Entry-level work skills, career training Decision-making skills Self-responsibility and initiative Matching interests/abilities to job information Understanding of others Know socioeconomic trends: career knowledge Sex role awareness Better parent-child communication	Same or better on basic skills scores U, better math (12th-grade girls) E P Specific job skills S E P U Career planning and choice: aids goalless Job exploration attitudes positive E How interests fit jobs, what to look for in job E: identity, explore career options C A Experience with world of work: head start C U S Career, occupational knowledge E Preparation for real world of work Experience in working with adults: P communicating with them better U	Less exposure to academic courses C	Personal development, identity, U E P Better communication with adults U S Self-confidence U E P S Increased attendance U Responsibility, motivation U C E P Staying in school (lower-level students) C A U Help goalless students A Improved peer relations U Getting permanent job S Parent-child communication P	Some students "get lost" again after a while U Some bide time, don't "deliver" U Program more effective with girls U Alienation from regular school activities C A S Irresponsibility, "can't handle freedom" P U
Masepa (E)	Improvement in full range of language arts skills (see at right) More on-task behavior Improved discipline	Increased skills: vocabulary U A P, spelling U A, phonetics Ux, punctuation U, reading comprehension Ux E, reading decoding U, grammar U, written expression U Low achievers more productive Ux	Retention levels not good U Too little diversity Student fatigue U	Concentration, study skills Fewer discipline problems U A More attentive to errors U Better academic self-concept U More enjoyment, enthusiasm U A Work with less supervision, more responsible A U Less time lost, more time on task U A E Rapid students progress faster E	Some lagging, failing Mastery tests U Boredom U
Moderate Impact					
Canon (L)	Increased achievement Clearer career interests Friendliness Improved self-concept as a learner More internal locus of control	Career knowledge U A C Work on new interests U		Achievement composite (use of resources) E Better classroom attitude U Attitude to school E U Self-concept as learner (HS) F Friendliness E Social studies (elem) Self-understanding E	Little effect on achievement U

CASES		Direct Outcome		Meta-Level Outcomes and Side Effects	
Impact	Program Objectives	Positive	Negative	Positive	Negative
Moderate Impact					
Calston (E)	Basic reading skills, plus use of reading as tool for learning: literature appreciation: reading for enjoyment	Increased criterion-referenced test scores A U More reading skills Ux		Learning to work independently, self-managing U A Self-motivation A: children like independent work U Children proud to come to school A Children not competing A Reduced discipline problems A	
Moderate to Low Impact					
Dun Hollow (L)	Eliminate stereotyping of Eskimos Knowledge of Eskimo history, customs, current life Create positive image of Eskimo culture	Some learning of culture, reduction of stereotypes U A More reading skills Ux	Information too detailed U		Some students behind in language arts <u>U</u>
Low Impact					
Burton (E)	Knowledge & practical skills re political/government/legal processes (voter education, state government, individual rights)	Concept learning, by being in different roles U Experience in active learning approach A	No effects discernible <u>U</u>		

Legend for sources of data:

U = user
A = administrator
C = counselor
P = parent
E = evaluator
S = student

<u>Underlined</u> letters refer to mention by at least two persons
x = presence of dissenting or conflicting opinion

(E) = externally - developed innovation
(L) = locally - developed innovation

Source: Miles, M. B., & Huberman, A. M. (1994). *Qualitative data analysis: An expanded sourcebook* (2nd ed.). Thousand Oaks, CA: Sage Publications.

CLOSURE AND TRANSITION

Most ordering displays are complex because we are attempting to multidimensionally and simultaneously document cases, ranks, variables, actions, time periods, outcomes, and/or assessments. Basic software literacy and access for most of us are limited to two-dimensional renderings when we wish we could draw in three dimensions or animate some of our graphics. But two-dimensional matrices, networks, and graphics bring us one step closer toward understanding complex participant processes.

Exploring, describing, and ordering data are necessary prerequisites for the next chapter's methods: *explaining*. Rich and insightful answers are generated from posing "how" and "why" questions.

METHODS OF EXPLAINING

CHAPTER SUMMARY

This chapter explores how displays can be used to construct explanations for interrelationships, change, and causation. Matrices, networks, and graphics are carefully designed and plotted to map research sequence stories of antecedent conditions, mediating variables, and outcomes.

INTRODUCTION

We've been profiling methods for developing coherent descriptions of *who, what, when,* sometimes *where,* and sometimes *how* things happen across a number of cases. In this chapter, we turn to questions of *why.*

Why things happen is at the forefront of the research experience, once you're past the basic problem of understanding just *what* is happening. That question is also a salient one for people in their day-to-day lives; questions of "why," "how come," and answers beginning with "because" appear constantly in day-to-day interactions.

The conventional view is that qualitative studies are good only for exploratory or descriptive forays, and that strong explanations, including causal attributions, can be derived only through quantitative studies, particularly the classic experimental–control design. We consider this view mistaken. Even the most sophisticated quantitative procedures can develop plausible possibilities only smoothed across many persons and situations. We consider qualitative analysis to be a very powerful method for assessing causation. But we have to go far beyond assertion, showing an empirical basis for the claim that Y is explained or caused/influenced and affected by X.

Good explanations need to link the explanations given by the people we are studying with explanations we develop as researchers. But people may not always offer rational reasons for why something happens. Some may reduce the complexity of an event to a single root cause. Munton, Silvester, Stratton, and Hanks (1999) offer that "beliefs about causality can, and often do, involve multiple causes and multiple outcomes. . . . In sequences of attributions, an outcome in one attribution can become a cause in the next" (p. 9).

Causes are not only multiple but also "conjunctural"—they combine to influence and affect each other as well as the outcomes or "effects." Furthermore, outcomes of multiple causes are not the same in all contexts, and different combinations of causes can turn out to have similar outcomes. Thus, to Saldaña (2003), *influences and affects* may be the more accurate way to reconceptualize the positivist construct of "cause and effect." (In this volume, *effects* as a term will sometimes be used to harmonize with the methodological display principles of causation established by Miles and Huberman, when appropriate.)

ANTECEDENT CONDITIONS, MEDIATING VARIABLES, AND OUTCOMES

Recall the primary principles of Causation Coding discussed in Chapter 4. The analyst searches for combinations of *antecedent conditions* influenced and affected by certain *mediating variables* that lead toward certain *outcome* pathways, symbolized as a CODE 1 → CODE 2 → CODE 3 sequence (→ means "leads to"), or

ANTECEDENT CONDITIONS → MEDIATING VARIABLES → OUTCOMES

But any three of those processes can include more than one condition, variable, and/or outcome working in combination that serves as connected parts of the causation sequence. Thus, a basic CODE 1 → CODE 2 → CODE 3 sequence might be more complexly represented as

Antecedent Conditions	Mediating Variables	Outcomes
CODE 1A + CODE 1B +	CODE 2A +	CODE 3A +
CODE 1C + CODE 1D	CODE 2B	CODE 3B

As an example of the above display, HLN-TV reported on the August 9, 2016, Delta Airlines "computer meltdown." A 6-hour power outage in Atlanta "caused" the reservation and flight systems to crash, leaving thousands of flights grounded and hundreds of thousands of passengers stranded in airports worldwide for days. But the news story noted that a "convergence of issues" actually led to a "perfect storm" of failure.

The four primary *antecedent conditions* (CODES 1A, 1B, 1C, and 1D) or things in place *before* the power failure occurred were as follows:

- CODE 1A: Mixed software systems (i.e., different programs for domestic and international flights, rather than a universal system for both)

- CODE 1B: Airline mergers (i.e., incompatible and complex software systems coming together from different companies)

- CODE 1C: Lack of investment (i.e., cash-strapped airlines not investing in infrastructural computing efficiency)

- CODE 1D: Human error in backup preparation (i.e., information technology personnel unsuccessfully safeguarding the airline's software and computing systems)

With these four antecedent conditions in place, two *mediating variables* (CODES 2A and 2B) triggered (i.e., influenced and affected) the Delta Airlines computer system shutdown:

- CODE 2A: The power outage—a local problem in Atlanta; this should not have been a problem in and of itself, but there was also a

- CODE 2B: Backup system failure—safeguards in place in the event of a power failure did not "kick in."

Thus, when this perfect storm of four major antecedent conditions and two crippling mediating variables combined, there were two primary *outcomes* (CODES 3A and 3B):

- CODE 3A: Over 2,000 flights cancelled

- CODE 3B: Thousands of people stranded in airports (not to mention individual related outcomes such as family vacation plans ruined, business meetings postponed or cancelled, lost opportunities for job interviews, airline reservations agents in distress with angry customers, etc.)

So, when you search for causation in qualitative data, extend beyond the quantitative paradigm's linear "cause and effect." In qualitative inquiry, we search for the often multiple and interacting *influences and affects*.

Display 9.1 is an example of how antecedent conditions, mediating variables (termed "Nonprofit Display Norms" for this particular study), and outcomes can be graphically displayed. Silard (2018) conducted 34 semi-structured interviews with individuals who have occupied leader and/or follower roles in nonprofit organizations. He examined the mutually strengthening interplay of emotion-related leader behaviors and organizational display norms in the nonprofit sector:

> These norms favor the expression of positive emotion and proscribe [forbid] the display of negative emotion. Nonprofit leaders who enact emotion-related behaviors congruent with these display norms generate the follower outcomes of engagement and loyalty. . . . Self-reported accounts point to the existence of two primary emotion display norms in nonprofits: a Cult of the Positive and a Proscription of the Negative. (pp. 304, 310)

Display 9.1 shows how Silard went beyond merely listing the antecedent conditions and mediating variables culled from his analysis. He illustrates their interrelationship and interplay through the use of bins, conceptual labels, and arrows to suggest the intertwined process of the individual and organizational emotional labor involved with nonprofit leadership. Interestingly, Silard's written report discusses the mediating variables first, then the antecedent conditions, because the latter ("Leader

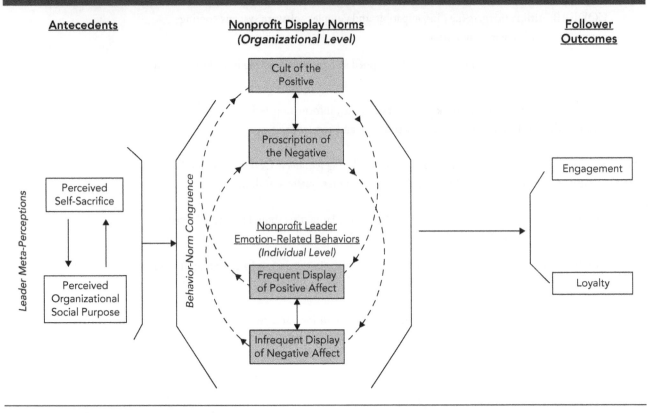

Source: Silard (2018), p. 310.

Meta-Perceptions" of a nonprofit's purpose and mission) is more closely related to the third part of the process: follower outcomes.

ON EXPLANATION AND CAUSATION

Morrison (2009) advises that we should carefully consider the nuanced differences between a cause, a reason, and a motive, and keep our focus primarily on people's intentions, choices, objectives, values, perspectives, expectations, needs, desires, and agency within their particular contexts and circumstances: "It is individuals, not variables [like social class, gender, ethnicity, etc.], which do the acting and the causing" (p. 116).

People are not like billiard balls, each progressing in its own direction after it's been struck. People have complex intentions operating in a complex web of others' intentions and actions. That is why we emphasize here that you examine not only people's actions but their *reactions* as well (Saldaña & Omasta, 2018). Another line of reasoning emphasizes the "disorderly" nature of social facts; they are more chaotic and less coherent than our minds make them. There need to be ways for us to understand how human events and meanings, actions, reactions, and interactions are chained over time, as slippery and disorderly as they may be.

Just as there's no clean boundary between description and explanation, there's no precise demarcation between general "explanation" and "causation." It's not fair to say that determining causation is necessarily a stronger form of explanation than others. At the minimum, we can note that causation decisively brings in the question of *time*: Prior events are assumed to have some connection with following events, even though that connection may not be neat and clear. We are concerned with finding out what led to what.

Assessing causation is essentially a retrospective matter. It can proceed by the creation and parsing of stories, the flow of connected events in context. In the *process* mode, we'll be likely to assemble chronologies, pay attention to time, and look for connections within the big picture. In the *variable* mode, we'll be likely to code small units of data, retrieve them, and look for similarities and conceptual patterns, with less regard to setting, sequence, and the passage of time. *Both* stances will be needed at different points in a study. The issue is being aware of your analytic assumptions and acting on them appropriately, moving back and forth between story and concept modes to deepen each.

Qualitative analysis, with its close-up look, can identify *mechanisms*, going beyond sheer association. It is unrelentingly local and deals well with the complex network of events and processes in a situation. It can sort out the *temporal* dimension, showing clearly what preceded what, either through direct observation or *retrospection*. It is well equipped to cycle back and forth between *variables* and *processes*—showing that stories are not capricious but include underlying variables, and that variables are not disembodied but have connections through time.

Explanatory matrices, networks, and graphics usually require more careful attention to various forms of ordering. And multiple cases are extraordinarily helpful in both generating explanations and testing them systematically. In a real sense, they are our best resource for advancing our assertions and theories about the way social life works. But we should not delude ourselves that scientific explanation is somehow lofty, wholly determinate, and precise. Research never "proves" anything; at best, it *suggests*.

In this chapter, the *Explaining Interrelationship* section examines how variables interact and interplay. *Explaining Change* looks at the multiple pathways leading toward outcomes. And *Explaining Causation* provides methods for displaying and narrating not just the "how" but the "why" of a study's outcomes.

EXPLAINING INTERRELATIONSHIP

Interrelationship is one of the foundation principles for methods of Explaining Change and Explaining Causation. The *Variable-by-Variable Matrix* first explores the interaction and interplay between multiple pairs of variables to see whether they apply to selected cases.

Variable-by-Variable Matrix

Description

A variable-by-variable matrix has two main variables in its rows and columns. Specific properties or components of each variable are individually listed and ordered by intensity. The cell entries, rather than being data bits, are case names, so that we can see which cases (themselves also ordered on a variable) include a specific type of interaction or interrelationship between the two main variables (see Display 9.2).

Applications

Sometimes, after cases have been analyzed carefully, you begin to notice that a few major variables are in play, underlying many specific phenomena, and you would like to know how these variables may be connected or interrelated. The problem is how to keep the richness of specific indicators of the main variables, so as to see in more depth what the core relationships might suggest.

DISPLAY 9.2 ● Variable-by-Variable Matrix: Coping Strategies and Problems, by Case

STYLE	Coping Strategies	Program Process	Program Content	Target Pop.	Skill Lacks	Attitudes	Crises	Competing Demands	Low Control	Physical Setting	Resources
	Can't determine	BURR	ALAMEDA						CARUSO		
DO NOTHING	None	CHESTER			CARUSO	CHESTER			CHESTER		
TEMPORIZE	Delaying/avoiding		CARUSO			CHESTER					
DO IT THE USUAL WAY	Short-run coping	CARUSO CHESTER	CARUSO							CARUSO	CARUSO
	Using existing meetings/roles	ALAMEDA BURR CARUSO CHESTER	CHESTER								ALAMEDA CARUSO
	Action-taking	CARUSO									
	People-shuffling		CARUSO?			AGASSIZ	CARUSO CHESTER				CARUSO
EASE OFF	Program modification		BURR	AGASSIZ BURR CARUSO	BURR?	BURR		BURR			
DO IT HARDER	Symbolic support					AGASSIZ CARUSO CHESTER		AGASSIZ			
	Rewards/incentives					AGASSIZ ALAMEDA BURR CHESTER					
	Negotiating										CHESTER
	Pressuring/requiring					BURR CHESTER					
BUILD PERSONAL CAPACITY	Person-changing	ALAMEDA		AGASSIZ ALAMEDA BURR?	AGASSIZ						

STYLE	Coping Strategies	Program Process	Program Content	Target Pop.	Skill Lacks	Attitudes	Crises	Competing Demands	Low Control	Physical Setting	Resources
BUILD SYSTEM CAPACITY	New orchestration structure	ALAMEDA CARUSO	CARUSO		ALAMEDA						ALAMEDA CARUSO
	New interaction arenas			BURR							
	Vision-building/ sharing		AGASSIZ			AGASSIZ ALAMEDA BURR					
	Monitoring		CARUSO								
	Rolling planning					ALAMEDA					
	Ongoing assistance		AGASSIZ								AGASSIZ
ADD NEW PEOPLE	Re-staffing					ALAMEDA BURR					
REDESIGN THE SYSTEM	Increasing control							AGASSIZ	BURR?		AGASSIZ?
	Empowering	AGASSIZ ALAMEDA BURR?				AGASSIZ ALAMEDA					
	Role redesign										AGASSIZ
	Organization redesign										AGASSIZ ALAMEDA

Legend

AGASSIZ High School [more successful]

ALAMEDA High School [more successful]

BURROUGHS [BURR] High School [moderately successful]

CARUSO High School [less successful]

CHESTER High School [less successful]

? = Cases with less researcher certainty

Source: Miles, M. B., & Huberman, A. M. (1994). *Qualitative data analysis: An expanded sourcebook* (2nd ed.). Thousand Oaks, CA: Sage Publications.

A variable-by-variable matrix arranges individual properties or components of variables into distinct row and column headings to detect what types of *associations* or intersections may be occurring within cases and their data. It is both descriptive and ordered, exploratory and explanatory, for it matches cases with two variables to encourage you to explain why the interrelationship is suggested in the matrix.

Strong statistical correlation does not imply causation or prediction, but it suggests that some type of relationship may exist between the variables being measured. It is up to the quantitative researcher to further explore what that relationship might be. The same principle applies to a variable-by-variable matrix. The display is a heuristic for examining possible qualitative associations between two variables, and the researcher's inferential implications of that relationship.

Example

In a study of urban high school reform (Louis & Miles, 1990; Miles, 1986), one of the questions of interest was how schools coped with the inevitable problems encountered during the change process. The researcher had clustered and categorized the types of *problems* reported and ordered them from most to least "tractable" or solvable (see the column headings of Display 9.2). Problems such as program process and program content were relatively easy to deal with; problems stemming from the school's physical setting or available financial resources were judged as more difficult to resolve, on the basis of prior studies of educational reform.

The researcher also developed, from the five high school cases at hand, a list of 23 coping strategies (the second column from the left): What do you do when faced with a problem? The strategies listed under coping strategies, such as delaying/avoiding, people-shuffling, vision-building/sharing, and role redesign, were sorted into nine stylistic clusters such as DO NOTHING, DO IT THE USUAL WAY, DO IT HARDER, and REDESIGN THE SYSTEM. These clusters were then ordered according to a major shallow–deep dimension, one end of which was "shallow, soft, informal" and the other "deeper, more structurally oriented, deliberate, and person-changing."

Once the conceptual work was done, the matrix design was plotted: Rows were coping strategies, and columns were problem types. The cell entries were the five high school case names: Agassiz and Alameda had the most successful implementation; one case, Burroughs, was moderately successful; and Caruso and Chester were least successful. Instances of problems and the associated coping strategies used were drawn from case report displays, field notes, and researcher judgments. The problem was sorted into the appropriate column, and the strategy used was identified by the researchers most knowledgeable through their fieldwork and case analysis. If more than one strategy had been used for the same problem, more than one cell entry was made. When the researcher was less certain about the problem–coping connection, the symbol "?" was added to the cell entry after a school's name.

Analysis

Variable-by-variable matrix analysis relies primarily on eyeballing the results and making inferences about the associations. The analyst, looking at the top part of the table, wrote,

> Most of the instances of "shallow" coping (DO NOTHING, TEMPORIZE, DO IT THE USUAL WAY) appear in the two less-successful sites: Caruso and Chester (tactic: **noting patterns, themes**).
>
> Second, moving to the lower region of the table, it is quite striking to note that the deeper managing and coping strategies (BUILD PERSONAL & SYSTEM CAPACITY, ADD NEW PEOPLE, REDESIGN THE SYSTEM) are used mostly by more-successful sites.

Except for the New orchestration structure and the Monitoring strategies at Caruso, such strategies are mostly absent in the less successful sites. The Burroughs moderately successful site employs a few "deep" strategies, but fewer than Agassiz and Alameda.

Then the analyst saw another pattern, a bit more complex. He focused on the Agassiz and Alameda sites and wrote the following:

> These sites actually use a very wide range of strategies, *except* for None and Delaying/avoiding. The feeling is one of actively doing whatever the problem seems to require, but having a repertoire that includes vigorous managing and capacity-building interventions where they are needed. . . . [They] show "deeper" coping for the more difficult problems.

To check the meaning of these findings further, the researcher returned to the case reports to a section where the analyst had described the typical *results* of problem–coping efforts and made a summary table shown in Display 9.3 (tactic: **replicating a finding**). This summary table not only synthesizes the findings, it helps pull together and support the variable-by-variable matrix associations.

The more properties and components of variables listed in the matrix rows and/or columns, the more preparatory work required to review the data corpus and fill in the cells. But it's a worthwhile investment of time and energy to learn whether any interaction and interplay exist. This can transcend basic descriptive association to potentially explanatory reasoning.

The time dimension can be added to a variable-by-variable matrix by identifying cell entries as occurring earlier or later during some time period. Each cell entry could also include a magnitude code indicating how "successful" a strategy turned out to be.

DISPLAY 9.3 ⬡ Summary Table: Typical Consequences of Coping, by Case	
Agassiz	Most problems have been acknowledged, addressed, and solved.
	Main consequence is an increase in individual and collective self-confidence (both teachers and students).
	More downtown (central office) respect for school.
Alameda	Reduced anxiety, built more constructive norms.
	Better mesh with staff development, met teacher needs.
	New roles and empowerment meant that principal could be reassigned [without disruption of program].
Burroughs	Increased respect for principal's authority.
	Staff schism: people either big fans or opponents.
	Little investment by new staff in program.
	As trained staff moved to other schools, new staff did not know or have skill in program.
Caruso	Problems slightly ameliorated, but will recur.
Chester	Moderate coordination of the curriculum alignment part of the program, but not of the remainder.
	Problems will continue.

Source: Miles, M. B., & Huberman, A. M. (1994). *Qualitative data analysis: An expanded sourcebook* (2nd ed.). Thousand Oaks, CA: Sage Publications.

Notes

The cut-and-paste functions of Word tables and Excel spreadsheets permit easy rearrangement of rows and columns for exploratory analyses. Most CAQDAS programs have the ability to quickly assemble and display variable-by-variable (or code-by-code or category-by-category) matrices, thus enabling convenient examination of what possible interrelationships may be present within specific cases. Most of these programs can also provide statistical information as to the strength of an association.

EXPLAINING CHANGE

These three profiles illustrate a research story's trajectory and outcome with a focus on change, but they also serve as foundation methods for explaining causation. An *Explanatory Matrix* is the initial plotting of possible causation for more in-depth analytic explanation. An *Outcomes Matrix* generally explains *what* eventually happened, while a *Case Dynamics Matrix* charts *how* the outcomes came to be.

Explanatory Matrix

Description

An explanatory matrix is a broad brushstroke chart that serves as an exploratory first step to answer why certain outcomes were achieved and what caused them—either generally or specifically (see Display 9.4).

Applications

An explanatory matrix helps clarify a domain in *conceptual* terms; it is a useful first-cut exploration, beginning to trace back—and forward—the emerging threads of causation. The matrix helps us understand things temporally, and thus, we may get a feel for the causal mechanisms that may be involved. It is a first draft, of sorts, for further analytic work on the intricacies of explanation.

Example

A researcher talked to users of an environmental studies program innovation, asking them from whom they had received day-to-day ongoing assistance (the conceptual domain of interest), what it actually consisted of, and what the effects or outcomes (both in the short and long run) seemed to be. The results are shown in Display 9.4. The researcher entered quotes and paraphrases, aiming to get at the essence of the interview material appropriate for each cell. In the last column, the researcher adds his own general explanation for each row's "story."

Analysis

The analyst scans across rows to get a sense of each one's narrative storyline. Referrals back to field notes, interviews, and other original data sources will help develop entries for the Researcher Explanation column at the far right. These cells serve not just as tracing summaries but as possible provisional hypotheses for later testing.

In Display 9.4, that tracing involves the issue of which types of assistance, from which roles, lead to which types of outcomes in users—and why. For example, the technical help provided by developers and the materials seems to induce clarity and legitimacy, while it may take peer and administrative support to increase actual user mastery of the new program (tactic: **making contrasts, comparisons**).

DISPLAY 9.4 ● Explanatory Matrix: Ongoing Assistance					
Location	User's Assessment	Types Provided	Short-Run Effects ("State" of Users)	Longer Run Consequences (Able/Unable to Do)	Researcher Explanation
Superintendent	0	None	"He's going along just for the money"	Building/expansion of program on their own	Supt was a money manager not involved with programs
Building Administrator Years 1–2	+	Met w/community Gave encouragement Buffered supt	"We have some help here" "We're not alone" "We'll fight our battles"	Left users more time to address program issues, students, site, buses	Admin'r supported innov. programs by providing needed help to teachers
Years 3–4	0	None	"We lost our friend"	Had to fight own battles and thus learned how	Admin'r's relative indifference probably solidified users
Developers	++	Gave ideas, help Provided framework Activity planning Positive outlook Resources	"They know their stuff" "It all makes sense" "Hey, I can do this!" "We can get equipment"	Expansion of science program to off-campus sites w/ community involvement	Dept needed money to do the program: one user needed direction and support and got both. Off they went.
Peer Users	+	Helped w/planning Gave ideas, sugg'ns Gave encouragement	How it could work Filled in gaps Not alone; there's help	Strong users of the off-campus program; they know how to do it	One user was experienced in this approach and brought others up to speed
Materials (Guides)	+	Overview, approach, and suggested activities in detail	This is really good stuff, well worked out, tried, useful	Good basis for development of own program	Mat'ls fulfilled their role: to stimulate & aid in development of local program

Source: Miles, M. B., & Huberman, A. M. (1994). *Qualitative data analysis: An expanded sourcebook* (2nd ed.). Thousand Oaks, CA: Sage Publications.

A look at the Researcher Explanation column shows us mostly straightforward summaries; we have not advanced the causation quest very much. It is hard to see the links between assistance types, roles, and effects more than impressionistically. Furthermore, each row is looked at one at a time as a causal sequence. It is hard to grasp the complexity of the *interactions* among rows. Thus, more detailed and thorough causation analysis usually requires other methods, such as those outlined later in this chapter.

Notes

The explanatory matrix is intended primarily as an initial heuristic for determining the *plot* or overall structure of your research story. Continued analysis may help you discover the objectives and nuanced motivations of the participant-characters as the story unfolds, possibly enabling you to construct the tale's moral (i.e., its theory).

Outcomes Matrix

Description

An outcomes matrix displays data on one or more outcomes, as the study requires. There is always an implicit predecessor (i.e., an antecedent condition and/or mediating variable), and the basic principle in an outcomes matrix is a focus on *dependent* variables (see Display 9.5).

Applications

In many studies, the researcher is interested in outcomes. An evaluator may want to know what changes a particular program or treatment brought about in its target population. A more descriptive researcher may simply want to know where things stood at the end of some process. A researcher aiming at explanations will usually want to have a good look at some main dependent variables of interest (e.g., reading scores, dropout rates, school social climate) before turning to predictor variables. These are examples of "ultimate" outcomes. This label may sound pretentious, but it means only that the variable is the last one being looked at in a temporal or causal chain.

DISPLAY 9.5 ⬗ Outcomes Matrix: Organizational Changes After Implementation of the ECRI Program				
	Early Use 1st and 2nd Years		Later Use 3rd Year	
Effect Type	**Primary Changes**	**Spin-Offs**	**Primary Changes**	**Spin-Offs**
Structural	Scheduling: ECRI all morning, rescheduling music, phys. ed. Helping teacher named: has dual status (teach/admin)	Cutting back on math, optional activities Two separate regimens in school Ambiguity of status and role	Integrated scheduling, cross-age grouping in Grades 2–6	Less individual latitude: classroom problems become organizational problems
Procedural	No letter grades, no norms Institutionalizing assistance via helping teacher	Parents uneasy 2 regimens in class Teachers insecure Loosens age-grading system In-house assistance mechanism implanted	ECRI evaluation sheets, tightening supervision More uniformity in work in all classes	Teachers more visible, inspectable Problems, solutions more common, public
Relational/ Climate	Users are minority, band together	Cliques, friction between users, non-users	Tighter academic press Perception by teachers of collective venture	Reduction in "fun activities," projects (e.g., Xmas) More lateral help More "public" distress

Source: Miles, M. B., & Huberman, A. M. (1994). *Qualitative data analysis: An expanded sourcebook* (2nd ed.). Thousand Oaks, CA: Sage Publications.

Example

When an organization, such as a school, implements an innovation, the possibility exists that the organization may change in some way as a consequence. Although some innovations can be "dropped into" an existing structure, most innovations turn out to make demands on the system and have ripple effects. The organizational response often shows up in the form of something new—new attitudes, new rules, new procedures, and new structures. In the school improvement study, we (Miles and Huberman) wanted to study the changes in local schools that were traceable to their having implemented an innovation. The Exemplary Center for Reading Instruction (ECRI) innovation in this example was a relatively demanding, rather structured, language arts program implemented in an elementary school.

First, we need to make clear what makes up the bundle called an "outcome"—in this case, organizational change. Display 9.5 shows how this worked out. The analyst decided that the outcome "organizational change" has three basic parts: structural changes, procedural or operating changes, and more general relational or social climate changes.

Second, the analyst, reflecting on the particular case at hand, believes that such aspects of organizational change should be displayed separately for the early use period (first and second years) and for later use, when 9 of the school's 11 teachers were users of the innovation.

Third, the analyst wants to distinguish between primary changes—those directly following from the requirements of the innovation's implementation—and those termed *spin-offs*—secondary outcomes, some of which may not have been fully anticipated. Because the usual convention (at least in a culture where the printed word is read from left to right) is that later events should be displayed to the right of earlier events, the analyst puts the time dimension in columns and the outcome types in rows.

The cell entries in Display 9.5 are brief phrases describing specific organizational changes found in the coded write-ups of field notes. The original question to teachers, their principal, and several central office personnel was, "Did any changes occur in the organization of the school or the district during this period?" Follow-up probes asked about specific structural or "set-up" changes, procedural changes, and climate or feeling shifts. The decision rule was that any change reported and verified by a document or at least one other respondent would be condensed to a summary phrase for entry into the matrix.

Analysis

A look at the left side of the matrix shows that the major structural change was rescheduling previously separate language arts activities into one integrated morning period; this change required rescheduling of the subjects taught by circulating teachers (music, physical education). This change, in turn (see the Spin-Offs column), created two separate daily regimens, because the scheduling was done for two ECRI users in the first year and five in the second year. Other teachers were on the old schedule.

Other early changes included use of mastery levels, rather than letter grades, and the creation of a new helping teacher role to assist new users of ECRI. We can see by moving vertically down the columns that (as has been found in much social psychological research) structural changes tend to lead to procedural changes and, in turn, to climate/attitudinal changes (tactic: **making conceptual/ theoretical coherence**). In this case, the pressure, insecurity, and special attention led to a "we unhappy few" climate change, where users banded together. Moving across the climate row, we can see the spin-off effect: cliques and friction.

Moving to the right half of the matrix (Later Use, 3rd Year), we can note that, because 9 of 11 teachers were now involved, scheduling became more integrated, and close supervision and uniformity were more typical. And it is suggested that the fuller-scale, more regulated implementation now is seen by teachers as a collective venture. Looking across from primary changes to spin-offs, we observe that teachers are both more likely and more able to express need for help and to give and receive it (tactic: **building a logical chain of evidence**).

This display lets us see how structural changes induce procedural and attitude changes. We can see how first-level changes lead to later consequences (spin-offs), and we can see how organizational changes flowed and developed over the 3-year period. Naturally, these conclusions all need to be confirmed, tested, and verified, but we have a good running start on what the outcomes added up to.

Outcomes matrices also can be organized by specific *persons*. You can show, for example, the changes in concepts, attitudes, and behavior experienced by several teachers as a result of their use of an innovation through quoted interview excerpts. Outcomes matrices might also employ magnitude codes such as + or – or numeric ratings of some kind to display users' perceptions of the outcomes.

Finally, outcomes can be sorted according to their immediate impact. Some outcomes are *direct*, like the primary changes just noted. Others are more general; they might be termed *meta-outcomes*, which go considerably beyond the immediate direct effects the innovation is supposed to have. And we can think of residual *side effects*, minor outcomes quite far away from the original intention.

Notes

It is most unlikely that any innovation is perfectly implemented and happily accepted by everyone involved. If your outcomes matrix does not include negative (undesired) outcomes, be prepared to give a good justification for the reader.

Case Dynamics Matrix

Description

A case dynamics matrix displays a set of forces for change and traces the consequential processes and outcomes. The basic principle is one of preliminary explanation (see Display 9.6).

Applications

The analyst, during and after data collection, is constantly trying to link data with explanations and trying to understand why specific things happen as they do and how people in the cases explain why things happen as they do. A case dynamics matrix illustrates, in a preliminary way, the explanations that seem relevant to a particular question.

Example

Suppose you were interested, as we (Miles and Huberman) were, in the question of how and why an educational innovation induces change in the organization implementing it. That is an important "why" question, because the history of many educational innovations is that they are either shrugged off or absorbed into routine operating procedures, disappearing without a trace. But under what conditions does this *not* happen?

If we are looking for causes, we might start with "dynamic" issues—things with a pushing or demanding quality. In this instance, they might be "demands," "requirements," or "strains" that the innovation carries with it. These can be in rows of the matrix. For columns, we could include underlying issues or assumptions about the meaning of these demands, the organizational coping responses, and how things finally settled down in terms of resulting organizational changes.

DISPLAY 9.6 ◆ Case Dynamics Matrix: The IPA Innovation as a Force for Organizational Change in the District and Its Schools

Strains, Difficulties Created	Underlying Issues (as seen by researcher)	How Coped With	How Resolved: Type of Resulting Change
Conflicting expectations: should parents or teachers do activities?	Work load. Parent-teacher role conflict.	"Explaining" that teachers could not take primary responsibility for out-of-school activities.	Increased use of "batched" activities, many set up by coordinator (P).
View that forms and procedures were "extra," overloading.	Work load. Autonomy, resistance to control.	In-service assistance.	Repeated revision and simplification of forms and procedures; production of an operating manual. Reduction of expectations (no home visits, fewer conferences) (P).
User uncertainty and resistance to use.	Autonomy.	In-service assistance. Management Team interviews of all staff.	See above. Also creation of in-service committee (S), with coordination through Management Team (P).
Extra time requirements.	Work load.	Initially, via volunteerism, high commitment.	Use of substitutes (P). Dismissal of school during conference days (P). Reduction of expectations (above).
Program is complex, demanding, externally funded.	Authority, coordination, accountability.	Early creation of Management Team, addition of elementary teachers.	Institutionalization of Management Team (S). Heightened expectations for teacher upward influence (C). Lowered morale when expectations violated (C).
Enthusiasm of "advocate" teachers led to peer criticism.	Autonomy.	Quieting conflicts through informal discussion. Informal coordination and referral.	Norms supporting flexibility and colleague influence within schools, and cross-school interaction (C). Increased linkage and closer interaction between schools (C). Hobby Day (P).

(S) Structural change
(P) Procedural change
(C) Climate change

Source: Miles, M. B., & Huberman, A. M. (1994). *Qualitative data analysis: An expanded sourcebook* (2nd ed.). Thousand Oaks, CA: Sage Publications.

Display 9.6 shows how this works out. The innovation is a program for doing individualized educational planning for all students in a school district, not just those involved in special education. As such, it had been deliberately designed locally to be an organizational, district-wide change, with its procedures to be used routinely by all staff.

Looking through coded field notes, the analyst can pick out units of material marked by relevant codes. In this case, the coded data were as follows:

- Implementation problems

- Organizational practice outcomes

- Organizational climate outcomes

- Explanations for organizational outcomes

The analyst has also decided to sort organizational outcomes into three general classes: structural, procedural, and climate.

Analysis

As always, any display forecloses some issues. Here, the analyst is looking at only those demand-caused outcomes that actually constituted an organizational change, and is tacitly excluding demands that caused no organizational outcomes, or are absorbed without a trace.

In this sort of matrix, much analysis occurs during the actual data entry, which is done by moving across each row. By the time the row is filled in, the analyst has a first sense of what the dynamics have been (tactic: **noting patterns, themes**). Analytic, summarizing text can be written by cycling back as needed to the written-up field notes for amplification and clarification.

We can also look at the types of resulting change in the last column (How Resolved), noting that genuine structural changes are fewer than procedural or climate changes (tactic: **counting**). And we can look down the Underlying Issues column to see that issues of work load and autonomy are occurring repeatedly (tactic: **clustering**). Cycling back to the How Resolved column, we can see that work load issues were generally resolved through routinization and reduction of effort.

Using the tactic of **making contrasts, comparisons**, we see that autonomy issues were resolved in an interesting, unexpected way: increased interdependence and colleague influence. When the analyst runs into such a conclusion, it poses a puzzle: how to shed light on an unpredicted finding. This calls for the tactic of **following up surprises**. Reviewing field notes further, the analyst comments:

> It appeared that the program induced more elementary-secondary contact and collaboration—partly because many teachers were themselves parents, and experienced the IPA program in that role (and could notice poor or partial implementation as well as benefits).

The data in this sort of matrix are at several removes from the actual field notes, so the display will work best as a summarizing, clarifying, puzzle-posing (but not always puzzle-solving) device. Cycling back to the field notes is often a helpful move.

Case dynamics matrices, rather than starting with "strains," as this example did, can start with "dilemmas." Columns could be labeled as follows with appropriate cell entries:

- Dilemmas (the problems)
- Issues (why they were perceived as problems)
- Who did what (actions taken by individuals to resolve the dilemmas)
- Final resolution (the outcomes of the actions)

Some cell entries may also include cases of nonchange. A column could be added easily that emphasizes stability and nonchange data—particularly on outcomes that might have been expected a priori to change as a result of the initial push or strain. That addition, in turn, suggests the need for an "explanations" column.

Notes

Review (or have a colleague review) the first versions of your matrix to see what you are excluding and what analyses you will and will not be able to make. Ask someone else to look at the completed matrix and tell you what your analytic assumptions seem to be.

EXPLAINING CAUSATION

The three methods in this section build on each other and incorporate selected principles from the Explaining Interrelationship and Explaining Change sections. *Causal Chains* illustrates the trajectory or path of an individual storyline in the data. *Causal Network: Within-Case Analysis* integrates several causal chains into an interrelated system, while *Causal Network: Cross-Case Analysis* builds on and combines several within-case networks. These last two are perhaps the lengthiest and most complexly described of the analytic methods thus far toward explanatory development.

Causal Chains

Description

A causal chain is a researcher-constructed linear display of actions and/or states that suggests a plausible, interrelated sequence of events (see Displays 9.7 and 9.8).

| DISPLAY 9.7 ● Causal Chain: Illustration |

Individualization/Pupil Centeredness → Pupil Self-pacing, Self-organization → Inability to Monitor (in-class, off-campus) → Development of Trust → Letting Go → Changed Self-Image as a Teacher

Source: Miles, M. B., & Huberman, A. M. (1994). *Qualitative data analysis: An expanded sourcebook* (2nd ed.). Thousand Oaks, CA: Sage Publications.

Applications

During the early stages of causal modeling, it helps to make simplifying assumptions about what leads to what in a linear chain. Such a chain helps the analyst lay out explicitly what may be causing certain phenomena. Although the chain does represent a simplification, that very simplification carries with it the seeds of a fuller explanation.

Causal chains are useful because they require little elaboration or textual explanation. They are a rapid, simple way to communicate with colleagues (and final readers) about the meaning of—that is, the mechanisms underlying—a process. They can be elaborated and linked with other chains to form causal models or to build within-case causal networks (discussed later in this chapter).

Example

Display 9.7 shows an analyst's effort to understand how teachers using an innovation that stressed Individualization and Pupil-Centeredness came to experience a change in themselves they called "Letting Go." The labels for each bin in between the arrows were developed by the researcher after a review of coded field notes and analytic reflection on a key teacher outcome from the study.

Analysis

A causal chain is similar to a story outline for a narrative—a condensed treatment, of sorts, before the full explanation is given for what led to what and why. The analyst expands on the processes suggested by Display 9.7:

> There is something like an implicit contract between parties that pupils going off campus will not "betray" their teachers in return for pastoral care . . . [or that] in classroom-bound

projects, pupils will complete their work and do the requisite exercises or mastery tests in return for individual help with difficult concepts or operations.

We have left out some steps [in this display]. For example, Pupil-Centeredness also leads to Relational Closeness (not shown) and to a better grasp of Individual Ability Levels and Emotional States. Trust then develops as a result of the Bond Between Staff and Pupils (Trust Violation was a common motif at many sites).

Causal chains can be used to study less constructive processes—sequences with negative outcomes. Display 9.8 presents one chain explaining why an initially ambitious innovation eventually was discontinued, with energy expenditures dwindling steadily. The labels of each action and/or state should be concise yet descriptive enough to give a reader with no background knowledge of the study a general idea of what happened through time.

DISPLAY 9.8 ● Causal Chain: Illustration

Source: Miles, M. B., & Huberman, A. M. (1994). *Qualitative data analysis: An expanded sourcebook* (2nd ed.). Thousand Oaks, CA: Sage Publications.

Keep a causal chain limited to seven descriptive blocks or bins maximum. Remember that this is a thumbnail sketch of a much larger portrait and is only one thread of sequences in a complex tapestry of interwoven field work stories. You can explore a sequence by tracing significant events forward in time (from *A* to *B* to *C*), or start with an outcome and work backward to determine its mediating variables and antecedent conditions (from *C* to *B* to *A*).

Notes

The causal chain seems to adhere to the positivist construct of "cause and effect" because the display design is linear. But networked, interwoven, and multidirectional causal chains (described next) will better illustrate qualitative influences and affects (see Saldaña, 2003).

Causal Network: Within-Case Analysis

Description

It is assumed that some variables exert an influence on others: Variable *X* brings variable *Y* into being, or variable *X* increases variable *Y* and decreases variable *Z*. A causal network is a display of the most important variables (represented in boxes) in a field study and the relationships among them (represented by arrows). The plot of these relationships is unidirectional rather than bidirectional or correlational to suggest that one or more variables lead to another variable(s). In a causal network, the analyst traces the emergence and outcomes of a particular theme and orchestrates it with others. To be useful, the display should have accompanying analytic text describing the meaning of the connections among variables (see Displays 9.9 [network fragment], 9.10 [network excerpt], and 9.13 [complete network]).

Applications

Participants walk around with a cognitive network or process map in their heads that provides a frame for perception and action and explains what causes what in their world. Much of field research

DISPLAY 9.9 ● Causal Fragment: Mastery of a New Educational Practice

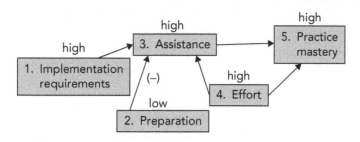

Source: Miles, M. B., & Huberman, A. M. (1994). *Qualitative data analysis: An expanded sourcebook* (2nd ed.). Thousand Oaks, CA: Sage Publications.

has to do with recording individuals' mental cause maps, putting them together, and making connections with your own evolving map of the setting. But causation is not unilateral. Thus, how do you get a reasonable handle on the overall "plot" of the research story—the flow of events in a particular case—and not get lost in a blur of everything affecting everything else?

A causal network illustrates through a study's variables how one thing led to another in linear yet interwoven patterns. A causal network builds a progressively integrated map of case phenomena and, for multiple cases, aligns their maps to make a cross-case map that contains more generalizable causal explanations. It neatly assembles and "anthologizes" into one thematic display all the stories of your individual cases.

A causal network is an abstracted, inferential picture organizing field study data in a coherent way. In this profile, we review how to do this for a single case; afterward, we outline a multiple- or cross-case approach. Developing good causal maps that respect complexity and are plausibly connected with those of respondents is the challenge. Meeting it helps the analyst avoid intellectual overload and produces results that are systematic and verifiable.

Example

Causal network construction necessitates a step-by-step outline of "how to." Thus, foundation principles will be discussed first, followed by their integration.

Inductive and Deductive Approaches to Building Causal Networks. Ideally, you have to plan from the beginning of data collection to produce a causal network display, so that successive rounds of data collection, interim analysis of all the data, and iterations of the network itself all build toward that end. There are two different ways of approaching the task: inductively and deductively.

In the *inductive* approach, the researcher discovers recurrent phenomena in the stream of field experiences and finds recurrent relations among them. These working hypotheses are modified and refined progressively as field work progresses. The causal network emerges piecemeal and inductively. It has regularity and pattern; some things happen only when others do or don't. These things and the links between them acquire their own names or labels, cluster into probable influences and affects they appear to engender, and the analyst has a causal network.

In the *deductive* strategy, the researcher has some a priori orienting concepts and propositions to test or observe in the field. These analytic units are operationalized and then matched with a body of field data.

Induction and deduction are actually dialectical rather than mutually exclusive research procedures. The deductive researcher *starts* with a preliminary causal network, and the inductive researcher *ends up* with one. Wolcott (1992) calls the approaches "theory-first" and "theory-later." In either approach, the initial version is amended and refined as it is tested against empirical events and characteristics. Both are substantiating an influences and affects network, but the deductive conceptualist has a top-down model, and the inductive constructivist has a built-up one.

In principle, you could draw a full causal network for the case during the early stages of a study, then go back to the field for cumulative testing and refining. We do not advise this. The risk is that a network vision sets in too early. A final "coherent" picture emerges before the individual parts of the picture have been carefully studied individually and in combination. The analyst constructs a premature causal network and begins to use it to (mis)interpret all the phenomena of interest. The better alternative is to save full causal network drawing and analysis for late in the project, making it perhaps the last analytic exercise.

Causal Fragments. Earlier in this chapter, causal chains were profiled and illustrated as a linear design. Many of those same principles will apply to the discussion of causal fragments below, but the linearity of the chain now "bends" and "branches" here and there to accommodate the complexity of network models.

Display 9.9 shows a causal fragment. This one puts together variables concerning the mastery of a new educational practice. The story can be told quickly, point by point or box by box:

Box 1. A demanding project with high Implementation requirements . . .

Box 2. began with low or inadequate Preparation, and was . . .

Box 3. bailed out by high levels of Assistance, which then . . .

Box 4. increased local Efforts, and ultimately. . .

Box 5. facilitated Practice mastery.

The minus sign (–) indicates inverse causal influence; low Preparation led to high Assistance in this particular case.

Try to assemble a few such fragments from your study without necessarily connecting one to another. Play around; do some causal noodling, fiddle with other fragments. Don't try to connect variables that don't go together empirically, even if on speculative grounds they "should." Some variables, like some blood types, don't commingle well.

In the style of causal mapping we're describing, we (Miles and Huberman) do not advise bidirectional arrows/flows from one box to another. They rapidly bewilder the mind ("after all, everything affects everything else"). For graphic and intellectual clarity, we have found it better to stick with one-way arrows that keep a temporal order to the diagrammed research story. For anything that justifiably "loops," accumulates, or cycles back (e.g., a bad economy leads to high prices, which lead to a worse economy, which leads to higher prices, which lead to . . .), show the recurring action through new boxes, not through bidirectional arrows. Saldaña advises that if bidirectional arrows *are* used, the narrative should explain and justify their use (see Display 5.2).

A useful next step is to take these fragments out to the field to see how and whether they work. This step can include showing the rough diagram to a case participant (tactic: **getting feedback from participants**) to get confirmation or revision recommendations.

If you're new to qualitative research, start with causal fragments. They can be profitably done early and repeatedly as a basis for discussion with your critical friends. Causal fragments are useful if your case is defined as an individual—and are very useful if you are studying several individuals.

Event-State Networks as Precursors of Causal Networks. Displays we have discussed up to now can inform and feed causal network analysis. Analyzing conceptually clustered matrices (Chapter 7), for example, lets you tease out the relationships within one of the variable families. Ordered and outcome matrices (Chapters 8 and 9) are exercises in identifying interconnected relations. In other words, causal analysis goes incrementally; you are testing individual paths more rigorously and, at the same time, building a cognitively meaningful, integrated causal map. The event-state network (Chapter 8) in particular gets us almost there.

Display 9.10 shows an excerpt from the final causal network, with the variable numbers keyed to the corresponding variables in the event-state network. Display 9.11 shows an excerpt from the original event-state network for the case in our illustration (Perry-Parkdale).

In most instances, case-specific events and states such as those in Display 9.11 can be turned into more generic network variables. They give you more powerful explanations, usable in other cases. Plus, there's much analytic power in working from a specifically temporal, process-oriented display (an event-state network) toward a variable-oriented display that still retains temporality (a causal network).

The lesson here is this: Use your previous analytic display work about your data for threads to weave your causal network tapestry.

Generating a Causal Network Variable List. Late during data collection, you may be ready to assemble the remaining fragments of the full causal network. But a useful first step is to generate the full set of network variables as a written list. This, too, is an exercise in playful brainstorming. The idea is to list all the antecedent conditions, mediating variables, and outcomes (in the form of events, actions, states, factors, processes, and so on) that seem to be important and then to turn them into variables. For instance, the several fights between employees will become "organizational conflict." The first pass should be exhaustive, the next one more selective. The first list should be combed for redundancies and overdifferentiation (e.g., three types of fighting between employees).

As an illustration, Display 9.12 presents a list of core variables generated in our school improvement study. (This was a complex, multi-case study; the list for single, simpler cases would be much shorter.)

Note the three general temporal categories:

1. *Antecedent conditions*—the baseline conditions within the field site that will later change

2. *Mediating variables*—those events, actions, states, factors, processes, and so on that initiate changes or other actions of some kind

3. *Outcomes*—the consequent results of antecedent conditions influenced and affected by mediating variables

Just as drawing causal fragments is effective preliminary work for a network display, composing a variable list is also important foundation work. It lets you know what specifically gets entered into

DISPLAY 9.10 ● Excerpt From a Causal Network: Perry-Parkdale School

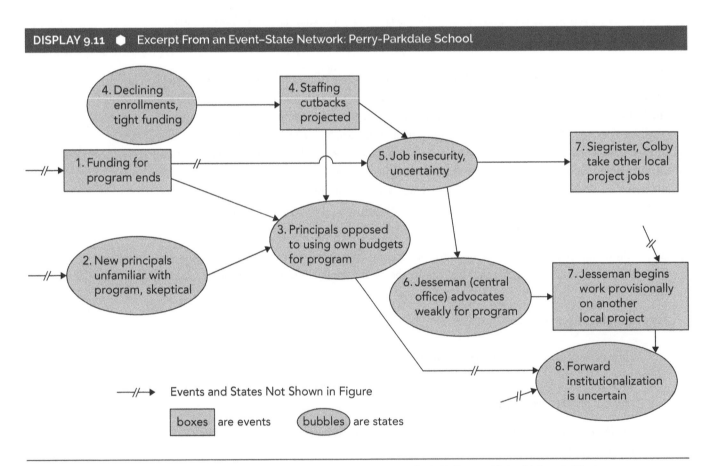

DISPLAY 9.11 ● Excerpt From an Event–State Network: Perry-Parkdale School

Source: Miles, M. B., & Huberman, A. M. (1994). Qualitative data analysis: An expanded sourcebook (2nd ed.). Thousand Oaks, CA: Sage Publications.

DISPLAY 9.12 ● List of Antecedent Conditions, Mediating Variables, and Outcomes: School Improvement Study		
Antecedent Conditions	**Mediating Variables**	**Outcomes**
Internal funds	External funds	Stabilization of use
Career advancement motivation	Program adoption (E)	Percentage of use
Assessed adequacy of local performance	Program concept initiative (L)	Student impact
Environmental turbulence	District endorsement	User capacity change
	Building endorsement	Institutionalization
	Influence of innovation advocate	Job mobility
	Implementation requirements	
	Adequacy of initial user preparation	
	Program-district fit	
	Program-building fit	
	Program-user fit	
	Assistance	
	User commitment	
	User skill	
	Program transformation	
	Teacher-administrator harmony	
	Validation effort (L)	
	Stability of program leadership	
	Stability of program staff	
	Organizational transformation	

Legend:
    (E) externally developed innovation
    (L) locally developed innovation

Source: Miles, M. B., & Huberman, A. M. (1994). *Qualitative data analysis: An expanded sourcebook* (2nd ed.). Thousand Oaks, CA: Sage Publications.

the boxes and encourages you to hypothesize about what led to what. Causation coding (Saldaña, 2016) is an effective way of generating lists of antecedent conditions, mediating variables, and outcomes for display work.

Assembling Data Fragments: Codes, Analytic Memos, and Summaries. As profiled earlier, Second Cycle Pattern Codes (Chapter 4) symbolically represent larger units of First Cycle coded data and often become candidates for inclusion in a causal network. In essence, they signal a *theme* or *pattern* that can be integrated into the network. For example, in our study of Perry-Parkdale, we noticed that teachers using innovations described their experiences in such terms as, "Finally I felt really on top of it," "It got easier when I knew how," "It's a snap now," and "Basically, I learned how to do it right." We labeled this pattern of responses and thus the underlying variable "User skill" and made a box for it.

Analytic memos and other analytic processes on interrelationship, coupled with exploratory and descriptive summaries, synthesize discrete pieces of data into an evidential chain that suggests causation. You think, roughly, "These variables are present or absent together (they covary), while others look random or unconnected." The tactic is **building a logical chain of evidence**. But with more knowledge, you begin to think more elaborately: "Some of these variables are coming into play *before* others, varying *with* others, or having an *influence and affect* on others, and the outcomes seem to change when *other* variables are taken into account." You now have the rudiments of a causal network that contains well-founded assertions about *directions* of influence among *sets* of variables.

Ideas ultimately need to get drawn on paper or on a monitor, and fragments of your thinking and analyses start coming together into one place by doing the following:

- Translate your preliminary analytic work into *variables*—that is, something that can be scaled (high to low, big to little, more to less).

- *Rate* the variable (e.g., high, moderate, low). How much of it is in the case?

- Draw a *line* between pairs of variables that *covary*, that is, that appear together consistently in the case, or that have some kind of relationship—for example, more of one variable goes with less of another.

- Draw a *unidirectional arrow* between each variable that comes first (temporally) and those later ones it appears to influence. *Influence* here means that more or less of one variable determines or affects to some extent the rating of another. The rating of the second variable might have been different had the first one not been there—a reasonable "mechanism" is involved.

- If two variables covary but seem to have only a tepid or oblique influence on each other, probably another latent variable needs to be found to join the two (tactic: **finding mediating variables**). Review the full list of codes to see whether one fits here.

It is important to note that not all variables may need accompanying ratings or scales (high, medium, low) to be eligible for inclusion as causal network boxes. The example used in this profile includes them since the original study had evaluation objectives.

Analysis

Display 9.13 shows the resulting causal network for one case. At first, it may look complex and forbidding. But look at one section of it (say, starting at the upper left) in conjunction with some text, like this:

> The first three antecedent conditions (1, 2, and 4) worked out this way: The state mandate (2) for well-planned career education programs, together with assessment of local performance as less than adequate (1), led to a search for new programs (3), which proved to be a good fit (7) with district characteristics, and hence to district endorsement (8), and to adoption of the program (9).
>
> But these were not sufficient causes of adoption. Inadequate local funds (4) to cover existing programs led to a ceaseless search for add-on funds (6) as almost a "way of life" for the district. That search led to getting temporary external funds (14) for a three-year period; they were the other basic causes of adoption (9).

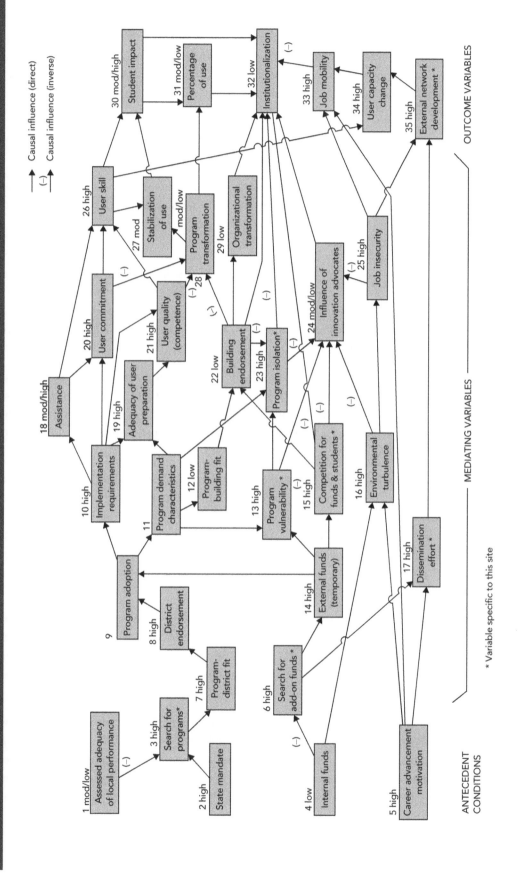

DISPLAY 9.13 ● Causal Network for Perry-Parkdale CARED Program

Causal influence (direct)
Causal influence (inverse)

ANTECEDENT CONDITIONS

MEDIATING VARIABLES

OUTCOME VARIABLES

* Variable specific to this site

1 mod/low Assessed adequacy of local performance
2 high State mandate
3 high Search for programs*
4 low Internal funds
5 high Career advancement motivation
6 high Search for add-on funds*
7 high Program-district fit
8 high District endorsement
9 Program adoption
10 high Implementation requirements
11 Program demand characteristics
12 low Program-building fit
13 high Program vulnerability*
14 high External funds (temporary)
15 high Competition for funds & students*
16 high Environmental turbulence
17 high Dissemination effort*
18 mod/high Assistance
19 high Adequacy of user preparation
20 high User commitment
21 high User quality (competence)
22 low Building endorsement
23 high Program isolation*
24 mod/low Influence of innovation advocates
25 high Job insecurity
26 high User skill
27 mod Stabilization of use
28 mod/low Program transformation
29 low Organizational transformation
30 mod/high Student impact
31 mod/low Percentage of use
32 low Institutionalization
33 high Job mobility
34 high User capacity change
35 high External network development*

Source: Miles, M. B., & Huberman, A. M. (1994). *Qualitative data analysis: An expanded sourcebook* (2nd ed.). Thousand Oaks, CA: Sage Publications.

245

The program, when adopted, proved to have substantial implementation requirements (10), which dictated the need for assistance (18), and also exerted a good deal of pressure for careful selection of high-quality staff (21), and for careful preparation (19) of them to carry out the program. The heavy implementation requirements (10), and to some degree the assistance provided (18), induced a good deal of user commitment (20) and, in turn, user skill (26), which was also high because of staff quality (21). High user skill, in conjunction with the fact that the program was quite well stabilized (27) by late 1980, brought about a reasonable degree of student impact (30).

Text and a network together communicate more than either could alone. We are moving toward an *explanation*—not just a description—of what happened at Perry-Parkdale. This network has taken more than 300 pages of field notes down to a few dozen boxed words and arrows on one page; the network and the text tell economically how and why things turned out as they did.

Streams. Drawing the network is done in the same way you analyze it: stream by stream. Some streams—unbroken chains of variables—are long: Look at the one that runs through these numbered boxes: 1 → 3 → 7 → 8 → 9 → 10 → 20 → 26 → 30 → 31 → 32. Others are conveniently shorter, like the bottom stream: 5 → 33 → 32. Within an unbroken stream, multiple channels usually lead in different directions or end up at the same place via a different route. Those also should be drawn in.

Streams can be drawn most easily—especially if the event-state network is used as the preceding try—from antecedent conditions forward in time. It is also possible to take a dependent variable and work backward, but then, it is important to run it forward again to be sure the links are coherent and empirically justified. You'll inevitably find cross-stream connections, and they can be drawn in as the network evolves.

Often, these streams can be given a name—a scenario or theme—and this labeling makes them easier to both analyze and report. For example, along the bottom stream, variables 5 → 17 → 35 → 34 have a "cosmopolitanizing" theme: People go outside their environments in connection with a new project, and the experience both stretches them and sets up career shifts. Or again, staying along the bottom of the network, boxes 4 → 16 → 25 → 33 add up to a "casualty" (*casualty*, not causality) stream: low money, high turbulence (usually in the form of budget cuts), staff instability, and ultimate staff reassignments.

Streams also can be labeled according to the level of dependent variables, such as *high student impact scenarios*, *low institutionalization scenarios*, or *high job mobility scenarios*. These similarly named scenarios can be very different, even within the same case. For instance, one high job mobility scenario involves a promotion or desirable transfer, whereas another involves an unwanted reassignment or even a layoff.

Finally, causal networks can have a predictive function. In drawing a variable stream with two or three substreams leading out to the dependent variables, you are in a position to say something like "Effect D is likely to occur when predictors A, B, and C occur in sequence," or "To get high levels of J, you need high antecedent levels of G, H, and I, but not necessarily of E and F." These statements have modest weight in a single-case analysis, but they perk up noticeably when several within-case sets show the same or a similar pattern.

We provide a proverb that may be helpful: "Where there's a stream, there's a theme."

The Causal Network Narrative. Drawing conclusions from the network goes along with its production. Like all time-related representations, this one tells a story—really, several stories. You can write out a chronological narrative including each of the major streams, starting at the beginning. Display 9.14 presents the complete narrative for the causal network shown in Display 9.13.

Writing the narrative usually does several things. First, it forces you to be less mechanistic and more coherent; turning a network into clear text requires you to be honest and explicit about what you

---

DISPLAY 9.14 ● Narrative for Causal Network: Perry-Parkdale CARED Program

The first three antecedent conditions (1, 2 and 4) worked out this way. The state mandate (2) for well-planned career education programs, together with assessment of local performance as less than adequate (1), led to a search for new programs (3), which proved to be a good fit (7) with district characteristics, and hence to district endorsement (8), and to adoption of the program (9).

But these were not sufficient causes of adoption. Inadequate local funds (4) to cover existing programs led to a ceaseless search for add-on funds (6) as almost a "way of life" for the district. That search led to getting temporary external funds (14) for a three-year period; they were the other basic cause of adoption (9).

The program, when adopted, proved to have substantial implementation requirements (10), which dictated the need for assistance (18), and also exerted a good deal of pressure for careful selection of high-quality staff (21), and for careful preparation (19) of them to carry out the program. The heavy implementation requirements (10), and to some degree the assistance provided (18), induced a good deal of user commitment (20), and in turn user skill (26), which was also high because of staff quality (21). High user skill, in conjunction with the fact that the program was quite well stabilized (27) by late 1980, brought about a reasonable degree of student impact (30).

The stream of causality refers essentially to internal program dynamics. What was happening at the *district and building* level?

Moving back to program demand characteristics (11), we note that certain aspects of the program (such as its removing students from high school control, and from high school courses and activities) caused poor fit between the program and the sending buildings (12). That poor fit led to lack of endorsement (22) from building principals, counselors, and teachers. Poor endorsement was further weakened by the presence of competition for funds and for students (15), induced by the fact that external funds (14) were temporary in nature.

Temporary funding, together with the program's demand characteristics (11) (for example, students were visible to employers, had to be responsible, and could easily behave like "assholes") also made for a good deal of program

vulnerability (13). As a consequence, the staff tended to operate the program in a rather isolated fashion (23), to buffer it against the consequences of vulnerability when the immediate environmental endorsement (22) was weak. Certain programs demand characteristics (11), such as the intensive time block, reinforced isolation (23) as well.

An added set of mediating variables was also in play. The career advancement motivation (5) of key central office staff and principals operated to induce a good deal of turbulence (16) in the district. This turbulence effectively reduced the influence of those who were advocating the innovation (24); for some advocates, influence was weakened by job insecurity (25).

So although the program was transformed and altered (28) to some degree to meet the objections stemming from low building endorsement (22), achieved a modest increase in percentage of use (31) for a while, and was, as we have seen, proving reasonably effective with students (30), these factors were not enough to ensure the program's institutionalization (being built into the system) (32).

Rather, the weak building endorsement (22), the program's isolation (23), the competition for funds and students (15), and the weak exercise of influence by innovation advocates (24) resulted in weak institutionalization (32). So, it seems likely, did the departure of program staff, whose mobility (33) was driven by both career advancement motivation (5) and job insecurity (25). It also seems likely that the very user capacity development (34) induced by experience with skillful use of the program (26), enhanced by the external network of contacts (35) generated through the dissemination effort (17), also contributed to the decision of staff members (and it seems, possibly the director) to move on.

Taken as a whole, these explanations seem baroque and complex. But there is fairly clear evidence that each causal link worked as described. The chart will look less complicated if one notes that the chart contains four basic streams: the *program development* stream across the top, the *building/district* stream in the middle, the *career stream* near the bottom, and the external *dissemination/networking* stream last. In many respects the final outcomes can be seen as stemming from conflicting pressures across the streams.

Source: Miles, M. B., & Huberman, A. M. (1994). *Qualitative data analysis: An expanded sourcebook* (2nd ed.). Thousand Oaks, CA: Sage Publications.

think is causing what. Second, it provides an opportunity for expansion: You can explain why variables are related, why they are rated differently, why some precede others, which ones matter more, and so on. Third, both products—the network display and the narrative text—are the basic material to be handed to a colleague for reaction and revision. It's nearly impossible to map a causal network "right" the first time. Someone else who knows the database can review it and suggest improvements. When a causal network and its narrative are revised to coherent form, they can be used to generate more general explanations at the multi-case level.

Final Recommendations. Be cautious about giving excessive weight to individual network variables. Presumably, the one with more arrows leading to it is more significant, but a variable with too many arrows leading to it multiplies the possible number of streams. Conversely, you may be building too much order and purpose into loose-ended, inconclusive events. Get others to propose a more complex view.

Doing a causal network forces a more inferential level of analysis that pulls together the data into a single summarizing form. You have to look at all the data and the preceding conclusions and map them in a coherent way. If you've done it right, you will have respected the complexity of local causality as it has played out over time and successfully combined "process" and "variable" analyses.

Notes

Remember that a causal network is only as good as the analyses whose shoulders it stands on: the original codes, conceptual clusters, and previously composed displays. Good causal models are only as good as the data and earlier analyses they derive from. Selected CAQDAS programs are equipped to help draw causal streams for you, based on your input during analytic entry. A few programs may prompt or suggest some type of interrelationship, but you must specify the connections of what leads to what.

Causal Network: Cross-Case Analysis

Description

A cross-case causal network analysis is both a display and a *thematic narrative* derived from systematic comparison of within-case causal network displays. All cases in a sample are analyzed using variables estimated to be the most influential in accounting for the outcome or core variable. You look at each outcome measure and examine, for each case, the stream of variables leading to or "determining" that outcome. Streams that are similar or identical across cases, and that differ in some consistent way from other streams, are extracted and thematically interpreted. The basic principle is that of developing one or more meta-networks that respect the individual case networks from which they have been derived (Huberman & Miles, 1989; see Display 9.15 for a subnetwork example).

Applications

Causal network *within-case* displays show how to make an inclusive, explanatory analysis of single-case data. A *cross-case* causal network, with its core list of variables found to have significance across several cases, is a way to move from case-specific explanations to more generalizable concepts and theory. We are going from local causation to clusters or "families" of cases sharing important attributes.

Example

Because cross-case causal networking involves manipulating several sets of boxes and arrows at the same time, it can be confusing to explain. So, let's break down the process into successive analytic steps. We'll work from a familiar example and take an outcome variable that lends itself easily to cross-case analysis.

DISPLAY 9.15 ● Subnetwork: Variable Streams Leading to High Job Mobility, Perry-Parkdale Case

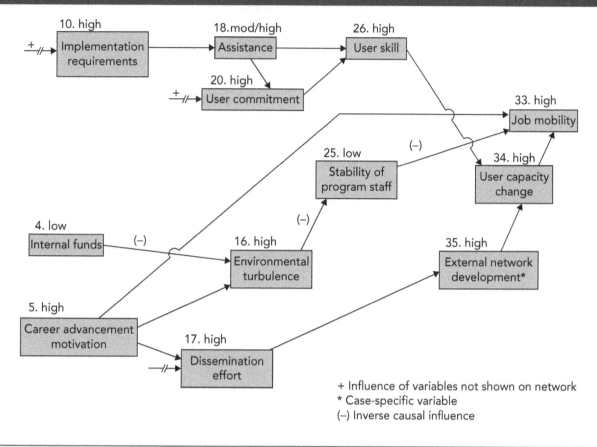

+ Influence of variables not shown on network
* Case-specific variable
(–) Inverse causal influence

Source: Miles, M. B., & Huberman, A. M. (1994). *Qualitative data analysis: An expanded sourcebook* (2nd ed.). Thousand Oaks, CA: Sage Publications.

Assembling the Causal Network. We will assume that you have the basic building blocks discussed in within-case causal networks above for each of your cases:

- The list of core variables (see Display 9.12 for an example)

- The causal network (see Display 9.13)

- The accompanying narrative (see Display 9.14)

In our (Miles and Huberman) school improvement study, for example, we had 12 such networks and narratives, incorporating a core list of some 35 variables, together with six case-specific variables. It helps to have each within-case causal network display printed out and posted on a wall or another display surface.

Isolating the Causal Streams for Each Case That Lead to the Dependent Variable Being Analyzed. This is the major task. Let's assume, for purposes of illustration, that you want to see how an outcome called "job mobility" is determined in a study of people's role and career shifts. We begin by looking at the predictors of that outcome for one case. We start with an exhibit we have seen already, the causal network for the Perry-Parkdale case (Display 9.13). But to make the cross-case causal network analysis easier to follow, let's extract the streams from the causal network that led to job mobility, as shown in Display 9.15.

We've pulled out the *subnetwork* of variables leading to the outcome of job mobility. The job mobility box (number 33) has three arrows leading to it from boxes 5, 25, and 34. Two of those boxes, in turn, have others leading to them along what we call a stream. The streams leading to "job mobility" are easy to see if you scan backward from Box 33 to the preceding boxes. It helps to go only two steps back from the outcome. The boxes reached in that way can be thought of as "immediate" causes of the outcome (i.e., mediating variables); earlier boxes on the causal stream are "remote" causes (i.e., preceding mediating variables and/or antecedent conditions).

To understand the five streams within the subnetwork, we have two tools. First, we can read across each stream to see what is happening—what the theme or logical succession is. To do that, we have the variable labels and their ratings. For instance, take the substream 5 → 17 → 35. The message here is that key participants at Perry-Parkdale were interested in getting promoted (5), which led to a more energetic effort to disseminate (17) the innovation they had developed to others outside their home district (35), where, presumably, some interesting jobs might be found.

Working from the bottom of the display, let's look at the five streams that led to job mobility (Box 33):

- 5 → 17 → 35 → 34 → 33
- 5 → 33
- 5 → 16 → 25 → 33
- 4 → 16 → 25 → 33
- 10 → 18 → 20 → 26 → 34 → 33

To be sure that such an interpretation is plausible, we have the second tool: the causal network narrative (see Display 9.14, the narrative for the case discussed here). The narrative nails down the context, shows the temporal and causal relationships mapped on the network, and explains why the variables are chained as they are.

But here is where analysis takes a real qualitative turn. Each job mobility stream in Display 9.15 is not just a causal chain but a *story* with an accompanying *theme* (remember the proverb: Where there's a stream, there's a theme):

- 4 → 16 → 25 → 33: This stream looks ominous—low funds, high turbulence, high job insecurity, low stability of program staff, high job mobility. Reading the narrative confirms our impression that this is a *casualty* scenario: Low funding led to local uncertainties about continuing the project, which caused project staff to be shifted to other jobs.

- 5 → 16 → 25 → 33: This stream adds the "career advancement motivation" variable and thereby strengthens the *casualty* theme; people did not get promoted or reassigned to desired job slots, even though they had hoped for that.

- 5 → 33: Some people got where they wanted via the project. For now, let's call this one an *opportunism* stream.

- 5 → 17 → 35 → 34 → 33: Some made desirable job shifts, but in what looks like a socially redeeming way. The dissemination effort may be fed by career advancement motives, but the process of spreading the project to other districts develops training and consulting skills (capacity changes) that then are used on the next job. Reading the narrative to get a clearer sense of what is happening here yields a *career crystallization* theme: People doing the disseminating realize they want to go on doing this kind of work, rather than return to their former jobs.

- 10 → 18 → 20 → 26 → 34 → 33: The stream itself is upbeat: Local staff take on a stiff project (high implementation requirements), receive decent assistance, develop strong commitment, master the project (high user skill), develop new capacities, and move to desirable new jobs. Let's call this stream *success-driven advancement*.

Don't try for a theme or scenario name until you have looked at several cases. A stream usually has a stray predictor or two, and you need to wait until these strays can be separated out from those variables appearing consistently, which will give the name to the stream.

Analysis

Pattern matching is discovering whether a pattern found in one case is replicated in other cases as well, suggesting a common scenario. Are the same patterns of core variables involved? Are the ratings (high, moderate, low) the same? Let's take another high "job mobility" case, extracting the streams leading to that outcome. Display 9.16 presents the result for the Calston case.

Only two streams lead to the "job mobility" variable, and both highlight the same scenario. If you look back at the *casualty* stream/theme for the Perry-Parkdale case (Display 9.15), three of the same variables (internal funds, environmental turbulence, stability of program staff) are here. Better still, they are in the same sequence and have identical ratings.

Let's try another case. Display 9.17 shows the extracted portion for Banestown.

This is yet another *casualty*-themed case. If we take out the case-specific "climate in district office" variable and the "external funds" variable, we have the same variables, identically rated, as in Perry-Parkdale, although not in the same order. Here, the "internal funds" variable comes after, not before, the "environmental turbulence" variable. But reading the case narrative produces the same, sad scenario of dashed career hopes; the shift in sequence means little.

Let's look at one more example in Display 9.18.

By now, you probably can dissect the network more rapidly. Three arrows lead to high "job mobility," but so do five possible streams. The first one—variables 20 → 18 → 26 → 36 → 37—is the

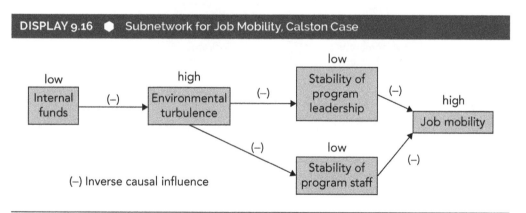

DISPLAY 9.16 ● Subnetwork for Job Mobility, Calston Case

Source: Miles, M. B., & Huberman, A. M. (1994). *Qualitative data analysis: An expanded sourcebook* (2nd ed.). Thousand Oaks, CA: Sage Publications.

DISPLAY 9.17 ● Subnetwork for Job Mobility, Banestown Case

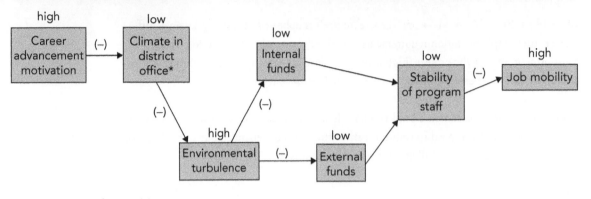

* Case-specific variable
(–) Inverse causal influence

Source: Miles, M. B., & Huberman, A. M. (1994). *Qualitative data analysis: An expanded sourcebook* (2nd ed.). Thousand Oaks, CA: Sage Publications.

DISPLAY 9.18 ● Subnetwork for Job Mobility, Plummet Case

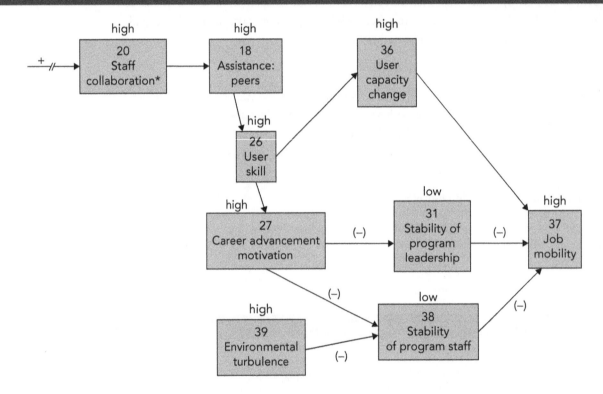

* Case-specific variable
+ Influence of variables not shown on network
(–) Inverse causal influence

Source: Miles, M. B., & Huberman, A. M. (1994). *Qualitative data analysis: An expanded sourcebook* (2nd ed.). Thousand Oaks, CA: Sage Publications.

success-driven advancement stream/theme we saw at Perry-Parkdale, at least in the immediate causal variables, those closest to the criterion measure: skill, capacity change. The sequence is the same and the ratings are identical.

Let's try another stream: 27 → 31 → 37; this looks like the *opportunist* scenario at Perry-Parkdale. Finally, let's take a third stream: 39 → 38 → 37. This is the same sequence as the final three predictors in the Calston *casualty* scenario, which itself is virtually identical to the Perry-Parkdale *casualty* scenario. (To confirm this, the analyst rereads the causal network narratives for the three cases.)

At the end of this analysis, the 40+ streams for the 12 cases fell into the four *thematic families* or "tale types" we identified along the way:

1. *Casualty* scenarios

2. *Opportunism* scenarios

3. *Success-driven advancement* scenarios

4. *Career crystallization* scenarios

Moreover, the analyst can move up an analytical notch and cluster *cases* rather than individual streams. For example, both Perry-Parkdale and Plummet have successful and unsuccessful job mobility scenarios; some people get what they are after, and others do not. This was also obtained for other cases; we could group them at the case level as a *win–lose* scenario/theme.

In a sample of cases, we have not only comparability but also *variability*. There are moderate and low job mobility cases, and we have to be sure their causal flows are either different from or contrary to the ones in the high job mobility cases. Ideally, the low cases would have some of the same *variables* in the same or similar *sequences* as for the high cases, but the *ratings* would be different. For example, high internal funds, combined with low environmental turbulence and high staff stability, would lead to low job mobility—the opposite of the casualty scenario, but with the same variables in the same order. That would strengthen the analysis and increase its explanatory power. We now can claim with more confidence that job mobility is caused by a *particular combination* of funding, turbulence, and staff stability, because both high and low mobility result from the same interaction of these variables.

Confirmation of the emerging scenarios/themes can range from research team discussion and consensus to a series of logic-based decision rules such as the following:

• The most immediate predictor/mediating variables—the two or three closest to the outcome measure—are the same and are in the same sequence.

• The common predictors have the same ratings (high, moderate, low).

• The outcome themes are different (or absent) in cases with a differently rated outcome variable (e.g., high, moderate, low).

In a single-case study, making and revising a variable list is fairly straightforward. In a multiple-case study for cross-case comparisons, the same variables will be used to analyze 5, 10, or 20 cases. For this to happen, ideally each of the variables should be empirically meaningful in all cases. Of course, you should leave slack for two likely situations: There will be some case-unique variables, and some variables will be influential in most but not all cases. In the former instance, the final causal network will contain some case-specific variables, labeled as such. In the latter instance, some network variables will be dropped (with an explanation) from the cases where they contribute little or nothing to the analysis.

Finally, back out of certain dead ends. Dead ends are streams that make no sense and need to be broken up, even though they seem common across cases. And if a cross-case scenario doesn't square with the network narrative, the scenario needs to be revised.

Notes

We've found that the basic operations for cross-case causal network analysis are very similar to those used for within-case causal networks. The lesson again here is to *use your previous analytic display work about your data for threads to weave your causal network tapestry.*

Displaying a cross-case causal network is possible, but we forgo an example here. This is one case in which words, in the form of themes and an accompanying explanatory narrative, are the stronger and more elegant display strategies for your analytic efforts. Selected CAQDAS programs can provide the software necessary for such complex modeling, but you must still, as the data analyst, initiate the boxes' labels, connections, and pathways.

For an excellent example of causal networking displays with multiple participants' data, see Aluko's (2015) study of safety challenges in commercial motorcycle operations.

CLOSURE AND TRANSITION

Remember that research never *proves* anything; it *suggests*, at best. Explaining through these methods why something happened the way it did is an evidence-based but nonetheless good-faith effort to map causation. It is a complex and slippery enterprise that requires the analyst to find the storylines in data, constructed through systematic investigation of "What happened next?"

With explaining comes the groundwork for predicting, the method outlined in the next chapter.

METHODS OF PREDICTING

CHAPTER SUMMARY

This chapter presents methods of displaying efforts that attempt to predict outcomes based on careful and nuanced analysis of antecedent conditions and mediating variables. These methods rely on earlier displays that serve as foundations for documenting and hypothesizing about possible future trajectories of action.

CONTENTS

INTRODUCTION

Futurists and inventors ask themselves three questions when they think about visions for the world:

- What is possible? (i.e., What *might* happen?)

- What is plausible? (i.e., What *could* happen?)

- What is preferable? (i.e., What *should* happen?)

These same questions also apply to qualitative researchers attempting to predict and theorize about their studies for future, comparable contexts.

But no one can predict the future with 100% accuracy. Even statisticians, with their sophisticated mathematical models, give themselves margins of error. Wong (2012) notes that human agency in unique social contexts generates "demi-regular" patterns, thus making generalizable predictions suspect. Research-based predictions and theories are well-informed but, nevertheless, provisional visions about what might, could, and should happen.

METHODS OF PREDICTING

Making and Testing Predictions outlines a series of heuristics for proposing hypotheses and building theory. A *Predictor–Outcome–Consequences Matrix* illustrates how to document, order, and chart antecedent conditions and mediating variables that lead toward primary outcomes and consequences. *Causal–Prediction Models* completes the series by showing how primarily matrix data transform into network displays for explanatory analysis, predictive construction, or theory building.

Making and Testing Predictions

Description

Predictions are inferences that a researcher makes about the probable evolution of case events or outcomes over the following months or years. The predictions are drafted at the time of analysis, held, and then submitted to case participants later (e.g., 6–12 months, but timing obviously depends on the nature of the cases and predictions involved). Participants respond to (a) the accuracy of the predictions, and (b) the accuracy of the reasons given to justify them. Although predictions can originate from virtually any research process, they are more solidly grounded when they derive from causal/explanatory displays (see Display 10.1).

DISPLAY 10.1 ◆ Prediction Feedback Form

School District _____ <u>Dun Hollow</u> _____   Name _____

<u>Our Predictions</u>   (Made with June 1980 data)   Date _____

1. <u>Institutionalization</u>: that is, the degree to which the Eskimo units have become a durable, built-in or routine part of the ongoing operation in the district.

Our Prediction

> The curriculum will not be incorporated into the district after the field test at Carr and Tortoise Area Schools.

<u>Your Description of the Actual Situation Since Then</u>

Actual Situation

There are probably many factors leading to the actual situation. The most important ones are:

A. _____
_____

B. _____
_____

C. _____
_____

D. _____
_____

E. _____
_____

F. _____
_____

Please rank these factors you have listed in their order of importance by putting next to the letter A – F nos. 1 for the most important, 2 for the next most important, etc.

Source: Miles, M. B., & Huberman, A. M. (1994). *Qualitative data analysis: An expanded sourcebook* (2nd ed.). Thousand Oaks, CA: Sage Publications.

Applications

History, Napoleon is supposed to have said, is the version of past events that people have decided to agree on. And field researchers, who depend heavily on local participants' perceptions in building a descriptive and explanatory write-up of the site, are likely to get sucked into collective perceptions that lend coherence to such a write-up. There are many ways to avoid biases in the data being collected, but there are fewer ways of getting around collective, consensual ones. Also, participants may not agree—either with parts of your write-up or with one another. People witnessing the same events may make sense of them in quite different ways and give discrepant accounts.

In three studies where we fed back causal networks, we found only modest discrepancies among participants, or between them and us. But there was some disagreement, and we were left sitting on it, trying to think of a way to get resolution. We did invent one approach: testing the validity of your findings by predicting what will happen in your case after 6 months or a year. Presumably, if the analysis is expressed clearly, it has some implications or consequences (using the **if-then** tactic). These can be spelled out and operationalized. The real-world results can be checked out later in a new field contact through the tactic of **getting feedback from participants**. The result is the qualitative researcher's rich, full-fledged prediction of a slice of social life, which in turn helps with current ways of working and living and forewarns us of potential obstacles as we strive toward our goals.

Generating predictions is a good experience. You have to take a hard look at the data and analyses and address their portent explicitly. It's a way of clarifying a general theory about your case by generating multiple predictions about different aspects of the case. It's also a validation device, even when participants' responses are equivocal.

Is prediction making worth the time? Yes, if you want to know how good your analysis really is or if much is riding on it. No, if your main thrust in a study is descriptive rather than explanatory or predictive.

Example

Making a Prediction. In our (Miles and Huberman) school improvement study, we had been looking retrospectively at 3 or 4 years of change efforts in schools. It made sense to plan for a follow-up, a year after field work ended, to see whether our analyses had not just explanatory but predictive power.

To see how this process works, take a look back at Display 9.13 and find variable/Box 32 on the network: *Institutionalization.* It has a "low" rating, indicating that the innovation at this site has not become a durable, routine part of ongoing operations. The rating on this variable is a function of the several paths leading to it, both from other outcome variables (e.g., 30 *Student impact,* and 31 *Percentage of use*) and from variables further back in the causal streams. Schematically, the causal network says that *Institutionalization* is as low as the combined function of the variables leading up to it; they are the likely causes of the *Institutionalization* outcome.

In testing the plausibility of the causal analysis, we asked two predictive questions: What is likely to happen to the innovation between now and next year at this time? On which factors are we basing that prediction?

Looking over the causal network and accompanying text, and reviewing our collective displays for the study, the analyst decided the program was in trouble. The data suggested that the innovation was a peripheral one, that its benefits were less than its demands on staff, that its support was soft, that competing practices had not been eliminated, and that its funding was uncertain.

But there were some promising signs: The program was operating on a regular, daily basis, and it was getting positive results with turned-off students, but they were buried in a pile of pessimistic indicators. The analyst predicted that *the project would be phased out gradually in the course of the following year.*

Justifying the Prediction. Now that a prediction has been made, it needs to be justified through the data. Here is where your earlier display work provides evidentiary support.

Back to our example: Display 9.13's causal streams leading to Box 32 *Institutionalization* look foreboding. The stories that the interrelated variables tell are as follows:

- The project makes for a poor program fit (Box 12) and is not supported by teachers or administrators (Box 22). It has not worked through to a better fit by changing the organization (Box 29).

- The project is vulnerable because of its demands, its isolation, and its dependence on soft money (Boxes 11, 13, 14, and 23).

- It competes for funds and students (Box 15).

- Its support in the central administrative office is uncertain for a variety of reasons (Box 24).

- Key project staff are about to leave (Box 33).

- The number of students projected for the following year is lower than for the previous year (Box 31).

These are the reasons for the dire prediction. You weight all of these indicators by their degree of influence; this is also a way of getting the number down to four or five, which is all that a participant can be asked to respond to. Display 10.2 shows the five factors that were settled on.

DISPLAY 10.2 ● Factors Supporting "Institutionalization" Prediction

A. Poor district record of institutionalizing soft-money programs.

B. Unlikelihood of strong support from new principals: some counselors indifferent; some elective-subjects teachers hostile.

C. Lukewarm support from central office.

D. Financial squeeze in district: declining enrollments, staff cutbacks, lowered external funds. Program vulnerable because of high unit costs.

E. "Tightening up" mandate to principal: Program may be seen as a "frill," with lax control over students.

Source: Miles, M. B., & Huberman, A. M. (1994). *Qualitative data analysis: An expanded sourcebook* (2nd ed.). Thousand Oaks, CA: Sage Publications.

Looking for Contrary Data. If you look only for the factors supporting a prediction, you'll probably make a poor one. Making a good guess is a function of weighting the odds for one outcome as against another. It's important to consider the factors that could work *against* the prediction (tactic: **looking for negative evidence**).

In the same example (Display 9.13) were indications that the project was well entrenched in routine operations, that it appeared to pay off for a normally hard-to-reach pupil public (Boxes 30 → 31 → 32), and that it had some central office support (Box 24). Pooling these indicators with a contextual and trend analysis of the case as a whole, the analyst came up with four factors shown in Display 10.3 that could "spoil" the pessimistic prediction.

DISPLAY 10.3 ● Factors Working Against "Institutionalization" Prediction

A. Possibility of dissemination funding, which would call for continued implementation.

B. Program meets needs (oasis, dumping ground, safety valve) for alienated, undecided students who are not college bound.

C. Program well installed (recruitment, job sites, monitoring, and instruction), well stabilized.

D. Program might be folded into new vocational education center and be funded through it.

Source: Miles, M. B., & Huberman, A. M. (1994). *Qualitative data analysis: An expanded sourcebook* (2nd ed.). Thousand Oaks, CA: Sage Publications.

Analysis

Selecting Participants to Confirm/Disconfirm the Prediction. Before the predictions are sent out, an ethical review is important: Can this information be damaging to these individuals or to their colleagues in any way? General predictions usually have little harmful potential, in contrast with person-specific information. But the question needs careful consideration.

The prediction and its justification are given to key participants at the site 1 year later, with a request for data on the current, actual situation about which the prediction was made. Normally, you choose participants who (a) have proven reliable, (b) are in a position to know the current situation, and (c) occupy differing roles and have somewhat differing perspectives.

Pertinence Ratings:
1 = not pertinent
2 = pertinent, but not important in causing current situation
3 = important factor in causing current situation

Our Prediction

The program will undergo a transitional year in 1980–81, during which time it will be phased out.

Factors we thought would support our prediction	Pertinence (write in appropriate number below)	Brief explanation (why you say this)
A. Poor district record of institutionalizing soft-money programs.	2	It could have been different with a more aggressive leader sold on the idea.
B. Unlikelihood of strong support from new principals; some counselors indifferent; some elective-subjects teachers hostile.	2	One new principal was supportive; the other not. Counselors reflected the principals' attitudes.
C. Lukewarm support from central office.	3	This is true. In four years neither the Supt. nor the Deputy have ever visited the room. The new Assistant spent 30 min. there last year.
D. Financial squeeze in district; declining enrollments, staff cutbacks, lowered external funds. Program vulnerable because of high unit costs.	3	
E. "Tightening up" mandate to principals: Program may be seen as a "frill," with lax control over students.	1	I wasn't aware of the "tightening up" toward the program. Student behavior—yes.

Factors we thought could work against our prediction	Pertinence (as things turned out)	Brief explanation
A. Possibility of dissemination funding, which would call for continued implementation.	3	As long as state funds are available, a demonstration program will be available.
B. Program meets needs (oasis, dumping ground, safety valve) for alienated, undecided students who are not college bound.	3	This year more students were less motivated than ever before.
C. Program well installed (recruitment, job sites, monitoring and instruction), well stabilized.	1	I don't think this matters at all to the decision makers.
D. Program might be folded into new vocational education center, and funded through it.	1	I have not heard this said regarding the voc. ed. center, though I've thought it has possibilities under state guidelines which allow for student community placement under contracts with employers.

Source: Miles, M. B., & Huberman, A. M. (1994). *Qualitative data analysis: An expanded sourcebook* (2nd ed.). Thousand Oaks, CA: Sage Publications.

Display 10.4 shows a response form from one of the three case participants. Factors A through E on the top part of the chart are the "supporting factors" we listed earlier; Factors A through D on the bottom part are the "spoilers." This respondent agrees that most of the supporting factors were pertinent in determining the way things turned out 1 year later. The other participants made similar, but not identical, judgments on all of the predictors (e.g., two thought central office support was stronger and the "tightening up" was a more pertinent predictor).

As for the factors working against the prediction, the two high "pertinence" estimates suggest that the analyst had underrated the possibility of more external funding and the importance of the "dumping ground" function of the project. (Two other participants agreed, but they also felt that C and D were influential factors that bettered the chances of institutionalization. So, we are still caught in the dilemma of differing perceptions among respondents—a dilemma that sometimes can be resolved by follow-up phone interviewing.)

Limit the number of variables or outcomes for which you make predictions (say, to four or five), and keep the explanatory factors for each to the same number or less. Define each of the outcome variables specifically, or else participants may give confusing responses. You should not ethically expect site personnel to carry out what amounts to professional work without some form of compensation. We offered a modest reader's fee for participants' time and feedback to our prediction response forms.

Assessing the Prediction. How about the researcher's prediction itself—that the program would be phased out? The prediction is probably in trouble because participants felt some of the "spoiler" factors are pertinent and important. As it turned out, our prediction was too pessimistic. The project was reduced in scale, and its status was transitional—but it was still around, though barely.

Central office support apparently was stronger than estimated, owing to the successful and still necessary dumping ground function and the possibility of receiving new external funds to disseminate the project to other districts. The district office had decided to fund the project for one more year but had cut project staff and students by half. We counted our accuracy as only moderate.

We did better at predicting *Institutionalization* at other field sites; one other was moderately accurate, and the rest were high/moderate to highly accurate. Furthermore, the explanations given by us and the site people overlapped reasonably well (58% of assigned causes were in full agreement).

As the causal network in Display 9.13 shows, this was a difficult prediction to make in light of the number of streams and the fact that not all led to the same conclusion. The predictions for the other outcome variables shown at the outcome end of the network (e.g., student impact and job mobility) were easier to make and were on the nose.

Notes

This exercise has some limits. Unless you go back to the field, you are relying solely on self-report data. And predictions can be wrong for reasons that have little to do with their internal validity. A few unanticipated events, such as a budget crisis or teachers' strike, can wreak havoc on the best-laid projections of an analyst. Though you may try to imagine the intrusion of unanticipated events as part of the predictive work, surprises and the idiosyncratic can never be fully anticipated.

Predictor–Outcome–Consequences Matrix

Description

A predictor–outcome–consequences matrix arrays cases and data on three components:

1. The main *antecedent conditions* and *mediating variables* that you think may be the most important contributors to

2. The main *outcome* or criterion variables, then

3. The predicted *consequences* of the outcomes.

The basic principle behind the three-component matrix is explanatory rather than purely descriptive; we want to see whether particular antecedent conditions, mediating variables, and outcomes predict or account for *consequences*—that is, the later outcomes of the outcomes.

This analytic model does not necessarily "predict the future," per se, for the specific cases you're investigating. Rather, you're strategically documenting what has already actually happened to the cases in order to discover whether, in retrospect, certain antecedent conditions or mediating variables, and in what combination, foreshadowed—that is, predicted—particular outcomes and consequences (see Display 10.5).

Applications

Cross-case matrices can be used to explore and test relationships between two, then among several, variables. It's also possible to do more directly explanatory work with cross-case matrices, moving beyond probabilistic predictions to more causal (deterministic) analyses. We can hook a chain of predictors to an outcome, and then show the later consequences of that outcome. Such a display is especially good when you are looking at a variable that is not construed as a "final" outcome.

Use a predictor–outcome–consequences matrix when you want to see how several contributing factors function *together* in relation to different levels of a criterion measure. It's variable oriented but keeps the configuration of variables for each case. This matrix and its accompanying analysis also provide opportunities to develop conditional hypotheses, though they may be site-specific only to the contexts of the cases.

Example

In the school improvement study, we (Miles and Huberman) found that some cases had an easy, smooth time during early use and that others had a rougher time. What accounted for this difference? In other words, which prime factors, coming before or during early use, were associated with more or less smoothness? We had already done some preliminary analysis on "preparedness factors" (e.g., available resources and materials, skills and training of school personnel), and we assigned magnitudes or *dynamic descriptors* to each case's variable under examination. For example, we assessed for each site whether

- the *Required practice changes* were major, moderate, or minor;
- the *Actual size and scope of the innovation* was large, moderate, or small;
- the *Actual classroom/organizational fit* of the innovation was good, moderate, or poor;
- the *Central office's commitment to change* was high, moderate, or low;
- the *Smoothness or roughness of early implementation* was very rough, rough, smooth, mostly smooth, or mixed; and
- other variables.

The use of these dynamic magnitude descriptors is not intended to reduce or seemingly quantify our observations. Rather, it is intended to make *comparative* analyses across cases and between variables more possible and manageable.

In Display 10.5, the first goal is to predict the degree of *Assistance* provided at the 12 field sites (which are ordered in the left-hand column). To do this, the analyst assembled the most likely predictors emerging from the individual cases and from preceding cross-case analyses.

DISPLAY 10.5 ● Predictor–Outcome–Consequences Matrix: Antecedents and Consequences of Assistance

SITES	Antecedent Conditions					Mediating Variables		Assistance	Consequences	
	Actual size/ scope of innovation	Required practice change	Actual classroom/ organizational fit	Strength of implementation requirements #	Scale of funding	Central office commitment to change	Admin. latitude	Outcome: Overall presence	Smoothness/ Roughness of early implementation	Practice-stabilization (later implementation)
Scale of Assistance	↑	↑	↑		↑	↑	↑			
Substantial assistance										
Masepa (E)	large	major	mod/good	12 of 15	$30-50K	high	low	**high**	very rough	mod
Plummet (L)	large	mod/ major	good/poor*	12 of 15	$300K	high	high	**high**	very rough	mod
Carson (L)	large	major	mod/good	12 of 15	$96K	high	mod	**mod/high**	rough	mod
Tindale (L)	large/mod	major	mod	12 of 15	$87K	high	low	**mod/high**	rough	high
Perry-Parkdale (E)	mod	mod/ major	mod	10 of 15	$300K@	mod	high	**mod/high**	mixed	mod/high
Banestown (E)	small/ mod	major	mod	10 of 15	$5.6K	high	high	**mod**	very rough	mod
Initial assistance, then minimal										
Lido (E)	small	mod	mod	7 of 15	$6.1K	low	high	**low/mod**	mostly smooth	mod/high
Astoria (E)	small	minor	good	3 of 15	none	high	high	**low/mod**	smooth	high
Calston (E)	small	mod	poor	9 of 15	none	mod/high	mod/ high	**low/mod**	mixed	mod/high
Nearly none										
Dun Hollow (L)	small	minor	poor	7 of 15	none	low	mod	**low**	rough	low
Proville (L)	mod	minor	mod	7 of 15	$180K	high/low	high	**low**	very rough	low
Burton (E)	small	minor	good	3 of 15	$3.1K	mod/high	high	**low**	smooth	mod

(E) = externally developed innovation
(L) = locally developed innovation
* = good at district level, poor for students
# = weighted sum of three variables at left, scaled 1-5
@ = local innovation funds, to adopt
+ = disseminate externally developed innovation

Source: Miles, M. B., & Huberman, A. M. (1994). Qualitative data analysis: An expanded sourcebook (2nd ed.). Thousand Oaks, CA: Sage Publications.

The first three *Antecedent Conditions* columns (*Actual size/scope of innovation*, *Required practice change*, and *Actual classroom/organizational fit*) deal with variables that are bundled together and are given a numerical weight in the fourth column signifying *Strength of implementation requirements*. A high "score" of 15 was possible.

Then we have three *Mediating Variables* columns (*Scale of funding*, *Central office commitment to change*, and *Administrative latitude*). The *Outcome: Overall presence* as a level of *Assistance* is listed in the next column. A mod/high or low/mod rating meant that our assessment fell in between the two words (i.e., "moderately high" and "low to moderate," respectively). We made these predictive ratings based on the antecedent conditions and mediating variables that came before them on the matrix, coupled with earlier analyses on preparedness factors, plus our insider research knowledge of the 12 cases' subtleties.

If we wanted to, we could have stopped the analysis here and ended up with a two-component predictor–outcome matrix. But the display can be helped with another objective: looking beyond *Assistance* to its *Consequences* during *early* implementation (next to last column) and during *later* implementation (last column). In other words, although the degree of *Assistance* was a dependent variable for an earlier analysis, it is, in turn, the chief predictor of the two later *Consequences*.

Analysis

The next step is to get into a *multivariate* prediction mode, taking those antecedent conditions or mediating variables that we have good reason to believe are contributing to outcomes and assessing their separate and combined effects for consequences.

The analyst is looking to see whether the predictors that best accounted for the degree of assistance make sense and lead to different levels of later outcome. So we have the rudiments of a *causal chain* appearing in the matrix. But we are going beyond a simple configuration in each case to understanding, if we can, the actual *causal mechanisms* involved.

The analyst begins to piece together this mosaic by looking for possible explanatory configurations and by cycling back to the case-level reports to see whether the emerging picture makes sense. Here the analyst saw one cluster of cases and variables (small practice change, high latitude, and small-sized innovation) with its countervailing cluster (large practice change, lower latitude, and large innovation size). He then could look back at the case reports to see whether such phenomena actually existed, and whether the hypothesis about *size* of attempted changes affecting early smoothness was plausible in each case or not (tactic: **replicating a finding**).

Of course, eyeballing the matrix and looking for patterns is the best way to compose predictions. One analyst developed three assertions using basic if-then logic:

1. When there is virtually no on-site preparation assistance for an innovation, later program stabilization will tend to be low.

2. Even when there is substantial on-site preparation assistance for an innovation, early program implementation will be rough, but later program stabilization will most likely be moderate.

3. The amount of on-site funding for an innovation does not appear to affect the program's eventual early implementation or later stabilization; but no funding at all generally equates to minimal on-site preparation assistance (which, in *some* cases, could lead to later lower program stabilization).

These assertions or statements about what *did* happen at 12 particular sites are written in the present tense, comparable to *hypotheses*—projections or predictions of what *could* happen or *most likely would* happen if another comparable program innovation were to be initiated in the future at these sites. Also notice that they are conditional, meaning that phrases such as "tend to," "does not appear to," "most likely," "in *some* cases," and so on, are woven into the statements. No one can predict the future with any exact certainty, not even statisticians. Therefore, couch your qualitatively derived predictions with a touch of humility.

Begin work with a manageable number of candidate antecedent condition and mediating variable predictors chosen on the basis of good sense, conceptual plausibility, and empirical groundedness. More than 12 at a time is a formula for overload. Don't let predictors balloon. Expect that one matrix will lead to another and that the next one will be smaller and better informed as a result of the first one.

Work with the matrix descriptively before you work with the relationships between the variables; that is, go down each column first (tactic: **noting patterns, themes**) and then start **comparing, contrasting** columns. If there is too little variation in the matrix, be content with what you can extract descriptively, or focus solely on the variables that *do* have some range.

Notes

Although this method is not necessarily designed to "predict the future" for the specific study you're working on, there's nothing that says you can't plausibly predict midway through your field work what might happen, and then later see if your predictions of outcomes and consequences were correct (or not). Depending on the scope of your study and the persuasiveness of your argument, there may be transferability of your predictions to other comparable settings, contexts, and conditions.

This profile illustrated a three-component model: predictor, outcome, and consequence. For small-scale or short-term studies, you may wish to explore a simpler two-part prediction and outcome model (discussed later in Display 10.7).

Causal–Prediction Model

Description

A causal–prediction model is a network of variables with causal connections among them, drawn from multiple-case analyses. Although empirically grounded, it is essentially a higher order effort to derive a testable set of hypotheses about the complete network of variables and interrelationships. The principle is one of theory building and thus prediction (see Display 10.6).

Applications

Carefully ordered meta-matrices, time-ordered matrices, or outcome matrices can begin to tell us a lot about what goes with what. Variable by variable, we can understand that X comes before Y; that more of X goes with more of Y; that less of Z goes with more of Y; and perhaps that W looks unrelated to X—unless you take varying levels of V into account. This is all rather atomistic, though; two problems remain.

The first problem is transcending mere association to arrive at *interrelationship*—something like a judgment that variable X not only precedes Y in time but also looks coherently connected to it: If X goes up for some reason, we would expect Y to go up (or down), as well.

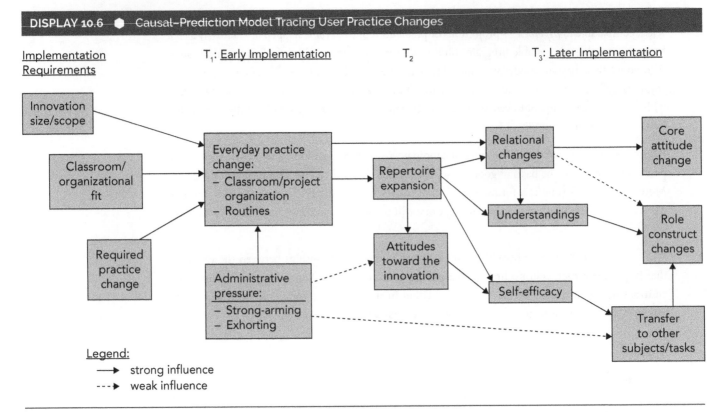

DISPLAY 10.6   ●   Causal–Prediction Model Tracing User Practice Changes

Source: Miles, M. B., & Huberman, A. M. (1994). *Qualitative data analysis: An expanded sourcebook* (2nd ed.). Thousand Oaks, CA: Sage Publications.

The second problem is how to go beyond mere list making to something like an integrated set of relationships among the variables: in short, a *model*. In practice, these problems usually need to be solved together, and they require a network rather than a matrix display.

We have discussed in Chapter 9 the practical problems of assessing causality and of forming a sensible, data-grounded causal network. The question at hand is this: Given multiple-case data in ordered matrix form and a set of variable-oriented conclusions, how can you integrate those findings into a general visual model of the variables involved that specifies causal and thus theoretical/predictive connections clearly? A causal–prediction model is proposed as one heuristic.

Example

Preliminary Displays: Variables and Outcomes. In the school improvement study, we (Miles and Huberman) asked the question, "In what way do users of an innovation change their 'practice' after using the innovation—and what determines greater or lesser amounts of practice change?" Because causal–prediction modeling is usually a second-order activity drawing on other displays, we need to discuss the preliminary displays first.

Throughout this book, there have been many displays related to the school improvement study, some of which have focused on exploring, describing, ordering, explaining, and predicting the antecedent conditions, mediating variables, actions, processes, phenomena, states, events, outcomes, consequences, and so on of the participants. We draw on those displays plus field notes and additional analytic insights made along the way to contribute ideas for the causal–prediction model.

Preliminary Display: Predictors and Outcomes. We first need to look at the question of which predictor variables might be associated with the particular outcomes in this study. For that we need to build a *case-ordered predictor–outcome meta-matrix* (see Display 10.7).

DISPLAY 10.7 ● Predictor-Outcome Matrix: Predictors of Magnitude of User Practice Change

Early Implementation Requirements

Magnitude of change, by sites	Required practice change *	Project size/scope	Classroom/ organizational fit	Index of early implementation requirements @	General attitude during implementation	Administrative pressure: Direct: Strong-arming	Administrative pressure: Indirect: exhorting, reinforcing
High Change							
Masepa (E)	major	large	mod/good	14	+	high	high
Plummet (L)	mod-major	large	good/poor #	12	+	low	high
Moderate Change							
Banestown (E)	major	small/mod	moderate	10	+	mod	high
Tindale (L)	major	large/mod	moderate	12	+	high	high
Carson (L)	major	large	moderate	13	+	low	high
Perry-Parkdale (E)	mod-major	mod	moderate	10	+	low	low/mod
Moderate-Low Change							
Calston (E)	moderate	small	poor	9	+	mod	mod
Lido (E)	moderate	small	moderate	7	+	low	mod
Small-No Change							
Burton (E)	minor	small	good	3	+	low	mod
Dun Hollow (L)	minor	small	poor	7	-	mod	low
Proville (L)	minor	moderate	moderate	7	-	mod	mod
Astoria (E)	minor	small	good	3	+	low	low

(E) = externally developed innovation

(L) = locally developed innovation

* = discrepancy between users' customary instructional practices and those required to implement the innovation at the time of initial use

= good in the district, poor for needs of incoming students

@ = sum of 5-point scales for first 3 columns

Source: Miles, M. B., & Huberman, A. M. (1994). Qualitative data analysis: An expanded sourcebook (2nd ed.). Thousand Oaks, CA: Sage Publications.

The analyst in this case chose to order the cases in terms of overall intensity of the outcome (high, moderate, moderate-low, small/no change) and selected a number of predictors that seemed to have been important on a case-by-case basis in inducing user practice change.

In this instance, the analyst concluded that *Required practice change*, *Project size/scope*, and *Classroom/organizational fit* were all associated with the degree of user practice change (tactic: **making contrasts, comparisons**). This conclusion also involved another tactic: **checking the meaning of outliers**. For example, the analyst noted that the moderate-sized program at Proville was sabotaged by dissatisfied users, so there was no opportunity for user practice change to occur. The analyst also noted that *General attitude during implementation* was a poor predictor because it was largely positive, except in cases where discontinuations took place (Dun Hollow, Proville).

Finally, the analyst saw that *Administrative pressure* of a *Direct* sort was, by itself, not a very good predictor. But if it was combined with *Indirect* pressure (exhorting, reinforcing), the consequences were clear: A carrot-and-stick approach was associated with greater user practice change (tactic: **finding mediating variables**).

Analysis

Building the Causal–Prediction Model. Now you begin reflecting: How can the associations noted in matrix displays be transformed and integrated into a meaningful explanatory network model? So far, the analysis has been mostly variable oriented. Let's apply four process-oriented rules of thumb:

1. Order the model *temporally*: Learn which relevant variables occur first in time, which occur along the way during implementation, and which might be seen as early and later outcomes.

2. Consider which variables might reasonably be expected to have a direct *influence* on other variables, both preceding them in time and having a plausible direct connection.

3. *Check case participants' explanations*: Consult the field notes. What causal linkages do *they* claim are present?

4. Consider what available *research and theory* have to say about causal connections and their predicted outcomes. (In this case, past studies of implementation and individual learning theory might suggest relationships among certain variables.)

Using these rules, you have to noodle for a while. As with other network displays, it helps to put variables on index cards or "sticky notes," move them around into various configurations, and look at the connections that seem plausible and sensible. If you have some user-friendly CAQDAS graphic software, use that. Display 10.6 shows the model that finally emerged from our own process. Let's look at some of its aspects.

First, the analyst concludes that the innovation's three *Implementation requirements* are logically prior to what happens when it is implemented. So he places *Innovation size/scope*, *Classroom/organizational fit*, and *Required practice change* as antecedents of some aspects of user practice change.

From the Display 10.7 matrix, we can suggest that the easiest (hence, possibly earliest) things to change are classroom routines. The analyst, reflecting a moment and reviewing case data, also realizes that such routines are being changed, not by magic, but by the form of organization of the project and the way it is carried out in classrooms. So those are drawn in Display 10.6 as the immediate *Everyday practice* changes during early implementation. The model is growing.

Where should *Administrative pressure* fit in the model? It occurs mainly during early implementation, the field notes show, and the analyst reasons that it probably has a direct effect on *Everyday practice change*: The strong-arming and exhorting serve to keep the immediate short-run practice changes in place. (Prior educational implementation research tends to support this linkage, contributing to the strength of the model's prediction component.)

The analyst also postulates that *Administrative pressure* has weaker, later effects as well (suggested through dashed lines in Display 10.6): It encourages positive *Attitudes toward the innovation* itself (through the strong-arming and exhorting) and makes it more likely that users will *Transfer* their learnings *to other subjects and tasks*.

From Early (T₁) Through Later (T₃) Implementation. Once the initial user changes in practice have taken place, what is a reasonable model that would get us to the other, "deeper" outcomes noted in Display 10.6? It almost surely is not a linear chain but a network. We have to consider how succeeding types of changes in teachers might influence and affect each other. The analyst also has the variables and outcomes from earlier relevant displays as an empirical start.

The analyst culled from previous displays and field notes that the project's *Routines*, given some teacher experience with them, led to *Repertoire expansion* (i.e., teachers have new things they know how to do). From this expansion came positive *Attitudes toward the innovation*.

These two practice changes have further consequences. An expanded repertoire leads to *Relational changes* (e.g., more willingness to share one's new knowledge with other teachers), and it deepens teachers' *Understandings*—of classroom dynamics; of their own and pupils' roles; and, in some cases, of school and district dynamics. Finally, both repertoire expansion and positive attitudes to the innovation lead to increased *Self-efficacy* (i.e., I am more skilled in doing this new thing; therefore, I feel good about myself professionally).

After a good deal of implementation, *Core attitude* changes (e.g., "I was learning to be flexible") come essentially from the teacher's working relations with peers, as well as with students themselves. The analyst also proposes that *Role construct* changes (e.g., reconceptualizing "structured" teaching as productive, rather than authoritarian) come essentially from basic understandings and from the successful experience of transfer to other subjects and tasks. *Transfer*, itself, comes mainly from *Self-efficacy* in this model: The better I feel about my competence, the more likely I am to try my new ideas and practices in other aspects of my work.

All of these variables were mapped into Display 10.6, the causal–prediction model. Think of the final result as a carefully interwoven series of causal chains from the school improvement study, with transferable possibilities to comparable sites and contexts. Each stream is a story about the project and its participants across time, and their points (or variables) of convergence are moments of interrelationship. The structure of the causal–prediction model, with its "what happens next?" scenarios, outlines the accompanying narrative we compose for readers to tell them: "This is what happened, and this is *why* it happened *in this particular sequence*." This implies that we are proposing a theory, and *theories are about prediction*.

Recommendations for Causal–Prediction Model Development. It sometimes helps to make submodels that are wholly linear ($W \rightarrow X \rightarrow Y \rightarrow Z$) as a simplifying strategy (see the methods profile for Causal Chains in Chapter 9). It's also useful to consider a backward mapping approach: You begin with final outcomes and reason back along the causal byways (Which antecedent conditions or mediating variables, in principle, would have to be changed in order to induce this change?).

It often happens that you feel blocked, unable to understand how variable *A* could lead to variable *C* in any plausible way. There must be one or more other variables in the picture that affect the outcome. Use the tactic of **finding mediating variables** to generate a variable *B* that comes between *A* and *C*.

You should subject the "final" causal model to verification, most easily through colleagues and participants, who can help you clarify the assumptions you are making and suggest alternative views (tactic: **checking out rival explanations**). Given a causal–prediction model with which you are reasonably satisfied intellectually, return once again to the written-up field notes for evidence of disconfirmation or needed revision. Of course, the true test of a causal–prediction model is if the same sequences occur in different settings in the future.

Notes

Expect to do several versions of the causal–prediction model. Use a simple technology that permits flexibility in rearrangement—index cards and "sticky notes" do indeed work well for the initial stages of display design. Once those are relatively set, transform the bins to digital representations with modeling software. Get advice from colleagues; don't close up too fast. Return repeatedly to field notes to check, test, and extend the model. It usually helps to refer back to preceding matrices, with a good look at **outliers** and **extreme cases**. When a specific, well-understood case does not fit the model, *change the model* to accommodate that information, rather than try to explain away the "inconvenient" information.

CLOSURE AND TRANSITION

Prediction is a slippery concept in qualitative inquiry, but there may be some occasions in which projection of what might, could, and should happen is a necessary goal of our research endeavors. We advise that you predict, propose, hypothesize, and theorize only after rigorous analysis and careful reflection on the consequences of your statements.

We have completed five chapters on methods of qualitative data analysis through display: exploring, describing, ordering, explaining, and predicting. The next chapter in Part Three offers several methods for further analytic work—ways of better ensuring the credibility and trustworthiness of your findings.

MAKING GOOD SENSE

PART III

DRAWING AND VERIFYING CONCLUSIONS

CHAPTER SUMMARY

This chapter offers additional analytic tactics for generating meaning from data and for testing or confirming findings. Standards for assessing the quality of conclusions are proposed, along with methods for documenting a researcher's analytic processes.

CONTENTS

INTRODUCTION

This is a substantial chapter, and one that fellow researchers have told us they've found most useful. As you work with any display, there's always a flow of specific analysis *tactics*—that is, ways of drawing and verifying conclusions that you use during the process. These tactics have been named in **boldface** in the preceding chapters. Now, we discuss each in detail. Following that, we turn to the question of the goodness or *quality* of the conclusions you reach. The chapter concludes with a look at the documentation of qualitative analyses.

Creativity scholar Sir Ken Robinson is credited with offering this cautionary advice about making a convincing argument: "Without data, you're just another person with an opinion." We add to that, "Without verification, you're just another researcher with a hunch." Twenty-six tactics are discussed in this chapter to assist with verification, but you do not have to employ all 26 of them in just one study. Some are default tactics used as "givens" for any study such as **noting patterns, themes**. Others may be utilized on an as-needed basis, such as **making metaphors** or **following up surprises**. And others will be more appropriate for selected qualitative research methodologies and data sets, such as **factoring** and **ruling out spurious relations**. We cannot prescribe which specific tactics are appropriate for your unique projects, but we do encourage using at least 3 to 5 of these 26 tactics in each study to better support your analysis.

TACTICS FOR GENERATING MEANING

In this section, we discuss 13 specific tactics for drawing meaning from a particular configuration of data in a display. People are meaning finders and meaning makers; we keep the world consistent and predictable by organizing and interpreting it as best we can. The critical question is whether the meanings you find in qualitative data are trustworthy and "right." The following section discusses tactics for testing or confirming meanings, minimizing bias, and ensuring to your best ability the quality of the conclusions.

First, here is a quick overview of tactics for generating meaning, numbered from 1 to 13. They are arranged roughly from the descriptive to the explanatory and from the concrete to the more conceptual and abstract.

(1) **Noting patterns, themes**; (2) **seeing plausibility**; and (3) **clustering** help the analyst see "what goes with what." (4) **Making metaphors**, like the preceding three tactics, is a way to achieve more integration among diverse pieces of data. (5) **Counting** is also a familiar way to see how much of "what's there."

(6) **Making contrasts, comparisons** is a pervasive tactic that sharpens understanding. Differentiation sometimes is needed too, as in (7) **partitioning variables**.

We also need tactics for seeing things and their relationships more abstractly: (8) **subsuming particulars into the general**; (9) **factoring**, an analogue of a familiar quantitative technique; (10) **noting the relations between variables**; and (11) **finding mediating variables**.

Finally, we can systematically assemble a coherent understanding of data by (12) **building a logical chain of evidence**, and (13) **making conceptual/theoretical coherence**.

1. Noting Patterns, Themes

When you're working with text or initial displays, you often note recurring patterns, overarching themes, or "gestalts" that pull together many separate pieces of data. Something jumps out at you and suddenly makes sense.

Some examples of patterns from the school improvement study were

- the frequent citing of a "miracle case" (e.g., a failing student who was rejuvenated by the innovation) as either an explanation or a justification for the project,

- "deep coping" as a problem-solving style in a high school staff group, and

- the use of "administrative latitude"—the freedom to alter an innovation in return for trying it at all.

What kinds of patterns can there be? As usual, we can expect patterns of *variables* involving similarities and differences among categories, and patterns of *processes* involving connections in time and space within a bounded context.

Pattern finding can be very productive when the number of cases and/or the data overload is severe. McCammon et al. (2012), for example, analyzed responses from 234 returned open-ended surveys. The patterns constructed from the mixed methods data resulted in 30 major categories, which were then synthesized into three major themes, then into one key assertion.

The human mind finds patterns almost intuitively; our brains are hardwired to do so. But patterns don't just happen; we construct them from our observations of recurring phenomena. The important thing is to be able to (a) see added evidence of the same pattern, and (b) remain open to disconfirming evidence when it appears. Patterns need to be subjected to *skepticism*—your own or that of others—and to conceptual and empirical testing before they can represent useful knowledge (Do we find it elsewhere in the data where it was expected? Are there any counterexamples?).

2. Seeing Plausibility

It often happens during analysis that a conclusion is plausible, makes good sense, and "fits." If a colleague asks you how you came to the conclusion or what you based it on, the initial answer is something like "I don't really know. It just feels right." Many scientific discoveries initially appeared to their authors in this guise; the history of science is full of global, intuitive understandings that, after laborious verification, proved to be true. So, plausibility with intuition as the underlying basis is not to be dismissed.

But people are meaning finders, even in the most genuinely chaotic data sets. Patterns can be found even in random data, as the activities of numerologically obsessed people show (see the films π [pi], *A Beautiful Mind*, and *The Number 23*). Plausibility can easily become the refuge of analysts who are too ready to jump to conclusions.

During the documentation of our own analysis efforts, we often found ourselves giving the "plausibility" basis for the conclusions we drew, particularly in the early stages of analysis. Nearly always, it turned out, plausibility was an initial impression that needed further checking through other tactics. Plausibility in this sense was a sort of *pointer*, drawing the analyst's attention to a conclusion that looked reasonable and sensible on the face of it—but what was the real basis involved?

Here's a brief illustration: McCammon et al. (2012) analyzed their survey data by *gender* to observe whether men and women responded differently to their high school arts experiences. Saldaña hypothesized and "felt sure" that major differences would appear, based on his earlier research with audience response trends. But after data analysis, no *major* gender differences were found. There were nuances of experience that women remembered and men did not, but the projected differences were just not present in the data. Saldaña even thought, "This can't be right," and he subjected the qualitative data to reanalysis tactics—**counting** and finding new ways of **making contrasts,**

comparisons with the data—but nothing new was discovered. (The most revealing differences actually occurred between other demographics, such as age cohort.)

So, the moral is, trust your "plausibility" intuitions but don't fall in love with them. Subject the preliminary conclusions to other tactics of conclusion drawing and verification.

Incidentally, a somewhat more trustworthy tactic involves noticing a *lack* of plausibility. When a conclusion someone is advancing just doesn't make sense, it's a bit safer to rule it out—but not completely safe. Counterintuitive or puzzling findings sometimes can be extraordinarily stimulating and rich, so they should be allowed their day in the sun. (We will discuss the tactic of **following up surprises** later.)

3. Clustering

In daily life, we're constantly clumping things into classes, categories, and bins: Things that do not move around but grow are called "plants"; things that move around and have babies are called "animals"; and things that move around, have four wheels, have an engine run by fossil fuels or electricity, and carry people are called "automobiles." Most categories have subcategories to further define them, such as "wheel," "engine," and "fuel."

The next step is to figure out what to call the clusters. For example, the process of transforming hundreds of pages of interview transcripts and field notes into a one-page matrix, network, or graphic display might be called "condensing" the data. But to others, it might be called "distilling," "synthesizing," "abstracting," "transforming," and even the abhorrent "reducing" the data. Even though these are different words and processes, they *kind of* mean the same thing. We have clustered them and now need to assign a word or phrase that represents all of them. Shall one of the six words be chosen as their representative? Or shall we compose a completely new umbrella label for the six of them? (This is where a thesaurus comes in handy. But, ultimately, it's your call as the analyst.)

Just as we are pattern-finding people, we are also cluster-making people. We organize and categorize the vast array of things in our lives to feel a sense of comfort and security in their ordering. Routines, rituals, rules, roles, and relationships are clusters of patterned actions—what some generically label as our habits (Duhigg, 2012; Saldaña & Omasta, 2018). Clustering is a tactic that can be applied at many levels to qualitative data: at the level of events or acts, individual participants, processes, settings/locales, sites or cases as wholes, time periods, and so on. In all instances, we're trying to understand a phenomenon better by *grouping* and then *conceptualizing* objects that have similar patterns or characteristics.

But occasionally, clusters are not always mutually exclusive and may overlap. For example, a student most often is in *either* an undergraduate *or* a graduate program. That's easy enough. But what's the undergraduate student's major? Well, it's complicated. He's a double major in social work and religious studies, *and* he's concurrently enrolled in the university's Honors program. Yes, he's male. And gay. And Hispanic. And a first-generation college student. And so on. Life is not neatly bounded and discrete as it once might have seemed. As the analyst works at clustering, the operations become more and more complex and extended—just as sorting things into "animals" and "plants" is a (perhaps deceptively) simpler task than sorting various kinds of wheeled machines (automobiles, trucks, golf carts, airplanes, ski-lift gondolas, and floor polishers) into sensible clusters. Clustering is our best attempt to categorize what seems to belong together, or what "looks alike" and "feels alike" (Lincoln & Guba, 1985).

Here are some additional examples.

Focusing on *participants*, we asked high school students to name the cliques they observed at their school. They identified clusters such as "preppies," "jocks," "goths," "skaters," "band kids," "stoners," "math geeks," "cheerleaders," and so on.

At the level of *processes*, we clustered the activities involved in coping with the problems of later implementation of an innovation: "reaching up," "improving," "debugging," "refining," "integrating," "adapting," and "extending." Processes are best identified in the form of gerunds ("-ing" words) to connote action.

At the level of both *processes* and *phases*, another example comes from our look at teachers' and administrators' job mobility, which clumped rather easily into these categories: "moving in," "moving out," "moving up," "moving in and up," "moving out and up," and "moving over."

It's also possible to cluster *settings* where site-specific *actions* occur. For example, in schools, we might sort places where people interact into the following clusters:

- Formal instructional (classroom, gym)

- Informal instructional (library, media center)

- Formal adult work (meeting room, office)

- Informal adult association (faculty lounge, corridor)

- Mixed (cafeteria, playground)

Clustering also can be seen as a process of moving to higher levels of abstraction (see **subsuming particulars into the general** later in this chapter).

Clustering is a general name given to the process of inductively forming *categories* and the iterative sorting of things—events, participants, processes, settings, and so on—into those categories. When less complex things are being sorted (events, participants, etc.), the clustering tactic typically relies on aggregation and comparison (What things are like each other/unlike each other?) and is closely interwoven with the creation and use of attribute codes.

Clustering techniques do not have to be completely self-invented. There is a long tradition of content-analytic, coding, and categorizing techniques dealing directly with issues of unitizing and clustering qualitative data that can be very helpful (see Richards, 2009; Saldaña, 2016; Schreier, 2012).

4. Making Metaphors

The notion that research should focus only on matter-of-fact, literal description, with cautious, later ventures into interpretation and meaning, is responsible for much intellectual poverty and misery.

That sentence itself is stuffed (a metaphor) with metaphors (cautious ventures, poverty, misery). Metaphors, seen as one major type of trope or literary device, involve comparing two things via their similarities and ignoring their differences. As Morgan (1980) notes, calling a boxer "a tiger in the ring" evokes fierceness, grace, and power—and ignores striped fur, fangs, and four-leggedness. Metaphors are thus a partial abstraction.

The people we study use metaphors constantly as a way of making sense of their experience. We do the same thing as we examine our data. The issue, perhaps, is not *whether* to use metaphor as an analysis tactic but to be *aware* of *how* we—and the people we study—use it.

The *richness and complexity* of metaphors are useful. They are *data-condensing devices*, taking several particulars and making a single generality of them. Qualitative researchers looking at mountains of field note write-ups are grateful for any device that will condense the bulk without locking out multiple avenues for analysis. For instance, the "scapegoat" metaphor pulls together into one package facts about group norms, the treatment of those perceived as "deviants," social rituals, and social rationalizations.

Metaphors are also *pattern-making devices*—for ourselves and for the people we study. For example, in the school improvement study, we found at one site that the remedial learning room was something like an "oasis" for the pupils sent there for part of each day. (A teacher used the word spontaneously, and we began to see the pattern.) The metaphor "oasis" pulls together separate bits of information: The larger school is harsh (like a desert); not only can students rest in the remedial room, but they also can get sustenance (learning); some resources are very abundant there (like water in an oasis); and so on. Such metaphors also help place the pattern noted in the larger context (in this case, the harsh, resource-thin school).

Metaphors are also excellent *decentering devices*. You step back from the welter of observations and conversations at the field site and ask, "What's going on here?" Because metaphors will not let you simply describe or denote a phenomenon, you have to move up a notch to a more inferential or analytical level. The remedial learning room does not look like an oasis, and most people are not actually describing it that way, nor is anyone behaving literally like an exhausted Bedouin under a date palm tree.

Finally, metaphors or analogies are ways of *connecting findings to theory*. The "oasis" metaphor makes you think of how institutions develop compensating mechanisms to reduce the stress they put on role occupants or of how they nurture as well as isolate. Metaphoric thinking effectively unites reason and imagination. Lakoff and Johnson's (1980) *Metaphors We Live By* is essential reading on this topic.

The metaphor is halfway from the empirical facts to the conceptual *significance* of those facts; it gets you up and over the particulars toward the basic social processes that give meaning to those particulars. So, we offer a few words of advice for metaphor makers:

- Stay aware of the metaphors you and people in your study are using, often with only partial awareness. Dig into them for implicit meanings, for more explicit exploration and testing.

- Don't look for overarching metaphors too early in the study. It distracts you from fieldwork, and it leads to hasty judgments that clamp down on the meaning of what you are studying. You start to look around less, and you project the metaphor onto things that are, at best, remotely related to it.

- Being cognitively playful helps generate metaphors. Ask yourself, "If I only had two words to describe an important feature at this site, what would they be?" or "What does it feel like?" The trick is to move from the denotative to the connotative. Instead of the social or the personal, go to biological, mechanical, or spatial domains to find useful metaphors.

- Interaction helps. Groups stimulate their members' thinking by increasing the inputs, bringing in ideas from a new angle, and creating a contagiously playful thinking environment.

- Know when to stop pressing the metaphor for its juice. When the "oasis" starts to have camels, camel drivers, a bazaar, and a howling sandstorm, you know you're forcing things. Use it as long as it's fruitful, and don't overmetaphorize. Remember that the two things compared in a metaphor always have differences.

Other literary devices are available to qualitative inquirers, such as irony (the view from the opposite, sometimes incongruous or paradoxical side); synecdoche (linking instances to a larger concept); and metonymy (representing a whole in terms of one or more of its parts). Gibbs (2018) describes how romance, tragedy, and other literary genres can be used effectively for narrative inquiry.

5. Counting

In qualitative research, numbers tend to get ignored. After all, the hallmark of qualitative research is that it goes beyond *how much* there is of something to tell us about its essential *qualities*.

However, a lot of counting goes on in the background when judgments of qualities are being made. When we identify a theme or a pattern, we're isolating something that (a) happens a number of times and (b) consistently happens in a specific way. The "number of times" and "consistency" judgments are based on counting. When we make a generalization, we amass a swarm of particulars and decide, almost unconsciously, which particulars are there *more often*, which *matter more* than others, which *go together*, and so on. When we say that something is "important," "significant," or "recurrent," we have come to that estimate, in part, by making counts, comparisons, and weights.

So it's important in qualitative research to know (a) that we are sometimes counting and (b) when it is a good idea to work self-consciously with frequencies *and when it's not*. There are three good reasons to resort to numbers: to see rapidly what you have in a large batch of data; to verify a hunch or hypothesis; and to keep yourself analytically honest, protecting against bias.

Seeing What You Have

Numbers, we noted earlier, are more economical and manipulable than words; you "see" the general drift of the data more easily and rapidly by looking at distributions. For instance, in the school improvement study, we asked participants why they were using the new school practices we were studying. We got a mass of answers from several participants at each of the 12 field sites. It seemed that many people were saying that they had been pushed, more or less gently, into these projects, rather than diving in voluntarily. To see more clearly, we did a content analysis of the responses, totaled them, and derived Display 11.1.

DISPLAY 11.1 ● Reasons Given for Adoption by Users	
Reasons/Motives	**Number of Respondents Mentioning Item (N = 56)**
Administrative pressure, constraint	35
Improves classroom practice (new resources, relative advantage over current practice)	16
Novelty value, challenge	10
Social (usually peer influence)	9*
Opportunity to shape projects	5
Professional growth	5
Gives better working conditions	3
Solves problems	2
Provides extra money	1
Total	86
	*Seven mentions from one site

Source: Miles, M. B., & Huberman, A. M. (1994). *Qualitative data analysis: An expanded sourcebook* (2nd ed.). Thousand Oaks, CA: Sage Publications.

It turns out that 62% (35 of the 56 respondents) mentioned administrative pressure and constraint. And, counterintuitively, very few of the practices were adopted to solve problems. There also seemed to be a general "professional development/capacity enhancement" theme (challenge, shaping projects, professional growth). Seeing that theme, gauging the importance of the "constraint" motive, and noting the infrequent problem-solving incentive were all helpful. We saw the overall trends, got some new leads, and saw some unexpected differences. All these findings helped in the subsequent nonquantitative analysis.

Verifying a Hypothesis

McCammon et al.'s (2012) mixed methods survey examined, in part, whether any gender differences occurred between adult men's and women's responses about their high school arts experiences. Saldaña hypothesized that there would be. On a 4.00 "strongly agree" scale, the female respondents' mean was 3.85 and the male respondents' mean was 3.93 to the prompt "I have good memories from my [high school] speech and/or drama participation." But when we "crunched the numbers" through a t test, there was no statistically significant difference on a $p < .05$ standard between these two mean ratings. And the *qualitative* content analysis of their narrative responses to this prompt also confirmed no major differences between men's and women's experiences. So counting in the form of a statistical operation disconfirmed the hypothesis and made for a more trustworthy analysis.

Keeping Yourself Analytically Honest

We had expected from the start that careers would be important in the school improvement projects we studied. The more data we got, the more it seemed that "innovating" was a vehicle for moving up, in, over, or out (seldom down). The finding seemed important, was potentially controversial, and might have been a result of our expectation. So, we actually counted the number of job moves (63 for 12 sites) and estimated how many could be attributed to the innovation (83% were). Afterward, we felt far more comfortable about the claims we were making. For example, it seemed that only 35% of the job-related shifts were upward ones, contrary to our earlier impression.

As qualitative researchers, we work to some extent by insight and intuition. We have moments of illumination—things "come together." The problem is that we could be wrong. Doing qualitative analysis with the occasional aid of numbers is a good way of testing for possible bias and seeing how robust our insights are. Microsoft Office and CAQDAS software, plus online programs such as Wordle, can perform quick word search and word counts with our data.

6. Making Contrasts, Comparisons

Although comparisons are supposedly odious, they are what we do naturally and quickly when faced with any life experience, including looking at a qualitative data display. How does X differ from Y? Comparison is a time-honored, classic way to test a conclusion; we draw a contrast or make a comparison between two sets of things—persons, roles, activities, variables, cases as a whole—that are known to differ in some other important respect. This is the classic "method of differences" heuristic. A few examples from our work described in earlier chapters are as follows:

- *Contrast tables* show how exemplary cases vary in extreme ranges of their change, from "high" to "low" to "negative" degrees of user change (see Display 6.21).

- *Growth gradients* display time on one axis and degree on another axis, enabling a comparison of changes across time (see Display 8.4).

- *Predictor–outcome–consequence matrices* array cases by high and low outcomes and use that leverage to examine the impact of possible predictors. In our example, the comparison was between the *magnitude* of change, showing which predictors were present in "high-change" sites but not in "small-/no-change" sites (see Display 10.5).

We advise you to make sure that the comparisons made are the right ones and that they make sense. Take a moment before you display a comparison and think, "How big must a difference be before it makes a difference?" You do not always need a statistical significance test to fall back on. The *practical* significance is what you need to assess.

7. Partitioning Variables

There are times when *differentiation* is more important than integration. It may occur to you at some point in your analysis: "Whoa—that variable is not really one variable but two, or maybe even three."

Partitioning or subdividing variables can occur at many points during analysis. At the stage of initial conceptualization, it pays to "unbundle" variables rather than assume a monolithic simplicity. For example, the general variable of "preparedness" to carry out an innovation can be partitioned into subvariables or components, ranging from the state of the user ("commitment," "understanding," "skills") to the availability of materials and the actions taken by administrators ("time allocation," "in-service workshops").

When you are designing matrix formats, variable partitioning is also useful; more differentiation lets you see differences that might otherwise be blurred or buried. Rather than a single column of *Outcomes*, it may help to partition that into two columns: *Short-Term Effects* and *Long-Term Consequences*.

When is variable partitioning a good tactic? The first answer: Divide variables in the early stages (coding, conceptualizing) to avoid monolithism and data blurring. The second answer: Partition a variable when it is not relating as well to another variable as your conceptual framework (or other available data) has led you to expect.

Finally, we should say that variable partitioning is not a virtue in itself. Extreme differentiation can lead to complexity and atomization, and poor mapping of events and processes. When you divide a variable, it should be in the service of finding coherent, integrated descriptions and explanations.

8. Subsuming Particulars Into the General

Clustering involves clumping together things that "go together" by using a single or multiple dimensions. A related tactic is to ask, "What is this specific thing an instance of? Does it belong to a more general class?" This tactic is similar to the analytic processes for pattern coding (see Chapter 4). Classic grounded theory calls this the "constant comparative method." You are trying to categorize a particular action, event, participant, state, and so on into a more abstractly defined class. That class may have been predefined, or it may have emerged as a result of coding or analytic memoing.

For example, in the school improvement study, we noted specific statements made by teachers and administrators, such as the following:

- "If you want to depart from the guide, ask me and also tell me why you want to do it and how it will fulfill the guide's objectives."

- "The basic philosophy is there, but the use of [the innovation] is flexible, and doesn't require use of all units."

- "In this program you're like a robot . . . but I learned that if I wanted to change something I would just go ahead and do it. . . . I learned to cut corners and do it just as well."

These statements can be subsumed into a more general class: the presence of high or low *administrative latitude* given to teachers to adapt or alter an innovation, a variable that turned out to be very important in explaining the amount of adaptation that occurred.

Subsuming particulars into more general classes is a conceptual and theoretical activity in which you shuttle back and forth between first-level data and more general categories that evolve and develop through successive iterations until the category is "saturated" (new data do not add to the meaning of the general category).

Arbitrary abstraction, however, gets you nowhere. Suppose you observed a teacher writing her name on the dry-erase board on the first day of school. That specific action can be subsumed into a larger class of "written communication," then into a larger class of "information transmission," and finally into a still larger class of "human action." That is a sort of taxonomic classification without useful meaning, however. You cannot decide in a vacuum which of these classes is "right" or "best." There must be a clear linkage to the study's conceptual framework and research questions.

9. Factoring

Factoring comes from factor analysis, a statistical technique for representing a large number of measured variables in terms of a smaller number of hypothetical variables. These second-order variables (factors) may have some "communality." So what is the qualitative researcher's version of factoring? Making patterns of patterns, or categories of categories, or themes of themes.

Most of the tactics we've discussed are designed to do two things: Condense the bulk of the data and find patterns in them. Noting patterns or themes, clustering, and making metaphors are all pattern-forcing exercises. The task essentially is saying to yourself, "I have a mountain of information here. Which pieces go together?" When you create a Pattern Code (see Chapter 4), you are proposing that several disparate but related pieces of data have something in common. What they do or are is the factor, and the process by which you generate it is factoring. In other words, we're condensing the data even further by making a smaller number of patterns from a larger number of patterns, or a smaller number of categories from a larger number of categories, or a smaller number of themes from a larger number of themes. Time for an illustration.

Hager, Maier, O'Hara, Ott, & Saldaña (2000; see also Saldaña, 2016) examined a state department of education's new arts standards document and how it was received by high school theatre teachers. (Long story short, the majority of teachers rejected it because it was poorly written and developed with virtually none of their input.) The focus group interview transcript data generated 52 different Versus Codes, which were then clustered into comparable groups to form eight descriptive categories:

1. Arts Standards Development

2. Curricula

3. Teacher Resistance

4. People

5. Political Ideologies

6. Testing and Graduation Requirements

7. Exclusion and Marginalization

8. Institutions

The next analytic step was to *factor* these categories—in other words, to categorize these eight categories into an even tighter and smaller number of categories. Given below is how the analyst factored the eight into the resulting three categories, which were labeled with war imagery because tensions were high among the participants and the metaphor seemed apt for this study:

Category 1: Human and Institutional Conflicts—The "Fighters"

Subcategories:

People

Institutions

Political Ideologies

Category 2: Standards and Curriculum Conflicts—The "Stakes"

Subcategories:

Curricula

Arts Standards Development

Testing and Graduation Requirements

Category 3: Results of Conflicts—The "Collateral Damage"

Subcategories:

Exclusion and Marginalization

Teacher Resistance

These three new categories were eventually transformed into "versus" phrases (e.g., Your Way vs. Our Way) that served to thematically represent the data.

The consequential question for this analytic tactic is "Do these factors make any meaningful difference, or are they essentially decorative?" The factors have to contribute to our understanding of the case or of its underlying dynamics. Otherwise, they are no more useful than the big, gift-wrapped boxes that unpack into a succession of smaller but equally empty gift-wrapped boxes, leaving us at the end with a shapeless heap of ribbon, paper, and cardboard.

10. Noting the Relations Between Variables

The idea of the interrelationship between variables has been discussed throughout the book thus far, but let's examine it as an analytic tactic.

Networks are most easily depicted as sets of bins and arrows; the bins are the variables, and the arrows show relationships between them. Once you are reasonably clear about what variables may be in play in a situation, the natural next query is "*How* do they relate to each other?" What sort of relationship can we envision between variables A and B? A variable is something that varies. Thus, we might have the following:

1. $A+$, $B+$ (both are high, or both are low at the same time)

2. $A+$, $B-$ (A is high, while B is low, or vice versa)

3. $A\uparrow$, $B\uparrow$ (A has increased, and B has increased)

4. $A\uparrow$, $B\downarrow$ (A has increased, and B has decreased)

5. $A\uparrow$, then $B\uparrow$ (A increased first, then B increased)

6. $A\uparrow$, then $B\uparrow$, then $A\uparrow$ (A increased, then B increased, then A increased some more)

These don't cover all of the possible permutations, of course.

Relationship 1 is a direct association: Both variables are high (or low) at the same time. For variables that are "all or nothing," this relationship can be read as follows: When A is present, B is also present, or both may be absent.

Relationship 2 is the inverse. With Relationship 3, we are noting that changes have occurred recently in A and in B in the same direction; Relationship 4 is the inverse. No claims are necessarily being made that the changes are linked; they are just present.

In Relationship 5, we verge toward causation: A changed, then B changed (and—not shown—there is a reasonable belief that A could have caused B). If A is an evening of heavy drinking and B is a headache the next morning, there is a presumptive connection. But little connection is likely—in most cases—if B is a morning headache and A is the announcement of the new city budget. (Still, if the headache belongs to the mayor, maybe.)

Finally, in Relationship 6, we see a mutual relation: A change in A leads to a subsequent change in B, then to a subsequent change in A. The strength of these associations can vary: We can have decisive, strong, clear relationships—or feeble, weak, ambiguous ones. And, as Morrison (2009) reminds us, causation can be direct or indirect, mediated through other variables.

The basic analysis tactic here involves trying to discover what sort of relationship—if any—exists between two (or more) variables. The important thing to keep in mind is that we are talking about *variables or concepts*, not necessarily specific actions.

Even when we focus on specific events, usually underlying or more general variables are involved. The event of an evening of heavy drinking and the event of the morning headache do not quite affect each other directly. All sorts of variables are at work: the presence of certain chemicals in the beverage involved and the body's ability to metabolize alcohol, the amount consumed, the time intervening, and so on.

How are relationships detected? We propose in this book that displays are an especially strategic way to see them: Data bearing on two or more variables can be arrayed for systematic inspection, and conclusions drawn. Network displays help us look at more complex configurations and show the temporal dimension more clearly.

People tend to think in causal terms. The risk in trying to understand relationships between two variables is jumping too rapidly to the conclusion that A "causes" B, rather than that A happens to be high and B happens to be high. Here, it helps to shift to verification tactics (discussed later), such as proposing and **checking out rival explanations**, **ruling out spurious relations**, or **using extreme cases**.

Drawing in skeptical colleagues to use one or more of these tactics can be very useful. One friend of ours says that any causal statement made about a social situation should be reversed immediately to see whether it looks truer that way:

- "The students are late to class because they hate the teacher." (resistance driven by dislike)

- "The students hate the teacher because they are late to class." (lateness, caused by other reasons, leads to dislike—perhaps mediated by the teacher's reactions to tardiness)

That example may sound a little fanciful, but the reversal exercise is useful. In our school improvement study, we considered this conventional statement: "Teacher involvement and commitment lead to more effort in using the innovation." Then, we considered the reverse: "High teacher effort leads to teacher involvement and commitment." That made good theoretical sense in terms of cognitive dissonance theory. And we had seen several examples of cases where early, strong teacher effort led to later increases in commitment.

11. Finding Mediating Variables

It often happens during analysis that two variables that "ought" to go together according to your conceptual expectations, or your early understanding of events in the case, have an inconclusive interrelationship. Another puzzle is the case of two variables that do go together, but without making much sense. The analyst cannot quite figure out *why* they go together.

In both of these conditions, looking for other variables that may be in the picture is a useful tactic. Your initial analysis may be showing that $A \rightarrow C$, but you may be thinking, "Yeah, but something's missing. Where's 'B'? And what *is* 'B' anyway?" To start the example, look at Display 11.2.

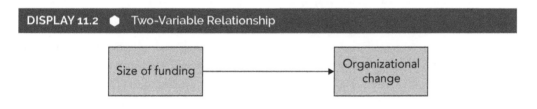

DISPLAY 11.2 ● Two-Variable Relationship

Source: Miles, M. B., & Huberman, A. M. (1994). *Qualitative data analysis: An expanded sourcebook* (2nd ed.). Thousand Oaks, CA: Sage Publications.

In the school improvement study, we observed that schools adopting innovations accompanied with large funding changed more than those adopting less well-funded innovations. That finding leaves a great deal unexplained. Why should it be that a well-funded innovation motivates more organizational change?

In this case, the analyst created a case-ordered matrix of other possible correlates of organizational change, such as "environmental pressure," "problem-solving orientation," "implementation requirements," and "administrative support." A careful scan showed that the original relation (Display 11.2) could be understood much more realistically when several other variables entered the picture (see Display 11.3). Here, we see that "Size of funding" is part of a web of other variables.

DISPLAY 11.3 ● Two-Variable Relationship With Mediating Variables

Source: Miles, M. B., & Huberman, A. M. (1994). *Qualitative data analysis: An expanded sourcebook* (2nd ed.). Thousand Oaks, CA: Sage Publications.

Larger innovations (Box 1) carry more funds with them (Box 2). The funds increase the support administrators give (Box 4), but so do the heavier implementation requirements (Box 3) of larger innovations. Organizational change (Box 6) comes from at least three sources: the direct requirements of the implementation itself (Box 3), administrative support (Box 4), and the degree to which implementation is successful (Box 5). As the network revealed, *Administrative support* is a very central mediating variable.

In this example, the effort to clarify a plausible but puzzling relationship led to a much clearer—if more complex—formulation. Simpler cases of finding mediating variables also exist. Finding mediating variables is easiest with multiple examples of the two-variable relationship to look at, contrast, and compare. See the discussion on antecedent conditions, mediating variables, and outcomes in Chapter 9.

12. Building a Logical Chain of Evidence

We've discussed **noting patterns**, **making metaphors**, **clustering**, **subsuming particulars into the general**, and **factoring**. With these tactics, discrete pieces of information come together to make a more economical whole that, analytically speaking, is more than the sum of its parts. How do you actually accomplish this? Is there some kind of heuristic you can use? Let's start with an example.

In the study of interorganizational arrangements between schools and universities, we happened on one especially successful case. It was a "teacher center" connected to a rural state college that undertook a variety of in-service training activities for schools within a radius of some 60 miles. We developed a logical chain of factors that could be leading to success, as seen from the state college side and from the school side (see Display 11.4). The logical chain of evidence goes like this.

DISPLAY 11.4 ⬤   Example of a Chain of Evidence Supporting an Observed Outcome

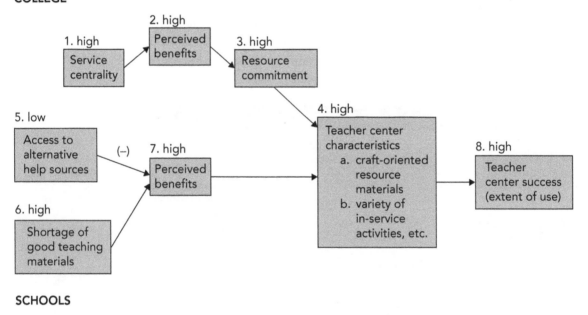

Note: (–) = inverse influence

Source: Miles, M. B., & Huberman, A. M. (1994). *Qualitative data analysis: An expanded sourcebook* (2nd ed.). Thousand Oaks, CA: Sage Publications.

The state college might regard service and outreach activities as very central (Box 1). Because of that, we would expect college staff to see the benefits (Box 2) of a teacher center as high (which they did). That should, in turn, lead to higher resource commitment (Box 3) to the center; such commitment was found in the form of money and staff.

Looking at the school side, we found few other opportunities for in-service help (Box 5) and a shortage of good teaching materials (Box 6); both of these should lead to high perceived benefits (Box 7) from using the center—if the center did, in fact, give good in-service help and provide new materials. As it turned out, the high resource commitment did permit that; teacher center assets (Box 4) and extent of use (Box 8) were high.

This example illustrates how to build an evidential chain. Some minimal conditions have to be met. *Several* participants with *different* roles have to emphasize the factors independently and *indicate the causal links* directly or indirectly (e.g., "We didn't have any other facility to go to in order to find out about new materials, so the center looked good" supports the link between Boxes 5 and 7). You have to *verify* the logical predictions and the claims (e.g., the actual funds committed, the lack of alternative resource sources, the activities actually undertaken). *Countervailing evidence* has to be accounted for.

How does building a chain of evidence differ from causal network methods? This approach is more tactically and specifically oriented. Building a chain of evidence requires painstaking verification *at each step*: Does this really happen, and what would we logically predict as an outcome or consequence—and does that outcome or consequence appear in the data? We are stringing together a series of **if-then** tactics: "If that were true, then we should find X. We do find X. Therefore . . . "

Furthermore, the *relationships have to make sense*: There must be a logical basis for the claim that "perceived college benefits" lead to "resource commitment." The chain must be complete; the stream from antecedent conditions to outcomes should have no gaps. For instance, in Display 11.4, the link between Boxes 3 and 4 is not so obvious. The college might have committed resources and might come up with another model or a center with different characteristics. Committing resources does not translate automatically into, say, craft-oriented resource materials. Something is missing in the logical chain and needs to be filled in.

You construct this evidential trail gradually, getting an initial sense of the main factors, plotting the logical relationships tentatively, testing them against the yield from the next wave of data collection, and modifying and refining them into a new explanatory map, which then gets tested against new cases and instances. This is the classic procedure of analytic induction.

At its most powerful, the method uses two interlocking cycles. One is called "enumerative induction," in which you collect a number and variety of instances all going in the same direction. The second is called "eliminative induction," in which you test your hypothesis against alternatives and look carefully for qualifications that bound the generality of the conclusion. When qualitative researchers invoke "progressive focusing," they are talking about enumerative induction; when they get into "constant comparisons" and "structural corroborations," they are switching into a more eliminative inductive mode of work. The "modus operandi" logic used in several professions as a troubleshooting device—for forensic pathologists, garage mechanics, doctors, detectives, classroom teachers—is a good example of a back-and-forth cycling between enumerative and eliminative induction.

13. Making Conceptual/Theoretical Coherence

When you're trying to determine what someone's actions "mean," the mental exercise involves connecting a discrete fact with other discrete facts, then grouping these into comprehensible and more abstract patterns. With the preceding tactics, we're moving up progressively from the empirical trenches to a more conceptual overview of the landscape. We're no longer dealing with just observables but also with unobservables, and we are connecting the two with successive layers of inferential glue.

The next step is to move from metaphors and interrelationships to *concepts*, and from there to *theories*. We need to tie the findings of our study to overarching, across-more-than-one-study propositions that can account for the "how" and "why" of the phenomena under study.

In the school improvement study, we came to notice that people at some of the field sites were literally exhausting themselves in the course of using new instructional practices. These very people were also making strong claims that the practice had substantially improved reading scores or children's attitudes toward school. The interesting part was that data to substantiate the outcome claims either were nonexistent or gave little support for them.

These are the "facts" from which we made a pattern. Field site participants could—and did—agree with the facts, but they didn't put them together as we did. To some extent, we were able to see the pattern only because things were happening otherwise at *other* sites—less investment, fewer claims, or more accurate claims. Multi-case field research is very useful in providing contrast and variance.

Let's call the pattern we saw "consensual delusion"—everyone agrees that more is happening with outcomes than there really is. The metaphors, in gerund form, might be "group thinking," "self-deluding," or "wish fulfilling." We also could sketch out a logical flowchart like the one shown in Display 11.4 to get a fix on how this happens at the several sites. But we are still within the confines of our study. The analyst now has to ask, "Do any broader constructs put these facts together the way I am putting them together?" In principle, gerunds should help. The first one (group thinking) points toward group behavior, the next one (self-deluding) toward individual cognitive processes, and the third one (wish fulfilling) toward motivational dynamics.

We picked up an appropriate and powerful concept from classic cognitive social psychology: *effort justification*. To justify the effort expended, you "see" more results than are objectively there. This action led us into the domain of *cognitive dissonance* and how people learn to love that for which they have suffered.

Where does this process get us? For starters, it tells us that our finding has a conceptual analogue, which lends more plausibility to the finding and to the concept, which is now empirically grounded in a new context. It also helps explain why such a pattern occurs. And it throws light on larger issues (e.g., how people, at our sites and more generally, cope with uncertainty). Finally, the concept can be trained back on our cases to explain related but puzzling phenomena. For example, we can now see why objective criteria (the test scores) are being systematically ignored when they are easily available.

We have progressed here from the bottom up—from the field to the concepts. The steps are (a) establishing the discrete findings, (b) relating the findings to each other, (c) naming the pattern, and (d) identifying a corresponding concept. We are making conceptual "additions" to the observed data to make them applicable more broadly.

It is perfectly legitimate, and sometimes necessary, to work from the top down—from a theory to the collection of information testing its validity. Of course, you have to stay open to the idea that the concept is inapplicable or has to be bent or discarded when you see the data. Concepts without corresponding support are hollow.

TACTICS FOR TESTING
OR CONFIRMING FINDINGS

We've spent some time on particular tactics for generating meaning making and interpreting findings at different levels of inference. Now, we need to confront the issue of *validity* or *trustworthiness*. Qualitative analyses can be evocative, illuminating—and wrong. The story, well told as it is, does not fit the data. Reasonable colleagues double-checking the case come up with quite different findings. The interpretations of case participants do not match those of the researchers. In this section, we review some general guidelines for judging the "goodness" of qualitative research—that is, what researchers can do at the tactical, operating level to test and confirm the findings.

When we read reports, they are most often heavy on the "what" (the findings, the descriptions) and rather thin on the "how" (how you got to the "what"). In most cases, we don't see a procedural account of the analysis, explaining just how the researcher got from 500 pages of field notes to the main conclusions drawn. So, we don't know how much confidence we can place in them. Researchers are not being cryptic or obtuse. It's just that there are few guidelines for explaining to their colleagues what they did, and how. (And, in all fairness, the page or word limit for journal articles also forces researchers to briefly sketch their methods paragraphs.)

We need to be mindful in qualitative research about the multiple sources of analytic bias that can weaken or even invalidate our findings. Some of these biases have been identified in mainstream research methods textbooks; the archetypical ones include the following:

1. *The holistic fallacy:* Interpreting events as more patterned and congruent than they really are, lopping off the many loose ends of which social life is made—that is, sloppy research

2. *Elite bias:* Overweighting data from articulate, well-informed, usually high-status participants and underrepresenting data from less articulate, lower-status ones

3. *Personal bias:* The researcher's personal agenda, personal demons, or personal "axes to grind," which skew the ability to represent and present field work and data analysis in a trustworthy manner

4. *Going native:* Losing your perspective or your "bracketing" ability, being co-opted into the perceptions and explanations of local participants

The language of confirming and verifying is bolder than what we can usually achieve. But the intent is still there: How can we increase our—and our readers'—confidence in what we've found? We describe 13 tactics, beginning with ones aimed at ensuring the basic quality of the data; then moving to those that check findings by examining exceptions to early patterns; and concluding with tactics that take a skeptical, demanding approach to emerging explanations.

Data quality can be assessed through (1) **checking for representativeness**; (2) **checking for researcher effects** on the case, and vice versa; and (3) **triangulating** across data sources and methods. These checks also may involve (4) **weighting the evidence**, deciding which kinds of data are most trustable.

Looking at "unpatterns" can tell us a lot. (5) **Checking the meaning of outliers**, (6) **using extreme cases**, (7) **following up surprises**, and (8) **looking for negative evidence** are all tactics that test a conclusion about a pattern by saying what it is *not* like.

How can we really test our explanations? (9) **Making if-then tests**, (10) **ruling out spurious relations**, (11) **replicating a finding**, and (12) **checking out rival explanations** are all ways of submitting our beautiful theories to the assault of brute facts.

Finally, a good explanation deserves attention from the very people whose actions it is about—the participants who supplied the original data. The tactic of (13) **getting feedback from participants** concludes our list.

1. Checking for Representativeness

When we develop a finding in a field study, we quickly assume it to be typical, an instance of a more general phenomenon. But is it? And if it is, *how* representative is it? People typically make a generalization and then illustrate it ("For example, my friend . . ."), but they would be hard put to come up with several more instances of a supposedly widespread occurrence. To compound the problem, people as information seekers—and processors—are far more likely to see *confirming* instances of original beliefs or perceptions than to see disconfirming instances, even when disconfirmations are more frequent.

Operating alone, without any standardized or validated instruments, the field researcher runs several risks of generalizing wrongly from specific instances. Here are some of the most common pitfalls and their associated sources of error.

The first pitfall, *sampling nonrepresentative participants*, highlights the fact that you can talk only with people who can be contacted; some people are harder to contact than others. This problem in itself signals something particularistic; their accessibility may be connected with workload, a lack of cooperativeness, or both. Anthropologists have often warned of fieldworkers' tendency to rely too much on articulate, insightful, attractive, and intellectually responsive participants; such people often turn out to be in the local elite.

The second pitfall, *generalizing from nonrepresentative events or activities*, results from the researcher's noncontinuous presence; you have to infer what is happening when you are not there. When you observe a dramatic event (a crisis, an argument), the tendency is to assume that it has "built up" when you were absent or that it symbolizes a more general pattern. These are plausible but certainly not well-grounded inferences.

The third pitfall, *drawing inferences from nonrepresentative processes*, is looking for underlying processes explaining what you've seen and heard. But if the samples of events and activities are faulty, the explanation cannot be generalized beyond them. If an emerging account makes good logical sense (to you) and fits well with other, independently derived analyses, you lock on to it and begin to make a stronger case for it. The problem is that you might have *plausibility* but not *confirmability*.

The real problem with selective sampling and hasty generalizing is that you can slide incrementally into these biases, with the first layer preparing the ground for the next. There is no longer any possibility, cognitively speaking, of standing back or reviewing critically what you have observed up to then. What you now understand has been accumulated very gradually from within, not drawn validly from without.

So, if you want to stand back and review critically, you need someone else to do it—or you must build in safeguards against self-delusion. We've already reinforced the former approach (critical friends, colleagues, other fieldworkers, research team members, auditors, dissertation supervisors) throughout the methods profiles, so let's offer some additional safeguards.

Automatically assume that you are selectively sampling and drawing inferences from a nonrepresentative sample of cases, be they people, events, or processes, in the first place. You are guilty until you prove yourself innocent by extending the "universe" of your study. How?

1. Increase the number of cases

2. Look purposively for contrasting cases (negative, extreme, countervailing)

3. Order the cases in various ways in a matrix to see who or what may be missing

4. Randomly sample people and phenomena within the site(s) you're studying

The last two procedures correspond to the "stratification" and "randomization" conventions used by experimental researchers to enhance internal validity. But while the experimental researcher uses the conventions *early*, as anticipatory controls against sampling and measurement error, the qualitative researcher typically uses them *later*, as verification devices. That use allows you to let in all the candidate people and data, so the most influential ones will have a chance of emerging. But you still have to carry the burden of proof that the patterns you ultimately pinpoint are, in fact, representative.

2. Checking for Researcher Effects

Outsiders to a group influence the insiders, and vice versa. So it is with the researcher who disembarks in a field setting to study the "researchees." You are likely, especially at the outset, to create social behavior in others that would not have occurred ordinarily. That behavior, in turn, can lead you toward biased observations and inferences, thus confounding the natural characteristics of the setting with the artificial effects of the researcher–researchee relationship. Unconfounding them is like moving through a hall of mirrors. We have two possible sources of bias here:

Bias 1:   the effects of the researcher on the case, and/or

Bias 2:   the effects of the case on the researcher

Field study researchers are often less worried about Bias 1 because they typically spend enough time on-site to become part of the local landscape. But that, of course, increases the hazard of Bias 2: being co-opted, going native, swallowing the agreed-on or taken-for-granted version of local events.

Although we discuss these biases as they occur during site visits, they influence the analysis deeply, both during and after data collection. The researcher who has gone native remains native during analysis. The researcher who has influenced the site in un-understood ways suffers unawares from that influence during analysis.

Bias 1 occurs when the researcher threatens or disrupts ongoing social and institutional relationships by doing nothing more than simply being there. People now have to figure out who this person is, why he or she is there, and what might be done with the information being collected. While they are figuring that out, participants typically will switch into an on-stage role or special persona, a presentation of self to the outsider. (They have other personae, of course, for fellow insiders, as Goffman [1959] shows so well.)

Even after this preliminary dance, participants will often craft their responses to appear amenable to the researcher and to protect their self-interests. For some analysts, local participants' interests are fundamentally in conflict with those of the researcher, who might penetrate to the core of the rivalries, compromises, weaknesses, or contradictions that make up much of the basic history of the site.

Insiders do not want outsiders—and sometimes other insiders—to know about such things. So the researcher, who is usually interested in uncovering precisely this kind of information, must assume that people will try to mislead and must shift into a more investigative mode.

Field research can be considered an act of betrayal, no matter how well-intentioned or well-integrated the researcher is. You make the private public and leave the locals to take the consequences. But that is not the only way Bias 1 can occur. In some instances, Biases 1 and 2 can team up to create "artifactual" effects as a result of the complicity between the researcher and local actors. This is Rosenthal's (1976) famous "experimenter" effect.

For instance, one field site in the school improvement project was about to phase out the project we had come to see. For some mysterious reason, the phase-out decision was cancelled during our time on-site. The reasoning, which we unraveled only after several more days, was that the practice *had* to be better than it appeared because university researchers had come from so far away to see it. There was also the desire to avoid a public indictment; the researcher and/or the public reading her research might convey the impression that the school had botched things.

Bias 1 can take still other forms. For example, local participants can implicitly or explicitly boycott the researcher, who is perceived as a spy, a voyeur, or a pest. Or the researcher can inhibit the local actors. After several days on-site and multiple interviews, people are not sure anymore how much the researcher has found out and assume—wrongly in most cases—that the researcher knows too much. This opinion then triggers Bias 2: The researcher accordingly becomes more reassuring or, alternatively, moves into the investigative-adversarial mode. Both strategies are likely to affect the data being collected.

Assuming, then, that you have only a few months, weeks, or even days on-site, how can these two interlocking forms of bias be countered? Below is a list of suggestions, many of which are treated in far more detail in field work–related literature.

A. Avoiding Biases Stemming From Researcher Effects on the Site

- Stay on-site as long as possible; spend some time simply hanging around, fitting into the landscape, taking a lower profile.

- Use unobtrusive measures where you can, such as reading the site's publicly accessible documents.

- Make sure your intentions are clear for participants: why you are there, what you are studying, how you will collect information, and what you will do with it.

- Consider co-opting a participant—asking that person to be attentive to your influence on the site and its inhabitants.

- Do some of your interviewing off-site in a congenial social environment (café, restaurant, participant's home), by way of reducing both your threat quotient and your exoticism.

- Don't inflate the potential problem; you are not really such an important presence in the lives of these people.

B. Avoiding Biases Stemming From the Effects of the Site on the Researcher

- Avoid the "elite" bias by spreading out your participants; include lower status participants and people outside the focus of your study (peripheral or former actors).

- Avoid co-optation or going native by spending time away from the site; spread out your site visits.

- Be sure to include dissidents, cranks, deviants, marginals, isolates—people with different points of view from the mainstream, people less committed to tranquillity and equilibrium in the setting.

- Keep thinking conceptually; translate sentimental or interpersonal thoughts into more theoretical ones.

- Consider finding a participant who agrees to provide background and historical information for you and to collect information when you are off-site (such co-optation may be more useful, in bias reduction terms, than the information provided).

- Triangulate with several data collection methods; don't overly depend just on talk, just on observation, or just on documents to make sense of the setting.

- If you sense you are being misled, try to understand and focus on why a participant would find it necessary to mislead you. Follow that trace as far upstream as you can.

- Do not casually show off how much you do know; this is a covert plea for confirmation that deludes only the person making it.

- Show your field notes to a colleague. Another researcher is often much quicker to see where and how you are being misled or co-opted.

- Keep your research questions firmly in mind; don't wander too far from them to follow alluring leads or drop them in the face of a more dramatic or momentous event.

As with all such lists, following some items gets you in trouble on others. For instance, if you have only a few days on-site, off-site interviewing may be too costly. Or you may be co-opted by the participant you are trying to co-opt.

Bias detection and removal take time. The more time you have, the more layers you can peel off the setting to get to the core explanatory factors and the less subject you are to Biases 1 and 2. However, we take that with a grain of salt. Long exposure can just push up Bias 2 and make Bias 1 harder to see.

We say again that people who are discreet, savvy in the environment under study, and conceptually ecumenical are often able to get to the core of a case in a matter of days, sidestepping both types of researcher bias and coming away with good-quality data. It's possible that the methodologists demanding months or years on-site before valid data can be obtained are confusing time with competence.

3. Triangulating

Much has been written about triangulation as a near-obligatory method of confirming findings. Stripped to its basics, triangulation is supposed to support a finding by showing that at least three independent measures of it agree with it or, at least, do not contradict it. But it's not as simple as that. For one thing, if two measures agree and one does not, you are stuck with a deeper question: Which do you believe? (See the film *Minority Report*.)

Triangulation is similar to the modus operandi approach used by those who diagnose in some way, such as detectives, auto mechanics, and primary care physicians. When the detective amasses fingerprints, hair samples, alibis, and eyewitness accounts, a case is being made that presumably fits one suspect far better than others; the strategy is pattern matching, using several data sources. Note the importance of having different kinds of measurements, which provides repeated verification. Diagnosing engine failure or chest pain follows a similar approach. The signs presumably point to one specific conclusion and/or rule out other conclusions.

What kinds of triangulation can there be? Following Denzin's (2001) classic distinctions, we can think of triangulation by *data source* (which can include persons, times, places, etc.); *method* (observation, interview, document); *researcher* (Investigator A, B, C, etc.); and *theory*. To this, we add *data type* (e.g., qualitative texts, audio/video recordings, quantitative data). How to choose which? The aim is to pick triangulation sources that have different foci and different strengths, so that they can complement each other.

As an example, Saldaña's studies on child audience responses to theatre employed multiple measures: (a) live audience observations and field notes of the events; (b) audio and video recordings of audience responses to the performance; (c) audio-recorded focus group interviews with children after the performance; (d) drawings or written assessments by children of the productions they viewed; (e) play script dramaturgical analyses; (f) interviews with selected teachers and adult production company members; (g) quantitative semantic differential surveys; (h) case study interviews with individual children; and (i) relevant theories from the professional research literature in areas such as child development, psychology, education, media, and performance studies.

What can we expect from triangulation? We may get *corroboration* from three different sources, which enhances the trustworthiness of our analysis. But sometimes we may get *inconsistent* or even directly *conflicting* findings. At best, this can push us to more closely examine the integrity of the data collection methods and even the data themselves. Inconsistent and conflicting findings force us to explain why they exist. It may be due to an undetected variability of something that we need to consider, or unanticipated anomalies and outliers in the phenomena we're studying that merit closer examination. Sometimes, the inconsistent and conflicting findings suggest that the researcher made a mistake somewhere along the way and needs to figure out what may have gone wrong. But sometimes, the conflicting findings are a blessing because different data collection methods gather different facets of data, and their combined effects *build* on each other to compose a more three-dimensional perspective of the phenomenon.

Perhaps our basic point is that triangulation is not so much a tactic as a way of life. If you self-consciously set out to collect and double-check findings, using multiple sources and modes of evidence, the verification process will largely be built into data collection as you go along. In effect, triangulation is a way to get to the findings in the first place—by seeing or hearing multiple *instances* of it from different *sources* by using different *methods* and by squaring the finding with others it needs to be squared with.

4. Weighting the Evidence

Any given preliminary conclusion is always based on certain data. There are events in the real world from which we capture only a partial record in the form of raw field notes, from which we further extract only certain information in the form of write-ups. There is, in turn, further condensation, selection, and transformation as these data are entered into various displays and reports.

Some of these data are better than others. Fortunately, you can exploit that fact beautifully in verifying conclusions. If the data on which a conclusion is based are known to be stronger and more valid than average, then the conclusion is strengthened. Conversely, a conclusion based on weak or suspect data can be, at the least, held lightly and, optimally, discarded if an alternative conclusion has stronger data to back it up.

There is a range of reasons why certain data are stronger (valid) or weaker (less valid) than others. First, data from some participants are simply "better." The participant may be articulate and reflective, and may enjoy talking about events and processes. Or the participant may be knowledgeable and close to the event, action, process, or setting with which you're concerned. In our (Miles and Huberman) study, for example, we gave more weight to school superintendents' judgments about district budget matters than we did to those of teachers about that topic.

Second, the circumstances of the data collection may have strengthened (or weakened) the quality of the data. Seeing with your own eyes what happened in a classroom is more reliable than overhearing faculty lounge gossip about the incident. Interviewing a participant during later rather than earlier stages of field work may get you richer responses since you've had time to build rapport and trust.

Third, data quality may be stronger because of a fieldworker's validation efforts. These may consist of several varieties (some of which are discussed elsewhere in this chapter):

- Checking for researcher effects and biases
- Checking for representativeness
- Getting feedback from participants
- Triangulating
- Looking for ulterior motives
- Looking for deception

Douglas (1976) emphasizes that regardless of the degree of trust a fieldworker may believe has developed, people in field sites nearly always have some reasons for omitting, selecting, or distorting data and also may have reasons for deceiving the fieldworker (not to mention deceiving themselves). If you have entertained such a view of certain respondents, and of the data from them, and have done something to validate the data, more confidence is justified. Douglas offers a few strategies, which we have adapted:

- Check against "hard facts."
- Check against alternative accounts.
- Look for the "trapdoor"—what is going on beyond the obvious.
- Share your own personal story to open up the respondent.
- Share what you genuinely think is going on and see how the respondent reacts.

Fieldworkers who rely mainly on trust may quail at such interventions or dismiss them as too intrusive. We have found that it pays to be skeptical, to expect to be lied to sometimes, to look for respondent self-deception, and to *gently* and *tactfully* question respondents from time to time on such matters.

We offer two additional suggestions. First, we've found it useful to keep a running log of data quality issues (often in the form of analytic memos or OCs—observer's comments—in field notes), together with recurrent efforts to improve data quality in subsequent site visits. Second, when approaching the final write-up of a case analysis, it's useful to summarize your views of data quality—both for yourself and for your eventual readers. Here is an example from a case report in our school improvement study, which appeared after the researcher listed the number of interviews (46), informal talks (24), and observations (17) held during three site visits:

> The data base is probably biased toward administrators and central program personnel (3–6 interviews apiece), and may underrepresent . . . normal program users, and certainly . . . peripheral (and more disenchanted) people. So, the information may be fuller about the ins and outs of operation as seen by key operators, and thinner on what day-to-day life in the Carson schools is like.

5. Checking the Meaning of Outliers

Any given finding usually has exceptions. The temptation is to smooth them over, ignore them, or explain them away. But *the outlier is your friend.* A good look at the exceptions, or the ends of a distribution, can test and strengthen the basic finding. It not only tests the generality of the finding but also protects you against self-selecting biases and may help you build a better explanation.

For example, in the school improvement study, we happened on one case where the new practice was seen by many teachers as a near-miraculous cure for local ills. Although teachers had difficulty getting on top of it, the project eventually led to dramatic increases in reading and composition scores. Enthusiasm was high.

But was it a "miracle cure"? To test the finding, we asked about people who either had not adopted the practice or had used it and found it wanting. Our interviews with these two groups of people were instructive. First, we found that their reasons for not adopting were opposite to—and thereby coherent with—the reasons given by the other participants for adopting. Then, we found that the dissident users had not really mastered the innovation in the way the contented users had. We already had good evidence linking technical mastery to positive results. So, our findings were strengthened, and we understood far better why deviant cases were deviant.

It became clearer that the innovation was like a "miracle cure," but only if it was technically well carried out. Furthermore, these outliers told us that there were more people like them around than the advocates had admitted. We realized then that we had oversampled the contented users and, in a sense, had been "sucked in" to the taken-for-granted version of events among the local teachers. In widening the sampling of discontented users thereafter, we got a somewhat different and more intricate picture of the case.

There are often more exceptions or deviant cases than you realize at first; you have to go looking for them. They usually do not come calling, nor do you usually think spontaneously of sampling for them. After all, they are inconvenient—not only hard to reach or observe but also spoilers of your artfully built, coherent version of case dynamics.

Remember, too, that outliers are not only people; they can consist of discrepant *cases,* atypical *settings,* unique *treatments,* or unusual *events.* You need to find the outliers and then verify whether what is present in them is absent or different in other, more mainstream examples (see **using extreme cases** next). Finding outliers is easier when you have well-ordered displays. Cases, roles, settings, events, and individuals can be shown in coherent relation to others. If you are still collecting data, display what you have and go for the outliers. If things are closely clumped (no apparent outliers), consider where you might go to find some outlying persons, events, or settings. And on following up, stay open to the eventuality that the exceptional cases can turn out to be prototypical ones.

In many cases, outlier analysis strengthens an original conclusion ("the exception proves the rule"). But be careful; don't force it. Stay open to the idea that the outlier is telling you something useful and important about how your conclusion needs modification.

6. Using Extreme Cases

We've just described the use of outliers in deepening preliminary conclusions. Outliers of a certain type, which we call extreme cases, can be very useful in verifying and confirming conclusions.

In Saldaña's (1995) exit interviews with sixth graders about their 7 years of theatre-viewing experiences since kindergarten, one interview question we posed to the young participants was, "Is theatre necessary?" All except one child said, "Yes"; the young boy who said "No" was the extreme case in this instance. His explanation that "we don't have to have" theatre was not unexpected, as he was one of the lowest rated participants in the study over the past 7 years. But his "no" became part of the data record, and we now had to explain why, after so many years of free and mostly high-quality theatre experiences, he alone out of 30 children felt that theatre was unnecessary. Long story short, his "no" forced us to closely examine the varying *value* children attribute to the arts, and thus the landscapes of meanings and payoffs they offered to their young participants. That single "no" helped crystallize the conclusions of the study. This is a tactic of "holding everything else constant"—looking for the most extreme case, where there should have been consensus but there wasn't.

The second sort of extreme case is persons known to have a strong bias. For example, suppose you are talking with a very conservative administrator who you know from past contact is rather defensive. You ask him why the teachers he works with are reluctant to try innovations. He answers that it's due to his own lack of cooperation and support. That answer is very persuasive because you wouldn't expect this particular administrator to make such a statement at all.

To put this another way, look for the person in a site who would have the most to gain (or lose) by affirming or denying something, and pop the question. If you get a surprising answer (e.g., the person who has much to gain by denying the statement/question, in fact, affirms it), then you can be more confident. This maneuver requires you to have a good prior understanding of the person's typical stance and biases.

7. Following Up Surprises

Surprises have more juice than outliers. When you are surprised, it usually means that something has occurred well outside the range of your expectations. Something that surprised Saldaña on his first day of fieldwork in an inner-city school in the mid-1990s Southwest was the combed back and "slicked" hairstyles of most of the Hispanic boys—a grooming nuance he realized had been within the culture since his own childhood 40 years ago. Also surprising was the realization that many young Hispanic girls did not wear shorts or pants but wore dresses to school—unlike the clothing observed at middle-class, predominantly White elementary schools. These small fashion details made him rethink the larger cultural dynamics he was now surrounded by and how selected traditions and values still played a role in these Hispanic children's lives.

Surprises and anomalies are fodder for *abductive thinking*—reflection on all the possibilities that could explain the surprise, and sound conclusion drawing of the most reasonable explanation. Like outliers, *surprises are your friend*. They disrupt the routine and thus the patterns in progress and force the researcher to rethink the accuracy of an emergent assertion, proposition, or theory.

Following up surprises has three aspects: You (a) reflect on the surprise to surface your violated theory, (b) consider how to revise it, and (c) look for evidence to support your revision. You may also work from (b) to (c), hunting in a sniffing mode, to find new aspects of the case that possibly could lead to a new theory.

Overall, outliers, extreme cases, and surprises are phenomena that should not be dismissed during analysis.

> There is a risk that novel data will be overlooked, and prevailing ideas will simply be verified rather than enhanced. This is likely to occur, because it is easier to verify conventional wisdom rather than to recognize and understand experiences and perspectives that fall outside the norm. (Finfgeld-Connett, 2018, p. 48)

8. Looking for Negative Evidence

The tactic **looking for negative evidence** is easy to describe but, given people's pattern-making proclivities, not naturally instinctive. When a preliminary conclusion is at hand, the tactic is to ask, "Do any data oppose this conclusion, or are any inconsistent with this conclusion?" This is a more extreme version of looking for **outliers** (discussed earlier) and for **rival explanations** (discussed later). You are actively seeking *dis*confirmation of what you think is true.

Einstein is supposed to have said, "No amount of evidence can prove me right, and any amount of evidence can prove me wrong." That is so, in the abstract, but most of us act as if the converse were true. Our beautiful theories need few data to convince us of their solidity, and we are not eager to encounter the many brutal facts that could doom our frameworks. A good case study of such an effort is Cressey's (1953) classic study of embezzlers. Cressey revised his working hypotheses five times, looking for negative cases for each version in turn, using prior data, newly collected data, and the studies of others, until there was no disconfirmation.

Miller (n.d.) advises that "disconfirming instances should be handled with care." Discarding your original hypothesis too quickly and modifying it hastily to accommodate the negative evidence are both undesirable. Miller suggests that although one instance of negative evidence may be enough to require reconsideration, the *proportion* of negative to positive evidence should probably play a part.

Commission a friendly but curmudgeonly skeptic to take a good look at your conclusion at hand, avoiding your data display and seeking data back in the written-up field notes that would effectively disconfirm your conclusion. If such evidence is found, proceed to the formulation of an alternative conclusion that deals with the evidence.

9. Making If-Then Tests

If-then tests are the workhorse of qualitative data analysis. They are focused propositions supporting a general analytic direction.

A formal statement is "If X, then Y." It is a proposition of expected relationship. Assuming X to be true (an important condition), we look to see whether Y is true. If Y is true, then we have a building block for understanding. We are a long way from a "law" about the relation of X and Y, which requires universality, linkage to a larger theory, and nontriviality, among other conditions. But we know more than we did and can take some next analytic steps—notably, making more if-then tests and connecting them into a general theory of what is happening.

Saldaña's (1999) study of adolescent social class and social consciousness was an opportunistic study that investigated why two different groups of teenagers, each from two very different social and economic backgrounds, responded quite differently to the same social issues-oriented workshop content. The lower socioeconomic group embraced the seriousness of the social issues addressed at a forum workshop and participated with respectful enthusiasm. But the upper socioeconomic group transformed the same content at their forum workshop into a parody and satire of the social issues we tried to address.

After reflection on these experiences, Saldaña put forth the following general proposition: "*If* adolescents are from an upper social class background, *then* their social consciousness may not be as heightened as those from a lower social class." Of course, a reflective practitioner might also develop the following proposition: "*If* workshop content is not relevant or meaningful for its participants, *then* they will reject the provided experiences." One can always think of exceptions or **negative evidence** that will force a revision of these propositions, but for this particular event, this is what was observed.

The use of the conditional future tense in the "then" statements helps remind us that we have to look to see whether the "then" has happened. Therefore, if-then statements are a way to formalize propositions for testing as *hypotheses*. The method of generating *predictions* involves linking together a large number of "ifs" to a single major "then." If-then statements are just a step away from constructing theories.

10. Ruling Out Spurious Relations

"Spurious" means something that's falsely attributed; a spurious relation means that you're connecting things together incorrectly. Tyler Vigen's (2015) amusing compilation of quantitative *Spurious Correlations* shows that, across a 10-year span, there was a 95.4% correlation between public high school student enrollment and sour cream consumption, and a whopping 99.5% correlation from 2003 to 2009 between computer science doctoral degrees awarded and aggregate comic book sales. The statistics align closely and well, but one did not cause the other. Qualitative researchers face a comparable dilemma with our logical reasoning.

Suppose you've been able, through assorted tactics, to establish that variable A is indeed related to B. Whenever we see A, we see B, and vice versa. Before breathing a sigh of relief and proceeding to the next conclusion, it pays to consider the picture you are drawing:

$$A \rightarrow B$$

may, in fact, be portrayed more accurately as

where some third factor is in play, causing both A and B to occur.

This is an old logic problem, and we can draw a nice example from a classic Wallis and Roberts (1956) study from the *Journal of the American Medical Association*. Researchers noted that polio patients who traveled longer distances (average, 85 miles) to a hospital were more likely to die than patients who traveled less (average, 7 miles) and were more likely to die sooner (50% died within 24 hours, vs. 20%). They concluded, "The greater mortality in the transported group, occurring shortly after admission to the hospital, is a manifestation of the effect of long transportation during the acute stage of illness" (p. 285).

Yet Wallis and Roberts also suggest that a third variable may be influencing both *A* (transportation) and *B* (mortality)—the *seriousness of the initial attack*. All of the patients were seen in a certain hospital: Willard Parker, a noted center for the treatment of contagious diseases. Polio patients who lived farther away were probably brought to Willard Parker only if their condition was serious; milder cases would be treated nearer their own homes. Thus, the picture develops as shown in Display 11.5. This interpretation can be checked out through the sort of display found in Display 11.6, with *N*s and mortality rates entered in the cells.

DISPLAY 11.5 ● Possible Explanation of Spurious Relationship

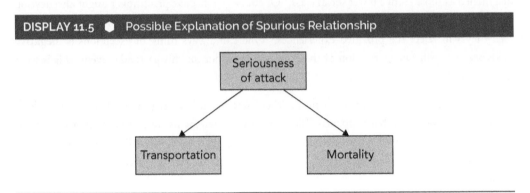

Source: Miles, M. B., & Huberman, A. M. (1994). *Qualitative data analysis: An expanded sourcebook* (2nd ed.). Thousand Oaks, CA: Sage Publications.

DISPLAY 11.6 ● Display for Testing Explanations in Display 11.5

	Local patients	Distant patients
Mild attack		
Severe attack		

Source: Miles, M. B., & Huberman, A. M. (1994). *Qualitative data analysis: An expanded sourcebook* (2nd ed.). Thousand Oaks, CA: Sage Publications.

As Wallis and Roberts faithfully point out, even if the reanalysis could be done and it supported "seriousness of initial attack" as the real issue, you would have to do additional ruling out. Perhaps those coming from a distance had poorer basic health to begin with. Perhaps they came from an area where a particularly virulent strain of polio was widespread. The Willard Parker researchers did think of a third variable—length of prior illness—which showed no real difference. Finding a candidate third variable is not always easy, especially if the original explanation "makes sense," as the transportation–mortality link seemed to at first glance.

The moral for qualitative researchers is the same. When two variables look correlated, especially when you think that they are causally associated, wait a bit and consider whether some third variable might be underlying/influencing/causing them both. Use a knowledgeable but detached colleague to help in the search. Then, consider new displays that will give you a clean look at third variables and their affects.

Earlier, we discussed the tactic of **finding mediating variables**, but there we were concerned with understanding a tepid relationship better. Here, the issue is *undoing* a relationship you think looks plausible and strong. Doing this procedure in a more than cursory way takes time, so it is worth it mainly when you have a major (but perhaps surprising) conclusion or one on which a lot is riding, in practical terms.

11. Replicating a Finding

As we showed earlier in the section on **triangulating**, findings are more dependable when they can be buttressed from several independent sources. Their validity is enhanced when they are confirmed by more than one data collection instrument measuring the same thing.

Still, the fact that usually one person is doing all of this measuring with customized instruments is a ground for precaution. Once you've latched on to a hypothesis that makes powerful sense of the case, it's the dickens to get rid of it. Confirmation seems, almost magically, to come from all quarters. New interviews, observations, and documents all appear to bring verification and to fit together coherently. Disconfirming evidence is absent or feeble. This is a heady and very slippery time, and it usually means you are knee-deep in the "holistic fallacy": putting more logic, coherence, and meaning into events than the inherent sloppiness of social life warrants. How do you protect against this?

One line of attack is to think in terms of study replication. If I can observe and reproduce the finding in a new context or in another part of the database, it is most likely a dependable one. If someone else can reproduce it, better still.

This tactic can be used in several ways. At the most basic level, you are replicating as you collect new information from new participants, from new settings and events. New data bolster or qualify old data by testing their validity and generality.

At a notch higher in the confidence scale, you can test an emerging hypothesis in another part of the case or data set. Such a test is more rigorous; it's harder to bootleg researcher bias into it. Even stiffer tests can be made by looking at multiple cases: finding a pattern in a cross-case display and then tracking carefully through all of the cases to see whether the pattern is repeated.

Even better, replicate in a brand new case, though we acknowledge that may be an extreme and ephemeral goal. Some brief words of advice:

- In cross-case studies, replication is an important part of the basic data collection effort. Emerging patterns from one case need to be tested in others. Be prepared in the course of fieldwork to do the kind of corroborative testing described here and in the section on **triangulation**.

- If provisions are not made in advance for replications, they will not happen; there is inevitably too little time and too much information still to compile.

- Doing replication at the very end of field work, during the final analysis and write-ups, is very difficult and less credible. To test a hypothesis in another part of the data set assumes that all of the requisite data are there for the test to be made. They usually are not, unless the researcher has made sure to collect them beforehand in anticipation of just such an exercise.

Reasonably early in your study, think forward a bit. Imagine that your findings will turn out to be truly amazing with profound implications for your field. Then, ask a friendly colleague to perform a rapid "replicability check." Based on a few hours' review of the project database and methods, how easy or difficult would it be *for your colleague* to repeat your study?

12. Checking Out Rival Explanations

Thinking that rival explanations may account for the phenomena you have carefully studied and masterfully unraveled is a healthy exercise in self-discipline and hubris avoidance. But that thought often gets lost in the shuffle. During data collection, you are often too busy making sense of the welter of stimuli. Later on, you tend to get married to your emerging account and usually opt for investing the scant time left to buttress, rather than to unhorse, your explanation. Then, during data analysis, it is often too late to test any other explanation than the one arrived at; the data necessary for doing that in any but a cosmetic way just aren't there.

But we think that the search for rival explanations is often more thorough in qualitative research than in most laboratory studies and that it's relatively easy to do. The competent field researcher looks for the most plausible, empirically grounded explanation of events from among the several competing for attention in the course of field work. You are not looking for one account, forsaking all others, but for the best of several alternative accounts.

The trick is to hold on to several possible (rival) explanations until one of them gets increasingly more compelling as the result of more, stronger, and varied sources of evidence. Looking at it from the other end, you give each rival explanation a good chance. Is it better than your main love? Do you have some biases you weren't aware of? Do you need to collect any new data?

One of the most intriguing yet puzzling findings in McCammon et al.'s (2012) survey of adults from various generations reflecting on their high school experiences was an outcome from data analysis of the most recent age cohort. When participants were asked about the challenges they faced as an adolescent, those who graduated during 2000–2010 described a general sense of disconnect and "fear" more than older age groups. Saldaña hypothesized this as the result of living in an uncertain post–9/11 world and affirmation of the then-current emotional angst in America's youth projected by Goleman (1995, 2007). But Saldaña was a researcher in his 50s who was trying to understand the responses of a generation that was in its 20s, so he turned to younger colleagues—his research assistants Matt Omasta and Angela Hines—for their perspectives. And they did indeed offer other factors to consider for hypothesis development, such as the generational search for "safe spaces" that school arts programs provided, the pervasive fear of gun violence in schools, and the sociopsychological effects on the most recent generation by rapidly developing social media and entertainment technology.

Foreclosing too early on alternative explanations is a harbinger of bias. You lock in to a particular way of construing the case and selectively scan the environment for supporting evidence. Discounting evidence is ignored, underregistered, or handled as exceptional—thus further increasing your confidence in your erroneous thesis.

We should also note that closing too *late* on alternative explanations builds too weak a case for the best one. It also adds great bulk to the corpus of data. So, rival explanations should be looked at fairly promptly in field work and sustained until they prove genuinely unviable—or prove to be better. This step should happen, if possible, before most of the fieldwork is done. The same principle applies to analysis done after field work. Check out alternative explanations early, but don't iterate forever.

It also helps to fasten onto discrepant information—things that do not fit or are still puzzling (tactics: **looking for negative evidence, following up surprises**). The trick is not to explain them away in light of your favorite explanation—that's a piece of cake—but rather to run with them, to ask yourself what kind of alternative case these bits of information could build, and then check them out further.

A useful subtactic is as follows: During the final analysis, first check out the merits of the next best explanation you or others can think of as an alternative to the one you preferred at the end of the field work. "Next bests" have more pulling power than fanciful alternatives.

13. Getting Feedback From Participants

One of the most logical sources of corroboration is the people you have talked with and watched. After all, an alert and observant participant in the setting is bound to know more than the researcher ever will about the realities under investigation. In that sense, local participants can act as judges, evaluating the major findings of a study through what has been labeled "member checking." Some of the display methods profiles encouraged feedback from case participants: commenting on a short summary of findings, evaluating the accuracy of a causal network, or verifying researcher predictions.

Feedback may happen during data collection, too. When a finding begins to take shape, the researcher may check it out with new and/or key participants. The delicate issue here, of course, is that of introducing bias (see **researcher effects**). Feeding things back in the course of a study may change participants' actions or perspectives. (In some genres, such as action research, critical ethnography, or community-based collaborative research, however, changing participants' actions and perspectives for the better *is* the goal.)

Still, we've seen some useful examples of thorough early feedback. In a phenomenological study, Melnick and Beaudry (1990) interviewed teachers and then, in a second interview, fed back the transcript, which had been annotated with marginal remarks on themes, and follow-up questions; the transcript became the basis for shared reflection. Warner (1991) not only had children run camcorders of adult–child interaction and added their comments, but he also played back the videotapes for yet more comments by the children. The more emic the study, the more useful early feedback is likely to be.

There are also good reasons for gathering feedback after the final analysis. For one thing, you know more. You also know what you do know *better*—you are less tentative, have more supporting evidence, and can illustrate it. In addition, you can get feedback at a higher level of inference: on main factors, on causal relationships, and on interpretive conclusions. Finally, the feedback process can be done less haphazardly. You can lay out the findings clearly and systematically and present them to the reader for careful scrutiny and comment.

It is crucial that the reader be able to connect to the feedback—understand it; relate it to local experience and perceptions; *do* something with it (draw on it, cross out parts and add others, etc.). So, *formatting* the feedback is crucial. Sending back an abstract, an executive summary, or the concluding chapter without transforming it into the language of the site—which the researcher has come to learn in the course of field research—is of little value if you are seriously after verification. Data feedback is an occasion to learn more about the *case*, not only about the feedback.

We offer some advice:

- If you don't plan deliberately for this exercise—setting aside the time, transforming write-ups into site-friendly language and formats, leaving time to incorporate the results of the exercise into your final write-up—it probably won't happen. There will be too many competing claims on your time.

- Think carefully about displays. As with analysis, matrices, networks, and graphics work much better than text alone to help participants access the information. They will find it easier to get an overview, to see how the pieces fit together.

- Providing information at more macro-analytical levels of inference (e.g., main factors and relationships, causation) has to be done very carefully by working up from particulars. If this is not done, participants may discount the whole exercise because the overarching findings look too abstract or incomprehensible. Or they may swallow these macro findings whole because these read so "scientifically." Format your data in a participant-friendly way.

- Think very carefully before feeding back any specific incident. Will anyone's self-esteem, job chances, or standing in the organization be damaged by the report? (One of us once fed back first-draft case reports to people in five cases and was threatened with lawsuits in four of the five because of specific incidents in the reports—even though the incidents were reported accurately.)

- Don't expect that participants will always agree with you or with one another. If they always did, life at the site would be more conflict-free than you probably found it to be. People often have widely varying perceptions of the same phenomenon. Interpretivists consider this natural and part of the data record.

STANDARDS FOR THE QUALITY OF CONCLUSIONS

We've reviewed 26 tactics for drawing and verifying conclusions. How will you, or anyone else, know whether the finally emerging findings are *good*? That term has many possible definitions: possibly or probably true, reliable, valid, dependable, reasonable, confirmable, credible, trustworthy, persuasive, useful, compelling, significant, empowering (add others of your choice). It's not enough to say that well-carried-out tactics will make for good conclusions.

In this section, we explore some practical standards that could help us judge the quality of conclusions. The battles in this domain have been extensive, and they continue. Many interpretivist researchers suggest that it is not really possible to establish standards or to specify criteria for good qualitative work—and that the effort to do so is somehow expert-centered and exclusionary, not responsive to the contingent, contextual, and personally interpretive nature of any qualitative study.

But the problem of quality, of trustworthiness, of authenticity of the findings will not go away. The fact is that some accounts read better than others. Although we may acknowledge that "getting it all right" may be an unrealistic goal, we should, as Wolcott (1990) suggests, try to "not get it all wrong" either.

Our view is that qualitative studies take place in a real social world and can have real consequences in people's lives; that there is a reasonable view of what happened in any particular situation (including what was believed, interpreted, etc.); and that we who render accounts of it can do so well or poorly and should not consider our work unjudgeable. These are matters of merit, rigor, integrity, ethics, and accountability.

We cannot enter here into a discussion of how goodness criteria flow from varied ontological and epistemological positions. Rather, we remain broadly in the critical realist tradition and discuss five main, somewhat overlapping, issues: the **objectivity/confirmability** of qualitative work, **reliability/dependability/auditability**, **internal validity/credibility/authenticity**, **external validity/transferability/fittingness**, and **utilization/application/action orientation**. Here, we are pairing traditional terms with those proposed as more viable alternatives for assessing the trustworthiness and authenticity of naturalistic research (Lincoln & Guba, 1985).

In each section, we describe the issues generally, without trying to straighten out all of the thorny problems involved. (Better people than us are still trying.) Then, we propose some practical guidelines that can be applied to qualitative work—your own or that of others. These are not rules to be stiffly applied but guidelines to consider when you reflect on the question "How good is my/this research report?"

Objectivity/Confirmability

The basic issue here can be framed as one of relative neutrality and reasonable freedom from unacknowledged researcher biases—at the minimum, explicitness about the inevitable biases that exist. This domain is sometimes labeled "external reliability," borrowed from classic quantitative terminology.

Some useful criteria to consider about this issue for a qualitative study are as follows:

1. The study's general methods and procedures are described explicitly and in detail. We feel that we have a complete picture, including "backstage" information.

2. We can follow the actual sequence of how data were collected, processed, condensed/transformed, and displayed for specific conclusion drawing.

3. The conclusions are explicitly linked with exhibits of condensed/displayed data.

4. There is a record of the study's methods and procedures, detailed enough to be audited by an outsider.

5. The researcher has been explicit and as self-aware as possible about personal assumptions, values and biases, and affective states—and how they may have come into play during the study.

6. Competing hypotheses or rival conclusions have been considered. The plausibility of rival conclusions has been examined.

7. The study's data are retained and available for reanalysis by others (as allowed by Institutional Review Board regulations and any researcher–participant agreements).

Reliability/Dependability/Auditability

The underlying issue here is whether the process of the study is consistent, reasonably stable over time and across researchers and methods. We are addressing issues of quality and integrity: Have things been done with reasonable care?

Some useful criteria to consider about this issue for a qualitative study are as follows:

1. The research questions are clear, and the features of the study design are congruent with them.

2. The researcher's role and status within the site have been explicitly described.

3. The findings show meaningful parallelism across data sources (participants, contexts, times).

4. Basic paradigms and analytic constructs are clearly specified. (Reliability depends, in part, on its connectedness to theory.)

5.   Data were collected across a full range of appropriate settings, times, respondents, and so on, as suggested by the research questions.

6.   If multiple fieldworkers are involved, they have comparable data collection protocols.

7.   When appropriate, intercoder agreement checks were made with adequate results.

8.   Data quality checks have been made (e.g., for bias, deceit).

9.   Multiple observers' accounts converge—in instances, settings, or times—when they might be expected to.

10.   Forms of peer or colleague review are in place.

Internal Validity/Credibility/Authenticity

Here, we arrive at the crunch question: truth value. Do the findings of the study make sense? Are they credible to the people we study and to our readers? Do we have an authentic portrait of what we were looking at?

Validity is a contested term among selected qualitative researchers. Some feel that this traditional quantitative construct (with its components of face, content, predictive, etc., validity) has no place in qualitative inquiry. Alternative terms such as *verisimilitude* and *a persuasively written account* are preferred. But other qualitative methodologists continue to use the term purposefully because it suggests a more rigorous stance toward our work.

Wolcott (1990) went so far as to reject validity in our field and proposed that we should come to a deep *understanding* instead. Maxwell's (1992) thoughtful review distinguishes among the types of understanding that may emerge from a qualitative study: *descriptive* (what happened in specific situations); *interpretive* (what it meant to the people involved); *theoretical* (the concepts, and their relationships, used to explain actions and meanings); and *evaluative* (judgments of the worth or value of actions and meanings).

Saldaña calls this domain the "That's right!" factor. When an oral presentation is made of one's research and people in the audience are nodding their heads affirmatively, saying "M-hm" in agreement and (even better) exclaiming out loud, "That's right!" to the speaker after an assertion has been made, you can feel confident that some sense of resonance has been achieved between the research and the audience. Call this domain what you will; it's the write-up itself that matters in the end.

Some useful criteria to consider about this issue for a qualitative study are as follows:

1.   Descriptions are context-rich, meaningful, and "thick" (Geertz, 1973).

2.   The account rings true, makes sense, seems convincing or plausible, and enables a vicarious presence for the reader.

3.   Triangulation among complementary methods and data sources produced generally converging conclusions. If not, the procedures for reconciling the differences and their results are explained.

4.   The data presented are well linked to the categories of prior or emerging theory. The measures reflect the concepts at work.

5.   Findings are clear, coherent, and systematically related—that is, unified (Charmaz, 2014; Saldaña & Omasta, 2018).

6. Confirmation procedures for assertions, propositions, hypotheses, theories, conclusions, and so on, are described.

7. Any areas of uncertainty have been identified.

8. Negative evidence was sought (and, if applicable, found and accounted for in the analysis and write-up).

9. Rival explanations have been actively considered.

10. When possible, findings have been replicated in parts of the database other than the one they arose from.

11. The conclusions were considered to be accurate by the original participants. If not, a coherent explanation is offered.

12. If predictions were made in the study, their accuracy is reported.

External Validity/Transferability/Fittingness

We need to know whether the conclusions of a study—a case study, in particular—have any larger import. Are they transferable to other contexts? Do they fit? How far can they be generalized?

Grounded theorists attest that the methodology develops concepts and abstractions at a level that supports their transferability to other populations and contexts (Glaser, 2005). Some methodologists suggest that any transfer of a study's findings to other contexts is the responsibility of the reader, not the researcher (Erickson, 1986). The generalizability of the case study has been a contentious issue, ranging from the researcher's analytic ability to find levels of universality in the case (Spradley, 1979, 1980) to frank admission that complex and site-specific contexts problematize the ability to construct theory and thus generalization (Clarke, Friese, & Washburn, 2018).

The generalizing process is far from mechanical. We again conclude that it's the write-up itself that matters in the end. How *persuasive* a case can the researcher make that the findings of $N = 1$ have meaning and resonance to other individuals, sites, and times?

Some useful criteria to consider about this issue for a qualitative study are as follows:

1. The characteristics of the original sample of persons, settings, processes, and so on, are fully and sufficiently described to permit adequate comparisons with other samples.

2. The report specifies any limits on sample selection and critically examines its ability to generalize to other settings and contexts.

3. The sampling is theoretically diverse enough to encourage broader applicability when relevant.

4. The findings include enough "thick description" for readers to assess the potential transferability and appropriateness for their own settings.

5. A range of readers report that the findings are consistent with their own experiences.

6. The processes and outcomes described in the conclusions are applicable in comparable settings.

7. The findings are congruent with, connected to, or confirmatory of prior theory.

8. Any new theories and their transferability are explicitly stated.

9. The report suggests settings where the findings could fruitfully be tested further.

10. When possible, the findings have been replicated in other studies to assess their robustness.

Utilization/Application/Action Orientation

Even if a study's findings are valid and transferable, we still need to know what the study does for its participants—both researchers and researched—and for its consumers.

Evaluation and policy studies in particular are supposed to lead to more positive and constructive change; whether or not they do, real people's lives are being affected, and large amounts of money are being spent (or misspent). Action research, critical ethnography, and other community-based research projects are designed to clarify and rectify particular local problems through participatory engagement. At the very least, they heighten awareness among participants of selected social issues that affect them directly.

These research genres also raise questions of ethics—who benefits from a qualitative study, who may be harmed, and what is its "evaluative validity" (Maxwell, 1992)? Whose judgments are made about the worth, legitimacy, or goodness of actions or meanings?

Some useful criteria to consider about this issue for a qualitative study are as follows:

1. Value-based or ethical concerns and dilemmas are raised explicitly in the report.

2. The findings are intellectually and physically accessible to potential users.

3. The findings stimulate and provide intellectual "payoff" for a reader, and possibly ideas for his or her own related research project.

4. The level of usable knowledge offered is worthwhile, ranging from consciousness raising and the development of insight or self-understanding, to broader considerations—a theory to guide action, or policy advice. Or it may be local and specific—corrective recommendations or specific actions.

5. The actions taken actually help solve a local problem.

6. Users of the findings have experienced a sense of empowerment or increased control over their lives (Lincoln & Guba, 1985).

7. Users of the findings have learned or developed new capacities.

ANALYTIC DOCUMENTATION

The Problem

Good qualitative research requires careful record keeping as a way of connecting with important audiences. The first audience is the *self*: well-organized electronic and hard-copy files that help keep track of what was done along the way, suggesting ways of improving next steps and documenting all logistical matters related to the study.

The second audience is the *readers* of the research reports, who need to know what was done and how, as a way of assessing the credibility and trustworthiness of the findings. Other researchers and journal peer reviewers make such judgments carefully, even obsessively. And other readers, such as local participants, policymakers, managers, and the general public, often raise questions such as

"Whom did you talk to, anyway?" "How do you know that?" "Why are you being so negative?" and "Where did you get that recommendation?"

The third audience is a subset of the second: *other researchers* who are interested in secondary analysis of the data, want to carry out a metasynthesis of several studies, or want to replicate your findings to strengthen or modify them.

For the latter two audiences, most journals require authors of empirical studies to report on their procedures as an integral part of the article. The formats are often so familiar that the author can almost fill in the blanks when writing sections on sampling, methods, and data analysis. For mixed methods studies, it's also expected that you report relevant statistical data in standardized display formats. The word or page limitations of journal article manuscripts generally require that these procedures be written in terse prose with little nuance or detail.

There is a traditional set of conventions for documenting empirical research and for reporting it, but the hybridity of qualitative inquiry has created multiple, open-ended reporting structures for progressive genres such as poetic inquiry, autoethnography, narrative inquiry, and others. And selected schools of thought reject the very notion of "conclusions," considering them abhorrent abuses of researcher power to force fixed meanings on an uncertain social world. (The irony, of course, is that these same schools of thought seem to authoritatively assert their stances as fixed meanings.)

Although qualitative studies are rich in descriptions of settings, people, events, and processes, they often say little about how the researcher got the information, and very little about how the conclusions were drawn. When procedures are left so opaque, we have only vague criteria for judging the goodness of conclusions: the "plausibility," the "coherence," or the "compellingness" of the study.

So, we have an unappealing double bind. Qualitative studies cannot always be verified because researchers don't always report clearly on their methodology, and they don't report clearly on their methodology because there are not always required conventions for doing so. (Epistemological reasons may be claimed as well—for instance, the idea that a qualitative study is such a person-specific, artistic, private/interpretive act that no one else can viably verify or replicate it—but that takes us far from shore just now.) What do we do?

Methods sections are much more typical in dissertations, theses, and journal reports of traditional qualitative methodologies. They tend to follow a conventional outline and sequence:

- Rationale for the study

- Central and related research questions

- Cursory literature review

- Conceptual or theoretical framework

- Methodology
  - Participants
  - Data collection methods
  - Data analysis procedures

We need to know a few additional things, if possible:

- Which kinds of qualitative designs do researchers actually use?

- How are sampling decisions actually made?

- What does the instrumentation look like, and how does the researcher know whether it is measuring accurately what it was meant to measure?

- How does field work actually proceed?

- How are the data aggregated, condensed, partitioned, displayed, analyzed, and interpreted?

- Most fundamentally, how do researchers get from hundreds if not thousands of pages of field notes, interview transcripts, and documents to a final report?

Until we can share clear descriptions of qualitative research procedures, we cannot talk about them intelligibly with one another—let alone set up conventions for verification. We have to begin, then, by logging and then describing our procedures clearly enough so that others can understand them, reconstruct them, and subject them to scrutiny.

Most of the conclusions drawn during analysis are substantive, based on the content. But the analyst is constantly drawing *procedural* conclusions along the way as well: to transpose two rows in a matrix, to add or discard a column, to revise a code or category label, or to change the analytic approach altogether midway. It's important to log and report the procedural decisions made.

Lincoln and Guba (1985) used the metaphor of the fiscal auditor who examines the books of a company to determine whether accounts have been kept satisfactorily and whether the "bottom line" is correct. Making such an audit depends on the auditee's having documented income, outlays, and transfers. Without such an audit trail, you cannot determine the dependability or the confirmability of the bookkeeping.

Thorough auditing, as such, is relatively rare as far as we know for qualitative studies. The audit metaphor is forbidding: It connotes an external, stern, obsessive expert and misses the idea that you, with close colleagues, can frequently look at documentation fruitfully on your own. There are also confidentiality issues to consider with outsiders looking at personal data; Institutional Review Board regulations may prohibit this unless approval has been granted in advance by the regulatory body.

The first and basic audience for good documentation is the *self*. Even if no audit is ever intended, devices such as the researcher's journal, research team meeting reports, and/or analytic memos strengthen the study *as it goes*. They also enable easy production of the final report's methods section. Also, a number of CAQDAS software programs automatically develop a dated log of analysis operations of certain sorts, such as code development, searches and queries, and analytic memo records.

Examples

First, analytic documentation occurs when the researcher logs the processes in a personal journal or in analytic memos. The notes can range from a simple description of the analytic moves undertaken, to deeper reflections about the qualitative data analytic process. One example comes from Saldaña's unpublished study on the phenomenology of being a qualitative researcher. In this memo, he reflects on the emergence of a new theme:

January 31, 2018

NEW THEME: "REPRESENTATIONAL RESPONSIBILITY"
    After my initial presentation of the study in progress, I was struck by one respondent's suggestion that we have a "responsibility" as researchers to tell other people's stories. That term made me think that we have other responsibilities as well: the responsibility to be ethical, to tell the truth, to maintain high standards, etc. If I were to make that term more

thematic, I would say that we have a "*representational* responsibility"—a responsibility to represent not just our participants, but a representational responsibility to our readers, our jurors, and even ourselves as scholars. "Representational responsibility" seems to fit best under the *Communal Grounding* category since it relies on our interactions with others. That makes it four themes under the category, which kind of irks me because it's not that magic number of 3 I always try to work for. But it's too important to leave out.

Analytic documentation also occurs in our final reports. As space permits, we should disclose to our readers not just the specific procedures but even the difficulties we encountered along the way. McHugh et al. (2013) detail their extensive coding and data-analytic procedures for focus group interview data in their *Urban Education* article, "Bridges and Barriers: Adolescent Perceptions of Student–Teacher Relationships." Though the passage below is lengthy, we present it as an exemplar of meticulous analytic documentation that serves its readers. The multiple supporting citations to the literature, themselves serving as evidence of good methods scholarship, have been deleted to focus exclusively on the coresearchers' analytic methods:

Coding Procedures and Data Analyses

Using the NVivo 9 software package, we descriptively micro-coded (units as small as phrases in a sentence, to full conversations) data and examined how frequently different codes occurred simultaneously to identify patterns and themes. Examining code co-occurrences between our structural codes and our content codes provided a multifaceted understanding of what the adolescent participants perceived as occurring in their student–teacher interactions, as well as provided insight into the likely implications of these relational assessments made by the adolescents. One challenge to a focus group method, however, is that topics may be abandoned and revisited multiple times within a relatively short span of time. Multiple processes were frequently discussed simultaneously by participants because (a) the participant reported experiencing them simultaneously; (b) the participant believed them to be interrelated in regard to a specific experience; or (c) the participant compared and contrasted dissimilar processes for instructive purposes. As a result, codes occasionally overlapped in unintentional ways. Therefore, to confirm the validity of our analyses, we manually verified all relevant coding co-occurrences. This instance-by-instance verification ensures that all counts of code co-occurrences are accurate and did not occur simply as artifacts of multiple sets of codes overlapping within the same one-paragraph coding unit. Throughout this coding process, we utilized three distinct types of codes: Mechanical codes, Conceptual codes, and Structural codes (see [Display 4.2 in this book] for an excerpt of our codebook). In the following paragraphs, we provide a brief overview of each distinct type of code.

Mechanical codes designated functional features of the focus group data such as the specific speaker (moderator, participant, or other), the specific actors referenced in any story or example provided by a youth participant (a student–teacher interaction, a youth–parent interaction, etc.), and which particular protocol item participants were discussing (continuum of opinion, identity cards, teacher educator, etc.). The mechanical codes facilitated data reduction. By selecting only data which referred to teacher–student interactions or regarded teacher-specific items of the protocol such as those reviewed above, we generated a succinct, focused dataset with which to explore our emergent research questions.

Conceptual codes consisted of emergent and literature-based concepts. We created conceptual codes through an iterative, cooperative process after multiple readings of several transcripts. These emergent codes allowed us to identify salient, repeated themes and concepts within the data, and form the heart of our analyses, as they represent the content of the adolescents' perceptions. Prior to independent coding, raters read and coded one transcript, compared the density of coding stripes, and calculated interrater reliability scores in order to ensure coding fidelity. To ensure that our codes were not redundant and had thematic unity, we examined the convergence and divergence of conceptually similar codes, and collapsed multiple codes into one, or split one code into multiples, as necessary. We also employed a few literature-generated codes specifically related to features of supportive relationships.

The final type of codes used, Structural codes, designated when participants expressed hypothetical social expectations or real observed social behaviors of teachers. This last set of classifications became especially important when organizing data relevant to the research questions. While conceptual codes explained the content of the data, structural codes designated whether or not the adolescent's story or example described something that the teacher did or did not do. Additionally, the structural codes reflected the adolescents' judgments and values of the story relayed, as to whether they felt it should or should not happen. Because applying the structural codes involved a subjective process of interpreting data, two or more researchers conducted this process collaboratively to reach a consensus of interpretation.

This type of coding deliberately labeled the perceived effect of the interaction on the closeness of the interpersonal relationship. As such, we were able to explore the driving question in this coding process, "Did the interaction *bridge* the two people to bring them closer together, or did it separate them or create a *barrier* between closeness developing?" Finally, by examining the thematic patterns identified, we gained a full understanding of the processes that the participants related to us. (adapted from McHugh et al., 2013, pp. 17–18)

A third method of analytic documentation is through display. When possible, researchers should not just narratively describe but visually illustrate their process of transforming codes into their consequent analytic products (e.g., major themes/concepts, key assertion, theory). A brief description of the journey from beginning to end, especially if it can be shown on just one page, helps readers see the big picture.

Brooks (2015) studied school principals in southern Thailand working in tension-filled communities and utilized for her data analysis a "conceptual framework that conceived of trust as five interrelated constructs: benevolence, honesty, openness, reliability, and competence" (p. 232). The five constructs served as a priori codes that helped formulate more detailed codes and thus six categories and thence into two emergent themes. Her one-page diagram of the entire analytic process (see Display 11.7) is an elegant overview of how one begins and progresses toward condensation and summation of qualitative data.

We offer these final recommendations for analytic documentation:

1. Be clear in your own mind why you are doing documentation for this study. Is it for study steering and revision, for your own personal learning, for getting feedback from a colleague or other critical friend, for methods section reportage, for a methodological article or technical report, or for actual audit?

2. Any study has more or less riding on it. A high-stakes study (e.g., an expensive one or controversial case) demands more care.

DISPLAY 11.7 ● Analysis of Data, Categories, and Emergent Themes		
A Priori Codes	**Codes**	**Categories**
Benevolence	Visits Invitations Good reputation Morality	Fostering goodwill between school and community
Honesty	Ethics Mothering Dependable Religious guidance	Need for community acceptance and community ties
Openness	Community approval Community participation Asking teachers questions	Community and teacher decision making
Reliability	Community support Community help Unknown others	Silence Neutrality
Competence	Lowest achieving Private Islamic schools and no oversight Integration of Islamic curriculum Negative presence of soldiers	Barriers to leadership
Categories		**Emergent themes**
Fostering goodwill Need for community acceptance Community and teachers as decision makers Silence Neutrality Barriers to leadership		Fear of the unknown Lack of communication

Source: Brooks (2015), p. 240.

3. Avoid "laundering" or retrospective enlightenment. If the analytic process was difficult (it almost always is), admit it. When in doubt, tell the truth.

4. It's not a good idea to do a thorough reflection on your analysis while doing the analysis. You need all the energy you can spare for the analysis itself. Compose jottings or brief analytic memos about your procedures for expanding at a later date.

CLOSURE AND TRANSITION

Tremendous amounts of tactics, guidance, advice, and recommendations were covered in this chapter. We do not mean to overwhelm you with this vast array of factors to consider in your data analyses, but we do feel they are important guidelines that can strengthen the quality and integrity of your qualitative work. Use these methods on an "as-needed" or "as-relevant" basis.

In the next chapter, we will explore the write-ups researchers must make for sharing their data-analytic efforts and findings with audiences.

WRITING ABOUT QUALITATIVE RESEARCH

CHAPTER SUMMARY

This chapter reviews various choices available to researchers when writing up the qualitative report. Extended examples are provided to illustrate selected elements and styles of writing. Brief advice for thesis and dissertation students is also provided.

CONTENTS

INTRODUCTION

Reporting study results to others is a necessary component of virtually all qualitative research projects. But in what form? The conventional formats long familiar to quantitative researchers, something like this, are too schematic and constraining:

- Statement of the problem

- Research questions

- Methods

- Results

- Discussion

- Conclusions

A qualitative write-up could follow that format (and many do), but it's not the only one available to us. Normally, we'd have other expectations for a qualitative report.

For example, we might expect a close description of the setting and the major participants. We might look for a more circular linkage between research questions, methods, data collection, and analyses. Qualitative data have special strengths: local groundedness, holism, temporality, access to causation, emphasis on meanings, and so on. Reporting formats can capitalize on them. Even for data segments within a study, a set of field observations can be rendered differently—as a series of vignettes, in poetic form, or compiled in a meta-matrix. A blurring of the frontiers seems to occur between social scientific reporting and figurative or rhetorical renditions of aesthetic material.

The reporting of qualitative data may be one of the most fertile fields going; there are no standardized formats (save for a journal's manuscript submission requirements such as APA, MLA, etc.), and the ways data are being analyzed and interpreted are getting more and more varied. As qualitative data analysts, we have few shared canons of how our studies *should* be reported. Should we have normative agreement on this? Probably not now—and, some would say, not ever.

Yet it's important to consider the choices you have in designing and writing reports. The challenge is to combine elegance and credibility appropriately with the many ways social events can be described, and to find intersections between the academic thinking of most conventional studies and more creative thinking. Just as a good analysis nearly always involves a blend of variable-oriented, categorizing, paradigmatic moves, and case-oriented, contextualizing, narrative ones, so does good reporting.

We do not offer a fixed set of ideas about reports and reporting but rather identify a series of *choices* you have in writing your accounts. They include choices about the report's audiences and the hoped-for effects on them, the voice or genre of the report, its style, its structure, and what can be done to ensure better use of the report.

Our stance is that these choices should be made clearly and deliberately in preliminary form—for interim reports, quite early, and for final reports, somewhat before the midpoint of a study. Wolcott (2009) has an even stronger position: "You cannot begin writing early enough. . . . Would that mean someone might write a first draft before venturing into the field to begin observations or interviews? Absolutely" (p. 18). The point here is not advocacy of data-free writing but of early and continuous writing as a way to make your ideas—more and more informed by data—explicit.

Reporting is not separate from thinking or analysis. Rather, writing *is* analysis. And from our perspective, *a report is a display*. Reports display your organized accounts of what happened in the field, and they display your carefully considered analytic explanations of those events. Your report triggers within your readers the memories of their own personal experiences, plus their comparative and critical faculties. At its best, writing as a form of display presents new, intriguing ideas and stimulates the reader to perceive social life in different and more insightful ways (Saldaña, 2018).

AUDIENCES AND EFFECTS

The Reader and the Writer

Reports are supposed to be written for specific audiences in order to achieve specific effects. But the familiar label "audience" obscures an important issue: You cannot exactly manage who reads your work or the effects you want to achieve with them. Rather, in Erickson's (1986) terms, the reader is a co-analyst, experiencing the original setting vicariously, looking at the evidence, weighing the writer's interpretations and perspective, and noting how they have changed along the way.

Generally speaking, you need to make choices of reader types from a list like this:

- *Local participants and respondents:* the people who provided data

- *Program administrators and operators:* in evaluation studies, people running and/or deciding about the program being looked at

- *Practitioners:* people engaged in the same sort of work as those studied but in different settings

- *Other researchers:*
    o Colleagues in your own setting
    o Colleagues in your academic field
    o Members of thesis/dissertation committees

- *Policymakers:* governing boards, legislators, and agency officials

- *General readers:* purchasers of trade and e-books

- *Mass readers:* purchasers of magazines and newspapers, readers of Internet news sources, websites, digital videos, and blogs.

Types of Effects

What are you hoping will occur when a particular type of reader engages with your report? Although that cannot be predicted or controlled, getting your *intentions* clear can make a profound difference in what the report will look like and how you produce it. Any qualitative research report may be written from certain general positions:

Scientific

- To heighten insight, illuminate, and deepen understanding

- To expand or revise existing concepts, explanations, and theory

- To convince the reader of the report's worth, truth, and value

- To advance the methodological craft of research

- To add to existing information on a topic

Aesthetic

- To entertain, amuse, and arouse feeling

- To enable vicarious experiencing

Moral

- To clarify and sharpen moral, ethical, and legal issues

- To emancipate, raise consciousness, and free the reader from unrealized oppression

Activist

- To show connections between findings and local problems
- To enable improved decisions and to provide guidance for action
- To empower the reader and to increase a sense of control
- To mobilize specific action
- To support the reader in future use of the findings

One of the critical considerations is *which* effects you intend for *which* types of reader. If your report is a dissertation and your first audience is your committee (and only secondarily other researchers), then the effects of theoretical and methodological advancement—or perhaps, mostly, convincing the readers of the report's credibility—are likely to be central. On the other hand, if your audiences are policymakers and trade book readers, your intended effects may be different—for example, the illumination, moral clarification, and mobilization that Jonathan Kozol (1991) doubtless intended in his riveting depiction of urban schools in *Savage Inequalities: Children in America's Schools*; and the insightful investigative journalism and social critique of America's minimum wage injustices in Barbara Ehrenreich's (2001) *Nickel and Dimed: On (Not) Getting by in America*.

VOICES AND STYLES

How do we speak to the reader? Many choices can be made, and no standard lexicon describes the overall tone, mode, and orientation of the report. Yet when we read a research report, we can almost immediately detect a pervasive voice, a *style* that defines the relationship between the writer and the reader.

Matters of style are connected with choice of voice. Using passive instead of active verbs, "objective" stances rather than honestly personal ones, and indirect locutions instead of straightforward talk have a long and dishonorable history in traditional research reporting. They serve only to wrap the writer in the mantle of "science" while mystifying and alienating the reader.

One common misconception some scholars have is that you need to "write smart" to be taken seriously or to prove that you know a lot, because it's a traditional discourse expected in scholarly/academic publications and presentations. Others "write smart" because they're arrogant elitists in love with their own intelligence, and they feel that lofty prose, obscure vocabulary, and abstract concepts are the only ways they can communicate their brilliance to others. We're not advocating that you "dumb down" your qualitative writing; we're advocating that you "smarten up" your voice. Things can still be complex without being complicated. Write simply, write clearly, and write believably. Keep it real.

van Maanen's (2011) eloquent and classic *Tales of the Field* distinguishes among several possible voices or research tale types, with many examples from his own and others' work. Several of these can be compatibly mixed and matched within a single report:

> ***Formal*** (also known as ***Analytic***): traditional and conventional scholarly writing. Details the methods, data collection, and data analysis procedures employed with a systematic overview of results and theories.
>
> ***Realist*** (also known as ***Descriptive***): a direct, highly detailed, matter-of-fact portrait, with methods left mostly undescribed.

Confessional: written from the fieldworker's viewpoint. This includes methodological dilemmas, admission of errors, ethical issues, and behind-the-scenes glitches.

Impressionist: personalized, atheoretical accounts, often story-like, aiming to link reality and the fieldworker and to enable the reader's vivid reliving of the experience.

Critical: focuses on sociopolitical implications of field work. Critically examines, usually through a Marxist lens, sociological and cultural underpinnings of human dynamics.

Literary: evocative narratives. Utilizes the power of literary tones, styles, and elements to develop characters in active storylines as in "creative nonfiction."

Jointly told: collaborative, coauthored accounts. The researcher and participants join together to create a polyvocal narrative of their collective experiences.

Structural (also known as *Interpretive*): a combination of theoretical reflection with first-person accounts. This writing links the local to the general.

Poststructural: "purposeful incompleteness and uncertainty." Inconclusive results to reinforce the flux of human nature.

Advocacy: takes a deliberate moral perspective. The work examines inequities and power struggles to achieve social justice and to empower the oppressed.

These voices have consequences for what is included in a report and what can be learned from it. For example, van Maanen notes that a realist, descriptive voice tends to rule out alternative interpretations and/or to pretend that the interpretations come straight from the respondents. Confessional tales may overfocus on the fieldworker as doing "vanity ethnography," blurring what happened, and may be seen as self-indulgent writing. An impressionist account may focus too much on the exemplary and dramatic moments of field work to the neglect of a site's mundane and patterned reality. (These are only sketchy summaries. We recommend van Maanen's *Tales of the Field: On Writing Ethnography* to the reader seeking an articulate, experienced researcher's reflections on writing.)

WRITING EXAMPLES AND RECOMMENDATIONS

There are excellent books devoted exclusively to writing up qualitative research; see the appendix for recommended titles. In this section, we offer just a few examples of what we consider to be important components of qualitative reportage, and some examples from published studies that exhibit (read: display) the necessities of exemplary writing.

Writing the Abstract

A journal article abstract or thesis/dissertation abstract may be the first narrative block a reader accesses after scanning your work's title. Certainly, this front matter should describe the study's purpose and design, but we emphasize that writers should also *include the project's major findings or conclusions* in the abstract, rather than simply relaying the topics that will be discussed. Giving us the study's "headlines" first better frames the reader for the full-length report, and makes searches more efficient for readers who may be reviewing a large number of works for a literature review or a qualitative metasynthesis. We recommend that at least one-half of an abstract's length be devoted to summarizing the study's conclusions.

As an example, Anthony Silard (2018; also see Display 9.1), in his *Nonprofit and Voluntary Sector Quarterly* journal article, "Emotions for a Cause: How the Emotion Expression of Nonprofit Leaders Produces Follower Engagement and Loyalty," suggests the results not only in his title, but also includes the major findings in his abstract. They are italicized below to highlight them:

Although emotion and leadership is a flourishing topic in organizational research, little is known about the actual emotion-related leader behaviors within the context of nonprofit organizations. Through an inductive, multiple-case study drawing from 34 semistructured interviews with individuals who have occupied leader and/or follower roles in nonprofit organizations, *a meso-level framework emerges that delineates the mutually strengthening interplay of emotion-related leader behaviors and organizational display norms in the nonprofit sector. These norms favor the expression of positive emotion and proscribe the display of negative emotion. Nonprofit leaders who enact emotion-related behaviors congruent with these display norms generate the follower outcomes of engagement and loyalty.* Implications for nonprofit leadership research and practice are discussed. (p. 304, emphasis added)

As a second example, Alessandro Stievano et al. (2016) explored "Nursing's Professional Respect as Experienced by Hospital and Community Nurses" in their *Nursing Ethics* journal article. An editorial requirement of this particular journal (and one we feel all journals, regardless of discipline, should adopt) is an extended yet succinct abstract that "front-loads" readers with a categorized summary of key components of the study. This textual display provides an at-a-glance overview for busy professionals who need essential information delivered concisely:

Background: There is growing awareness that patient care suffers when nurses are not respected. Therefore, to improve outcomes for patients, it is crucial that nurses operate in a moral work environment that involves both recognition respect, a form of respect that ought to be accorded to every single person, and appraisal respect, a recognition of the relative and contingent value of respect modulated by the relationships of the healthcare professionals in a determined context.

Research question/aim: The purpose of this study was to develop better understandings of perceptions of nursing's professional respect in community and hospital settings in England.

Research design: The research design was qualitative. Focus groups were chosen as the most appropriate method for eliciting discussion about nursing's professional respect.

Participants and research context: A total of 62 nurses who had been qualified for at least a year and were working in two localities in England participated in this study.

Methods: Data were collected using 11 focus group sessions. The data were analysed by means of an inductive content analysis, extracting meaning units from the information retrieved and classifying the arising phenomena into conceptually meaningful categories and themes.

Ethical considerations: To conduct the research, permission was obtained from the selected universities.

Results: Recognition respect of human beings was perceived as ingrained in the innermost part of nurses. Regarding appraisal respect, a great importance was placed on: the interactions among healthcare professionals, the time to build trust in these relationships, the influences of the workplace characteristics and nurses' professional autonomy and decision-making.

Conclusion: Recognition respect of persons was embedded in the inmost part of nurses as individuals. Concerning appraisal respect, it was thought to be deeply enshrined in the inter- and intra-healthcare professional interactions. The forging of trusting relationships over time was deemed to be strongly associated with good quality interactions with other healthcare professionals. (pp. 1–2)

Even if you're not submitting your manuscript to a journal that requires an extended abstract like the one above, we feel you should write one at the conclusion of your study as a way of condensing the primary elements of your study. This narrative display also functions as an executive summary for a private, commissioned report and can serve as a template for a thesis/dissertation abstract write-up.

Writing About Methodology and Methods

We must provide readers a necessary account of what and how we went about doing what we did in the field and in front of a computer monitor. The methodology section of a report details the overall framework of the investigation, while the methods section describes the procedures we followed to collect information of various types and from whom. It is an evidentiary warrant, of sorts—not of data, but of the researcher's systematic ways of working—that authenticates the qualifications of the investigator and the quality of the study's design and execution.

Dana L. Miller, John W. Creswell, and Lisa S. Olander (1998) explored the writing of a field work project in three different ways for their compelling *Qualitative Inquiry* journal article, "Writing and Retelling Multiple Ethnographic Tales of a Soup Kitchen for the Homeless." This first excerpt demonstrates an exemplar of qualitative research writing's front matter: their modified conceptual framework, purpose of the study, field work setting, and major research questions—in other words, the *methodology*:

> The soup kitchen becomes a microcosm for studying the homeless population . . . and we can learn much from an ethnographic study that explores alternative narratives about the culture of a soup kitchen.
>
> The purpose of this ethnographic study was to describe and interpret the cultural setting of the St. Tabor Soup Kitchen, located in a small Midwestern city called Midtown. St. Tabor is housed in a multipurpose complex with Daily Refuge (a daytime shelter for the homeless and near-homeless) and Community Thrift Shop. Three research questions emerged during the study: How might the soup kitchen, as a cultural setting, be described? What are the cultural themes of the soup kitchen? How can we become advocates for the soup kitchen, day-shelter and the homeless population? (p. 472)

Other necessary elements for this ethnographic report are documentation of the data collection methods, the selection of key informants, and how the coresearchers' findings were verified. Notice how the amounts and forms of data and the explanation of triangulation procedures establish a sense of trustworthiness for the forthcoming account—these are the *methods*:

> We observed homeless guests for 4 months during the noon lunch hour at St. Tabor Soup Kitchen. Our methodology was qualitative, involving ethnographic procedures . . . and an evolving design to best understand the culture of the soup kitchen and the needs of the low-income and homeless population in Midtown.
>
> The noon lunch at St. Tabor was provided by Daily Refuge. Gaining access through the director of Daily Refuge, we volunteered for 4 months, serving meals in the soup kitchen

and helping with clean-up. Data collection consisted of 35 observations, and formal and informal interviews. In addition, we collected documents describing the low-income population in the city, sign-in sheets that provided census data about guests, written materials about Daily Refuge, daily food menus, and we took photographs of the facility, town and guests. Our personal fieldnotes included conversations with guests, volunteers, and staff; notes from our research team meetings; and our interpretations and personal reflections.

Information-rich key informants were purposefully selected to participate in the study, including the director of Daily Refuge, the facility manager, and a homeless man who volunteered as a cook for many days during our visit. With these individuals, we periodically shared our emerging cultural description of St. Tabor. Throughout the study, we verified the accuracy of our account by taking our report back to key informants and by triangulating among multiple participants, investigators, and data collection methods. We use pseudonyms throughout this report to protect the anonymity of the site and participants. (p. 472)

The coresearchers do not label the above sections as ways of rendering van Maanen's *formal* style of writing and tale-telling, but that is what they have done. The formal (or *analytic*) tale presents the researcher's systematic procedures and thinking of how the data come together to explain how things work.

"Being There"

Careful description of the settings, people, and events we witnessed is one of the main contributions of qualitative research. But such descriptions also have an analytic and interpretive purpose: to illuminate the constant, influential, and determining factors shaping the course of events and what it all means in the grander scheme of things.

A classic ethnographic mandate is to give readers a vivid sense of "being there" at the social setting we observed. Descriptive and realistic accounts remain firmly rooted in the data themselves, and this style of writing may help the reader imagine the site in his or her mind and lend a sense of credibility to the author's experiences—in other words, "I was there, and this is what I saw and heard" (Saldaña, 2011b, p. 147).

A purely methods laden account makes our reports sterile and less "human." One of qualitative research's strengths is its ability to convey the social dimensions of life through evocative prosaic renderings. Giving readers a virtual experience of "being there" in the field with us can be accomplished through what Saldaña calls "significant trivia"—rich visual imagery. In this excerpt from the soup kitchen for the homeless study, Miller et al. (1998) provide a description of the setting using small but inference-laden details:

The Soup Kitchen, run by a Catholic church, provides dinner 7 days a week and lunch on weekends. Daily Refuge rents the kitchen on weekdays to serve free lunches. St. Tabor's dining area is one modest sized room, about 45 by 30 feet. Guests sit around three rows of tables (2 by 24 feet each) covered with green, plastic, flannel-backed tablecloths with tiny paw prints. When not in use, chairs line one of the walls of the room. The dining area is modern and clean, with sparse accessories—a couple of trash cans, a small cross hanging on the wall, a bulletin board advertising services available to the homeless, and a few community service awards. A long serving counter divides the dining area from the kitchen—a modern, clean cooking area with a stove; commercial size oven; microwave; stainless steel, locked refrigerator; dishwasher; and mops and buckets for clean-up. (p. 474)

"Being there" accounts for what the researcher both saw *and heard*. Occasional quotes from participants throughout the report both document the data and honor the voices of those we studied. We have read a few reports in which the researcher's point of view dominated the text and neglected to report what others said in the field, opting instead to summarize their responses rather than quoting them directly. Selected monologic and dialogic excerpts from field notes and interview transcripts give not just a voice but a "face" to the people in our investigation.

Chapter 7's Vignettes profile offers an evocative way to render a substantive moment of social action in narrative form that includes both action and dialogue. As another example, we provide excerpts from a 2006 *Management Communication Quarterly* article by Sarah J. Tracy, Pamela Lutgen-Sandvik, and Jess K. Alberts: "Nightmares, Demons, and Slaves: Exploring the Painful Metaphors of Workplace Bullying."

Ten in-depth interviews and two focus groups with nine and eight participants respectively were conducted with adult participants who self-identified as bullied workers. The coresearchers also employed creative drawing with them, a restorative approach for people experiencing trauma or pain, and which provides an outlet for expressing complex and subtle information that is difficult to verbalize (p. 156). The drawings served as stimuli for individual and focus group discussions, and they later became provocative displays in the final published report.

The coresearchers observed that participants related their workplace bullying experiences through selected metaphors, and thus the analysis focused on how these metaphors were used to describe their painful experiences. In this excerpt, notice how the participants are quoted throughout:

More than any other metaphor, narratives and drawings characterized bullying as a contest or battle. This metaphor continuum ranged from playing a game to outright war, including killing and death. On the less destructive end of the spectrum, those targeted described feeling as though bullying was a matching of wits with an opponent who played unfairly. Participants spoke in terms of bullying as strategic attack, defense, and a set of shifting rules saying, for instance, that bullying was "playing a game," "playing their game," and "I had no rights . . . and they played on that." Dale, who worked in a security business, said the bully was "up to his old tricks." These metaphors of play and game suggest a less-than-serious issue and something that all members ostensibly should also be able to negotiate. However, as illustrated below, targets viewed the rules of the game as unfair and playing the game as dangerous and threatening.

Targeted workers characterized the contest as fixed or unfairly weighted in the bully's favor. They said bullies created the rules, changed them without notice or input and, as an aircraft mechanic named Ben explained, did so "behind closed doors." Dolly, a dental office administrative assistant, noted that bullies "make their own rules." Stephanie, a call center employee, said that the only way the bully would win was "to play dirty," whereas Jack, the director of an online university program, said that bullying "really has to do with making up the rules as you go along." Sadly, this metaphor of a game that is difficult to win extended to targets' seeking external help through the courts. Going to court was a gamble and "a crap shoot." Furthermore, in this "game," abused workers could see themselves as the prey of the hunt; Dale explained, "everybody's fair game" for bullying. Hunting, of course, can result in significant and even lethal injury. (pp. 159–160)

Again, we emphasize that text, too, is a display; and a participant quote is a "verbal display" that represents and presents data vividly about the study's phenomenon of interest.

Analytic Storytelling With Displays

Chapter 11 includes an extended example about the detailed write-up of coding and data analysis procedures, and we refer you to its "Analytic Documentation" section for review. Here, we discuss how narrative and displays work together in a report.

Throughout this book, we've stressed two basic modes of presentation: text (with varying degrees of detail and organization), associated with organized displays in matrix, network, or graphic form. We think these modes are an enormous help in drawing coherent meaning from data and in confirming and deepening conclusions. By extension, they communicate clearly and well to readers.

We return to Stievano et al.'s (2016) study on nursing's professional respect as an example. Recall that 62 participants distributed among 11 focus group interview sessions offered their perspectives on the topic. A few discussion questions posed to the nurse participants included the following: "Could you describe some indicators of nursing's professional respect in degrees of importance?" "Have you witnessed an episode where nursing's professional respect was violated?" "Have you ever witnessed a situation where the behaviour of a health professional (physiotherapist, speech therapist, radiographer, etc.), support staff or clerical staff, damaged or reinforced nursing's professional respect? Could you give some examples?" (p. 5).

From a content analysis of the transcripts, "Codes were reduced, connected together based on their similarities and differences, and abstracted into 14 main categories. Six connecting themes were identified" (p. 7). Display 12.1 shows how the 14 categories clustered into those 6 themes.

Display 12.1 in and of itself is an effective graphic that illustrates the transformation of condensed data from one form to another. But the research team took it a step further and *integrated* the themes in a second graphic. They progressed from an *analysis* in Display 12.1 to a *synthesis* in Display 12.2. "Appraisal respect," a meta-theme based on the literature review and conceptual framework, is a relational engagement "embedded in time and place and is identified and expressed at various levels. . . . Appraisal respect will value morally virtuous personal attributes such as honesty, integrity, fairness, compassion, reciprocal trust and responsibility" (p. 3).

The complete article describes the interwoven nature of the six themes and how they work in concert with each other for professional appraisal respect. The narrative alone might have sufficed for astute readers to grasp the analytic work, but the two graphics greatly enhance the audience's cognitive grasp of the resulting themes. Display 12.1 is elegant and straightforward enough to speak for itself. But Display 12.2's ideas are more richly complex, and the analytic narrative, *in combination with and reference to the display*, explains the study's findings better than words or images alone. One excerpt from the report, to be read in concert with Display 12.2, reads as follows:

> Concerning appraisal respect, an extrinsic respect for the qualities of other individuals—generated asymmetrically in the relationships among persons—was thought to be deeply enshrined in the relationships among healthcare professionals. These interactions qualified the respect for nurses. In fact, it was during these interactions between nurses and other healthcare professionals, primarily physicians, that the respect was defined, could be lost or violated, or possibly never recognized. This was decisive because the realization of the appraisal respect for nurses was clearly figured out so as not to dismiss others or to ignore others or to keep distance in virtue of a superior rank, or to objectify others who were regarded just for their usefulness and not as ends in themselves. (p. 14)

DISPLAY 12.1 ● Elements That Influence Nursing's Professional Respect: Summary of the Analysis

Source: Stievano et al. (2016), p. 8.

Some stories without pictures are ultimately abstract and unconvincing. But a story with vivid pictures enhances the narrative and leaves a more memorable impression. Think of all the illustrated picture books you read as a child. Most likely some of those images are embedded strongly in your mind and remembered fondly. The same principle applies with matrices, networks, and graphics in our research reports. We may not be able to recite verbatim what we read long ago in an academic journal article, but there may be traces of any accompanying visual images from that study still lingering in our long-term memories.

Source: Stievano et al. (2016), p. 10.

TRADITIONAL PRESENTATION MODES

As we emphasize throughout the book, data analysis includes selecting, condensing, and transforming data; displaying these data in an organized way; and drawing and verifying conclusions from the condensed, displayed data. Any interim or final report will deal, more or less explicitly, with this flow of analytical processes and their resulting products.

But scholarly text does not have to be sterile. Qualitative researchers characteristically employ a range of literary devices. The description of the study's context is often rendered in quasi-pictorial form ("Yellow Falls lies at the end of a fertile valley, with small farms in its hollow and a creek meandering through the flood plain"). Important events or interactions may be reported in the form of vignettes ("This happened near the entrance to the outpatient clinic, when the cardiologist, two residents, and several patients were within earshot.").

Many codes—especially pattern codes—are captured in the form of metaphors ("dwindling efforts" and "interactive glue"), where they can synthesize large blocks of data in a single trope. Metaphor, irony, and metonymy—even comedy, satire, tragedy, and farce—are seen as workable tools. But qualitative research reports are both something more and something less than traditional fictional literature. Our tropes are about something that we have realistic reasons for believing in. Evidentiary warrants are behind our assertions and claims.

How are qualitative reports organized? Not surprisingly, there are no standard setups, except at a very general level. Each researcher must craft a report structure that fits the intellectual and local context of the particular study, combined with the in-house requirements of a journal editor, book publisher, or university graduate program. A study's research questions, context, and audiences drive the design of reports more than any general canon could. Nevertheless, we humbly offer what we feel are minimum guidelines for a traditional qualitative report:

1. The report should tell us what the study was about or came to be about.

2. It should communicate a clear sense of the social and historical context of the setting(s) where data were collected.

3. It should provide us with what Erickson (1986) calls the "natural history of the inquiry," so we see clearly what was done, by whom, and how. More deeply than in a sheer "methods" account, we should see how key concepts emerged over time, which variables appeared and disappeared, and which categories or themes led to important insights.

4. A good report should provide basic data, preferably in focused form (vignettes, organized narratives, or data displays) so that the reader can, in concert with the researcher, draw warranted conclusions.

5. Researchers should address the conclusions' broader meaning in the worlds of ideas and actions they affect. (This guideline brings us full circle to the "goodness" questions we explored in Chapter 11.)

6. Bottom line: Don't be boring.

PROGRESSIVE PRESENTATION MODES

Miller et al. (1998) insightfully rendered their field work account about a soup kitchen for the homeless through three different tale types or styles—the realist, confessional, and critical. But other possibilities exist. Imagine if their field work could also have been represented through poetry, as a short documentary film posted on YouTube, as a series of monologues and scenes performed on stage, or as a photography exhibit of images taken by the homeless participants themselves with accompanying audio recordings of their life stories—a method called *photovoice*. The genre(s) you select for telling your research story should be the most effective one(s) for presenting an account that is persuasive yet provocative, emotionally rich yet factually grounded, and analytically rigorous yet elegantly presented.

Reports can go beyond words. We've restricted our analytic and presentation modes in this book, but some qualitative researchers have created studio art installations of their research, and others have posted interactive websites dedicated to their field work and findings. There are other qualitative report possibilities such as slam poetry, ethnodramas, novels, and even comic books. Such accounts are typically "larger than life." Like all good fiction, they make these accounts compelling to the reader because they describe situations that are more extreme or archetypal than most instances of daily life. Yet compellingness and novelty are not enough to ensure the goodness of a progressive qualitative report. These progressive presentation modes must, first and foremost, be excellent artistic products based on excellent research. The trick is to find a proper balance between the academic and the aesthetic—a genre coined as *faction*.

Though progressive forms of qualitative inquiry are not the primary focus of this book's purpose, we acknowledge that they can be just as revelatory and rigorous as more traditional approaches. See Knowles and Cole (2008), Leavy (2018), Norris (2009), and Saldaña (2011a) for more on these innovative arts-based genres.

ON THESES AND DISSERTATIONS

One of the primary readers of this book is the graduate student. So, we offer a few recommendations for guidance through the qualitative thesis and dissertation document process and refer you to the appendix for excellent titles on writing up qualitative research. Since each college/university has its own unique protocol for graduate programming and document preparation, we can discuss only a few general guidelines.

Support and Supervision

First, have a separate meeting and conversation with your mentor or supervisor on writing after the prospectus has been approved—not necessarily on your research topic or field work matters, but on *writing* itself. It's assumed that the supervisor has written a comparable document of some type, plus other works such as articles, books, and so on. Discuss the writing process itself—personal ways of working, dilemmas, self-discipline, emotional roadblocks, problem solving, and so on. Sharing stories about the craft and art of writing with a mentor demystifies the process and creates a sense of community about what is primarily a solitary act.

Peer support, we've learned from our students, can be either a blessing or a curse. Some students enjoy shop-talking with each other about their particular research projects, and their dialogue informs each other about method, the literature, theory, and the like. Other students prefer that a peer serve primarily as a form of social and emotional support—a friend to go out with for dinner or a movie to just "get away from it all," and to be there when a desperate phone call or text message signals the need for compassionate understanding in moments of academic angst. And some students are lone wolves who prefer to work privately by themselves, and who perceive others' outreach efforts as an annoying interference rather than a sincere attempt to connect.

Don't hesitate to tell peers what kind of student you are and what you need (or don't need) from them. Most doctoral students we've supervised have traveled a rough road toward their degrees, mostly from the stress of looming deadlines, an erratic work-life balance, and the need for affirmation that what they're doing is worthy and worthwhile. An occasional cry is the norm, not the exception. We do not intend to paint a bleak picture about graduate life; we just want you to know that *virtually every student working toward a graduate degree we've supervised has experienced these same feelings.*

Select a mentor or thesis/dissertation supervisor carefully. He or she should be someone you trust and someone who "has your back." Committee members and readers should be those who have expertise in your topic and who can offer constructive feedback on your document. Don't hesitate to come to them for assistance; their job is to help you succeed and complete your degree. If they don't perceive their roles that way, then select different committee members who do.

This final piece of advice is directed toward thesis and dissertation supervisors: Conduct monthly reality checks with your students. Research suggests that students are more likely to "deliver" their work (even late work) when their teachers give the impression, "I've got my eyes on you, and I'm watching you like a hawk." Sometimes, we assume that the master's or doctoral student is mature enough to work independently and responsibly without our intervention and to successfully complete major tasks such as a thesis or dissertation by an expected deadline. But periodic follow-up adds a little pressure and motivation to make progress and keeps lines of communication open. These reality checks can be as simple as a phone call, e-mail, text message, or submission of a one-page summary progress report at the end of each month.

Writing Fundamentals

From the very beginning, create the template or shell of the thesis or dissertation document itself in finished form with strict adherence to format manual guidelines prescribed by your college or university. Saldaña tells his students, "Make your first draft *look* like a dissertation, and it'll start *feeling* like a dissertation." Creating the front matter such as the title page, abstract, table of contents/figures, and acknowledgments pages (even if there's nothing below the headings at these early stages) gets you prepared for what eventually needs to go in them. When you start separate files for your chapter drafts, set the page margins, spacing, fonts, page numbers (one of the most frequently missing items), and all other technical format matters from the very start. What you actually write on the pages can be a first draft or messy prose as a start, but it's the shell or template for the document that's always in finished format.

Write at least one page a day; and in a year, you'll have a draft or two—if not the finished document itself. This sounds like a relatively simple and simplistic formula, but you'd be surprised how many do not follow it and end up spending 4 to 6 years writing (or mostly procrastinating) a work that could have been completed in 1 to 2 years. Granted, field work has to be completed before your conclusions can be confidently asserted, but a good amount of the document can be drafted during the prospectus and field work stages. One page a day may motivate you to continue and write two additional pages, or even five or more. But hold yourself to one page a day *minimum*.

Also, don't assume you have to write Chapter 1 first, then Chapters 2, 3, 4, and so on. Write on whatever can be written about when you sit in front of a monitor, regardless of where it appears in the document. If you're in the middle of field work and caught up on your transcription work, you can tighten up your literature review section. If you're tired and feel unmotivated to write, then start assembling or cleaning up your references or bibliography. Imagine yourself as a time traveler, who can jump back and forth from one portion of your document to another as the need arises. Each day, write on whatever can be written about.

Warning: Never show a supervisor or committee chair a rough draft, unedited, or unproofread document. The reader will be so distracted by spelling, grammatical, punctuation, and format errors that his or her mind won't be able to focus on the contents and ideas in the work. The thesis/dissertation displays you at your scholarly best, and it must be nothing less than perfect—even in the second-draft stage. Drafts that are for-your-eyes-only can be as messy as you're comfortable with. But substandard early work for a supervisory reader makes a bad first impression and reduces the chances of constructive feedback for revision you might receive.

Finally, *stick to deadlines*. That may sound like obvious advice, but not everyone adheres to it. A recent televised news story reported that "personal drama" was the major reason for the loss of a worker's productivity. And as we reflect on that reason, it seems to apply to college and university students as well. Personal drama (e.g., extended illness, caretaking responsibilities, relationship difficulties, financial matters, and emotional upheaval) interferes with field work, writing, and meeting deadlines. Certainly, each individual should reconcile what gets personal priority during those inconvenient and tumultuous periods of daily living. Sometimes, family needs to come first; and keeping a roof over your head is vital for other good things to happen. But if you want to meet thesis or dissertation deadlines, try as much as possible to eliminate the personal drama—yours or someone else's—from your life. Having a detailed, long-range calendar of due dates for tasks (e.g., prospectus approved, Institutional Review Board application submitted, field work completed, first draft of Chapter 1 completed) and fiercely sticking to it also helps.

CLOSURE AND TRANSITION

The vast majority of graduate students, scholars, and research practitioners can write *competently*. But only a few individuals from these groups write *well*. We advocate that if you want to become a better writer of qualitative research, then read a lot of it—with conscious attunement to the author's word choices, sentence structures, overall organization, report genre, and general style. The purpose is not to imitate other outstanding writers' ways of documenting social life, but to acquaint yourself with a broad spectrum of possibilities for reporting qualitatively.

The final chapter now follows. It brings closure to the book by recapping the qualitative research process and offering final strands of advice.

CLOSURE

CHAPTER SUMMARY

This final chapter reviews the book's qualitative analytic methods through a network model, then offers closing reflections and advice for researchers.

CONTENTS

Qualitative Analysis at a Glance
Reflections
Final Advice

QUALITATIVE ANALYSIS AT A GLANCE

Display 13.1, adapted from training workshops we (Miles and Huberman) have led, pulls together all of the aspects of the approaches to qualitative data analysis we have explored in this book. The purpose is to provide an integrated overview. As with causal networks, it helps to walk through the figure, piece by piece. The time dimension, for once, goes vertically, from top to bottom.

Starting at the top, we see the early mutual influence of the conceptual framework and research questions. Both lead to plans for sampling (within and across cases) and instrumentation. Once the sampling plan is clear, access to cases starts and data collection begins.

During this time, it's a good idea to build a well-defined data management system, which will be used—with evolutionary changes—throughout the project. We also advocate building a documentation scheme for regular tracking of project data analysis activities.

The first experiences of data collection nearly always have back effects (dashed lines), which induce reconsideration not only of sampling and instrumentation but also of the conceptual framework itself. Initial processing of the data often leads to interim summaries of various kinds, which also

DISPLAY 13.1   ◆   Overview of Qualitative Data Analysis Processes

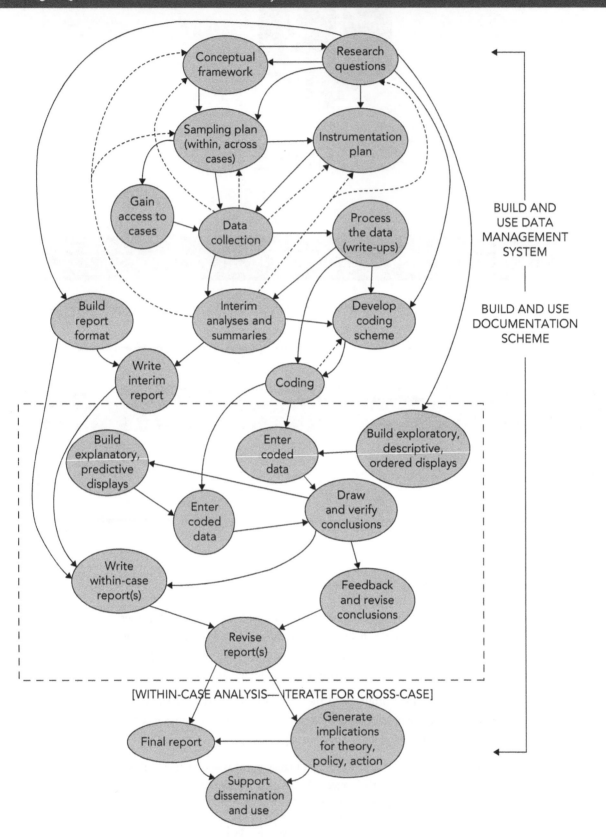

BUILD AND
USE DATA
MANAGEMENT
SYSTEM

BUILD AND USE
DOCUMENTATION
SCHEME

[WITHIN-CASE ANALYSIS—ITERATE FOR CROSS-CASE]

Source: Miles, M. B., & Huberman, A. M. (1994). *Qualitative data analysis: An expanded sourcebook* (2nd ed.). Thousand Oaks, CA: Sage Publications.

have effects back to the sampling and instrumentation approaches being taken as well as, more conceptually, to the framework and the research questions.

The initial coding scheme is usually influenced by the research questions, but it develops and iterates steadily as further coding is carried out. Interim analyses also make a clear contribution here. If interim reports are contemplated, a format is designed at this point, and the interim summaries are fed into it.

After assuming a body of coded data (not necessarily complete or full), the next move is into within-case analysis. The general strategy is to build, first, *exploratory*, *descriptive*, and *ordered* display formats designed to answer the research questions. Coded data are entered and, from them, conclusions of a descriptive sort are drawn and verified. With those conclusions in hand, *explanatory* (and, if needed, *predictive*) displays can be built; coded data can be entered; and explanatory conclusions can be drawn.

Both descriptive and explanatory conclusions can be fed back for verification and revision. By now, a format for within-site reporting, based as always on the research questions as well as on the interim results, has been prepared. Within-case reports are written and then revised on the basis of respondent feedback.

If more than one case is included, this entire cycle of within-case analysis is repeated to draw cross-case conclusions. These conclusions and the within-case results go into the final report, which will include implications for theory, policy, and action. Depending on the study's audiences and intentions, some degree of support for dissemination and use of the findings will be provided.

Any particular project will always loop among the nodes of Display 13.1 in idiosyncratic ways. The issue is to be aware of where you are in the flow right now, and where you want to be by a later date.

REFLECTIONS

Writing and revising this book has been a long, sometimes arduous, and always fascinating journey. We have encountered many new and thoughtful treatments of qualitative data analysis. The experience has reconfirmed the old saying that trying to teach something deepens your understanding of it—or, as the folk saying goes, "To teach is to learn twice." The process of clarifying, reformulating, and synthesizing the ideas in this fourth edition has extended and enriched our thinking about qualitative data analysis methods.

Throughout the book, we have tried to stay practical, "talking aloud" as we went, offering both methods and advice. Some qualitative data analysis texts tend toward the abstract, with brief examples that always seem to work out clearly, even effortlessly. Yet when you actually come to grips with collecting and analyzing real-life data, things seldom work out that way. Research-in-use is almost always messier and more disjointed than research-in-theory, and we have tried to take careful account of that fact. In short, *doing* qualitative analysis is the way you get better at it—and we believe that holds true not just for novices and new entrants to qualitative work but for seasoned researchers as well.

We believe that methodological quagmires, mazes, and dead ends are not necessarily a product of researcher incapacity but of qualitative data themselves. Like the phenomena they mirror, they are usually complex, ambiguous, and sometimes downright contradictory. Doing qualitative analysis means living for as long as possible with that complexity and ambiguity, coming to terms with it, and passing on your conclusions to the reader in a form that clarifies and deepens understanding.

It's not surprising that the mechanics of analysis seem formidable or elusive even to experienced analysts—and that researchers have often shied away from making them fully explicit.

It's right to say that qualitative data analysis is a *craft*—one that carries its own methodical and technical ways of working. We've found that making the steps of analysis explicit makes them less formidable and uncertain, and more manageable. The core requisites for qualitative analysis seem to be a little systematic doggedness, some good conceptual sensibilities, and cognitive flexibility—the capacity to rapidly undo your way of construing or transforming the data and to try another, more promising approach.

But qualitative data analysis is also an *art*—one that requires creative thinking, innovative problem solving, adaptive inventiveness, and the ability to render data in visual forms and formats. It asks you to think conceptually, symbolically, and metaphorically. The entire social research enterprise demands that you have keen insight into people's actions and feelings, and a deep understanding of their complex routines, rituals, rules, roles, and relationships (Saldaña & Omasta, 2018). In revising this book, we have continued our hope from the first three editions: To create a self-help book for researchers, rather than standardizing an accessible set of methods.

Qualitative researchers come in many varieties and flavors. The views we have expressed will almost certainly be seen as narrow-minded, perhaps even outdated, by some of our colleagues. We don't want to be seen as pretending to be ideology-free, or that our biases are noblest, or that we are just being old fashioned, plain folks—pragmatic and practical without understanding the issues.

To those who believe that analysis is an intuitive, nearly incommunicable act, we have insisted that analyses can be workably replicated, and that to be taken seriously, you should be fully explicit about what is being done at each step of the way.

To those who believe that qualitative data analysis requires years of training and apprenticeship, we have offered an expanded set of working methods that can be tried on for size and adapted or modified for particular projects—all in the service of a stronger methodology.

To those enamored of long narrative accounts as the sole route to understanding, we have counterposed the idea of focused, organized displays that permit systematic analyses and enhance confidence in findings.

To those who believe that nowadays we can put forth only our ambiguities, uncertainties, and unanswered questions as conclusions, we acknowledge the social complexities of contemporary life, but we also reinforce that the purpose of research is ultimately to reveal, clarify, and construct significant awareness, understanding, and meaning.

To those colleagues who are pleased with what we have done in this fourth edition, we express our gratitude, along with our hope for continuous testing and revision of these methods, so that we all can advance our craft and art.

FINAL ADVICE

Throughout the book, we've provided detailed advice on a method-by-method basis. Here, we offer some generalized last words of encouragement to our colleagues, of whatever persuasion.

Think display. Given a research question or a puzzling issue in a qualitative database, consider what forms of display—matrices, networks, or graphics—are most likely to bring together relevant, transformed data in a way that will permit good conclusion drawing and the strengthening of those conclusions.

Be open to invention. The wide range of methods we and many others have created reinforces our belief that the repertoire of useful displays is very large and, like other collections, constantly expanding. Don't shy away from more progressive forms of data display such as poetry and performance.

Expect iteration. The modes of analysis we've advocated throughout the book involve shuttling among data condensation, display, and preliminary and verified conclusions. New data enter the picture, new display forms evolve, and conclusions get reshaped and revised. All of these will have iterative effects on each other, effects that are crucial to the evolving analysis.

Seek formalization, and distrust it. We have steadily emphasized a structured approach to drawing meaning from qualitative data. Becoming more systematic, whatever your epistemological position, strikes us as a priority for those who wish to advance analysis methodology. Of course, increased formalization carries its own risks: narrowness, overconfidence, obsessiveness, and blindness to the emergent—and the risk of arrogant orthodoxy. Patience, trying to do things better, humility, collaboration, and accepting multiple perspectives are more like it.

Entertain mixed methods and models. Quantitative and qualitative inquiry can support and inform each other. Narratives and statistics need to interpenetrate and collaborate. Realists, idealists, and critical theorists can do better by incorporating other ideas than by remaining pure. Think of it as hybrid vigor, or eclectic rigor.

Stay self-aware. Our own experience showed us vividly how useful it is to maintain a part of your attention on the processes involved in analysis—from the selection of research questions through coding, the creation of displays, data entry, conclusion drawing, and verification. Only through such sustained reflexive awareness can regular self-correction occur—not just during specific analysis episodes but over time, as the methods themselves iterate and develop.

Share methodological learnings. The methodological sections of most reports of qualitative studies are still thin. Articles focusing directly on analysis issues and approaches are emerging but are still relatively few in number. We believe that anyone who wants to advance the craft and art of qualitative analysis owes it to colleagues to communicate what he or she has learned to others. We advise stronger methodological emphasis in articles and books, and we encourage reports of training methods in courses and workshops that have successfully expanded analysis skills.

In sum, we hope that more and more qualitative researchers and data analysts will share with each other, concretely and specifically, just how they went about their research and what they learned. Perhaps we can all be as vivid and rich in describing our own work as we are in describing the inner and outer lives of the people we study.

APPENDIX

An Annotated Bibliography of Qualitative Research Methods Resources

This appendix includes a selected listing of recommended titles for learning more about qualitative inquiry. It is limited to English-language works and primarily monographs. We cannot possibly include everything in print and online; we provide only a representative sample of resources.

REFERENCE TEXTS FOR QUALITATIVE INQUIRY

Bothamley, J. (1993). *Dictionary of theories*. London: Gale Research International. Reference guide to theories from all disciplines, including the arts, sociology, psychology, history, and the natural sciences—useful for terminology reference, definitions, and associated names.

Given, L. M. (Ed.). (2008). *The SAGE encyclopedia of qualitative research methods*. Thousand Oaks, CA: Sage. Superior reference for summaries of philosophical and methodological principles of qualitative inquiry.

Schwandt, T. A. (2015). *Dictionary of qualitative inquiry* (4th ed.). Thousand Oaks, CA: Sage. Extended dictionary of terms in the field; many entries include origins of the terms, applications across various social science fields, and references for additional investigation.

QUANTITATIVE AND QUALITATIVE RESEARCH DESIGN (GENERAL TEXTBOOKS)

Creswell, J. W., & Creswell, J. D. (2018). *Research design: Qualitative, quantitative, and mixed methods approaches* (5th ed.). Thousand Oaks, CA: Sage. Excellent overview of all three paradigms for the beginning researcher.

Durdella, N. (2019). *Qualitative dissertation methodology: A guide for research design and methods*. Thousand Oaks, CA: Sage. Overview of designing and writing about qualitative approaches, specifically for dissertation content and format.

Leavy, P. (2017). *Research design: Quantitative, qualitative, mixed methods, arts-based, and community-based participatory research approaches*. New York: Guilford. Introductory overview of five methodologies for research approaches.

Mertens, D. M. (2015). *Research and evaluation in education and psychology* (4th ed.). Thousand Oaks, CA: Sage. Introductory text that surveys various approaches to research but focuses more on the quantitative approach; compares various paradigms (emancipatory, feminist, etc.) and offers detailed guidelines for research design or evaluation of research.

Wilkinson, D., & Birmingham, P. (2003). *Using research instruments: A guide for researchers*. London: Routledge. User-friendly introduction to techniques such as survey construction, interview questions, focus group facilitation, participant observation, content analysis, and so on.

QUALITATIVE RESEARCH (GENERAL TEXTBOOKS)

Bhattacharya, K. (2017). *Fundamentals of qualitative research: A practical guide*. New York: Routledge. An activities-based introduction to key facets of inquiry. Provides questions and prompts for student participation and reflection.

Creswell, J. W. (2016). *30 essential skills for the qualitative researcher*. Thousand Oaks, CA: Sage. Thirty modules, ranging from research design to write-ups, are offered with practical guidance.

Creswell, J. W., & Poth, C. N. (2018). *Qualitative inquiry and research design: Choosing among five approaches* (4th ed.). Thousand Oaks, CA: Sage. Describes and compares the unique features of narrative research, phenomenology, grounded theory, ethnography, and case study research; includes article examples.

Gibson, W. J., & Brown, A. (2009). *Working with qualitative data*. London: Sage. An introductory overview with an emphasis on philosophical foundations of inquiry and data collection in various forms.

Glesne, C. (2016). *Becoming qualitative researchers: An introduction* (5th ed.). Boston: Pearson Education. Excellent overview and introductory text on the nature and process of qualitative research/ethnography.

Lofland, J., Snow, D. A., Anderson, L., & Lofland, L. H. (2006). *Analyzing social settings: A guide to qualitative observation and analysis* (4th ed.). Belmont, CA: Wadsworth. Highly systematic techniques for qualitative studies; a dense but comprehensive "how to" text.

Marshall, C., & Rossman, G. B. (2016). *Designing qualitative research* (6th ed.). Thousand Oaks, CA: Sage. Overview of considerations for the preparatory phases of qualitative studies; written for doctoral students; provides numerous illustrative vignettes.

Mason, J. (2002). *Qualitative researching* (2nd ed.). London: Sage. Overview of qualitative research based on ontological, epistemological, and methodological decision making; includes a series of questions to consider during all phases of research.

Maxwell, J. A. (2013). *Qualitative research design: An interactive approach* (3rd ed.). Thousand Oaks, CA: Sage. Particularly thorough book for preparing research proposals by considering how research design elements link together.

Morse, J. M. (2012). *Qualitative health research: Creating a new discipline*. Walnut Creek, CA: Left Coast Press. A rich and insightful primer on researching a disciplinary practice from one of its premiere methodologists; recommended reading for those not in health care.

Richards, L., & Morse, J. M. (2013). *Readme first for a user's guide to qualitative methods* (3rd ed.). Thousand Oaks, CA: Sage. Introduction to principles of qualitative research for phenomenology, ethnography, and grounded theory.

Saldaña, J. (2011). *Fundamentals of qualitative research*. New York: Oxford University Press. A survey of qualitative research methods with an emphasis on qualitative data analysis; good resource for undergraduates.

Saldaña, J. (2015). *Thinking qualitatively: Methods of mind*. Thousand Oaks, CA: Sage. A reader of over 60 modules for thinking about qualitative inquiry, data, and analysis; utilizes principles of brain-based learning for metacognition and research reflection.

Saldaña, J., & Omasta, M. (2018). *Qualitative research: Analyzing life.* Thousand Oaks, CA: Sage. An introductory textbook that utilizes data analysis as a frame and through-line for conducting social inquiry; includes sample articles.

Savin-Baden, M., & Major, C. L. (2013). *Qualitative research: The essential guide to theory and practice.* New York: Routledge. A comprehensive overview of all facets of inquiry, intended as an all-in-one text on the topic.

Stake, R. E. (2010). *Qualitative research: Studying how things work.* New York: Guilford. Introduces global principles of qualitative inquiry, with a focus on interpretation and assertion development.

MIXED METHODS RESEARCH

Bazeley, P. (2018). *Integrating analyses in mixed methods research.* London: Sage. A sophisticated text on how the properties of quantitative and qualitative data analytically integrate; includes numerous examples and graphics from published studies.

Creamer, E. G. (2018). *An introduction to fully integrated mixed methods research.* Thousand Oaks, CA: Sage. Superior introduction to mixed methods and specific strategies for each data paradigm's integration during design, collection, analysis, and write-up.

Creswell, J. W., & Plano Clark, V. L. (2018). *Designing and conducting mixed methods research* (3rd ed.). Thousand Oaks, CA: Sage. Primer on mixing quantitative and qualitative paradigms and data in research studies; includes sample articles.

Morgan, D. L. (2014). *Integrating qualitative & quantitative methods: A pragmatic approach.* Thousand Oaks, CA: Sage. Offers philosophical, methodological, and design guidance for the structure of mixed methods studies.

Morrison, K. (2009). *Causation in educational research.* London: Routledge. Superior overview of the intricacies and nuances of causation in both quantitative and qualitative research; recommended for researchers from all fields of study.

O'Dwyer, L. M., & Bernauer, J. A. (2014). *Quantitative research for the qualitative researcher.* Thousand Oaks, CA: Sage. Introduction to statistics and statistical tests and their integration with the qualitative paradigm.

Plano Clark, V. L., & Ivankova, N. V. (2016). *Mixed methods research: A guide to the field.* Thousand Oaks, CA: Sage. Comprehensive and systematic overview of mixed methods principles and practices; extensive references to the literature.

Tashakkori, A., & Teddlie, C. (Eds.). (2010). *SAGE handbook of mixed methods in social and behavioral research* (2nd ed.). Thousand Oaks, CA: Sage. Extensive chapters on the current trend in mixing the quantitative and qualitative paradigms for research.

Thomas, R. M. (2003). *Blending qualitative and quantitative research methods in theses and dissertations.* Thousand Oaks, CA: Corwin. Overview of methods from both paradigms, but primarily a collection of brief prospectus examples from 20 student works that illustrate the blending of data forms.

METHODOLOGICAL FOUNDATIONS/ HANDBOOKS OF QUALITATIVE RESEARCH

Becker, H. S. (1998). *Tricks of the trade: How to think about your research while you're doing it.* Chicago: University of Chicago Press. A classic in methodology; not a "how to" book but a compelling reader on strategic thinking for inquiry.

Denzin, N. K., & Lincoln, Y. S. (Eds.). (2018). *The SAGE handbook of qualitative research* (5th ed.). Thousand Oaks, CA: Sage. A collection of chapters on various topics of qualitative research by selected experts in the field.

Ellingson, L. L. (2009). *Engaging crystallization in qualitative research: An introduction.* Thousand Oaks, CA: Sage. Strategies for blending two or more approaches to qualitative inquiry, ranging from arts-based approaches to traditional constructivist methodologies (e.g., grounded theory).

Hesse-Biber, S. N., & Leavy, P. (2008). *Handbook of emergent methods.* New York: Guilford. Chapters on new methods of qualitative and selected quantitative inquiry at the beginning of the 21st century, including research with media, mixed methods, documents, and so on.

Leavy, P. (Ed.). (2015). *The Oxford handbook of qualitative research.* New York: Oxford University Press. Chapter collection of practical approaches to all components of qualitative inquiry.

Lincoln, Y. S., & Denzin, N. K. (2003). *Turning points in qualitative research: Tying knots in a handkerchief.* Walnut Creek, CA: AltaMira. Collection of seminal essays and articles in the field of qualitative research by writers such as Clifford Geertz, Margaret Mead, Dwight Conquergood, and others.

Lincoln, Y. S., & Guba, E. G. (1985). *Naturalistic inquiry.* Beverly Hills, CA: Sage. Detailed argument on the naturalistic paradigm as a valid framework for research and analysis; includes methods for establishing trustworthiness and audits.

Packer, M. J. (2011). *The science of qualitative research.* New York: Cambridge University Press. A title on the ontologies and epistemologies of qualitative inquiry; extensive scholarship and overview of knowledge construction.

Pascale, C.-M. (2011). *Cartographies of knowledge: Exploring qualitative epistemologies.* Thousand Oaks, CA: Sage. Overview of theoretical and historical foundations that shape current practices of qualitative research; focuses on analytic induction, symbolic interaction, and ethnomethodology.

SYMBOLIC INTERACTIONISM

Blumer, H. (1969). *Symbolic interactionism: Perspective and method.* Englewood Cliffs, NJ: Prentice Hall. Collection of essays by Blumer detailing the interpretive process of human and group action, labeled "symbolic interactionism"; a seminal method for later research methodologists.

Denzin, N. K. (1992). *Symbolic interactionism and cultural studies: The politics of interpretation.* Cambridge, MA: Blackwell. Commentary and critique on proponents and opponents of symbolic interactionism; Chapter 6, "Interactionist Cultural Criticism," has applicability to arts and multicultural researchers.

Prus, R. C. (1996). *Symbolic interaction and ethnographic research: Intersubjectivity and the study of human lived experience.* New York: SUNY Press. Detailed explanations and approach to symbolic interactionism and its function in ethnography; excellent discussion and outline of social processes and studying emotions in sociological research.

ETHNOGRAPHY/ANTHROPOLOGY

Angrosino, M. V. (2007). *Doing cultural anthropology: Projects in ethnographic data collection* (2nd ed.). Prospect Heights, IL: Waveland. Excellent primer on ethnographic data collection, with various projects for individuals and groups.

Atkinson, P. (2015). *For ethnography.* London: Sage. Insights and reflections on selected topics of ethnographic practice from one of its foremost writers.

Bernard, H. R. (2018). *Research methods in anthropology: Qualitative and quantitative approaches* (6th ed.). Lanham, MD: Rowman & Littlefield. Reader-friendly and exhaustive overview of research methods in both paradigms; more for advanced researchers with a focus on traditional anthropological field work.

Brown, I. C. (1963). *Understanding other cultures*. Englewood Cliffs, NJ: Prentice Hall. A layperson's introduction to anthropology; despite the early publication date, the book has a remarkable timelessness; surveys basic human constructs such as religion, arts, kinship, values, work, and so on.

Coffey, A. (2018). *Doing ethnography*. London: Sage. An excellent primer of the fundamentals of ethnographic field work and writing; lacks illustrative examples (of field notes, interview transcripts, etc.) but presents an elegant overview of the research method.

Collins, S. G., & Durington, M. S. (2015). *Networked anthropology: A primer for ethnographers*. New York: Routledge. Excellent discussion of how digital and ethnographic practices interface in contemporary field work.

Fetterman, D. M. (2010). *Ethnography: Step by step* (3rd ed.). Thousand Oaks, CA: Sage. Excellent overview of methods and techniques involved with field research from an ethnographic approach; includes information on computer utilization, websites, and data management.

Galman, S. C. (2019). *Shane, the lone ethnographer: A beginner's guide to ethnography* (2nd ed.). Lanham, MD: Rowman & Littlefield. Humorous cartoon drawing overview of a graduate student learning how to conduct an ethnography.

Geertz, C. (1973). *The interpretation of cultures*. New York: Basic Books. Seminal essays on ethnographic writing in anthropology, including "Thick Description: Toward an Interpretive Theory of Culture," and "Deep Play: Notes on a Balinese Cockfight."

Geertz, C. (1983). *Local knowledge: Further essays in interpretive anthropology*. New York: Basic Books. Chapters 1 to 7 present intriguing essays on topics such as "blurred genres," "common sense," and "art" as culturally constructed systems.

Gobo, G., & Molle, A. (2017). *Doing ethnography* (2nd ed.). London: Sage. Detailed introduction to ethnographic practices with an emphasis on the mechanics of field work.

Hammersley, M. (1992). *What's wrong with ethnography?* New York: Routledge. Essays on methodological questions and issues about validity, generalizability, quantitative vs. qualitative, and so on, in ethnographic practice; requires reader background experience in ethnography.

Hammersley, M., & Atkinson, P. (2007). *Ethnography: Principles in practice* (3rd ed.). London: Routledge. A distinctively U.K. approach to the research genre; rigorous and rooted in traditional approaches.

Handwerker, W. P. (2001). *Quick ethnography*. Walnut Creek, CA: AltaMira. Qualitative and quantitative methods for short-term ethnographic work; systematic procedures for extracting variability of cultural variables.

Handwerker, W. P. (2015). *Our story: How cultures shaped people to get things done*. Walnut Creek, CA: Left Coast Press. A brief and intriguing reader on aspects of cognitive anthropology; superior insights on human motivations.

Madden, R. (2017). *Being ethnographic: A guide to the theory and practice of ethnography* (2nd ed.). London: Sage. Excellent conceptual and practical overview of foundations for ethnographic field work; not many examples of "how to" but a solid narrative overview of "what" and "why."

McCurdy, D. W., Spradley, J. P., & Shandy, D. J. (2005). *The cultural experience: Ethnography in complex society* (2nd ed.). Long Grove, IL: Waveland. For undergraduate ethnography courses, provides an overview of ethnographic interviewing and taxonomic domain development; includes students' sample reports.

Norris, J., Sawyer, R. D., & Lund, D. (Eds.). (2012). *Duoethnography: Dialogic methods for social, health, and educational research*. Walnut Creek, CA: Left Coast Press. A collaborative methodology in which two or more researchers exchange perceptions of personal life histories to better understand a social phenomenon.

Pink, S. (2013). *Doing visual ethnography* (3rd ed.). London: Sage. An overview of the use of photography, video, and hypermedia in ethnographic field work for representation and presentation.

Pink, S., Horst, H., Postill, J., Hjorth, L., Lewis, T., & Tacchi, J. (2016). *Digital ethnography: Principles and practice*. London: Sage. Excellent discussion of how digital culture is examined through an ethnographic lens; explores relationships, events, materiality.

Sunstein, B. S., & Chiseri-Strater, E. (2012). *FieldWorking: Reading and writing research* (4th ed.). Boston: Bedford/St. Martin's. User-friendly introduction to ethnographic field work; includes numerous student samples of writing.

Thomas, J. (1993). *Doing critical ethnography*. Newbury Park, CA: Sage. Monograph on critical approaches to qualitative research to examine power structures, race relationships, and so on, for social change.

Wiseman, B., & Groves, J. (1997). *Lévi-Strauss for beginners*. London: Icon Books. An introduction to the major cultural theories by one of the 20th century's most noted structural anthropologists.

Wolcott, H. F. (2005). *The art of fieldwork* (2nd ed.). Walnut Creek, CA: AltaMira. An overview of fundamental principles and sage advice on educational anthropology from one of the leaders in the field.

Wolcott, H. F. (2008). *Ethnography: A way of seeing* (2nd ed.). Walnut Creek, CA: AltaMira. For those with some ethnographic background, a foundational text on the purposes and charges of ethnography; superior chapter (Chapter 11) on the concept of culture.

GROUNDED THEORY

Birks, M., & Mills, J. (2016). *Grounded theory: A practical guide* (2nd ed.). London: Sage. General descriptive overview of the method; includes a few examples for guidance.

Bryant, A. (2017). *Grounded theory and grounded theorizing: Pragmatism in research practice*. New York: Oxford University Press. Superior methodological discussion of the various approaches to and components of grounded theory.

Bryant, A., & Charmaz, K. (2007). *The SAGE handbook of grounded theory*. London: Sage. Chapters on the nuances of grounded theory methodology; not for beginners of the method.

Charmaz, K. (2014). *Constructing grounded theory* (2nd ed.). London: Sage. A clear and concise overview of grounded theory method; provides an excellent theoretical and explanatory overview of the classic procedures developed by Strauss, Glaser, and Corbin.

Clarke, A. E., Friese, C., & Washburn, R. S. (2018). *Situational analysis: Grounded theory after the interpretive turn* (2nd ed.). Thousand Oaks, CA: Sage. Adaptation of grounded theory, which acknowledges the complexity and context of social process through the development of situational maps, charts, and graphics; extensive background on epistemological foundations for the method.

Corbin, J., & Strauss, A. L. (2015). *Basics of qualitative research: Techniques and procedures for developing grounded theory* (4th ed.). Thousand Oaks, CA: Sage. The fourth edition does not systematically focus on techniques; it does, however, profile analytic memo writing extensively.

Gibson, B., & Hartman, J. (2014). *Discovering grounded theory*. London: Sage. Offers a detailed overview of the classical/traditional approaches to grounded theory with excellent guidance on analytic memoing.

Glaser, B. G., & Strauss, A. L. (1967). *The discovery of grounded theory: Strategies for qualitative research.* Hawthorne, CA: Aldine de Gruyter. Premiere work on the constant-comparative method of data analysis to generate grounded theory.

Holton, J. A., & Walsh, I. (2017). *Classic grounded theory: Applications with qualitative & quantitative data.* Thousand Oaks, CA: Sage. An overview of traditional grounded theory principles as originally conceived and their execution with projects.

Stern, P. N., & Porr, C. J. (2011). *Essentials of accessible grounded theory.* Walnut Creek, CA: Left Coast Press. An elegant summary and synthesis of "classic" Glaserian grounded theory.

Urquhart, C. (2013). *Grounded theory for qualitative research: A practical guide.* London: Sage. Follows traditional models and procedures for grounded theory research; excellent discussion on how theory derives from data analysis and memoing.

PHENOMENOLOGY

Brinkmann, S. (2012). *Qualitative inquiry in everyday life: Working with everyday life materials.* London: Sage. Fascinating self-exploration of and research about everyday experiences, including our interactions with humans, media, fiction, and artifacts.

Smith, J. A., Flowers, P., & Larkin, M. (2009). *Interpretative phenomenological analysis: Theory, method and research.* London: Sage. Interpretative phenomenological analysis from a psychological perspective; clear description of the origins and processes; includes sample studies that use interpretative phenomenological analysis.

Vagle, M. D. (2018). *Crafting phenomenological research* (2nd ed.). New York: Routledge. Elegant overview of phenomenological philosophy and practices through a "post-intentional" lens.

van Manen, M. (1997). *Researching lived experience: Human science for an action sensitive pedagogy* (2nd ed.). New York: Routledge. A classic of the field; focus is on phenomenology and its reporting, plus the purposes of this type of research, primarily in education.

CASE STUDY RESEARCH

Denzin, N. K. (2001). *Interpretive interactionism* (2nd ed.). Thousand Oaks, CA: Sage. Methodology and methods for biographical research of an individual's epiphanies.

Stake, R. E. (1995). *The art of case study research.* Thousand Oaks, CA: Sage. "Artistic" approach to profiling the case study; a good introduction to the method.

Yin, R. K. (2018). *Case study research and applications: Design and methods* (6th ed.). Thousand Oaks, CA: Sage. Overview of research design principles for case studies of individuals, organizations, and so on; somewhat post-positivist in its approach, but a good overview of the fundamentals of design and analysis.

EVALUATION RESEARCH

Patton, M. Q. (2015). *Qualitative research and evaluation methods: Integrating theory and practice* (4th ed.). Thousand Oaks, CA: Sage. Designed for evaluation research initially, now an excellent overview of paradigms, methods and techniques for observation and interviews.

Patton, M. Q. (2008). *Utilization-focused evaluation* (4th ed.). Thousand Oaks, CA: Sage. Exhaustive resource for evaluation methods, especially for programs and organizations.

Wadsworth, Y. (2011). *Everyday evaluation on the run: The user-friendly introductory guide to effective evaluation* (3rd ed.). Walnut Creek, CA: Left Coast Press. A layperson's guide, but includes a broad overview of basics and models.

AUTOETHNOGRAPHY

Adams, T. E., Jones, S. H., & Ellis, C. (2015). *Autoethnography.* New York: Oxford University Press. Introductory overview of the principles and methods of writing autoethnography.

Chang, H. (2008). *Autoethnography as method.* Walnut Creek, CA: Left Coast Press. Systematic approach to autoethnographic research; includes an excellent overview of cultural concepts.

Ellis, C., & Bochner, A. P. (Eds.). (1996). *Composing ethnography: Alternative forms of qualitative writing.* Walnut Creek, CA: AltaMira. Collection of autoethnographies focusing on social issues such as domestic violence, bulimia, detoxification, and discrimination.

Jones, S. H., Adams, T. E., & Ellis, C. (Eds.). (2013). *Handbook of autoethnography.* Walnut Creek, CA: Left Coast Press. Comprehensive collection of chapters on method and exemplars of autoethnographic writing.

Poulos, C. N. (2009). *Accidental ethnography: An inquiry into family secrecy.* Walnut Creek, CA: Left Coast Press. Autoethnographic stories and writing prompts for personal and family history.

Spry, T. (2011). *Body, paper, stage: Writing and performing autoethnography.* Walnut Creek, CA: Left Coast Press. Selected works from Spry, plus theoretical and practical approaches to performance studies.

NARRATIVE INQUIRY

Clandinin, D. J., & Connelly, F. M. (2000). *Narrative inquiry: Experience and story in qualitative research.* San Francisco: Jossey-Bass. Methods of three-dimensional renderings of participants in narrative inquiry.

Daiute, C. (2014). *Narrative inquiry: A dynamic approach.* Thousand Oaks, CA: Sage. Offers specific analytic approaches to narratives, focusing on features such as values, plot, significance, character, and time.

Gubrium, J. F., & Holstein, J. A. (2009). *Analyzing narrative reality.* Thousand Oaks, CA: Sage. Not a "how to" book, but an excellent overview of what to be aware of and look for when analyzing narrative texts from field work.

Holstein, J. A., & Gubrium, J. F. (2012). *Varieties of narrative analysis.* Thousand Oaks, CA: Sage. Chapter collection of varied approaches to the analysis of narrative texts, ranging from mixed methods to psychological interpretations.

Kim, J.-H. (2016). *Understanding narrative inquiry: The crafting and analysis of stories as research.* Thousand Oaks, CA: Sage. Provides an overview of the method, ranging from theoretical foundations, data collection, and write-ups as narratives.

Riessman, C. K. (2008). *Narrative methods for the human sciences.* Thousand Oaks, CA: Sage. Not necessarily a "how to" text, but surveys with examples of four major approaches to narrative analysis; contains representative examples about children and adolescents.

DISCOURSE AND CONVERSATION ANALYSIS

Bischoping, K., & Gazso, A. (2016). *Analyzing talk in the social sciences.* London: Sage. Three strategies for analyzing talk—narrative, conversation, and discourse analysis—are profiled with examples and guidance.

Boréus, K., & Bergström, G. (Eds.). (2017). *Analyzing text and discourse: Eight approaches for the social sciences.* London: Sage. Chapter collection of approaches such as content analysis, narrative analysis, argumentation analysis, discourse analysis, metaphor analysis, and so on.

Gee, J. P. (2014). *How to do discourse analysis: A toolkit* (2nd ed.). New York: Routledge. A series of questions and perspectives to consider when analyzing language in documented data and narratives; considers aspects such as grammar, vocabulary, intertextuality, identity, politics, and so on.

Lester, J. N., & O'Reilly, M. (2019). *Applied conversation analysis.* Thousand Oaks, CA: Sage. An introduction to the method for graduate students and novices; utilizes the Jefferson notation system for data documentation and analysis.

Rapley, T. (2018). *Doing conversation, discourse and document analysis.* London: Sage. A primer in the topic areas with examples; includes good recording and transcription recommendations.

ARTS-BASED RESEARCH

Ackroyd, J., & O'Toole, J. (2010). *Performing research: Tensions, triumphs and trade-offs of ethnodrama.* Stoke on Trent, England: Trentham Books. Treatise on the genre (terminology, ethics, representation, etc.) and six case studies of ethnodrama projects in Australia and Hong Kong.

Barone, T., & Eisner, E. W. (2012). *Arts based research.* Thousand Oaks, CA: Sage. Two pioneers in the genre offer methodological and aesthetic perspectives and criteria for this approach to qualitative inquiry.

Batty, C., & Kerrigan, S. (Eds.). (2018). *Screen production research: Creative practice as a mode of enquiry.* Cham, Switzerland: Palgrave Macmillan. Chapter collection of scholarly pieces on screenplays and film production as forms of qualitative research.

Butler-Kisber, L. (2018). *Qualitative inquiry: Thematic, narrative and arts-based perspectives* (2nd ed.). London: Sage. Overview of various modalities of qualitative inquiry, including approaches such as narrative, phenomenology, collage, poetry, photography, and performance.

Cahnmann-Taylor, M., & Siegesmund, R. (Eds.). (2018). *Arts-based research in education: Foundations for practice* (2nd ed.). New York: Routledge. Chapter collection from leading figures in the field on the use of the arts with and as educational research.

Denzin, N. K. (1997). *Interpretive ethnography: Ethnographic practices for the 21st century.* Thousand Oaks, CA: Sage. Inspirational reading about new, progressive forms of ethnography including performance texts, journalism, and poetics.

Eisner, E. W. (1993). *The enlightened eye: Qualitative inquiry and the enhancement of educational practice.* New York: Macmillan. An "artistic" approach to qualitative inquiry. Does not profile methods but provides an intriguing, commonsense approach to knowledge construction by the researcher.

Gergen, M. M., & Gergen, K. J. (2012). *Playing with purpose: Adventures in performative social science.* Walnut Creek, CA: Left Coast Press. Overview of arts-based modalities in qualitative inquiry—narrative, drama, visual art—and their theoretical groundings.

Janesick, V. J. (2015). *"Stretching" exercises for qualitative researchers* (4th ed.). Thousand Oaks, CA: Sage. A series of arts-based exercises for honing observation, interview, and conceptualization skills of researchers.

Knowles, J. G., & Cole, A. L. (2008). *Handbook of the arts in qualitative research: Perspectives, methodologies, examples, and issues.* Thousand Oaks, CA: Sage. Collection of essays on arts-based research, including theatre.

Leavy, P. (2015). *Method meets art: Arts-based research practice* (2nd ed.). New York: Guilford. Chapter overview of arts-based research techniques, with representative samples of the genre.

Leavy, P. (Ed.). (2018). *Handbook of arts-based research.* New York: Guilford. Chapter collection of premiere writers and artists in the field showcasing their methods and work.

Madison, D. S., & Hamera, J. (2006). *The SAGE handbook of performance studies.* Thousand Oaks, CA: Sage. Collection of essays on the field of performance studies; includes a few good selections.

Nisbet, R. (1976). *Sociology as an art form.* New York: Oxford University Press. Comparison of how the fine arts, humanities, and sociology have historic parallels in paradigm development and conceptual approaches; also addresses modern parallels in the goals and functions of both disciplines.

Norris, J. (2010). *Playbuilding as qualitative research: A participatory arts-based approach.* Walnut Creek, CA: Left Coast Press. Norris examines how playbuilding original devised work both employs and serves as a qualitative research modality/genre.

Saldaña, J. (2005). *Ethnodrama: An anthology of reality theatre.* Walnut Creek, CA: AltaMira Press. Collection of nine examples of play scripts developed from qualitative and ethnographic research (interviews, participant observation).

Saldaña, J. (2011). *Ethnotheatre: Research from page to stage.* Walnut Creek, CA: Left Coast Press. A playwriting textbook for ethnodramatic forms of research representation and presentation; includes extensive bibliographies of plays, articles, media, and texts.

ACTION/PARTICIPATORY ACTION RESEARCH

Altrichter, H., Feldman, A., Posch, P., & Somekh, B. (2008). *Teachers investigate their work: An introduction to action research across the professions* (2nd ed.). New York: Routledge. Superior text on action research; includes practical examples and techniques for generating a focal point and analyzing data.

Coghlan, D., & Brannick, T. (2014). *Doing action research in your own organization* (4th ed.). London: Sage. Dense, but practical, manual on the logistics of action research in business and education; not much on data analysis, but superior foregrounding, especially on the human aspects of change.

Fox, M., Martin, P., & Green, G. (2007). *Doing practitioner research.* London: Sage. Superior overview of practitioner research for those in the service and helping professions; provides excellent foundations for clinical and educational research.

Hitchcock, G., & Hughes, D. (1995). *Research and the teacher: A qualitative introduction to school-based research* (2nd ed.). London: Routledge. General survey of how the teacher can also play the role of researcher in the classroom; examples tailored to the British school system, but the methods are universal.

Schön, D. A. (1983). *The reflective practitioner: How professionals think in action.* New York: Basic Books. Methodological basis of "reflection-in-action" in selected professions; describes the cognitive and communicative processes of problem solving; a foundational book for action researchers.

Stringer, E. T. (2014). *Action research* (4th ed.). Thousand Oaks, CA: Sage. Detailed methods for community and collaborative research projects to improve or change existing social practices.

Thomas, R. M. (2005). *Teachers doing research: An introductory guidebook.* Boston: Pearson Education. General overview of teacher-as-researcher models in quantitative and qualitative studies; provides brush-stroke description and examples.

Wadsworth, Y. (2011). *Do it yourself social research* (3rd ed.). Walnut Creek, CA: Left Coast Press. An introductory overview of basic social research principles for community program evaluation.

LONGITUDINAL/LIFE COURSE RESEARCH

Giele, J. Z., & Elder, G. H., Jr. (Eds.). (1998). *Methods of life course research: Qualitative and quantitative approaches.* Thousand Oaks, CA: Sage. Collection of essays on longitudinal (retrospective and prospective) research with individuals and populations; exceptional chapter by John Clausen, "Life Reviews and Life Stories."

Holstein, J. A., & Gubrium, J. F. (2000). *Constructing the life course* (2nd ed.). Dix Hills, NY: General Hall. Reconceptualizes for the reader how traditional life course constructs (cycles, development, stages, etc.) have been socially constructed and potentially misused for assessment in education and therapy.

McLeod, J., & Thomson, R. (2009). *Researching social change.* London: Sage. Complex but rich ways of researching change through ethnographic, longitudinal, oral history, and other methods.

Saldaña, J. (2003). *Longitudinal qualitative research: Analyzing change through time.* Walnut Creek, CA: AltaMira. Methods book on long-term fieldwork and data analysis; uses three education studies as examples throughout the text.

SOCIOLOGY (GENERAL TEXTBOOKS)

Charon, J. M. (2013). *Ten questions: A sociological perspective* (8th ed.). Belmont, CA: Wadsworth Thomson Learning. Superior overview of basic sociological principles and theories, such as social reality, inequality, ethnocentrism, social change, and so on.

Churton, M., & Brown, A. (2010). *Theory and method* (2nd ed.). New York: Palgrave Macmillan. From sociology, an excellent overview of traditional, modern, and postmodern theories of the field.

Cuzzort, R. P., & King, E. W. (2002). *Social thought into the twenty-first century* (6th ed.). Orlando, FL: Harcourt. An overview of the major works of 17 prominent social thinkers, such as Marx, Goffman, Freud, and Mead; each chapter profiles the writer's prominent theories through everyday examples.

Massey, G. (2016). *Ways of social change: Making sense of modern times* (2nd ed.). Thousand Oaks, CA: Sage. A superior and rich discussion of the ways change occurs in such social domains as the state, technology, war, business, culture, and so on.

Meer, N., & Gabler, J. (2011). *Sociology for dummies.* Hoboken, NJ: Wiley. A thorough yet readable overview of sociological principles, writers, and concepts.

PSYCHOLOGY AND QUALITATIVE RESEARCH

Brooks, J., & King, N. (Eds.). (2017). *Applied qualitative research in psychology.* London: Palgrave. Chapter collection of methodological pieces using different approaches to inquiry (phenomenology, discourse analysis, appreciative inquiry, etc.).

Camic, P. M., Rhodes, J. E., & Yardley, L. (Eds.). (2003). *Qualitative research in psychology: Expanding perspectives in methodology and design.* Washington, DC: American Psychological Association. Chapter collection of qualitative methods for psychological research, therapy, and so on; good overview of some approaches commonly referenced in the area.

Chirkov, V. (2016). *Fundamentals of research on culture and psychology.* New York: Routledge. Superior text on conceptual foundations and thinking for studies that blend the ethnographic and psychological. Provides insider knowledge of psychological facets in studies of culture.

Forrester, M. A. (Ed.). (2010). *Doing qualitative research in psychology: A practical guide.* London: Sage. A handbook of the methodology; includes pragmatic sections on discourse analysis, grounded theory, phenomenology, and conversation analysis.

Rohleder, P., & Lyons, A. C. (Eds.). (2015). *Qualitative research in clinical and health psychology.* London: Palgrave. Chapter collection of methodological pieces using different approaches to inquiry (phenomenology, conversation analysis, discourse analysis, grounded theory, thematic analysis, etc.).

Smith, J. A. (Ed.). (2015). *Qualitative psychology: A practical guide to research methods* (3rd ed.). London: Sage. Not just for psychology but for all social science fields; excellent chapter overviews of methods such as grounded theory, plus narrative, discourse, conversation analysis, and so on.

COMMUNICATION AND QUALITATIVE RESEARCH

Hansen, A., & Machin, D. (2013). *Media & communication research methods.* New York: Palgrave Macmillan. Overview of research approaches (content analysis, discourse analysis, focus groups, surveys, etc.) with media content and talk.

Lindlof, T. R., & Taylor, B. C. (2019). *Qualitative communication research methods* (4th ed.). Thousand Oaks, CA: Sage. General textbook overview of qualitative research in human communication.

Tracy, S. J. (2013). *Qualitative research methods: Collecting evidence, crafting analysis, communicating impact.* Oxford, UK: Wiley-Blackwell. An excellent introductory methods text with multiple student exercises and ancillary materials.

QUALITATIVE RESEARCH IN EDUCATION (GENERAL TEXTBOOKS)

Bogdan, R. C., & Biklen, S. K. (2007). *Qualitative research for education: An introduction to theory and methods* (5th ed.). Boston: Allyn & Bacon. Excellent overview of the method, with an emphasis on field work; includes good sections on development of qualitative research, photograph analysis, and the novice researcher.

Eisner, E. W. (1998). *The kind of schools we need: Personal essays.* Portsmouth, NH: Heinemann. Several essays provide foundations for research in the arts and arts-based approaches to research; sections include "The Arts and Their Role in Education," "Cognition and Representation," and "Rethinking Educational Research."

Lancy, D. F. (1993). *Qualitative research in education: An introduction to the major traditions.* New York: Longman. A survey of types of qualitative research, with examples in fields such as anthropology, sociology, and education.

LeCompte, M. D., & Preissle, J. (1993). *Ethnography and qualitative design in educational research* (2nd ed.). San Diego, CA: Academic Press. Detailed methods for the design and execution of qualitative studies in the classroom.

Merriam, S. B., & Tisdell, E. J. (2016). *Qualitative research: A guide to design and implementation* (4th ed.). San Francisco: Jossey-Bass. Superior introductory textbook, primarily for those in education; elegantly written and clear procedures.

Wolcott, H. F. (2003). *Teachers vs. technocrats: An educational innovation in anthropological perspective* (Updated ed.). Walnut Creek, CA: AltaMira. A case study that illustrates the concept of "moieties" (dual/opposing cultures) in education between teachers and administrators.

RESEARCH WITH CHILDREN AND ADOLESCENTS

Christensen, P., & James, A. (Eds.). (2017). *Research with children: Perspectives and practices* (3rd ed.). New York: Routledge. Collection of essays about theoretical and social dimensions of researching children; includes chapters on working with children in war-affected areas, street children, and the disabled.

Clark, C. D. (2011). *In a younger voice: Doing child-centered qualitative research.* New York: Oxford University Press. Wonderful insider knowledge and nuances on researching children; excellent coverage of interpersonal dynamics between adults and youth.

Corsaro, W. A. (2015). *The sociology of childhood* (4th ed.). Thousand Oaks, CA: Sage. Outstanding resource on sociological dimensions of children and youth; cross-national comparisons and current U.S. statistics and trends presented.

Fine, G. A., & Sandstrom, K. L. (1988). *Knowing children: Participant observation with minors.* Newbury Park, CA: Sage. Monograph on the techniques and ethical issues of research with preschoolers through adolescents.

Freeman, M., & Mathison, S. (2009). *Researching children's experiences.* New York: Guilford. Superior, straightforward survey of researching children from a constructivist perspective.

Galman, S. C. (2019). *Naptime at the O.K. Corral: Shane's beginner's guide to childhood ethnography.* New York: Routledge. Galman presents, in comic book format, an introduction to the theories, history, methods, and ethics of research with children.

Graue, M. E., & Walsh, D. J. (1998). *Studying children in context: Theories, methods, and ethics.* Thousand Oaks, CA: Sage. Overview of methods of social science research with children; includes sample studies and excellent advice through all stages of the research process.

Greene, S., & Hogan, D. (2005). *Researching children's experience: Approaches and methods.* London: Sage. Excellent chapters on qualitative research with children, from interviews to participant observation to arts-based methods.

Greig, A. D., Taylor, J., & MacKay, T. (2013). *Doing research with children: A practical guide* (3rd ed.). London: Sage. Overview of classic/traditional and contemporary methods of data gathering from children; focuses primarily on preschool and younger children; excellent theoretical overview.

Hatch, J. A. (Ed.). (2007). *Early childhood qualitative research.* New York: Routledge. Collection of essays, including digital video, action research, focus groups, and so on, on research with young children.

Heiligman, D. (1998). *The New York Public Library kid's guide to research.* New York: Scholastic. Designed for upper elementary grades, an overview of basic research strategies and tools, including the Internet, conducting interviews and surveys, and fieldwork.

Holmes, R. M. (1998). *Fieldwork with children.* Thousand Oaks, CA: Sage. Practical advice on interviewing and observing children and gaining entry to their world; focuses on how gender interplays with rapport.

Lancy, D. F., Bock, J., & Gaskins, S. (Eds.). (2010). *The anthropology of learning in childhood*. Walnut Creek, CA: AltaMira. Outstanding chapters on how children from various cultures "learn," in its broadest sense; rich concepts, yet written in accessible language; not a "how to" book but an exceptional model for documenting participant observation.

Mukherji, P., & Albon, D. (2015). *Research methods in early childhood: An introductory guide* (2nd ed.). London: Sage. Readable overview of quantitative and qualitative research design approaches to research with young children; emphasizes British perspectives but applicable to U.S. youth.

O'Reilly, M., & Dogra, N. (2017). *Interviewing children and young people for research*. London: Sage. Excellent overview of all aspects of interviewing youth; includes insightful strategies for adult researchers' language use and interactions.

Pellegrini, A. D. (2013). *Observing children in their natural worlds: A methodological primer* (3rd ed.). New York: Psychology Press. A primarily quantitative and systematic approach to observing young people's behaviors; includes a chapter by John Hoch and Frank J. Symons on new technology methods for data collection and analysis.

Roberts-Holmes, G. (2014). *Doing your early years research project: A step-by-step guide* (3rd ed.). London: Sage. Geared for U.K. schools; provides an elegant overview of research design and data collection methods for graduate student projects.

Thomson, P. (Ed.). (2008). *Doing visual research with children and young people*. London: Routledge. Excellent collection of chapters on using photography, video, scrapbooks, drawings, and other visual materials as data when researching children.

Tisdall, E. K., Davis, J. M., & Gallagher, M. (2009). *Researching with children and young people: Research design, methods and analysis*. London: Sage. Superior collection of methods and case study profiles for designing and conducting research with children; geared toward U.K. programs but still has relevance for U.S. readers.

QUALITATIVE DATA COLLECTION

Braun, V., Clarke, V., & Gray, D. (Eds.). (2017). *Collecting qualitative data: A practical guide to textual, media and virtual techniques*. Cambridge, UK: Cambridge University Press. Outstanding collection of chapters on newer forms of data collection (social media, talk radio, blogs, e-mail interviews, instant messaging, etc.) for analysis.

Guest, G., Namey, E. E., & Mitchell, M. L. (2013). *Collecting qualitative data: A field manual for applied research*. Thousand Oaks, CA: Sage. Detailed methods for sampling, participant observation, interviews, focus groups, and data management.

INTERVIEWING

Brinkmann, S., & Kvale, S. (2015). *Interviews: Learning the craft of qualitative research interviewing* (3rd ed.). Thousand Oaks, CA: Sage. Overview of interview methods for qualitative inquiry.

Gubrium, J. F., Holstein, J. A., Marvasti, A. B., & McKinney, K. D. (Eds.). (2012). *The SAGE handbook of interview research: The complexity of the craft* (2nd ed.). Thousand Oaks, CA: Sage. Superior collection of chapters on all aspects of interviewing, including methods, analysis, and ethics.

Janesick, V. J. (2010). *Oral history for the qualitative researcher: Choreographing the story*. New York: Guilford. Includes an overview of oral history documentation with multiple examples; includes references to many resources for learning more about the genre.

Krueger, R. A., & Casey, M. A. (2015). *Focus groups: A practical guide for applied research* (5th ed.). Thousand Oaks, CA: Sage. Detailed manual on techniques for planning and moderating focus groups for corporate and nonprofit research.

Mears, C. L. (2009). *Interviewing for education and social science research: The gateway approach.* New York: Palgrave Macmillan. Outstanding resource on interviewing participants, with transformation of transcripts into poetic mosaics.

Morgan, D. L. (1997). *Focus groups as qualitative research* (2nd ed.). Thousand Oaks, CA: Sage. The design, dynamics, and analysis of group interviews.

Roulston, K. (2010). *Reflective interviewing: A guide to theory and practice.* London: Sage. Superior treatise on interviewing participants, ranging from theory to technique.

Rubin, H. J., & Rubin, I. S. (2012). *Qualitative interviewing: The art of hearing data* (3rd ed.). Thousand Oaks, CA: Sage. Excellently detailed overview of designing and conducting interviews, with numerous examples from the authors' studies.

Seidman, I. (2013). *Interviewing as qualitative research: A guide for researchers in education and the social sciences* (4th ed.). New York: Teachers College Press. Specific techniques and methods for conducting three-series, in-depth interviews with adult participants.

Spradley, J. P. (1979). *The ethnographic interview.* New York: Holt, Rinehart & Winston. Essential reading for interviewing techniques; analytic methods are exclusively Spradley's, but they have become "standard" to some methodologists.

PARTICIPANT OBSERVATION

Adler, P. A., & Adler, P. (1987). *Membership roles in field research.* Newbury Park, CA: Sage. Describes three types of participant observation for researchers in field settings.

Angrosino, M. V. (2007). *Naturalistic observation.* Walnut Creek, CA: Left Coast Press. Not a "how to" book but an excellent primer on all facets of ethnographic participant observation.

DeWalt, K. M., & DeWalt, B. R. (2011). *Participant observation: A guide for fieldworkers* (2nd ed.). Lanham, MD: AltaMira. Geared toward anthropological studies, the text reviews methods of taking field notes and interviewing participants.

Emerson, R. M., Fretz, R. I., & Shaw, L. L. (2011). *Writing ethnographic fieldnotes* (2nd ed.). Chicago: University of Chicago Press. Superior overview of the field note-taking process and how it springboards to analysis and write-up.

Spradley, J. P. (1980). *Participant observation.* New York: Holt, Rinehart & Winston. Companion volume to Spradley's *The Ethnographic Interview*; much is reiterated in this text, but the focus is on observation techniques.

ARTIFACTS, VISUAL AND MATERIAL CULTURE

Banks, M. (2018). *Using visual data in qualitative research.* London: Sage. Provides theoretical, methodological, and applied foundations for the analysis of visual materials (photographs, film, etc.), with case references to exemplars in the field.

Banks, M., & Zeitlyn, D. (2015). *Visual methods in social research* (2nd ed.). London: Sage. Overview of the analysis and making of digital visual materials such as photographs, film, and multimedia.

Berger, A. A. (2014). *What objects mean: An introduction to material culture* (2nd ed.). New York: Routledge. Elegant and clearly explained approaches to the critical and cultural analysis of artifacts.

Brown, S., Clarke, A., & Frederick, U. (Eds.). (2015). *Object stories: Artifacts and archeologists.* Walnut Creek, CA: Left Coast Press. Chapter collection of brief profiles of archeologists reflecting on the meanings of significant artifacts from field work.

Ledin, P., & Machin, D. (2018). *Doing visual analysis: From theory to practice.* London: Sage. Superior compendium of design elements and their connotations for the visual analysis of materials such as photographs, documents, space, and product/advertising media.

Margolis, E., & Pauwels, L. (Eds.). (2011). *The SAGE handbook of visual research methods.* London: Sage. An exhaustive collection of chapters devoted to visual analysis of photographs, film, digital work, material culture, and so on.

Moss, J., & Pini, B. (Eds.). (2016). *Visual research methods in educational research.* New York: Palgrave Macmillan. Chapter collection on the uses of visual research with young people; several selections offer intriguing ideas and discuss unique projects.

Spencer, S. (2011). *Visual research methods in the social sciences: Awakening visions.* New York: Routledge. Fieldwork practices with data collection and analysis of visual materials; explores place, identity, and the use of media technology in analysis.

QUALITATIVE DATA ANALYSIS

Abbott, A. (2004). *Methods of discovery: Heuristics for the social sciences.* New York: Norton. Excellent overview of current methodological debates in social science research and examples of problem-solving strategies used in landmark studies; provides guidance for seeing data and their analyses in new ways.

Auerbach, C. F., & Silverstein, L. B. (2003). *Qualitative data: An introduction to coding and analysis.* New York: New York University Press. Systematic procedures for finding "relevant text" in transcripts for pattern and thematic development; very readable, with good examples of procedures.

Bazeley, P. (2013). *Qualitative data analysis: Practical strategies.* London: Sage. Comprehensive compendium of analytic approaches ranging from data management to coding to theory building.

Bernard, H. R., Wutich, A., & Ryan, G. W. (2017). *Analyzing qualitative data: Systematic approaches* (2nd ed.). Thousand Oaks, CA: Sage. The emphasis is on systematic rather than interpretive approaches, meaning forms of content analysis, discourse analysis, and so on.

Boeije, H. (2010). *Analysis in qualitative research.* London: Sage. Primarily explicates the grounded theory model of qualitative research and data analysis, yet does a good job of explaining its procedures.

Bryman, A., & Burgess, R. G. (Eds.). (1994). *Analyzing qualitative data.* London: Routledge. Series of chapters describing the behind-the-scenes coding and analytic work of researchers.

Dey, I. (1993). *Qualitative data analysis: A user-friendly guide for social scientists.* London: Routledge. An excellent overview of specific techniques such as creating categories and splitting, splicing, linking, and connecting data.

Erickson, F. (1986). Qualitative methods in research on teaching. In M. C. Wittrock (Ed.), *Handbook of research on teaching* (3rd ed., pp. 119–161). New York: Macmillan. Classic chapter on an intuitive approach to qualitative inquiry through heuristics of assertion development.

Ezzy, D. (2002). *Qualitative analysis: Practice and innovation.* London: Routledge. Readable introduction to and overview of qualitative inquiry; explains conceptual ideas clearly.

Fielding, N. G., & Fielding, J. L. (1986). *Linking data*. Beverly Hills, CA: Sage. Monograph on the technique of triangulation with multiple methods of data gathering.

Flick, U. (Ed.). (2014). *The SAGE handbook of qualitative data analysis*. London: Sage. Chapter collection of international authors addressing various facets of qualitative data analysis.

Freeman, M. (2017). *Modes of thinking for qualitative data analysis*. New York: Routledge. Superior methodological guidance for five modes of analytic thought (categorical, narrative, dialectical, poetical, and diagrammatical).

Galman, S. C. (2013). *The good, the bad, and the data: Shane the lone ethnographer's basic guide to qualitative data analysis*. Walnut Creek, CA: Left Coast Press. A comic-based overview of fundamental principles of analysis; a sequel to Galman's *Shane, The Lone Ethnographer*.

Gibbs, G. R. (2018). *Analyzing qualitative data* (2nd ed.). London: Sage. Monograph with an overview of fundamental data-analytic techniques, with excellent content on narrative analysis and comparative analysis.

Grbich, C. (2013). *Qualitative data analysis: An introduction* (2nd ed.). London: Sage. Not a "how to" guide but an introductory overview of the types of analysis (e.g., grounded theory, narrative analysis, content analysis) available to qualitative researchers.

Guest, G., & MacQueen, K. M. (2008). *Handbook for team-based qualitative research*. Lanham, MD: AltaMira. Chapters on team research, including ethics, politics, coding, and data management.

Guest, G., MacQueen, K. M., & Namey, E. E. (2012). *Applied thematic analysis*. Thousand Oaks, CA: Sage. Systematic qualitative and quantitative procedures for segmenting and analyzing themes (in their broadest sense) for research reports; emphasizes team research collaboration.

Knowlton, L. W., & Phillips, C. C. (2013). *The logic model guidebook: Better strategies for great results* (2nd ed.). Thousand Oaks, CA: Sage. Graphic displays for program and theory of change models; illustrates possible complex interconnections.

LeCompte, M. D., & Schensul, J. J. (2012). *Analysis and interpretation of ethnographic data: A mixed methods approach* (2nd ed.; Ethnographer's Toolkit Series, Book 5). Lanham, MD: AltaMira. Overview of primarily qualitative analytic strategies for traditional ethnographies; provides a systematic approach to data management, analysis, and integration with quantitative data.

Lyons, E., & Coyle, C. (2016). *Analysing qualitative data in psychology* (2nd ed.). London: Sage. Overview of four approaches to data analysis in psychology: interpretative phenomenological analysis, grounded theory, discourse analysis, and narrative analysis—the latter includes a superior interview protocol for autobiographical/biographical work.

Northcutt, N., & McCoy, D. (2004). *Interactive qualitative analysis: A systems method for qualitative research*. Thousand Oaks, CA: Sage. For focus group synthesis—the development of flow charts for process through systematic qualitative analytic procedures.

Richards, L. (2015). *Handling qualitative data: A practical guide* (3rd ed.). London: Sage. An overview of data management principles before and during analysis; excellent content on category construction.

Saldaña, J. (2016). *The coding manual for qualitative researchers* (3rd ed.). London: Sage. Profiles 32 different methods for coding qualitative data; includes examples, along with ways to develop analytic memos.

Schreier, M. (2012). *Qualitative content analysis in practice*. London: Sage. Systematic procedures for qualitative content analysis; a hybrid blend of qualitative and quantitative approaches.

Sullivan, P. (2012). *Qualitative data analysis using a dialogical approach*. London: Sage. Intriguing methods for qualitative data analysis, particularly for thematic and discourse analysis; first three chapters are heavy on theory but lay the foundation for Sullivan's analytic methods in the remaining chapters.

Vogt, W. P., Vogt, E. R., Gardner, D. C., & Haeffele, L. M. (2014). *Selecting the right analyses for your data: Quantitative, qualitative, and mixed methods*. New York: Guilford. Emphasis in this book is placed on the quantitative, but the discussion on coding for both paradigms is worthwhile reading for mixed methods researchers.

Wertz, F. J., Charmaz, K., McMullen, L. M., Josselson, R., Anderson, R., & McSpadden, E. (2011). *Five ways of doing qualitative analysis: Phenomenological psychology, grounded theory, discourse analysis, narrative research, and intuitive inquiry*. New York: Guilford. A detailed examination of an interview transcript through five methods of data analysis: phenomenological psychology, grounded theory, discourse analysis, narrative research, and intuitive inquiry; includes reflexive statements by the analysts and the interview participant herself.

Wheeldon, J., & Ahlberg, M. A. (2012). *Visualizing social science research: Maps, methods, and meaning*. Thousand Oaks, CA: Sage. Overview of quantitative, qualitative, and mixed methods research and how diagrams (e.g., concept maps and mind maps) can be employed during all phases of the research project.

Wolcott, H. F. (1994). *Transforming qualitative data: Description, analysis, and interpretation*. Thousand Oaks, CA: Sage. Anthology of Wolcott's work, with accompanying narrative on three levels of qualitative data analysis.

TECHNOLOGY AND CAQDAS (COMPUTER ASSISTED QUALITATIVE DATA ANALYSIS SOFTWARE)

Altheide, D. L., & Schneider, C. J. (2013). *Qualitative media analysis* (2nd ed.). Thousand Oaks, CA: Sage. Reviews search, collection, and analysis strategies for media documents from television broadcasts, the Internet, social media, and other sources.

Bazeley, P., & Jackson, K. (2013). *Qualitative data analysis with NVivo* (2nd ed.). London: Sage. Reference guide to computer-assisted qualitative data analysis with the program software NVivo.

Berger, A. A. (2019). *Media analysis techniques* (6th ed.). Thousand Oaks, CA: Sage. Paradigms for media analysis of television programs, films, print advertisements, and popular technology (e.g., mobile phones, the Internet).

Friese, S. (2014). *Qualitative data analysis with ATLAS.ti* (2nd ed.). London: Sage. Detailed technical manual for the functions of ATLAS.ti software; focuses primarily on program features.

Gaiser, T. J., & Schreiner, A. E. (2009). *A guide to conducting online research*. London: Sage. Overview of electronic methods of data gathering through e-mail, websites, social networking sites, and so on.

Gibbs, G. R. (2002). *Qualitative data analysis: Explorations with NVivo*. Berkshire, UK: Open University Press. The version of NVivo demonstrated in this book is outdated, but there is still an excellent overview of data-analytic strategies with the software.

Hahn, C. (2008). *Doing qualitative research using your computer: A practical guide*. London: Sage. Step-by-step instructions for using Microsoft Word, Excel, and Access for qualitative data management and coding.

Haw, K., & Hadfield, M. (2011). *Video in social science research: Functions and forms*. London: Routledge. Reference for theoretical applications of video; contains excellent guidelines for video production by young people as a form of participatory research.

Heath, C., Hindmarsh, J., & Luff, P. (2010). *Video in qualitative research: Analysing social interaction in everyday life*. London: Sage. Focuses on microanalysis of video data fragments; shows transcription models for talk and action; excellent guidelines for working with video cameras in the field.

Ignatow, G., & Mihalcea, R. (2017). *Text mining: A guidebook for the social sciences.* Thousand Oaks, CA: Sage. Though text mining is a strategy for software engineers, the book offers qualitative researchers insider knowledge on how text is analyzed from algorithmic perspectives.

Kozinets, R. V. (2015). *Netnography: Redefined* (2nd ed.). London: Sage. Exceptionally well-detailed guide to online ethnographic research; includes excellent considerations for entrée, data collection, and ethical/legal matters.

Makagon, D., & Neumann, M. (2009). *Recording culture: Audio documentary and the ethnographic experience.* Thousand Oaks, CA: Sage. Methods for creating audio documentation of field work, including soundscapes, interviews, citizen journals, and so on.

Paulus, T., Lester, J. N., & Dempster, P. G. (2014). *Digital tools for qualitative research.* London: Sage. Excellent discussion of how digital tools (Internet, media, software, hardware) can be used for data collection and analysis.

Salmons, J. (2016). *Doing qualitative research online.* London: Sage. Excellent manual on collecting/mining data from Internet sources.

Shrum, W., & Scott, G. (2017). *Video ethnography in practice: Planning, shooting, and editing for social analysis.* Thousand Oaks, CA: Sage. Technical and procedural recommendations for digital video equipment and its use in field work and post-production.

Silver, C., & Lewins, A. (2014). *Using software in qualitative research: A step-by-step guide* (2nd ed.). London: Sage. Critically compares and illustrates the basic procedures for three CAQDAS programs: ATLAS.ti, MAXQDA, and NVivo; excellent introductory survey and accompanying reference manual.

Woolf, N. H., & Silver, C. (2018). *Qualitative analysis using ATLAS.ti: The five level QDA method.* New York: Routledge. Explains a branded approach to qualitative analysis, followed by its integration with ATLAS.ti analytic software.

DATA DISPLAY

Evergreen, S. D. H. (2017). *Effective data visualization: The right chart for the right data.* Thousand Oaks, CA: Sage. Offers well-designed templates and ideas for quantitative and qualitative data display in presentations and reports.

Evergreen, S. D. H. (2018). *Presenting data effectively: Communicating your findings for maximum impact* (2nd ed.). Thousand Oaks, CA: Sage. Superior, full color resource on the design principles for visual display of graphics, text, statistics, and so on in presentations and reports.

THEORY DEVELOPMENT AND APPLICATIONS

Alvesson, M., & Kärreman, D. (2011). *Qualitative research and theory development: Mystery as method.* London: Sage. Approach to theory development through problematizing the data and resolving "breakdowns" in patterns and field work observations.

Jackson, A. Y., & Mazzei, L. A. (2012). *Thinking with theory in qualitative research: Viewing data across multiple perspectives.* New York: Routledge. Approaches data analysis through theoretical lenses rather than codification; applies the principles of theorists such as Derrida, Foucault, and Butler to an interview data set from female professors.

Koro-Ljungberg, M. (2016). *Reconceptualizing qualitative research: Methodologies without methodology.* Thousand Oaks, CA: Sage. Provocative, polyvocal reader on challenges to the philosophical assumptions of inquiry and conventional thought and practices.

Maxwell, J. (2012). *A realist approach for qualitative research.* Thousand Oaks, CA: Sage. Approaches about realist ontology toward ethnographic inquiry; excellent discussions on causation and research design.

Ravitch, S. M., & Riggan, M. (2017). *Reason and rigor: How conceptual frameworks guide research* (2nd ed.). Thousand Oaks, CA: Sage. Explanation with examples of how a conceptual framework functions as a through-line during all phases and stages of the research process, from design to data analysis and from fieldwork to write-up.

Tavory, I., & Timmermans, S. (2014). *Abductive analysis: Theorizing qualitative research.* Chicago: University of Chicago Press. An intriguing discussion of the analytic heuristic and how it serves social science analysis.

QUALITATIVE METASYNTHESIS

Finfgeld-Connett, D. (2018). *A guide to qualitative meta-synthesis.* New York: Routledge. An elegant overview of meta-synthesis principles with three complete examples of the author's analytic work in the field of domestic violence.

Hannes, K., & Lockwood, C. (Eds.). (2012). *Synthesizing qualitative research: Choosing the right approach.* Hoboken, NJ: Wiley-Blackwell. Chapter collection of various approaches to synthesis with a disciplinary focus on studies in health care and medicine.

Major, C. H., & Savin-Baden, M. (2010). *An introduction to qualitative research synthesis: Managing the information explosion in social science research.* London: Routledge. Excellent theoretical and practical overview of qualitative research synthesis; includes extended examples.

Sandelowski, M., & Barroso, J. (2007). *Handbook for synthesizing qualitative research.* New York: Springer. Detailed methods book on metasummary and metasynthesis of related qualitative studies; for advanced researchers.

Saini, M., & Shlonsky, A. (2012). *Systematic synthesis of qualitative research.* New York: Oxford University Press. Descriptive overview of research study synthesis procedures with a disciplinary focus on social work.

WRITING QUALITATIVE RESEARCH

Allen, M. (2016). *Essentials of publishing qualitative research.* Walnut Creek, CA: Left Coast Press. Superior insider's guide from a publisher on the development and marketing of articles, book chapters, and book manuscripts in academic fields.

Belcher, W. L. (2009). *Writing your journal article in 12 weeks: A guide to academic publishing success.* Thousand Oaks, CA: Sage. Step-by-step and detailed procedures for revising drafts of papers for publication submission.

Booth, W. C., Colomb, G. G., Williams, J. M., Bizup, J., & Fitzgerald, W. T. (2016). *The craft of research* (4th ed.). Chicago: University of Chicago Press. A handbook of basics in logic, argumentation, writing, outlining, revising, and crafting the research report.

Goodall, H. L., Jr. (2008). *Writing qualitative inquiry: Self, stories, and academic life.* Walnut Creek, CA: Left Coast Press. Overview of writing and writing for the profession (journals, books, in the academy, etc.).

Higgs, J., Horsfall, D., & Grace, S. (Eds.). (2009). *Writing qualitative research on practice.* Rotterdam: Sense. Chapter collection of writing up research; includes excellent chapters on question development; argument construction; and genres (narrative inquiry, arts-based research, etc.).

Holliday, A. (2016). *Doing & writing qualitative research* (3rd ed.). London: Sage. Guidance for the beginning researcher's scholarly composition about theory, methods, data, and analysis.

Miller, A. B. (2009). *Finish your dissertation once and for all! How to overcome psychological barriers, get results, and move on with your life.* Washington, DC: American Psychological Association. Focuses on the cognitive/emotional barriers of progress and completion, plus the practical matters of timelines, project management, and writing.

Saldaña, J. (2018). *Writing qualitatively: The selected works of Johnny Saldaña.* London: Routledge. Anthology of the writer's scholarly articles, book chapters, keynote addresses, and arts-based research with introductory and accompanying commentary on the genres, elements and styles of research write-ups.

van Maanen, J. (2011). *Tales of the field: On writing ethnography* (2nd ed.). Chicago: University of Chicago Press. Contemporary classic on structuring and writing ethnography in various story forms (realistic, confessional, impressionist, etc.).

Wolcott, H. F. (2009). *Writing up qualitative research* (3rd ed.). Thousand Oaks, CA: Sage. Excellent monograph on writing reports clearly and briefly from the first draft to publication.

Woods, P. (2006). *Successful writing for qualitative researchers* (2nd ed.). London: Routledge. Offers specific strategies for writing up final reports; especially good with transitioning from data analysis to reporting; includes numerous examples.

ONLINE RESOURCES

Forum: Qualitative Social Research. The multilingual (English, German, Spanish) peer-reviewed e-journal includes articles, interviews with leading figures in the field, commentary, and book reviews: qualitative-research.net/index.php/fqs

Methodspace. Hosted by Sage Publications; a community networking site for researchers from various social science disciplines; members can join interest groups such as Qualitative Inquiry, Narrative Research, and Performative Social Science: methodspace.com

Pacific Standard. A print and online publication of the Miller-McCune Center for Research, Media and Public Policy; includes articles ranging from health to culture, bringing research to a general readership: psmag.com

ResearchTalk. An organization that conducts intensive workshops and camps in the United States throughout the year on various topics in qualitative research: researchtalk.com

Sage Research Methods. An online subscription platform of Sage Publications that includes access to books and book chapters, videos, case study profiles, and downloadable data: methods.sagepub.com

The Qualitative Report: Hosted by Nova Southeastern University; an online journal with a weekly newsletter featuring recent publication links; the site also includes an extensive list of Internet addresses of other organizations devoted to qualitative research: nsuworks.nova.edu/tqr/

REFERENCES

Adler, T. (1991, December). Outright fraud rare, but not poor science. *Monitor on Psychology*, 11.

Allen, W. T., Jr., & Hunsaker, S. L. (2016). Teacher conceptions, curriculum ideologies, and adaptations to linear change in River School District: Implications for gifted and talented. *Journal for the Education of the Gifted*, *39*(3), 195–220. doi: 10.1177/0162353216657183

Aluko, O. (2015). Improving audit trail in the use of qualitative data in developing conceptual models. *International Journal of Engineering & Technical Research*, *3*(3), 168–172.

Ballestra, L. V., Cardinali, S., Palanga, P., & Pacelli, G. (2017). The changing role of salespeople and the unchanging feeling toward selling: Implications for the HEI programs. *Journal of Marketing Education*, *39*(3), 176–189. doi: 10.1177/0273475317724842

Baral, N., & Pokharel, M. P. (2017). How sustainability is reflected in the S&P 500 companies' strategic documents. *Organization & Environment*, *30*(2), 122–141. doi: 10.1177/1086026616645381

Belli, R. F., Stafford, F. P., & Alwin, D. F. (Eds.). (2009). *Calendar and time diary methods in life course research*. Thousand Oaks, CA: Sage.

Bernard, H. R. (2011). *Research methods in anthropology: Qualitative and quantitative approaches* (5th ed.). Walnut Creek, CA: AltaMira.

Bernard, H. R. (2018). *Research methods in anthropology: Qualitative and quantitative approaches* (6th ed.). Lanham, MD: Rowman & Littlefield.

Bernard, H. R., Wutich, A., & Ryan, G. W. (2017). *Analyzing qualitative data: Systematic approaches* (2nd ed.). Thousand Oaks, CA: Sage.

Bogdan, R. C., & Biklen, S. K. (2007). *Qualitative research for education: An introduction to theories and methods* (5th ed.). Boston: Pearson Education.

Brooks, M. C. (2015). School principals in Southern Thailand: Exploring trust with community leaders during conflict. *Educational Management Administration & Leadership*, *43*(2), 232–252. doi: 10.1177/1741143213513191

Casey, R. C. (2017). Hard time: A content analysis of incarcerated women's personal accounts. *Affilia: Journal of Women and Social Work*, 1–13. doi: 10.1177/0886109917718233

Chapman, H. J., Veras-Estévez, B. A., Pomeranz, J. L., Pérez-Then, E. N., Marcelino, B., & Lauzardo, M. (2017). The role of powerlessness among health care workers in tuberculosis infection control. *Qualitative Health Research*, *27*(14), 2116–2127. doi: 10.1177/1049732317731317

Charmaz, K. (2001). Grounded theory. In R. M. Emerson (Ed.), *Contemporary field research: Perspectives and formulations* (2nd ed., pp. 335–352). Prospect Heights, IL: Waveland.

Charmaz, K. (2014). *Constructing grounded theory* (2nd ed.). Thousand Oaks, CA: Sage.

Clark-Ibáñez, M. (2008). Gender and being "bad": Inner-city students' photographs. In P. Thomson (Ed.), *Doing visual research with children and young people* (pp. 95–113). New York: Routledge.

Clarke, A. E., Friese, C., & Washburn, R. S. (2018). *Situational analysis: Grounded theory after the interpretive turn* (2nd ed.). Thousand Oaks, CA: Sage.

Cloyes, K. G., Rosenkranz, S. J., Wold, D., Berry, P. H., & Supiano, K. P. (2014). To be truly alive: Motivation among prison inmate hospice volunteers and the transformative process of end-of-life peer care service. *American Journal of Hospice and Palliative Medicine*, *31*(7), 735–748. doi: 10.1177/1049909113506035

Cochran-Smith, M., McQuillan, P., Mitchell, K., Terrell, D. G., Barnatt, J., D'Souza, L., Jong, C., Shakman, K., Lam, K., & Gleeson, A. M. (2012). A longitudinal study of teaching practice and early career decisions: A cautionary tale. *American Educational Research Journal*, *49*(5), 844–880. doi: 10.3102/0002831211431006

Coffey, A. (2018). *Doing ethnography*. London: Sage.

Cranmer, G. A., Anzur, C. K., & Sollitto, M. (2017). Memorable messages of social support that former high school athletes received from their head coaches. *Communication & Sport*, *5*(5), 604–621. doi: 10.1177/2167479516641934

Creamer, E. G. (2018). *An introduction to fully integrated mixed methods research*. Thousand Oaks, CA: Sage.

Cressey, D. R. (1953). *Other people's money: A study in the social psychology of embezzlement*. New York: Free Press.

Creswell, J. W., & Plano Clark, V. L. (2018). *Designing and conducting mixed methods research* (3rd ed.). Thousand Oaks, CA: Sage.

Denzin, N. K. (1993). *The alcoholic society: Addiction and recovery of the self*. Piscataway, NJ: Transaction.

Denzin, N. K. (2001). *Interpretive interactionism* (2nd ed.). Thousand Oaks, CA: Sage.

Denzin, N. K., & Lincoln, Y. S. (2018). *The SAGE handbook of qualitative research* (5th ed.). Thousand Oaks, CA: Sage.

Douglas, J. (1976). *Investigative social research*. Beverly Hills, CA: Sage.

Duhigg, C. (2012). *The power of habit: How we do what we do in life and business*. New York: Random House.

Ehrenreich, B. (2001). *Nickel and dimed: On (not) getting by in America*. New York: Henry Holt.

Emerson, R. M., Fretz, R. I., & Shaw, L. L. (2011). *Writing ethnographic fieldnotes* (2nd ed.). Chicago: University of Chicago Press.

Erickson, F. (1986). Qualitative methods in research on teaching. In M. C. Wittrock (Ed.), *Handbook of research on teaching* (3rd ed., pp. 119–161). New York: Macmillan.

Evergreen, S. D. H. (2018). *Presenting data effectively: Communicating your findings for maximum impact* (2nd ed.). Thousand Oaks, CA: Sage.

Finfgeld-Connett, D. (2018). *A guide to qualitative meta-synthesis*. New York: Routledge.

Geertz, C. (1973). Thick description: Toward an interpretive theory of culture. In *The interpretation of cultures* (pp. 3–30). New York: Basic Books.

Gibbs, G. R. (2018). *Analysing qualitative data*. London: Sage.

Glaser, B. G. (2005). *The grounded theory perspective III: Theoretical coding*. Mill Valley, CA: Sociology Press.

Gobo, G., & Molle, A. (2017). *Doing ethnography* (2nd ed.). London: Sage.

Godwin, E. E., Foster, V. A., & Keefe, E. P. (2013). Hurricane Katrina families: Social class and the family in trauma recovery. *The Family Journal: Counseling and Therapy for Families and Couples*, *21*(1), 15–27. doi: 10.1177/1066480712458224

Goetz, J. P., & LeCompte, M. D. (1984). *Ethnography and qualitative design in educational research*. New York: Academic Press.

Goffman, E. (1959). *The presentation of self in everyday life*. Garden City, NY: Doubleday.

Goleman, D. (1995). *Emotional intelligence*. New York: Bantam.

Goleman, D. (2007). *Social intelligence: The new science of human relationships*. New York: Bantam.

Gubrium, J. F., Holstein, J. A., Marvasti, A. B., & McKinney, K. D. (2012). *The SAGE handbook of interview research: The complexity of the craft* (2nd ed.). Thousand Oaks, CA: Sage.

Hager, L., Maier, B. J., O'Hara, E., Ott, D., & Saldaña, J. (2000). Theatre teachers' perceptions of Arizona state standards. *Youth Theatre Journal*, *14*(1), 64–77. doi: 10.1080/08929092.2000.10012518

Hlava, P., & Elfers, J. (2014). The lived experience of gratitude. *Journal of Humanistic Psychology*, *54*(4), 434–455. doi: 10.1177/0022167813508605

Hora, M. T. (2016). Navigating the problem space of academic work: How workload and curricular affordances shape STEM faculty decisions about teaching and learning. *AERA Open*, *2*(1), 1–19. doi: 10.1177/2332858415627612

Huberman, M. (1989). The professional life cycle of teachers. *Teachers College Record*, *97*(1), 31–57.

Huberman, A. M. (1993). *The lives of teachers*. London: Cassell.

Huberman, M., & Miles, M. (1989). Some procedures for causal analysis of multiple-case data. *Qualitative Studies in Education*, *2*(1), 55–68.

Humphreys, L. (1970). *Tearoom trade: Impersonal sex in public places*. Chicago: Aldine.

Irvine, J. M. (2016). Mapping the walk of shame: Incorporating emotions into concepts and methods. *Social Currents*, *3*(3), 207–216. doi: 10.1177/2329496516656871

Jang, E. E., McDougall, D. E., Pollon, D., Herbert, M., & Russell, P. (2008). Integrative mixed methods data analytic strategies in research on school success in challenging circumstances. *Journal of Mixed Methods Research*, *2*(3), 221–247. doi: 10.1177/1558689808315323

Kell, D. G. (1990). *Multimethod approach to analyzing effects of computers on classroom teaching and learning*. Andover, MA: Author.

Knowles, J. G., & Cole, A. L. (2008). *Handbook of the arts in qualitative research: Perspectives, methodologies, examples, and issues*. Thousand Oaks, CA: Sage.

Knowlton, L. W., & Phillips, C. C. (2013). *The logic model guidebook: Better strategies for great results* (2nd ed.). Thousand Oaks, CA: Sage.

Kozol, J. (1991). *Savage inequalities: Children in America's schools*. New York: Crown.

Kvale, S., & Brinkmann, S. (2015). *Interviews: Learning the craft of qualitative research interviewing* (3rd ed.). Thousand Oaks, CA: Sage.

Lakoff, G., & Johnson, M. (1980). *Metaphors we live by*. Chicago: University of Chicago Press.

Lancy, D. F., Bock, J., & Gaskins, S. (Eds.). (2010). *The anthropology of learning in childhood*. Walnut Creek, CA: AltaMira.

Leavy, P. (Ed.). (2018). *Handbook of arts-based research*. New York: Guilford.

Ledin, P., & Machin, D. (2018). *Doing visual analysis: From theory to practice*. London: Sage.

Lincoln, Y. S., & Guba, E. G. (1985). *Naturalistic inquiry*. Beverly Hills, CA: Sage.

Lofland, J., Snow, D., Anderson, L., & Lofland, L. H. (2006). *Analyzing social settings: A guide to qualitative observation and analysis* (4th ed.). Belmont, CA: Thomson/Wadsworth.

Louis, K. S., & Miles, M. B. (1990). *Improving the urban high school: What works and why.* New York: Teachers College Press.

Mages, W. K. (2007). Motivation, classroom management, and pedagogical vision: An investigation of the psychosocial development of two actor-educators. *Youth Theatre Journal, 21*(1), 94–112. doi: 10.1080/08929092.2007.10012599

Major, C. H., & Savin-Baden, M. (2010). *An introduction to qualitative research synthesis: Managing the information explosion in social science research.* London: Routledge.

Marsh, J. A., Bush-Mecenas, S., Strunk, K. O., Lincove, J. A., & Hugunet, A. (2017). Evaluating teachers in the Big Easy: How organizational context shapes policy responses in New Orleans. *Educational Evaluation and Policy Analysis, 39*(4), 539–570. doi: 10.3102/0162373717698221

Maxwell, J. A. (1992, December). *A synthesis of similarity/continuity distinctions.* Poster presented at the annual meeting of the American Anthropological Association, San Francisco.

McCammon, L. A., & Saldaña, J. (2011). *Lifelong impact: Adult perceptions of their high school speech and/or theatre participation.* Unpublished manuscript, School of Theatre and Film, Arizona State University, Tempe.

McCammon, L., Saldaña, J., Hines, A., & Omasta, M. (2012). Lifelong impact: Adult perceptions of their high school speech and/or theatre participation. *Youth Theatre Journal, 26*(1), 2–25. doi: 10.1080/08929092.2012.678223

McCurdy, D. W., Spradley, J. P., & Shandy, D. J. (2005). *The cultural experience: Ethnography in complex society* (2nd ed.). Long Grove, IL: Waveland.

McHugh, R. M., Horner, C. G., Colditz, J. B., & Wallace, T. L. (2013). Bridges and barriers: Adolescent perceptions of student–teacher relationships. *Urban Education, 48*(1), 9–43. doi: 10.1177/0042085912451585

McVea, K. (2001, April). *Collaborative qualitative research: Reflections for a quantitative researcher.* Paper presented at the annual conference of the American Educational Research Association, Seattle, WA.

Mears, C. L. (2009). *Interviewing for education and social science research: The gateway approach.* New York: Palgrave Macmillan.

Melnick, C. R., & Beaudry, J. S. (1990, April). *A qualitative research perspective: Theory, practice, essence.* Paper presented at the annual meeting of the American Educational Research Association, Boston.

Miles, M. B. (1986, April). *Improving the urban high school: Some preliminary news from five cases.* Paper presented at the annual meeting of the American Educational Research Association, San Francisco.

Miles, M. B. (1990). New methods for qualitative data collection and analysis: Vignettes and pre-structured cases. *Qualitative Studies in Education, 5*(1), 37–51.

Miles, M. B., & Huberman, A. M. (1994). *Qualitative data analysis: An expanded sourcebook.* Thousand Oaks, CA: Sage.

Miller, D. L., Creswell, J. W., & Olander, L. S. (1998). Writing and retelling multiple ethnographic tales of a soup kitchen for the homeless. *Qualitative Inquiry, 4*(4), 469–491.

Miller, S. I. (n.d.). *Qualitative research methods: A philosophical and practical inquiry* [Prospectus for a monograph]. Chicago: Loyola University.

Morgan, G. (1980). Paradigms, metaphors, and puzzle solving in organizational theory. *Administrative Science Quarterly, 25*(4), 605–622.

Morine-Dershimer, G. (1991, April). *Tracing conceptual change in pre-service teachers.* Paper presented at the annual meeting of the American Educational Research Association, Chicago.

Morrison, K. (2009). *Causation in educational research.* London: Routledge.

Morse, J. M., & Bottorff, J. L. (1992). The emotional experience of breast expression. In J. M. Morse (Ed.), *Qualitative health research* (pp. 319–332). Newbury Park, CA: Sage.

Munton, A. G., Silvester, J., Stratton, P., & Hanks, H. (1999). *Attributions in action: A practical approach to coding qualitative data.* Chichester, England: Wiley.

Neuendorf, K. A. (2017). *The content analysis guidebook* (2nd ed.). Thousand Oaks, CA: Sage.

Noblit, G. W., & Hare, R. D. (1988). *Meta-ethnography: Synthesizing qualitative studies* (Qualitative Research Methods Series, Vol. *11*). Newbury Park, CA: Sage.

Norris, J. (2009). *Playbuilding as qualitative research: A participatory arts-based approach.* Walnut Creek, CA: Left Coast Press.

O'Shaughnessy, T., & Burnes, T. R. (2016). The career adjustment experiences of women early career psychologists. *The Counseling Psychologist, 44*(6), 786–814. doi: 10.1177/0011000016650264

Patton, M. Q. (2008). *Utilization-focused evaluation* (4th ed.). Thousand Oaks, CA: Sage.

Patton, M. Q. (2015). *Qualitative research and evaluation methods* (4th ed.). Thousand Oaks, CA: Sage.

Prendergast, M., Leggo, C., & Sameshima, P. (Eds.). (2009). *Poetic inquiry: Vibrant voices in the social sciences.* Rotterdam, Netherlands: Sense.

Ragin, C. C. (1987). *The comparative method: Moving beyond qualitative and quantitative strategies.* Berkeley: University of California Press.

Rapley, T. (2018). *Doing conversation, discourse and document analysis.* London: Sage.

Ravitch, S. M., & Riggan, M. (2016). *Reason and rigor: How conceptual frameworks guide research* (2nd ed.). Thousand Oaks, CA: Sage.

Reyes, D. V. (2015). Inhabiting Latino politics: How colleges shape students' political styles. *Sociology of Education, 88*(4), 302–319. doi: 10.1177/0038040715602753

Richards, L. (2009). *Handling qualitative data: A practical guide* (2nd ed.). London: Sage.

Richardson, D. M., Pickus, H., & Parks, L. (2017). Pathways to mobility: Engaging Mexican American youth through participatory photo mapping. *Journal of Adolescent Research*, 1–30. doi: 10.1177/0743558417713303

Rosen, T., Bloemen, E. M., LoFaso, V. M., Clark, S., Flomenbaum, N. E., Breckman, R., Markarian, A., Riffin, C., Lachs, M. S., & Pillemer, K. (2016). Acute precipitants of physical elder abuse: Qualitative analysis of legal records from highly adjudicated cases. *Journal of Interpersonal Violence*, 1–25. doi: 10.1177/0886260516662305

Rosenthal, R. (1976). *Experimenter effects in behavioral research.* New York: Irvington.

Rubin, H. J., & Rubin, I. S. (2012). *Qualitative interviewing: The art of hearing data* (3rd ed.). Thousand Oaks, CA: Sage.

Saldaña, J. (1995). "Is theatre necessary?": Final exit interviews with sixth grade participants from the ASU longitudinal study. *Youth Theatre Journal, 9*, 14–30.

Saldaña, J. (1997). "Survival": A white teacher's conception of drama with inner city Hispanic youth. *Youth Theatre Journal, 11*, 25–46.

Saldaña, J. (1998). "Maybe someday, if I'm famous . . .": An ethnographic performance text. In J. Saxton & C. Miller (Eds.), *Drama and theatre in education: The research of practice, the practice of research* (pp. 89–109). Brisbane, Queensland, Australia: IDEA.

Saldaña, J. (1999). Social class and social consciousness: Adolescent perceptions of oppression in forum theatre workshops. *Multicultural Perspectives, 1*(3), 14–18.

Saldaña, J. (2003). *Longitudinal qualitative research: Analyzing change through time.* Walnut Creek, CA: AltaMira.

Saldaña, J. (2005). Theatre of the oppressed with children: A field experiment. *Youth Theatre Journal, 19*(1), 117–133. doi: 10.1080/08929092.2005.10012580

Saldaña, J. (2008). Analyzing longitudinal qualitative observational data. In S. Menard (Ed.), *Handbook of longitudinal research: Design, measurement, and analysis* (pp. 297–311). Burlington, MA: Academic Press.

Saldaña, J. (2011a). *Ethnotheatre: Research from page to stage.* Walnut Creek, CA: Left Coast Press.

Saldaña, J. (2011b). *Fundamentals of qualitative research.* New York: Oxford University Press.

Saldaña, J. (2016). *The coding manual for qualitative researchers* (3rd ed.). London: Sage.

Saldaña, J. (2018). *Writing qualitatively: The selected works of Johnny Saldaña.* New York: Routledge.

Saldaña, J., & Mallette, L. A. (2017). Environmental coding: A new method using the SPELIT Environmental Analysis Matrix. *Qualitative Inquiry, 23*(2), 161–167. doi: 10.1177/1077800416679143

Saldaña, J., & Omasta, M. (2018). *Qualitative research: Analyzing life.* Thousand Oaks, CA: Sage.

Sandelowski, M., & Barroso, J. (2007). *Handbook for synthesizing qualitative research.* New York: Springer.

Santiago-Brown, I., Jerran, C., Metcalfe, A., & Collins, C. (2015). What does sustainability mean? Knowledge gleaned from applying mixed methods research to wine grape growing. *Journal of Mixed Methods Research, 9*(3), 232–251. doi: 10.1177/1558689814534919

Scales, R. Q., Wolsey, T. D., Lenski, S., Smetana, L., Yoder, K. K., Dobler, E., Grisham, D. L., & Young, J. R. (2018). Are we preparing or training teachers? Professional judgment in and beyond teacher preparation programs. *Journal of Teacher Education, 69*(1), 7–21. doi: 10.1177/00224871177025

Schillemans, L. et al. (n.d.). *Treating victims of incest.* Antwerp, Belgium: Flemish Institute for General Practice, and University of Antwerp, Department of Family Medicine.

Schreier, M. (2012). *Qualitative content analysis in practice.* London: Sage.

Seidman, I. (2013). *Interviewing as qualitative research: A guide for researchers in education and the social sciences* (4th ed.). New York: Teachers College Press.

Shaked, H., & Schechter, C. (2017). Systems thinking among middle school leaders. *Educational Management Administration & Leadership, 45*(4), 699–718. doi: 10.1177/1741143215617949

Sieber, J. E. (1992). *Planning ethically responsible research: A guide for students and internal review boards* (Applied Social Research Methods Series, Vol. *31*). Newbury Park, CA: Sage.

Silard, A. (2018). Emotions for a cause: How the emotion expression of nonprofit leaders produces follower engagement and loyalty. *Nonprofit and Voluntary Sector Quarterly, 47*(2), 304–324. doi: 10.1177/0899764017737383

Spradley, J. P. (1979). *The ethnographic interview.* Fort Worth, TX: Harcourt Brace Jovanovich.

Spradley, J. P. (1980). *Participant observation.* Fort Worth, TX: Harcourt Brace Jovanovich.

Stake, R. E. (1995). *The art of case study research.* Thousand Oaks, CA: Sage.

Steyn, G. M. (2015). Creating a teacher collaborative practice in a South African primary school: The role of the principal. *Journal of Asian and African Studies, 50*(2), 160–175. doi: 10.1177/0021909613515626

Stievano, A., Bellass, S., Rocco, G., Olsen, D., Sabatino, L., & Johnson, M. (2016). Nursing's professional respect as experienced by hospital and community nurses. *Nursing Ethics*, 1–19. doi: 10.1177/0969733016664972

Stievano, A., De Marinis, M. G., Russo, M. T., Rocco, G., & Alvaro, R. (2012). Professional dignity in nursing in clinical and community workplaces. *Nursing Ethics*, *19*(3), 341–356. doi: 10.1177/0969733011414966

Sun, M., Ryan, C., & Pan, S. (2015). Using Chinese travel blogs to examine perceived destination image: The case of New Zealand. *Journal of Travel Research*, *54*(4), 543–555. doi: 10.1177/0047287514522882

Sunstein, B. S., & Chiseri-Strater, E. (2012). *FieldWorking: Reading and writing research* (4th ed.). Boston: Bedford/St. Martin's.

Tracy, S. J., Lutgen-Sandvik, P., & Alberts, J. K. (2006). Nightmares, demons, and slaves: Exploring the painful metaphors of workplace bullying. *Management Communication Quarterly*, *20*(2), 148–185. doi: 10.1177/0893318906291980

Tufte, E. R. (1986). Designing statistical presentations. *Social Science*, *7*(1), 75–80.

van Maanen, J. (1979). The fact of fiction in organizational ethnography. *Administrative Science Quarterly*, *24*, 539–611.

van Maanen, J. (1983). The moral fix: On the ethics of fieldwork. In R. M. Emerson (Ed.), *Contemporary field research* (pp. 269–287). Prospect Heights, IL: Waveland.

van Maanen, J. (2011). *Tales of the field: On writing ethnography* (2nd ed.). Chicago: University of Chicago Press.

Vigen, T. (2015). *Spurious correlations*. New York: Hachette.

Wallis, W. A., & Roberts, H. V. (1956). *Statistics: A new approach*. New York: Free Press.

Warner, W. (1991, February). *Improving interpretive validity of camera-based qualitative research*. Paper presented at the Qualitative Health Research Conference, Edmonton, Alberta, Canada.

Weinstein, E. (2018). The social media see-saw: Positive and negative influences on adolescents' affective well-being. *New Media & Society*, 1–27. doi: 10.1177/1461444818755634

Westerman, N. K., Cobham, V. E., & McDermott, B. (2017). Trauma-focused cognitive behavior therapy: Narratives of children and adolescents. *Qualitative Health Research*, *27*(2), 226–235. doi: 10.1177/1049732315627795

Wolcott, H. F. (1990). On seeking—and rejecting—validity in qualitative research. In E. W. Eisner & A. Peshkin (Eds.), *Qualitative inquiry in education: The continuing debate* (pp. 121–152). New York: Teachers College Press.

Wolcott, H. F. (1992). Posturing in qualitative inquiry. In M. D. LeCompte, W. L. Millroy, & J. Preissle (Eds.), *The handbook of qualitative research in education* (pp. 3–52). New York: Academic Press.

Wolcott, H. F. (1994). *Transforming qualitative data: Description, analysis, and interpretation*. Thousand Oaks, CA: Sage.

Wolcott, H. F. (2009). *Writing up qualitative research* (3rd ed.). Thousand Oaks, CA: Sage.

Wong, G. (2012). The Internet in medical education: A worked example of a realist review. In K. Hannes & C. Lockwood (Eds.), *Synthesizing qualitative research: Choosing the right approach* (pp. 83–112). West Sussex, UK: Wiley-Blackwell.

Yin, R. K. (2018). *Case study research and applications: Design and methods* (6th ed.). Thousand Oaks, CA: Sage.

INDEX